LEGAL ASPECTS OF ECONOMIC INTEGRATION IN AFRICA

Richard Frimpong Oppong challenges the view that effective economic integration in Africa is hindered by purely socio-economic, political and infrastructural problems. Inspired by the comparative experiences of other regional economic communities and imbued with insights from constitutional, public and private international law, he argues that even if the socio-economic, political and infrastructural challenges were to disappear, the state of existing laws would hinder any progress. Using a relational framework as the fulcrum of analyses, he demonstrates that, in Africa's economic integration processes, community–state, interstate and inter-community legal relations have been neither carefully thought through nor situated on a solid legal framework, and that attempts made to provide a legal framework have been incomplete and, sometimes, grounded on questionable assumptions. To overcome these problems and aid the economic integration agenda that is essential for Africa's long-term economic growth and development, the author proposes radical reforms to community and national laws.

RICHARD FRIMPONG OPPONG is a lecturer at Lancaster University Law School. He specializes in regional economic integration and private international law, focusing particularly on African countries. He studied law at the University of Ghana, Ghana School of Law, University of Cambridge, Harvard Law School and University of British Columbia.

LEGAL ASPECTS OF ECONOMIC INTEGRATION IN AFRICA

RICHARD FRIMPONG OPPONG

CAMBRIDGE
UNIVERSITY PRESS

CAMBRIDGE
UNIVERSITY PRESS

University Printing House, Cambridge CB2 8BS, United Kingdom

One Liberty Plaza, 20th Floor, New York, NY 10006, USA

477 Williamstown Road, Port Melbourne, VIC 3207, Australia

4843/24, 2nd Floor, Ansari Road, Daryaganj, Delhi - 110002, India

79 Anson Road, #06-04/06, Singapore 079906

Cambridge University Press is part of the University of Cambridge.

It furthers the University's mission by disseminating knowledge in the pursuit of education, learning and research at the highest international levels of excellence.

www.cambridge.org
Information on this title: www.cambridge.org/9781107007178

First published 2011

A catalogue record for this publication is available from the British Library

Library of Congress Cataloging in Publication data
Oppong, Richard Frimpong, 1978–
Legal Aspects of Economic Integration in Africa / Richard Frimpong Oppong.
p. cm
Includes bibliographical references and index.
ISBN 978-1-107-00717-8 (Hardback)
1. Africa–Economic integration. I. Title.
KQC742.O67 2011
343.6′07–dc22 2010050538

ISBN 978-1-107-00717-8 Hardback

Dedicated with love to my wife and daughter
Joyce Okofo Adjei and Mary Adjei

CONTENTS

TABLES

ACKNOWLEDGEMENTS

This book is based on a doctoral thesis completed at the University of British Columbia. I thank my supervisors – Professors Joost Blom, Elizabeth Edinger, Ljiljana Biukovic and Philippe Le Billon – for their critical and constructive comments. I also thank Professors Vaughan Black, Francis Botchway, Kofi Oteng Kufuor and Yuval Shany, and Mr Robert G. Miller for their comments on chapters of the book.

This book would not have been possible without the immense support and contribution of my family. Nothing can convey the depth of gratitude I feel to my beautiful and loving wife, Joyce Okofo Adjei, and most adorable baby, Mary Adjei. Joyce endured many lonely and cold nights while I researched and wrote this book. By cutting back on her playtime, Mary ensured that this book reached the world a little sooner! I am especially indebted to my parents James Kwadwo Frimpong and Mary Adjei who believed in me and spent all they had to educate me.

I thank the staff at Cambridge University Press, including Finola O'Sullivan, Richard Woodham, Sarah Roberts and Sophie Rosinke for making this book possible. I am equally indebted to two anonymous reviewers whose comments went a long way to improving this book. I pray that the prophetic words of one of the reviewers that this book 'would be a leading work on legal issues in African economic integration for some time' will come to pass.

I acknowledge the generous support I received from the Killam Trust in completing this book. Chapters of this book rely on materials gathered with the help of a grant from the British Academy for a book – *Private International Law in Commonwealth Africa* – which I am working on. The support of the Academy is accordingly acknowledged.

TABLE OF TREATIES

African Union, Decision on the Moratorium on the Recognition of Regional Economic Communities, Assembly/AU/ Dec.112 (VII), 2006

Agreement between the EFTA States on the Establishment of a Surveillance Authority and a Court of Justice, [1994] OJ L344/3

Agreement Establishing the Caribbean Court of Justice, 2001, online: www.caricom.org/jsp/secretariat/legal_instruments/agreement_ccj.pdf

Agreement on the European Economic Area, 17 March 1993, 1793 UNTS I-31121

Agreement on the Foundation of the EURASIAN Economic Community, 10 October 2000, 2212 UNTS I-39321

Agreement on the Statute of the Central American Court of Justice, 10 December 1992, 1821 UNTS I-31191, 34 ILM 921

Charter of the Organization of African Unity, 25 May 1963, 2 ILM 766

Charter of the Organization of American States, 30 April 1948, 119 UNTS 3

Charter of the Union of Central African States, 2 April 1968, 7 ILM 725

Charter of the United Nations, 26 June 1945, 1 UNTS XVI

Consolidated Version of the Treaty on European Union, 13 December 2007, [2010] OJ C83/13

Consolidated Version of the Treaty on the Functioning of the European Union, 13 December 2007, [2010] OJ C83/47

Constitutive Act of the African Union, 11 July 2000, (2005) 13 Afr. J. Int'l Comp. L. 25

Convention on the Settlement of Investment Disputes between States and Nationals of other States, 18 March 1965, 575 UNTS 159

Council Regulation (EC) No. 864/2007 of the European Parliament and of the Council of 11 July 2007 on the Law Applicable to Non-contractual Obligations (Rome II), OJ L199/40

Council Regulation (EC) No. 44/2001 of 22 December 2000 on Jurisdiction and the Recognition and Enforcement of Judgments in Civil and Commercial Matters, [2001] OJ L12/1

Council Regulation (EC) No. 2201/2003 of 23 November 2003, concerning Jurisdiction and the Recognition and Enforcement of Judgments in Matrimonial Matters and the Matters of Parental Responsibility, repealing Regulation (EC) 1347/2000, [2003] OJ L338/1

Decision on Differential and more Favourable Treatment, Reciprocity and Fuller Participation of Developing Countries, 28 November 1979, GATT BISD (1980)

ECOWAS 1979 Protocol A/P.1/5/79 relating to Free Movement of Persons, Residence and Establishment

ECOWAS 1985 Supplementary Protocol A/SP.1/7/85 on the Code of Conduct for the implementation of the Protocol on Free Movement of Persons, the Right of Residence and Establishment

ECOWAS 1986 Supplementary Protocol A/SP.1/7/86 on the Second Phase (Right of Residence) of the Protocol on Free Movement of Persons, the Right of Residence and Establishment

ECOWAS 1989 Supplementary Protocol A/SP.1/6/89 amending and complementing the provisions of Article 7 of the Protocol on Free Movement, Right of Residence and Establishment

ECOWAS 1990 Supplementary Protocol A/SP.2/5/90 on the implementation of the Third Phase (Right of Establishment) of the Protocol on Free Movement of Persons, Right of Residence and Establishment

General Agreement on Tariffs and Trade, 15 April 1994, Marrakesh Agreement Establishing the World Trade Organization, Annex 1A, 1867 UNTS 187, 33 ILM 1153

General Agreement on Trade in Services, 15 April 1994, Marrakesh Agreement Establishing the World Trade Organization, Annex 1B, 1869 UNTS 183, 33 ILM 1167

General Convention on Privileges and Immunities of the Organization of African Unity, 25 October 1965, online: www.africa-union.org/root/au/Documents/Treaties/treaties.htm

Hague Convention on the Service Abroad of Judicial and Extra-Judicial Documents in Civil or Commercial Matters, 15 November 1965, 20 UST 361

Hague Convention on the Taking of Evidence Abroad in Civil or Commercial Matters, 18 March 1970, 23 UST 2555

Inter-American Convention on Jurisdiction in the International Sphere for the Extraterritorial Validity of Foreign Judgments, 24 May 1984, 24 ILM 468

Inter-American Convention on the Extraterritorial Validity of Foreign Judgments and Arbitral Awards, 8 May 1979, 1439 UNTS I-24392, 18 ILM 1224

Inter-American Convention on the Law Applicable to International Contracts, 17 March 1994, 33 ILM 732

Lugano Convention on Jurisdiction and Enforcement of Judgments in Civil and Commercial Matters, [2007] OJ L339/3

Marrakesh Agreement Establishing the World Trade Organization, 15 April 1994, 1867 UNTS I-31874, 33 ILM 1144

North American Free Trade Agreement between the United States of America, Canada and Mexico, 17 December 1992, 32 ILM 296

Olivos Protocol for the Settlement of Disputes in MERCOSUR, 18 February 2002, 42 ILM 2

Protocol A/P.1/7/91 on the Community Court of Justice of the High Contracting Parties as amended by Supplementary Protocol A/SP.1/01/05 Amending the Protocol Relating to the Community Court of Justice

Protocol of Tegucigalpa of Reforms to the Charter of the Organization of the Central American States, 13 December 1991

Protocol of the Court of Justice of the African Union, 11 July 2003, (2005) 13 Afr. J. Int'l & Comp. L. 115

Protocol on Relations between the African Economic Community and the Regional Economic Communities, 25 February 1998, (1998) 10 Afr. J. Int'l & Comp. L. 157

Protocol on Relations between the African Union and the Regional Economic Communities, July 2007, online: www.afrimap.org/english/images/treaty/AU-RECs-Protocol.pdf

Protocol on the Commission of Mediation, Conciliation and Arbitration, 21 July 1964, 3 ILM 1116

Protocol on the Establishment of the East African Community Common Market, 20 November 2009, online: www.eac.int/advisory-opinions/cat_view/68-eac-common-market.html

Protocol on the role of National Parliaments in the European Union, 13 December 2007, [2010] OJ C83/203

Protocol on the Statute of the African Court of Justice and Human Rights, 1 July 2008, online: www.africa-union.org/root/au/Documents/Treaties/text/Protocol%20on%20the%20Merged%20Court%20-%20EN.pdf

Protocol to the African Charter on Human and Peoples' Rights on the Establishment of an African Court on Human and Peoples' Rights, 10 June 1998, online: www.africa-union.org/root/au/Documents/Treaties/Text/africancourt-humanrights.pdf

Protocol to the Southern African Development Community Tribunal and the Rules of Procedure Thereof, 7 August 2000, online: www.sadc-tribunal.org/docs/Protocol_on_Tribunal_and_Rules_thereof.pdf

Protocol to the Treaty Establishing the African Economic Community Relating to the Pan-African Parliament, 2 March 2001, (2005) 13 Afr. J. Int'l & Comp. L. 86

Revised Agreement Establishing the Caribbean Court of Justice Trust Fund, 12 January 2004, online: www.caribbeancourtofjustice.org/legislation.html

Revised Treaty Establishing the Economic Community of West African States, 24 July 1993, 35 ILM 660, (1996) 8 Afr. J. Int'l & Comp. L. 187

Revised Treaty of Chaguaramas Establishing the Caribbean Community Including the CARICOM Single Market and Economy, 5 July 2001, 2259 UNTS I-40269, online: www.caricom.org/jsp/community/revised_treaty-text.pdf

Southern African Customs Union Agreement, 21 October 2002, online: www.sacu.int/main.php?include=docs/legislation/2002-agreement/main.html

Southern African Development Community Protocol on Immunities and Privileges, online: www.sadc-tribunal.org/docs/ImmunitiesAndPrevileges.pdf

Statute of the African Union Commission on International Law, 4 February 2009, online: www.africa-union.org/root/au/Documents/Treaties/text/STATUTE%20OF%20THE%20AUCIL-Adopted%20-%20Feb%202009.pdf

Statute of the International Court of Justice, 26 June 1945, 59 Stat. 1055

Treaty Concerning the Establishment and Statute of the Benelux Court of Justice, 31 March 1965, 924 UNTS 13176

Treaty Creating the Court of Justice of the Cartagena Agreement, 28 May 1979, 18 ILM 1203, as revised by the Protocol Modifying the Treaty Creating the Court of Justice of the Cartagena Agreement, 28 May 1996, online: www.comunidadandina.org/ingles/normativa/ande_trie2.htm

Treaty Establishing a Central African Economic and Customs Union, 8 December 1964, 4 ILM 699

Treaty Establishing the African Economic Community, 3 June 1991, 30 ILM 1241

Treaty Establishing the Benelux Union, 3 February 1958, 381 UNTS 5471 (as revised by the Treaty Revising the Treaty Establishing the Benelux Economic Union, 17 June 2008)

Treaty Establishing the Common Market for Eastern and Southern Africa, 5 November 1993, 33 ILM 1067

Treaty Establishing the Economic Community of West African States, 28 May 1975, 1010 UNTS I-14843, 14 ILM 1200

Treaty Establishing the European Atomic Energy Community, 25 March 1957, 298 UNTS 140

Treaty Establishing the European Coal and Steel Community, 18 April 1951, 261 UNTS 140

Treaty Establishing the European Economic Community, 25 March 1957, 298 UNTS 11

Treaty for East African Cooperation, 6 June 1967, 6 ILM 932

Treaty for the Establishment of a Common Market between the Argentine Republic, the Federative Republic of Brazil, the Republic of Paraguay and the Eastern Republic of Uruguay, 26 March 1991, 2140 UNTS I-37341

Treaty for the Establishment of the East African Community, 30 November 1999, 2144 UNTS I-37437

Treaty for the Establishment of the Preferential Trade Area for Eastern and South African States, 21 December 1981, 21 ILM 479

Treaty of the Southern African Development Community, 17 August 1992, 32 ILM 120

Treaty on the Harmonization of Business Law in Africa, 1 November 1997, Official Journal of OHADA No. 4, p. 1

UN Convention on the Recognition and Enforcement of Foreign Arbitral Awards, 10 June 1958, 330 UNTS 3

UNCITRAL Model Law on International Commercial Arbitration, 21 June 1985, 24 ILM 1302

Vienna Convention on the Law of Treaties, 23 May 1969, 1155 UNTS 331, 8 ILM 679

TABLE OF CASES (INTERNATIONAL/REGIONAL COURTS)

Regional courts in Africa

African Court of Human and Peoples Rights

In the Matter of Michelot Yogogombaye v. *Republic of Senegal*, Application No. 001/2008 (African Court of Human and Peoples' Rights, 2009)

COMESA Court of Justice

Building Design Enterprise v. *Common Market for Eastern and Southern Africa*, Application No. 1 of 2002 (COMESA Court of Justice, 2002)

Eastern and Southern African Trade and Development Bank v. *Nyagamukenga*, Reference No. 3 of 2006 (COMESA Court of Justice, 2009)

Eastern and Southern African Trade and Development Bank v. *Ogang* [2001] 1 East Afr. LR 46

Eastern and Southern African Trade and Development Bank v. *Ogang (No. 2)* [2002] 1 East Afr. LR 54

Eritrea v. *Ethiopia* [1999] LawAfr. LR 6

Intelsomac v. *Rwanda Civil Aviation Authority*, Reference No. 1 of 2009 (COMESA Court of Justice, 2010)

Muleya v. *Common Market for Eastern and Southern Africa* [2003] 1 East Afr. LR 173

Muleya v. *Common Market for Eastern and Southern Africa (No. 2)* [2003] 2 East Afr. LR 623

Muleya v. *Common Market for Eastern and Southern Africa (No. 3)* [2004] 1 East Afr. LR 173

Ogang v. *Eastern and Southern African Trade and Development Bank* [2003] 1 East Afr. LR 217

Standard Chartered Financial Services, A. D. Gregory and COMESA. Cahill v. *Court of Appeal for the Republic of Kenya*, Reference No. 4/2002 (COMESA Court of Justice, 2002)

East African Court of Justice

AG of the Republic of Kenya v. *Anyang' Nyong'o*, Application No. 5 of 2007 (East African Court of Justice, 2007)

Anyang' Nyong'o v. *AG of the Republic of Kenya* [2008] 3 KLR 397; [2007] 2 East Afr. LR 5

Calist Andrew Mwatela v. *East Africa Community* [2007] 1 East Afr. LR 237

Christopher Mtikila v. *AG of the United Republic of Tanzania*, Application No. 8 of 2007 (East African Court of Justice, 2007)

East African Community v. *Republic of Kenya* (1970) 9 ILM 561; [1970] EA 512

East African Law Society v. *AG of Kenya* [2008] 1 East Afr. LR 95

East African Law Society v. *AG of the Republic of Kenya* [2007] 1 East Afr. LR 5

James Katabazi v. *Secretary General of the East African Community*, Reference No. 1 of 2007 (East African Court of Justice, 2007)

Matter of a Request by the Council of Minister of the East African Community for an Advisory Opinion, Application No. 1 of 2008 (East African Court of Justice, 2009)

Modern Holdings (EA) Ltd v. *Kenya Ports Authority*, Reference No. 1 of 2008 (East African Court of Justice, 2009)

ECOWAS Court of Justice

Alhaji Hammani Tidjani v. *Federal Republic of Nigeria*, Suit No. ECW/CCJ/APP/01/06 (ECOWAS Court of Justice, 2007)

Chief Ebrimah Manneh v. *The Gambia*, Suit No. ECW/CCJ/JUD/03/08 (ECOWAS Court of Justice, 2008)

Chukwudolue v. *Republic of Senegal*, Judgment No. ECW/CCJ/APP/07/07 (ECOWAS Court of Justice, 2007)

Djoy Bayi v. *Federal Republic of Nigeria*, Suit No. ECW/CCJ/APP/10/06 (ECOWAS Court of Justice, 2009)

Etim Moses Essien v. *Republic of Gambia*, Case No. ECW/CCJ/APP/05/07 (ECOWAS Court of Justice, 2007)

Executive Secretary of ECOWAS v. *Tokunbo Lijadu Oyemade*, Suit No. ECW/CCJ/APP/01/05 (ECOWAS Court of Justice, 2006)

Executive Secretary of ECOWAS v. *Tokunbo Lijadu Oyemade*, Suit No. ECW/CCJ/APP/04/06 (ECOWAS Court of Justice, 2006)

Frank Ukor v. *Alinnor*, Suit No. ECW/CCJ/APP/01/04 (ECOWAS Court of Justice, 2005)

Jerry Ugokwe v. *The Federal Republic of Nigeria*, Case No. ECW/CCJ/APP/02/05 (ECOWAS Court of Justice, 2005)

Mme Hadijatou Mani Koraou v. *The Republic of Niger*, Suit No. ECW/CCJ/JUD/06/08 (ECOWAS Court of Justice, 2008)

Odafe Oserada v. *ECOWAS Council of Ministers*, Judgment No. ECW/CCJ/JUD/01/08 (ECOWAS Court of Justice, 2008)

Olajide Afolabi v. *Federal Republic of Nigeria* [2005] 52 WRN 1

Parliament of ECOWAS v. *Council of Ministers*, Suit No. ECW/CCJ/APP/03/05 (ECOWAS Court of Justice, 2005)

Qudus Gbolanhan Folami v. *Community Parliament (ECOWAS)*, Judgment No. ECW/CCJ/6/10/08 (ECOWAS Court of Justice, 2008)

Tokunbo Lijadu Oyemade v. *Council of Ministers*, Suit No. ECW/CCJ/APP/02/08 (ECOWAS Court of Justice, 2009)

Tokunbo Lijadu Oyemade v. *ECOWAS Council of Ministers*, Judgment No. ECW/CCJ/JUD/02/08 (ECOWAS Court of Justice, 2008)

Tokunbo Lijadu Oyemade v. *Executive Secretary of ECOWAS*, Suit No. ECW/CCJ/APP/01/04 (ECOWAS Court of Justice, 2006)

Tokunbo Lijadu-Oyemade v. *Executive Secretary of ECOWAS*, Suit No. ECW/CCJ/APP/01/05 (ECOWAS Court of Justice, 2005)

Southern African Development Community Tribunal

Albert Fungai Mutize v. *Mike Campbell (Pvt) Ltd*, Case No. SADC (T) 8/08 (SADC Tribunal, 2008)

Bach's Transport (Pty) Ltd v. *The Democratic Republic of Congo*, Case No. SADC (T) 14/2008 (SADC Tribunal, 2010)

Ernest Francis Mtingwi v. *The SADC Secretariat*, Case No. SADC (T) 1/2007 (SADC Tribunal, 2008)

Gideon Stephanus Theron v. *The Republic of Zimbabwe*, Case No. SADC (T) 2/08; 3/08; 4/08; 6/08 (SADC Tribunal, 2008)

Louis Karel Fick v. *The Republic of Zimbabwe*, Case No. SADC (T) 01/2010 (SADC Tribunal, 2010)

Mike Campbell (Pvt) Ltd v. *The Republic of Zimbabwe*, Case No. SADC (T) 2/2007 (SADC Tribunal, 2008)

Mike Campbell (Pvt) Ltd v. *The Republic of Zimbabwe*, Case No. SADC (T) 2/2007 (SADC Tribunal, 2007)

Nixon Chirinda v. *Mike Campbell (Pvt) Ltd*, SADC (T) Case No. 09/08 (SADC Tribunal, 2008)

United Republic of Tanzania v. *Cimexpan (Mauritius) Ltd*, Case No. SADC (T) 01/2009 (SADC Tribunal, 2010)

William Michael Campbell v. *The Republic of Zimbabwe*, Case No. SADC (T) 03/2009 (SADC Tribunal, 2009)

International courts outside Africa

Allianz SpA v. *West Tankers Inc.* (C-185/07) [2009] ECR I-663
Amministrazione delle Finanze dello Stato v. *Simmenthal SpA* (106/77) [1978] ECR 629; 3 CMLR 263
Amsterdam Bulb v. *Produktschap voor Siergewassen* (50/76) [1976] ECR 137
Brazil-Measures Affecting the Importation of Retreaded Tyres (2007), WT/DS332/AB/R (Appellate Body Report)
Chorzow Factory case, PCIJ Ser. A., No. 17, 1928, p. 33
Flaminio Costa v. *ENEL*, Case 6/64, [1964] ECR 585
Hombre Sobrido v. *The French State*, Judgment No. 266/2000 (Court of Appeal of Saint Denis, 2000)
Ingmar GB Ltd v. *Eaton Leonard Technologies Inc.* (C-381/98) [2000] ECR I-9305
Jurisdiction of the Courts of Danzig (Pecuniary Claims of Danzig Railway Officials who have Passed into the Polish Service, against the Polish Railways Administration) PCIJ, Ser. B., No. 15, 1928, p. 12
Krombach v. *Bamberski* (C-7/98) [2000] ECR I-1935
Loewen Group Inc. v. *United States*, 42 ILM 811
Merce Pesca Co. v. *The French State*, Judgment No. 267/2000 (Court of Appeal of Saint Denis, 2000)
Mexico-Tax Measures on Soft Drinks and other Beverages (2006), WT/DS308/AB/R (Appellate Body Report)
Mondev International Ltd v. *United States*, 42 ILM 85
Opinion 1/91, *Draft Agreement between the Community and the Countries of the European Free Trade Association relating to the Creation of the European Economic Area* [1991] ECR I–06079
Opinion 1/00, *Proposed Agreement between the European Community and non-Member States on the establishment of a European Common Aviation Area* [2002] ECR I–03493
Owusu v. *Jackson* (C-281/02) [2005] ECR I-1383
Parliament v. *Council* (C-302/87) [1988] ECR 5616
Parliament v. *Council* (C-70/88) [1990] ECR I-2041
Regie Nationale des Usines Renault SA v. *Maxicar SpA* (C-38/98) [2000] ECR I-2973
Reparation for Injuries Suffered in the Service of the United Nations, Advisory Opinion, [1949] ICJ Reports 174
Trinidad Cement Ltd v. *The Caribbean Community* [2009] CCJ 2 (OJ)
Trinidad Cement Ltd v. *The Co-operative Republic of Guyana* [2008] CCJ 1 (OJ)
Trinidad Cement Ltd v. *The State of the Co-operative Republic of Guyana* [2009] CCJ 1 (OJ)
Turner v. *Grovit* (C-159/02) [2004] ECR I-3565
United States – Standards for Reformulated and Conventional Gasoline (1996), WTO Doc. WT/DS2/AB/R (Appellate Body Report)

United States: Sections 301–310 of the Trade Act of 1974 (1999), WT/DS/152/R (Panel Report)

Van Gend en Loos v. *Nederlandse Administratie der Belastingen* (26/62) [1963] ECR 1; [1963] CMLR 105

Von Colson and Kamann v. *Land Nordrhein-Westfalen* (14/83) [1984] ECR 1891

Yassin Abdullah Kadi and Al Barakaat International Foundation v. *Council of the European Union and Commission of the European Communities* (C-402 and 415/05) [2008] ECR I-6351

TABLE OF CASES (NATIONAL COURTS)

National courts in Africa

Abacha v. *Fawehinmi* [2000] 6 NWLR 228
Administrator, Transvaal v. *Traub* 1989 (4) SA 731
Afinta Financial Services (Pty) Ltd v. *Luke Malinga T/A Long Distance Transport*, Civ. Case No. 123/2001 (High Court, Swaziland, 2001)
AG v. *Dow* 1992 BLR 119
American Flag plc v. *Great African T-shirt Corp.* 2000 (1) SA 356
A.O. Agunanne v. *Nigeria Tobacco Co. Ltd* [1979] 2 FNLR 13
Argos Fishing Co. Ltd v. *Friopesca SA* 1991 NR 106
B & W Industrial Technology Ltd v. *Baroutsos* 2006 (2) SA 135
Baldwin v. *Baldwin* [1967] RLR 289
Bank of Baroda v. *Iyalabani Co. Ltd* [2002] 40 WRN 13
Barclays Bank of Swaziland v. *Koch* 1997 BLR 1294
Barclays Bank of Swaziland Ltd v. *Mnyeketi* 1992 (2) SA 425
Barlows Central Finance Corp. Ltd v. *Joncon Ltd*, Case No. 2491/99 (High Court, Swaziland, 1999)
Berrange NO v. *Hassan* 2009 (2) SA 339
Bid Industrial Holding v. *Strang* 2008 (3) SA 355
Bizy Holdings Ltd v. *Eso Management Ltd* 2002 (2) BLR 125
Blanchard, Krasner & French v. *Evans* 2002 (4) SA 144
Blanchard, Krasner & French v. *Evans* 2004 (4) SA 427
Bozimo Trade and Development Ltd v. *First Merchant Bank of Zimbabwe Ltd* 2000 (1) ZLR 1
Broderick v. *Northern Engineering Product* [1991] 2 GLR 88
Burchell v. *Anglin* 2010 (3) SA 48
Burdock Investment v. *Time Bank of Zimbabwe Ltd* HH 194/03 HC 9038/02 (High Court, Zimbabwe, 2003)
Cairo Bank v. *Mohamed Ali Bahaydar* 1966 (1) ALR Comm. 33
Charles Thys v. *Herman Steyn* [2006] eKLR
Chihana v. *Republic*, MSCA Criminal Appeal No. 9 of 1992 (Supreme Court, Malawi, 1992)
Chiraga v. *Msimuko* 2004 (1) SA 98

Chloride Batteries Ltd v. *Viscocity*, Civil Cause No. 1896 of 2006 (High Court, Malawi, 2006)
Chong Sun Wood Products Ltd v. *K & T Trading Ltd* 2001 (2) SA 651
Coluflandres Ltd v. *Scandia Industrial Product Ltd* 1969 (2) RLR 431
Commercial Farmers Union v. *Minister of Lands and Rural Resettlement*, Judgment No. SC 31/10 (Supreme Court, Zimbabwe, 2010)
Coutts v. *Ford* 1997 (1) ZLR 440
De Gree v. *Webb* 2007 (5) SA 184
Delmas America Africa Line Inc. v. *Kisko Products Ghana Ltd* [2005-6] SCGLR 75
Detmold v. *Minister of Health and Social Services* 2004 NR 175
Dow v. *AG* 1991 BLR 233
Drive Control Services Ltd v. *Troycom Systems Ltd* 2000 (2) SA 722
Eastern and Southern African Trade v. *Hassan Basajjabalaba* [2007] Uganda Commercial Court 30
Echodelta Ltd v. *Kerr and Downey Safaris* 2004 (1) SA 509
Eden v. *Pienaar* 2001 (1) SA 158
Edicomesa International Inc. v. *Citec International Estates Ltd* [2006] 4 NWLR 114
Ekkehard Creutzburg v. *Commercial Bank of Namibia* [2006] All SA 327
Emmanuel Bitwire v. *The Republic of Zaire* [1998] I Kampala LR 21
Fasco Trading Co. Ltd v. *Goodearth Ltd* [2000] LawAfr. LR 1236
Fattal v. *Fattal* [1999–2000] 1 GLR 331
Fick v. *Government of the Republic of Zimbabwe*, Case No. 77881/2009 (North Gauteng High Court, South Africa, 2010)
Fonville v. *Kelly* [2002] 1 East Afr. LR 71
Friday Anderson Jumbe v. *Humphrey Chimpando*, Constitutional Case Nos. 1 and 2 of 2005 (High Court, Malawi, 2005)
Friendship Container Manufacturing Ltd v. *Mitchell Cotts Ltd* [2001] East Afr. LR 338
George Lipimile v. *Mpulungu Harbour Management*, Judgment No. 22 of 2008 (Supreme Court, Zambia, 2008)
Georgina Ngina v. *Inter Freight East Africa Ltd* [2006] eKLR
Ghassan Halaoui v. *Grosvenor Casinos Ltd* [2002] 17 NWLR 28
Gramara (Pvt) Ltd v. *Government of the Republic of Zimbabwe*, HC 33/09 (Zimbabwe, High Court, 2010)
Hay Management Consultants (Pty) Ltd v. *P3 Management Consultants (Pty) Ltd* 2005 (2) SA 522
Healthwise Pharmaceuticals Ltd v. *Smithkline Beecham Consumer Healthcare Ltd* [2001] LawAfr. LR 1279
Herbst v. *Surti* 1990 (2) ZLR 269
Heyns v. *Demetriou* [2001] Malawi High Court 52
Higgs v. *Minister of National Security* [2000] 2 WLR 1368
Hoffman v. *South African Airways* 2001 (1) SA 1

Hulse-Reutter v. *Godde* 2001 (4) SA 1336
In the Matter of an Application by Evan Maina, Case No. 7/1969 (Kenya)
International Trade Administration Commission v. *SCAW South Africa (Pty) Ltd* [2010] ZACC 6
Italframe Ltd v. *Mediterranean Shipping Co.* [1986] KLR 54
Jammal v. *Abdalla Hashem* 1975 (2) ALR Comm. 141
John Holt v. *Christoph Nutsugah* (1929–1931) Gold Coast Divisional Court 75
K v. *K* 1999 (4) SA 691
Kells v. *Ako Adjei*, Case No. CA 8/2000 (Supreme Court, Ghana)
Lamus Agricultural Services Co. Ltd v. *Gwembe Valley Dev. Ltd* [1999] Zambia LR 1
Lepota v. *Hyland*, CIV/APN/280/87 (High Court, Lesotho, 1991)
Lesotho Express Delivery Services Ltd v. *Ravin Panambalana*, Civ/T/634A/02; Civ/T/APN/469/02 (High Court, Lesotho, 2006)
Lisse v. *The Minister of Health and Social Services* 2004 NR 107
MAK (Pty) Ltd v. *St Paul Insurance Co. SA Ltd* 2007 (1) BLR 210
Makwindi Oil Procurement Ltd v. *National Oil Co. of Zimbabwe* 1988 (2) SA 690
Makwindi Oil Procurement Ltd v. *National Oil Co. of Zimbabwe* 1989 (3) SA 191
Mashchinen Frommer GmbH v. *Trisave Engineering & Machinery Supplies (Pty) Ltd* 2003 (6) SA 69
Metlika Trading Ltd v. *Commissioner, South African Revenue Service* 2005 (3) SA 1
Microsoft Corp. v. *Mitsumi Computer Garage Ltd* [2001] KLR 470
Mike Campbell (Pvt) Ltd v. *Minister of National Security Responsible for Land, Land Reform and Resettlement*, Judgment No. SC 49/07 (Zimbabwe, Supreme Court, 2008)
Minister for Welfare and Population Development v. *Fitzpatrick* 2000 (3) SA 422
Minister of Immigration and Ethnic Affairs v. *Teoh* (1995) 183 CLR 273
Molifi v. *Independent Electoral Commission*, Civil No. 11/05, CC: 135/05 (Court of Appeal, Lesotho, 2005)
Molly Kiwanuka v. *Samuel Muwanga* [1999] Swaziland High Court 13
Moolla Group Ltd v. *Commissioner, South African Revenue Service* 2003 (6) SA 244
Movement for Democratic Change v. *President of the Republic of Zimbabwe*, HC 1291/05 (Zimbabwe, High Court, 2007)
Mtui v. *Mtui* 2000 (1) BLR 406
New Patriotic Party v. *Inspector General of Police* [1993–94] 2 GLR 459
Nika Fishing Co. Ltd v. *Lavinia Corp.* [2001] 16 NWLR 556
Nku v. *Nku* 1998 BLR 187
Noble Builders (U) Ltd v. *Sandhu* [2004] 2 East Afr. LR 228
Okunda v. *Republic* (1969) 91 ILM 556; [1970] East Afr. LR 453
Okunda v. *Republic* [1970] East Afr. LR 457
Owens v. *Owens* [1959] EA 909
Pakou v. *Rudnap Zambia Ltd* (1998) ZR 233
Pastificio Lucio Garofalo SPA v. *Security & Fire Equipment Co.* [2001] KLR 483

Patel v. *Bank of Baroda* [2001] 1 East Afr. LR 189
Peter Anyang' Nyong'o v. *AG* [2007] eKLR (Kenya High Court, 19 March 2007)
Pioneer General Assurance Society Ltd v. *Zulfikarali Nimji Javer* [2006] eKLR
Progress Office Machines v. *South African Revenue Services* 2008 (2) SA 13
R. v. *Obert Sithembiso Chikane*, Crim. Case No. 41/2000 (High Court, Swaziland, 2003)
Rage Mohammed Ali v. *Abdullahim Maasai* [2005] eKLR
Raytheon Aircraft Credit Corp. v. *Air Al-Faraj Ltd* [2005] 2 KLR 47
Re Lowenthal and Air France 1966 (2) ALR Comm. 301
Re the Maintenance Orders Enforcement Ordinance (1954) 27 KLR 94
Republic of Angola v. *Springbok Investment Ltd* 2005 (2) BLR 159
Republic of Kenya v. *Coastal Aquaculture* [2003] 1 East Afr. LR 271
Republic v. *Kenya Revenue Authority, ex parte Aberdare Freight Services Ltd* [2004] 2 KLR 530
Richard Thomas Etheredge v. *Minister of State for National Security Responsible for Lands, Land Reform and Resettlement*, Suit No. 3295/08 (High Court, Zimbabwe, 2008)
Richman v. *Ben-Tovim* 2006 (2) SA 591
Richman v. *Ben-Tovim* 2007 (2) SA 283
Riddlesbarger v. *Robson* [1958] East Afr. LR 375
Roger Parry v. *Astral Operations Ltd* 2005 (10) BLLR 989
Rono v. *Rono* [2005] KLR 538
Royal Dutch Airlines (KLM) v. *Farmex Ltd* [1989–90] 1 GLR 46
S v. *Shaik* 2008 (5) SA 354
SDV Transmi (Tanzania) Ltd v. *MS STE Datco*, Civil Application No. 97 of 2004 (Court of Appeal, Tanzania, 2004)
Sello v. *Sello (No. 2)* 1999 (2) BLR 104
Shah v. *Aperit Investment SA* [2002] KLR 1
Shah v. *Manurama Ltd* [2003] 1 East Afr. LR 294
Showlag v. *Mansour* [1995] 1 AC 431
Signal Oil & Gas Co. v. *Bristow Helicopters Ltd* [1976] 1 GLR 371
Sikunda v. *Government of the Republic of Namibia* 2001 NR 86
Silverston Ltd v. *Lobatse Clay Works* 1996 BLR 190
Sylvanus Juxon-Smith v. *KLM Royal Dutch Airline*, Civil Appeal No. J4/19/2005 (Supreme Court, Ghana, 2005)
Société de Transports International Rwanda v. *H. Abdi*, Civil Application No. NAI 298 of 1997 (Court of Appeal, Kenya, 1997)
Society of Lloyd's v. *Price* 2006 (5) SA 393
Ssebaggala & Sons Electric Centre Ltd v. *Kenya National Shipping Line Ltd* [2000] LawAfr. LR 931
Steinberg v. *Cosmopolitan National Bank of Chicago* 1973 (4) SA 564
Sunrise Travel and Tours Ltd v. *Wanjigi* [2002] LawAfr. LR 5933
Supercat Inc. v. *Two Oceans Marine* 2001 (4) SA 27

Tononoka Steels Ltd v. *East & Southern African Trade & Development Bank* [2002] 2 East Afr. LR 536
Transroad Ltd v. *Bank of Uganda* [1998] UGA J. No. 12
United Watch & Diamond Co (Pty) Ltd v. *Disa Hotels Ltd* 1972 (4) SA 409
Valentine Investment Co. Ltd v. *Federal Republic of Germany* [2006] eKLR
Von Abo v. *The Government of the Republic of South Africa* 2009 (2) SA 526
Von Abo v. *Government of the Republic of South Africa* 2010 (3) SA 269
Wachter v. *Harlley* [1968] GLR 1069
Willow Investment v. *Mbomba Ntumba* [1997] TLR 47

National courts outside Africa

The Atlantic Star [1973] QB 364
Beals v. *Saldanha* [2003] 3 SCR 416; 234 DLR (4th) 1
Blackburn v. *AG* [1971] 1 WLR 1073
Committee of United States Citizens Living in Nicaragua v. *Ronald Wilson Reagan* 859 F.2d 929
Hunt v. *T & N plc* [1993] 4 SCR 289; 109 DLR (4th) 16
J.H. Rayner (Mincing Lane) Ltd v. *Department of Trade and Industry* [1989] Ch. 72
J.H. Rayner (Mincing Lane) Ltd v. *Department of Trade and Industry* [1990] 2 AC 418
John Pfeiffer Ltd v. *Rogerson* (2000) 203 CLR 503
Jose Ernesto Medellin v. *Texas* 128 S. Ct 1346 (2008)
Macarthys Ltd v. *Smith* [1979] ICR 785
Macarthys Ltd v. *Smith* [1981] QB 180
Morguard Investments Ltd v. *De Savoye* [1990] 3 SCR 1077; 76 DLR (4th) 256
Pfizer Inc. v. *Canada (T.D.)* [1999] 4 FC 441; (1999) 2 CPR (4th) 298
R. v. *Jones (Margaret)* [2007] AC 136
Regie National des Usines Renault SA v. *Zhang* (2002) 210 CLR 491
Socobel v. *Greek State* (1951) 18 Int'l L. Rep. 3
Thoburn v. *Sunderland CC* [2003] QB 151
Tolofson v. *Jensen* [1994] 3 SCR 1022; 120 DLR (4th) 289
Trendtex Trading Corp. v. *Central Bank of Nigeria* [1977] QB 529

ABBREVIATIONS

AEC	African Economic Community
AEC Treaty	Treaty Establishing the African Economic Community
AMU	Arab Maghreb Union
Assembly Rules	Rules of Procedure of the Assembly of the African Union
AU	African Union
AU Court Protocol	Protocol of the Court of Justice of the African Union
Benelux Treaty	Treaty Establishing the Benelux Union
Brussels I Regulation	Council Regulation (EC) No. 44/2001 of 22 December 2000 on Jurisdiction and the Recognition and Enforcement of Judgments in Civil and Commercial Matters
Caribbean Court Agreement	Agreement Establishing the Caribbean Court of Justice
CARICOM Treaty	Revised Treaty of Chaguaramas Establishing the Caribbean Community Including the CARICOM Single Market and Economy
CEMAC	Central African Economic and Monetary Community
CENSAD	Community of Sahel-Saharan States
CEPGL	Economic Community of Great Lakes Countries
COMESA	Common Market for Eastern and Southern Africa
COMESA Arbitration Rules	Common Market for Eastern and Southern Africa Court of Justice Arbitration Rules
COMESA Treaty	Treaty Establishing the Common Market for Eastern and Southern Africa
EAC	East African Community
EAC Arbitration Rules	East African Court of Justice Arbitration Rules
EAC Treaty	Treaty for the Establishment of the East African Community
EALA	East African Legislative Assembly
ECCAS	Economic Community of Central African States
ECJ	Court of Justice of the European Union
ECOMOG	ECOWAS Monitoring Group

ECOWAS	Economic Community of West African States
ECOWAS Court Protocol	Protocol A/P.1/7/91 on the Community Court of Justice of the High Contracting Parties as amended by Supplementary Protocol A/SP/.1/01/05 Amending the Protocol Relating to the Community Court of Justice
ECOWAS Treaty	Revised Treaty Establishing the Economic Community of West African States
ECSC	European Coal and Steel Community
ECSC Treaty	Treaty Establishing the European Coal and Steel Community
EEA Agreement	Agreement on the European Economic Area
EFTA Court Agreement	Agreement between the EFTA States on the Establishment of a Surveillance Authority and a Court of Justice
EU	European Union
EU Treaty	Consolidated Version of the Treaty on the Functioning of the European Union
Executive Council Rules	Rules of Procedure of the Executive Council
ICJ	International Court of Justice
ICSID	International Centre for Settlement of Investment Disputes
ICSID Convention	Convention on the Settlement of Investment Disputes between States and Nationals of other States
IGAD	Inter-Governmental Authority on Development
IOC	Indian Ocean Commission
MERCOSUR	Mercado Comun del Cono Sur (Southern Cone Common Market)
MRU	Mano River Union
NAFTA	North American Free Trade Agreement
New York Arbitration Convention	UN Convention on the Recognition and Enforcement of Foreign Arbitral Awards
NGO	Non-Governmental Organization
OAS	Organization of American States
OAU	Organization of African Unity
OAU Charter	Charter of the Organization of African Unity
OHADA	Organisation for the Harmonization of Business Laws in Africa
OHADA Treaty	Treaty on the Harmonization of Business Law in Africa
Protocol on Relations	Protocol on Relations between the African Union and the Regional Economic Communities, July 2007

Protocol on Relations – 1998	Protocol on Relations between the African Economic Community and the Regional Economic Communities, February 1998
Protocol on the African Court of Justice	Protocol on the Statute of the African Court of Justice and Human Rights
Protocol on the Pan-African Parliament	Protocol to the Treaty Establishing the African Economic Community Relating to the Pan-African Parliament
PTA	Preferential Trade Area
PTA Treaty	Treaty for the Establishment of the Preferential Trade Area for Eastern and South African States
REC	Regional Economic Community
SACU	Southern African Customs Union
SADC	Southern African Development Community
SADC Treaty	Treaty of the Southern African Development Community
SADC Tribunal Protocol	Protocol to the Southern African Development Community Tribunal and Rules of Procedure Thereof
Statute of the African Court of Justice	Statute of the African Court of Justice and Human Rights
Treaty of Rome	Treaty Establishing the European Economic Community
UEMOA	Union Economique et Monétaire Ouest Africaine (West African Economic and Monetary Union)
UMA	Union du Maghreb Arabe (Arab Maghreb Union)
UN	United Nations Organization
UNCTAD	UN Conference on Trade and Development
UNECA	UN Economic Commission for Africa
WTO	World Trade Organization
WTO Agreement	Marrakesh Agreement Establishing the World Trade Organization

Introduction

> The piercing of national borders by transnational norms finds its strongest expression in the formation of regional communities of states which seek to develop a common fund of legal rules, concepts and principles among their members (Ulrich Scheuner, forward to C. J. Mann, *The Function of Judicial Decision in European Integration* (1971))

African states that have, for decades since their independence, held on to the idea of nation-state and national sovereignty appear to be on the path towards rejecting both. The immediate post-independence era saw a zealous assertion of national sovereignty by African states and attempts to develop stronger and more stable national institutions. In recent times, and with the resurgence of 'African consciousness' – African renaissance – calls have been made for the transfer of sovereignty away from the state to regional and continental institutions. National separatism is being abandoned in favour of regional and continental integration. Through numerous treaties, African states have positioned themselves on a path to economic integration. The route is complex, tortuous and fraught with social, economic, political and legal challenges. The ultimate goal is to create an African Economic Community (AEC). To get there, eight regional economic communities (communities) have been recognized by the African Union (AU) and given the mandate to progress gradually, ultimately with the view to merging to form the AEC.

The idea of integrating Africa, economically and politically, has a long history. But successive attempts have been largely ineffective and unsuccessful. As Hazlewood once observed, 'studies of economic and political integration between African states have as much or more to say about the weakening of existing ties than about the coming together of those who were apart. . . . Economic integration, however, has fared little better than political integration, and from the viewpoint of economic development this is greatly to be regretted.'[1] These views were expressed in 1967. It is gratifying to report that, unlike the previous attempts at economic integration, the current efforts are making significant progress, albeit slowly.[2]

At present, the need for African states to integrate their economies to enhance their growth and development is widely accepted. How it should be pursued, however, remains contested and well debated. The economic, social and political significance and dimensions of the endeavour are far-reaching. They have been well explored in many treatises. This book does not attempt to rehearse these issues; rather, its focus is a much neglected aspect – the *legal* aspects of Africa's economic integration processes. It uses a relational framework as the medium of analysis. It examines how what I have characterized as relational issues of law in economic integration are being approached in Africa. At their core, relational issues deal with the legal interactions among community, national, regional and international legal systems within the context of economic integration. The theory is that effective economic integration is the product of properly structuring and managing – within well-defined legal frameworks – vertical, horizontal and vertico-horizontal relations among states, legal systems, laws and institutions. Put differently, an economic community must have well-structured and managed relations between itself and other legal systems as a necessary condition for its effectiveness.

This book expounds this theory and applies it to Africa's economic integration processes. It uses four of the AU recognized communities – the Economic Community of West African States (ECOWAS), the Common Market for Eastern and Southern Africa (COMESA), the East African Community (EAC) and the Southern African Development Community (SADC) – as its principal focus. These communities, which are at varying stages of development, have many aims; but they all aim to create regions in Africa, and ultimately a continent, in which goods, services, labour and capital are able to and will circulate freely. These objectives are to be achieved in successive stages largely consistent with a linear model of economic integration – free trade area, customs union, common market and economic union.

The first chapter sets the stage for the discussion in the subsequent chapters. It defines some of the key concepts that are used in the book,

[1] Hazlewood (1967), pp. 3–4.
[2] United Nations Economic Commission for Africa (2010), pp. 7–35.

introduces the various communities which are the focus of this study, and provides a brief overview of the socio-economic and political context within which the current economic integration efforts are being pursued in Africa. Chapter 2 develops the thesis that effective economic integration is the product of properly structuring and managing, within well-defined legal frameworks, vertical, horizontal and vertico-horizontal relations among states, legal systems, laws and institutions. The chapter draws on the comparative jurisprudence, treaties and experiences of various economic communities, including some in Africa. It takes on board perspectives from constitutional, public and private international law. From these, the chapter distils and examines principles that are used by economic communities to manage relational issues. The extent to which these principles are reflected in community laws in Africa, their limitations and the factors that condition their effective use are the subject of subsequent chapters.

Chapter 3 addresses the complex and perplexing problem of the relationships between the AU, AEC and Africa's communities, as well as those between the Regional Economic Communities (RECs). Untangling and understanding this complex web of relations is essential to appreciate some of the institutional deficiencies that currently bedevil Africa's integration processes, especially at the continental level. The chapter draws on the emerging scholarship on international regime complexity and argues, to an extent, the character of international institutional density in Africa's economic integration is unique and presents its own challenges. The legal framework for regulating this institutional density is examined. The examination exposes a number of issues – present and future – that could undermine attaining the AEC's objectives. Some of these issues, especially regarding enforcement of AEC law, are further explored in Chapter 6.

Chapter 4 continues with the focus on the AEC. It examines aspects of the AEC Treaty with an eye on issues such as the nature of the AEC's legal system, supremacy of community law and harmonization of national laws. Although the discussion focuses on the AEC, it is equally relevant and applicable to the other communities. Without underplaying the importance of the issues examined in Chapters 3 and 4, it must be cautioned that, given the state of development of the AEC – it is still in formation and its own development is largely contingent on that of the constituent RECs – many of the issues examined in both chapters are likely to become more concrete in the future.

Chapter 5 shifts the focus to the COMESA, EAC, ECOWAS and SADC by drawing on their concrete experiences with relational issues. It uses their constitutive treaties and the jurisprudence of their respective community courts or tribunals as the basis of the analysis. Although the jurisprudence is comparatively scant (albeit expanding) and has mainly dealt with issues not directly related to economic integration, the few cases that have been decided offer very useful insights into how the courts can help to address some of the relational issues and limitations on their work. With the experiences of COMESA, EAC, ECOWAS and SADC in mind, and against the background of the theory that structured relations between community and national institutions are important for effective economic integration, Chapter 6 re-focuses on the AEC. The chapter examines the adequacy of the executive, legislative and judicial institutions of the AEC in meeting the demands of effective economic integration. It devotes particular attention to the structure and jurisdiction of the African Court of Justice and Human Rights. This court will ultimately be responsible for adjudicating economic integration issues in Africa. The chapter examines whether the court is adequately designed to meet the needs of economic integration, especially as regards its subject matter and personal jurisdiction, and its relationship with national courts.

Individuals play a central role in economic integration. Like institutions, they also serve as media for creating relations between legal systems. Their actions, especially through litigation, are important for the enforcement of community law. But their actions, which are aimed at ensuring the effectiveness of community law, can often be hampered by existing national legal infrastructure. These provide the background to Chapter 7, which assesses the implementation of community law within member states. This is an issue of direct concern to individuals who seek to benefit from community law in those member states. The chapter examines how national implementation of community law is approached within Africa's communities and member states. It also assesses how national constitutions and jurisprudence may constrain or enhance the communities' vision of the place of their laws in member states and, concomitantly, the ability of individuals to benefit from such laws.

Community–state and interstate relations are often discussed using perspectives from public international law and national constitutional law. The preceding chapters are situated within that discourse. However, as Chapter 2 demonstrates, a place exists for private international law in dealing with the relationship between legal systems in the context of economic integration. For example, effective economic integration demands strengthened interstate relations that create an enabling climate for economic transactions. Chapters 8 and 9 examine the role of private international law in managing interstate and community–state relations in Africa's economic integration processes. Chapter 8 examines some relational issues arising from the communities' constitutive treaties and laws on which public and private international law principles may have an impact. The chapter examines the impact that public and private international law may have on the effective operation of community institutions, especially the community courts. Among the issues examined are the arbitral jurisdiction of community courts, enforcement of their judgments, conflict of jurisdiction between community courts and judicial cooperation between community and national courts.

Chapter 9 uses private international law as a barometer to measure the extent to which African national legal systems are integrated. Private international law principles coordinate or regulate relations between legal systems. They can aid or constrain economic integration processes and economic transactions which take place within them. A principal issue addressed in the chapter is the recognition and enforcement of foreign judgments. Enforcing foreign judgments is, perhaps, the best manifestation of how sovereign legal systems relate to each other; they validate and give effect to each other's norms. The chapter examines existing foreign judgment enforcement regimes and their suitability for the demands of economic integration. It also provides a general assessment of private international law in Africa and suggests values that should inform the development of a regime that can meet the needs of economic integration. Chapter 10 provides the conclusion.

A common thread running through the chapters is that Africa's economic integration processes have not paid the necessary attention to relational issues: the issues have not been properly addressed. At present, there is no solid or carefully thought through framework to manage relations between community and member states' legal systems, among the various communities, as well as among member states' legal systems. Attempts to provide such a legal framework have been incomplete, unsatisfactory or grounded on questionable assumptions. This book argues that such shortfalls should be remedied to ensure the effectiveness of Africa's economic integration. To that end, the book, in various sections, proposes amendments to community and national laws.

1

Africa's economic integration – an introductory overview

1.1 Introduction

Economic integration is defined 'as the elimination of economic frontiers between two or more economies'.[1] In this regard, an economic frontier represents a demarcation – often the geographical boundaries of a state – into which the flow of goods, labour and capital is restricted. Economic integration involves the removal of obstacles to trans-boundary economic activities which occur in the fields of trade, movement of labour, services and the flow of capital. Economists have identified various stages in the process of economic integration. According to Bela Balassa, economic integration passes through five stages, namely: 'a free trade area, a customs union, a common market, an economic union, and complete economic integration'.[2] In a free-trade area, tariffs and quantitative restrictions on trade between the participating countries are abolished, but each country retains its own tariffs against non-members. Establishing a customs union involves, besides the suppression of discrimination in the field of commodity movements within the union, the equalization of tariffs in trade with non-member countries. A common market is a higher form of economic integration. In a common market, both restrictions on trade and factor movements are abolished. An economic union combines the suppression of restrictions on commodity and factor movements with some degree of harmonization of national economic policies to remove discrimination due to the disparities in these policies. Finally, total economic integration presupposes the unification of monetary, fiscal, social and countercyclical policies and requires the setting-up of a supranational authority, the decisions of which are binding on member states.

The first three stages involve negative integration. The stages entail the removal of discrimination in national economic rules and policies under

[1] Pelkmans (1986), p. 318. [2] Balassa (1962), p. 2.

joint and authoritative surveillance and, generally, placing limitations on national economic decision-making.[3] These are difficult stages in integration. They entail restrictions on countries' sovereign rights to take decisions affecting the socio-economic well-being of their residents. An economic union and complete economic integration are characterized as positive integration. They involve 'the transfer of public market-rule-making and policy-making powers from the participating polities to the union level'.[4] Balassa's linear model of economic integration has been criticized,[5] but it is still widely followed by economists.[6] It has shaped many economic integration initiatives, including some in Africa.

Economic integration is important to Africa and is currently being pursued at regional and continental levels. The urgency with which it must be pursued was expressed by the United Nations Economic Commission for Africa (UNECA) in these words: 'This shift [the global move to integrate economies] is nowhere more urgent than in Africa, where the combined impact of our relatively small economies, international terms of trade, and the legacy of colonialism, mis-rule, and conflict has meant that we have not yet assumed our global market share – despite our significant market size.'[7] It is envisaged that uniting African economies will permit economies of scale, make them more competitive, provide access to wider trading and investment environments, promote exports to regional markets, provide the requisite experience to enter global markets and provide a framework for them to cooperate in developing common services for finance, transportation and communication.[8] The economic philosophy that underlies these visions is neo-liberal economic thinking that emphasizes, among others, free trade and the removal of obstacles to investment.

The need to integrate African economies is widely accepted. But its nature, scope, focus and theoretical underpinning remain contested.[9] Some have questioned the state-centred formal economy focus of Africa's economic integration processes and advocated a re-focus on informal trading structures that exist within and among African countries. Others have advocated cooperation on specific projects in areas such

[3] Pelkmans (1986), p. 321. [4] Balassa (1962), p. 2.
[5] McCarthy (2008), pp. 24–40. [6] Pelkmans (1986), pp. 324–6.
[7] United Nations Economic Commission for Africa (2004), p. ix; and United Nations Conference on Trade and Development (2009).
[8] United Nations Economic Commission for Africa (2002), pp. 2–11.
[9] Boas (2001), p. 27; Meagher (2001), p. 41; Lesser and Moise-Leeman (2008); Mazzeo (1984), p. 165; and Senghor (1990), p. 17.

as agriculture, infrastructure and technology. Similarly, while some advocate regionalism, others emphasize the need for immediate, continent-wide integration. This debate in Africa can be seen as part of the wider international economic law debate on regionalism and multilateralism. Regionalism in Africa has benefits.[10] It will allow for region-specific initiatives. The relatively small size of RECs, in terms of the number of countries engaged, also makes for easy management and decision-making. Africa consists of fifty-three sovereign countries. Thus, perhaps, regionalism is the only manageable option. Competition among RECs may also be an avenue for development through efficiency gains. Regionalism in Africa also has disadvantages. It can reduce member states' commitment to ensuring the emergence of continent-wide integration. Multiple commitments given by states to RECs, resulting from multiple memberships of such organizations, can lead to non-compliance and jurisdictional conflicts. Additionally, countries with relatively large and developed economies may benefit at the expense of the smaller regional members.

While the above discussions are interesting, very little has been discussed about the legal issues arising from Africa's economic integration processes.[11] A difficult problem in economic integration is what I characterize as relational issues of law in economic integration (hereafter relational issues), which take on various forms, including: the relations between the laws of a community (community law[12]), its institutions and those of its member states; mechanisms for normative exchange or communication between a community and its member states and member states *inter se*; jurisdictional conflicts between a community and its member states; the allocation of competences between a community and its member states; individuals' access to community institutions; and the recognition and enforcement of member state and community normative acts.

These issues become more prominent especially when the economic integration process progresses through the various stages of integration. A free-trade area may exist without well-structured and managed relations between the community and national legal systems, but a customs

[10] Mulat (1998). [11] Kulusika (2000), p. 20; Salami (2008); and Akinrinsola (2004).

[12] Community law takes the form of treaty provisions, protocols, regulations and judicial decisions. Although not laws as such, the objectives, principles and undertakings of member states as outlined in the communities' treaties are of legal consequence. Like laws, they are meant to guide conduct and are enforceable.

union, common market or economic union cannot operate effectively without attention to relational issues. This is because the interactions between legal systems deepen as economic integration progresses through the various stages of integration. In Africa, relational issues are further complicated by Africa's unique approach to achieving continental integration. The approach uses pre-existing RECs as building blocks for a continent-wide economic community called the African Economic Community (AEC).[13] Other RECs have adopted an approach that involves expansion through the addition of new states to a core of founding members.

The emphasis on relational issues is meant to bring to the fore the importance of law as an instrument for economic integration. A purely economic or socio-political approach to, or analysis of, economic integration should be viewed with caution, as it fails to appreciate the important fact that obstacles to trans-boundary economic activity are not only economic or socio-political, but are also sometimes legal. National and international laws limit the movement of persons, goods, services and capital. These limitations may be informed by economic and socio-political considerations, but it is through the medium of law that the limitations are realized. An understanding of economic integration that envisages laws as an instrument for integration should immediately position law at the forefront of the process. As Pescatore has observed: 'The process of integration can have no real consistency and, above all, no real stability or lasting force unless we succeed in giving it a sufficiently solid institutional and legal framework.'[14] Attention to relational issues is an important aspect of this endeavour. The role of law in economic integration can be discussed from multiple perspectives. This book focuses mainly on legal and institutional structures, law-making processes, interactions between different legal systems, and implementation and enforcement of laws. One could argue that law should not be given any role or a major role to play in economic integration; rather, the emphasis should be placed on informal institutional structures, cooperation, voluntary compliance and the good faith of politicians to implement agreed objectives.[15] This is neither a view to which I subscribe, nor which the book advances.

[13] Treaty Establishing the African Economic Community, 3 June 1991, 30 ILM 1241 (hereafter, AEC Treaty).

[14] Pescatore (1974), p. 2.

[15] Gathii (2009–2010).

Contrary to that view, the relational framework used in this book, in essence, presupposes, or creates, a very high degree of legal integration and expectation of it. As Michael Ewing-Chow has observed, 'weak legalization . . . is perhaps an unusual basis for a regional integration project'.[16] At present, this degree of legal integration is a feat only achieved within the European integration experience. However, the fact that to date that degree of legal integration has been achieved only within Europe does not mean that it cannot be achieved in Africa or elsewhere.[17] It is worth remembering that the high degree of legal integration that currently exists in Europe was not achieved in a day. It is the result of a process that dates back to the 1950s, during which time many African countries were still under colonial rule. The economic integration processes in Africa which are dealt with in this book are of recent origins. They date back to the middle and late 1990s. Accordingly, one should not expect to see today in Africa the same level of legal integration as that achieved by Europe over a period of more than half a century. However, this should not be a reason to despair or argue that only Europe can do it. This book advocates the existence of such a high degree of legal integration as a necessary – but not a sufficient – condition for the effectiveness of economic integration in Africa.

The notion of effectiveness[18] is used in the book to measure the extent to which the communities are, and will be, able to achieve the objectives that they have clearly outlined in their respective treaties. From a legal perspective an effective community should demonstrate: the free flow of goods, services, person, capital and property, including judgments within the community consistent with the stage of economic integration it has reached; the existence and development of a significant body of community laws including judicial decisions to regulate the integration process; integration of community law into the laws of member states; the existence of a carefully structured legal framework for addressing and managing the multiple relationships (for example, community–state, interstate, inter-community, inter-institutional) created by economic integration; the existence of institutions adequately designed, mandated and resourced to ensure the application of community law; the existence of well-outlined

[16] Ewing-Chow (2008), p. 237.

[17] See generally Winters (1997). Comparatively, some writers have argued for greater legalization within the Association of South East Asian Nations. See Ewing-Chow (2008); and Davidson (2008).

[18] Ingram (1983).

procedures for monitoring and addressing breaches of community law; adherence to community law in member states; and the existence and development of constituencies with interest in the community and their full integration into the activities and operations of the community at both national and community levels. These criteria of effectiveness can be used to judge a community as a whole or on its individual policies. It is also important to emphasize that there could be varying degrees of achievement on these criteria; thus, what is entailed here is a process rather than a stage that is attained instantly. Put differently, these criteria should be viewed as elements along a continuum: the more effective a community is, the more it would exhibit elements of the criteria.

To emphasize the role of law in Africa's economic integration processes is not to underestimate the importance of socio-economic and political factors in these processes. Indeed, economic integration should be well grounded in the socio-economic and political realities of a region. These realities can, and often do, shape the workings or effectiveness of law in the processes. The emphasis placed on law is meant to challenge the existing literature, which is vast and sees progress in economic integration in Africa as being hindered by socio-economic, political, cultural and infrastructural problems. Without denying the importance of these problems, this book aims to demonstrate that even if all of the problems were to disappear, many legal issues, if unaddressed, would still hinder the effectiveness of Africa's economic integration processes. In summary, this book focuses on a very specific aspect of economic integration. It does not pretend to offer – and should not be read as an attempt to offer – a comprehensive treatise on all of the challenges that face or are likely to be faced by economic integration processes in Africa.

Additionally, Africa is host to a multiplicity of RECs, but the book focuses on only four of the AU-recognized RECs.[19] These are the East African Community (EAC),[20] the Common Market for Eastern and

[19] The four excluded from this study (the Arab Maghreb Union, the Community of Sahel-Saharan States, the Inter-Governmental Authority on Development and the Economic Community of Central African States) have witnessed very little progress in their economic integration processes.

[20] Treaty for the Establishment of the East African Community, 30 November 1999, 2144 UNTS I-37437 (hereafter, EAC Treaty). EAC is a 'resurrection' of the defunct East African Community established under the 1967 Treaty for East African Cooperation, 6 June 1967, 6 ILM 932.

Southern Africa (COMESA),[21] the Economic Community of West African States (ECOWAS)[22] and the Southern African Development Community (SADC).[23] All of these communities have the African Economic Community (AEC) as their umbrella organization. The communities do not vary too significantly in their structures; they share the common objective of creating a larger economic space for trade among their members through the gradual elimination of tariff and non-tariff barriers to trade. The AEC, which currently operates as an integral part of the African Union (AU), is to result from the ultimate merger of all the RECs in Africa. The choice of these communities is apposite. Geographically, they cover all the regions of Africa, namely Central, East, North, Southern and West Africa. Cumulatively, they have a membership that encompasses forty-one of the fifty-three African countries. All are active in the field of economic integration, envisage progress on the stages of economic integration and are indeed progressing on the stages, albeit at different paces.

1.2 Relational issues and Africa's integration

Relational issues are endemic in economic integration processes and they become more visible as the processes progress through the various stages of integration. Africans have had a long-standing commitment to economic integration. However, it appears that, against the background of the professed political enthusiasm to integrate, not much attention has been devoted to articulating the relational issues that bedevil Africa's economic integration processes, the effect they have on the processes and how they should be approached or resolved. To some scholars, Africa's economic integration processes have generally shied away from addressing the serious legal issues that precede and come with economic integration. The

[21] Treaty Establishing the Common Market for Eastern and Southern Africa, 5 November 1993, 33 ILM 1067 (hereafter, COMESA Treaty). COMESA began its life under the 1982 Eastern and Southern African States: Treaty for the establishment of a Preferential Trade Area, 21 December 1981, 21 ILM 479.

[22] Revised Treaty Establishing the Economic Community of West African States, 24 July 1993, 35 ILM 660; (1996) 8 Afr. J. Int'l & Comp. L. 187 (hereafter, ECOWAS Treaty). ECOWAS began life under the 1975 Treaty Establishing the Economic Community of West African States, 28 May 1975, 1010 UNTS I-14843; 14 ILM 1200 (hereafter, ECOWAS Treaty 1975).

[23] Treaty of the Southern African Development Community, 17 August 1992, 32 ILM 120 (hereafter, SADC Treaty).

processes have been mere political constructs – with no attention to the importance of solid legal frameworks.[24] Indeed, a recently concluded report of the UNECA found the existing legal framework for Africa's integration to be 'ambiguous and imprecise'.[25]

Perhaps, the best manifestation of Africa's economic integration processes' inattention to relational issues is the disjunction between the national and community legal systems. This disjunction is, in part, reflected in the absence of national legislation necessary to implement decisions taken by Africa's RECs. National constitutions and courts also appear ambivalent to the demands of economic integration. They appear to be ill-prepared to accommodate community laws. Obligations assumed by states at the community level have not been translated into domestic rights and benefits for individuals. And individuals face formidable legal obstacles when they seek to benefit from community law in member states. In general, national legal systems appear insensitive to the demands imposed upon them by economic integration.

A similar problem is manifest in the field of interstate and inter-community relations. The issue of interstate recognition and enforcement of judgments, and the general role of private international law as a means of regulating interstate relations, have not received any systematic attention in the communities' laws. In general, within member states, judgments and laws of other states do not enjoy any preferential status as far as the principles of private international law are concerned. There is also no precise legal framework for regulating relations between the many RECs in Africa.

In addition, there is the absence of a consideration of the relations between Africa's economic integration processes and other international economic arrangements, such as the World Trade Organization (WTO). Indeed, the very foundation of most regional economic integration processes is in WTO law, especially Article XXIV of the General Agreement on Tariffs and Trade or the Decision on Differential and More Favourable Treatment Reciprocity and Fuller Participation of Developing Countries. Regional economic integration processes must comply with WTO law. Thus, the relations between Africa's economic integration processes and the WTO, the status of WTO law within the framework of community law and national law, how the multiple commitments of African states under community law and WTO law can be reconciled, and

[24] Kufuor (1994); Joerges (2002–2003); and Joerges (1996).

[25] United Nations Economic Commission for Africa (2006), p. 21.

the rules for resolving conflicts between WTO law, community law and national law are all important issues. However, so far, they have not been articulated and addressed in writings on Africa's economic integration processes. These issues are important for the stability of both the world trading system and Africa's economic integration. Irreconcilable differences between community laws and national laws, vis-à-vis WTO law, are susceptible to challenge under the WTO dispute settlement system. Currently, forty-two African countries are members of the WTO and a number of African RECs have already been notified to the WTO. Thus, although it will not be explored in this book,[26] the issue of their relations with the WTO is not merely academic.

Against this background, this book addresses numerous issues, including: the extent to which relational issues are visible in Africa's economic integration processes; how the existing community laws and jurisprudence have approached or resolved them; the extent to which national legal systems are attentive to them, especially from the perspective of national constitutions and jurisprudence; how community and national approaches to such issues can affect or enhance the effectiveness of the economic integration processes; the contribution that principles of public and private international law can make in addressing such issues; and how attention or the lack of it to such issues in Africa's integration processes impacts on their effectiveness. It is remarkable that, notwithstanding the importance of relational issues to the effective development of Africa's economic integration processes, little or no attention has been devoted to them. Indeed, works on the legal aspects of Africa's economic integration processes are scant. A cursory look at the pages of leading African journals reveals this. Monographs and treatises are similarly rare. Other RECs outside Africa have confronted relational issues and addressed them through various means. The body of learning accumulated by the non-African RECs is a useful comparative source for this book.

1.3 Selected RECs – an overview

Africa is home to a bewildering array of economic integration processes. Each geographical region contains an average of three to four organizations, each with a mandate to carry out economic

[26] Ng'ong'Ola (1999); Kessie (1999); and Mutai (2007).

integration. In West Africa, ECOWAS coexists with the West African Economic and Monetary Union (UEMOA), the Mano River Union (MRU), and the Community of Sahel-Saharan States (CENSAD). In Central Africa, the Economic Community of Central African States (ECCAS) coexists with the Central African Economic and Monetary Community (CEMAC) and the Economic Community of Great Lakes Countries (CEPGL). In Southern Africa, the Southern African Development Community (SADC), the Southern African Customs Union (SACU) and the Indian Ocean Commission (IOC) share space with COMESA, which also covers East Africa and parts of North and Central Africa. In addition, East Africa has the EAC and Inter-Governmental Authority on Development (IGAD). North Africa also has the Arab Maghreb Union (AMU/UMA). The UNECA puts the total number of organizations at fourteen and notes that the proliferation of institutions and protocols means that out of the fifty-three member states of the African Union, twenty-six belong to two of the fourteen inter-governmental organizations, twenty belong to three of them, and one country belongs to four.[27] Table 1 provides the membership of the eight RECs recognized by the African Union, as well as the countries that are members of the WTO.

Table 1 *AU-recognized regional economic communities and their membership*

COUNTRIES	ECOWAS	EAC	COMESA	SADC	IGAD	AMU	ECCAS	CENSAD	AEC/AU	WTO
Algeria						X			X	
Angola				X			X		X	X
Benin	X							X	X	X
Botswana				X					X	X
Burkina Faso	X							X	X	X
Burundi		X	X				X		X	X
Cameroon							X		X	X
Cape Verde	X								X	X
Cen. Afr. Republic							X	X	X	X
Chad							X	X	X	X
Comoros			X						X	
Congo							X		X	X
Congo DR	X		X	X			X		X	X

[27] United Nations Economic Commission for Africa (2006), p. x.

Table 1 (*cont.*)

COUNTRIES	ECO WAS	EAC	COM ESA	SADC	IGAD	AMU	ECC AS	CEN SAD	AEC/ AU	WTO
Côte d'Ivoire									X	X
Djibouti			X		X			X	X	X
Egypt			X			X		X	X	X
Equatorial Guinea							X		X	
Eritrea			X					X	X	
Ethiopia			X		X				X	
Gabon							X		X	X
Gambia	X							X	X	X
Ghana	X								X	X
Guinea	X								X	X
Guinea Bissau	X								X	X
Kenya		X	X		X				X	X
Lesotho				X					X	X
Liberia	X								X	
Libya			X			X		X	X	
Madagascar			X	X					X	X
Malawi			X	X					X	X
Mali	X							X	X	X
Mauritania						X			X	X
Mauritius			X	X					X	X
Morocco						X		X	X	X
Mozambique				X					X	X
Namibia				X					X	X
Niger	X							X	X	X
Nigeria	X							X	X	X
Rwanda		X	X				X		X	X
SaoTome & Principe							X		X	
Senegal	X							X	X	X
Seychelles			X						X	
Sierra Leone	X								X	X
Somalia					X			X	X	
South Africa				X					X	X
Sudan			X		X			X	X	
Swaziland			X	X					X	X
Tanzania		X		X					X	X
Togo	X							X	X	X
Tunisia						X		X	X	X
Uganda		X	X		X				X	X
Zambia			X	X					X	X
Zimbabwe			X	X					X	X
TOTAL	**15**	**5**	**19**	**14**	**6**	**6**	**11**	**18**	**53**	**42**

1.3.1 African Economic Community

The history of the need for continental economic integration in Africa dates back to the formation of the Organization of African Unity (OAU) (now AU) in 1963.[28] One purpose of the OAU was to coordinate and strengthen cooperation between member states to improve the lives of their people.[29] To this end, they were enjoined to 'co-ordinate and harmonize their general policies' in economic and other fields.[30] However, it was not until 1980 that a major continental step was taken towards economic integration. Before then, resolutions and declarations were made to promote integration, and various RECs emerged and achieved different levels of integration.[31] At an extraordinary summit in 1980, the OAU adopted the Lagos Plan of Action, which culminated in the signing of the Treaty Establishing the African Economic Community (AEC Treaty). The AEC Treaty came into force in May 1994, envisaging an integrated economic area covering all of Africa.[32] Following the establishment of the AU in 2002, the AEC became an integral part of its constitutional structure.[33]

The AEC's objectives include the promotion of economic development and the integration of African economies to increase self-sufficiency, the promotion of endogenous and self-sustained development, and the fostering of the gradual establishment of the African Economic Community[34] through coordination and harmonization among existing

[28] Charter of the Organization of African Unity, 25 May 1963, 2 ILM 766 (hereafter, OAU Charter). The OAU has been replaced by the African Union. See Constitutive Act of the African Union, 11 July 2000, (2005) 13 Afr. J. Int'l Comp. L. 25 (herafter, Constitutive Act). For a discussion on the structure, characteristics and workings of the African Union, see Magliveras and Naldi (2002); Udombana (2002–3b); Udombana (2002); Maluwa (2001); and Maluwa (2007).

[29] OAU Charter, art. 2(1)(b). [30] OAU Charter, art. 2(2). [31] Kouassi (2007).

[32] As of September 2010, fifty-two African countries had signed the treaty and forty-nine had ratified it. However, unlike the EAC Treaty, I am unaware of any countries (especially common law countries) that have domestically implemented the AEC Treaty through legislation. See generally Ajomo and Adewale (1993).

[33] AEC Treaty, art. 98. Constitutive Act, art. 33. In this book, unless a contrary provision exists in the Constitutive Act, references are made to the institutional structures established under the AEC Treaty for consistency and clarity. On some of the difficulties of making the AEC an integral part of the AU, see Jackson (2003a), p. 140.

[34] The AEC both is and is to be! Understandably, this may sound confusing for the reader. In this book, 'AEC' will be used to refer to the current organization irrespective of the stage in its development, while reference to the ultimate stage of the AEC will be written in full as 'the African Economic Community'.

and future economic communities.[35] To ensure the attainment of these objectives, the AEC is enjoined to ensure: (i) the harmonization of national policies, particularly in the fields of agriculture, industry, transport and communication, energy, natural resources, trade, money and finance, human resources education, culture and technology; (ii) the adoption of a common trade policy with regard to third-party states; (iii) the establishment and maintenance of a common external tariff; (iv) the establishment of a common market; (v) the gradual removal of obstacles among member states to the free movement of persons, goods, services and capital; and (vi) the right of residence and establishment.[36]

The AEC Treaty provides for the gradual establishment of the African Economic Community through six stages over a period of thirty-four years.[37] This process is to be completed in 2028. The first stage involves the 'strengthening of existing regional economic communities'.[38] The second involves the stabilization of tariff and non-tariff barriers, custom duties and internal taxes at the level of the RECs and the strengthening of sectoral integration at the regional and continental levels. The third stage envisages the establishment of a free-trade area and a customs union at each regional level. The fourth focuses on the coordination and harmonization of tariff and non-tariff systems among the RECs, with a view to establishing a continental customs union. The fifth stage calls for the establishment of an African common market through the adoption of common policies, harmonization of monetary, financial and fiscal policies, and the application of the principles of the free movement of persons and the right of residence and establishment. Finally, the sixth stage focuses on, among other things: the strengthening of the African common market; the application of the free movement of people, goods, capital and services; the integration of the social, economic, political and cultural sectors; the establishment of a single domestic market;

[35] AEC Treaty, art. 4. [36] AEC Treaty, art. 4(2).

[37] AEC Treaty, art. 6(1). The following are the timelines for the evolution of the African Economic Community: '1. Creation of regional blocs in regions where such do not yet exist (to be completed in 1999) 2. Strengthening of intra-REC integration and inter-REC harmonization (to be completed in 2007) 3. Establishing of a free trade area and customs union in each regional bloc (to be completed in 2017) 4. Establishing of a continent-wide customs union (to be completed in 2019) 5. Establishing of a continent-wide African Common Market (to be completed in 2023) 6. Establishing of a continent-wide economic and monetary union (and thus also a currency union) and pan-African Parliament (to be completed in 2028) 7. End of all transition periods by 2034 at the latest.' United Nations Economic Commission for Africa (2008), p. 28.

[38] AEC Treaty, art. 6(2).

a Pan-African Economic and Monetary Union; a Pan-African Parliament;[39] and a single African currency.[40] It is worth noting that these stages follow the Balassian model of economic integration.

A distinct feature of the framework for integration under the AEC Treaty is the use of RECs as building blocks for the African Economic Community. With a membership of more than fifty states, this approach ensures a degree of manageability in the initial development of the community. As noted above, there are more than fourteen RECs at various stages of development in Africa. These communities have their separate institutions, members, objectives and legal personalities. It is also not uncommon to find states that are members of more than one of these communities. This book argues that, from a relational perspective, these pose significant legal challenges to the success of the AEC.[41]

The principal institutions of the AEC are the: Assembly of Heads of State and Government; Council of Ministers; Pan-African Parliament; Economic and Social Commission; Court of Justice; General Secretariat; and Specialised Technical Committees.[42] The Assembly is the supreme organ of the Community.[43] It is responsible for implementing the Community's objectives,[44] namely (amongst other things): determining the general policy and major guidelines of the Community, and giving directives, coordinating and harmonizing the economic, scientific, technical, cultural and social policies of member states; taking any action to attain the objectives of the Community; overseeing the functioning of Community organs as well as the follow-up of the implementation of its objectives; approving the organizational structure of the Secretariat; electing the Secretary-General and his deputies, and appointing the financial controller, accountant and external auditors; adopting the Staff Rules and Regulations of the Secretariat; taking decisions and giving directives concerning the RECs in order to ensure the realization of the objectives of the Community; approving the Community's programme of activity and budget, and determining the annual contribution of each member state; referring any matter to the Court of Justice when it confirms that a member state or organ of the Community has not

[39] Protocol to the Treaty Establishing the African Economic Community Relating to the Pan-African Parliament, 2 March 2001, (2005) 13 Afr. J. Int'l & Comp. L. 86 (hereafter, Protocol on the Pan-African Parliament). The Parliament was inaugurated in 2003.

[40] AEC Treaty, art. 6.

[41] Kiplagat (1995–1996); and Jackson (2003a), pp. 151–4.

[42] AEC Treaty, art. 7.

[43] Ibid., art. 8(1).

[44] Ibid., art. 8(2).

honoured any of its obligations, has acted beyond the limits of its authority or has abused the powers conferred on it by the provisions of the Treaty, by a decision of the Assembly or a regulation of the Council; and requesting the Court of Justice to give advisory opinion on any legal question.[45]

The Council is responsible for the functioning and development of the Community,[46] namely, amongst other things: making recommendations to the Assembly on any action aimed at attaining the objectives of the Community; guiding the activities of the subordinate organs of the Community; submitting to the Assembly proposals concerning programmes of activity and budget of the Community as well as the annual contribution of each member state; proposing to the Assembly the appointment of the financial controller, accountant and external auditors; requesting the Court of Justice to give advisory opinion on any legal questions; and carrying out all other functions assigned thereto under this Treaty and exercising all powers delegated to it by the Assembly.[47]

The Pan-African Parliament was set up to ensure that Africans are fully involved in the economic development and integration of the continent.[48] The composition, functions, powers and organization of the Pan-African Parliament are outlined in a protocol adopted after the AEC Treaty came into force.[49] Currently, it has only consultative and advisory powers.[50] Each member state is represented by five parliamentarians, at least one of whom must be a woman. At present, the parliamentarians are elected or designated by their respective national parliaments or any other deliberative organs of the member states, from among their members.[51] The ultimate aim is for it to evolve into an institution with full legislative power, with the members elected by universal suffrage.[52]

The Commission is composed of ministers responsible for the economic development, planning and integration of each member state. They may be assisted, as and when necessary, by other ministers. Representatives of RECs participate in meetings of the Commission and its subsidiary organs. The Commission's functions include: preparing programmes, policies and strategies for cooperation in the fields of economic and social development among African countries, on the one hand, and between Africa and the international community, on

[45] Ibid., art. 8(3). [46] Ibid., art. 11(2).
[47] Ibid., art. 11(3). [48] Ibid., art. 14. [49] Protocol of Pan-African Parliament.
[50] Ibid., art. 2(3)(i). [51] Ibid., arts. 4 and 5. [52] Ibid., art. 2(3).

the other, and making appropriate recommendations to the Assembly, through the Council; coordinating, harmonizing, supervising and following up the economic, social, cultural, scientific and technical activities of the Secretariat, the Committees and any other subsidiary body; examining the reports and making recommendations to the Assembly, through the Council, and ensuring their follow-up; making recommendations to the Assembly, through the Council with a view to coordinating and harmonizing the activities of the different RECs; and supervising the preparation of international negotiations, and assessing the results thereof and reporting thereon to the Assembly through the Council.

The composition and function of the Court of Justice is discussed in detail in Chapter 6. The Secretary-General directs the activities of the Secretariat and is its legal representative. The Secretary-General performs the following functions: following up and ensuring the implementation of the Assembly's decisions and the application of the regulations of the Council; promoting development programmes as well as projects of the Community; preparing proposals concerning the programme of activity and budget of the Community and, upon their approval by the Assembly, ensuring the implementation thereof; submitting a report on the activities of the Community to all meetings of the Assembly, the Council and the Commission; preparing and servicing meetings of the Assembly, the Council, the Commission and the Committees; carrying out studies, with a view to attaining the objectives of the Community, and making proposals likely to enhance the functioning and harmonious development of the Community; and recruiting the staff of the Community and making appointments to defined posts.[53]

It is important to set out the relationship between the AEC and the AU. In its founding treaty, the AEC is described as forming an 'integral part' of the OAU.[54] As an integral part of the OAU, the AEC is a distinct organization with economic integration as its objective. Its budget is linked to that of the OAU. In theory, the AEC could have maintained its separate institutions. In practice, that did not happen; the functions of its institutions were taken over by the coordinate organs of the OAU. Indeed, articles 11(1) and 15(1) of the AEC Treaty expressly provided that the Council of Ministers and Economic and Social Commission (of the AEC) shall be the Council of Ministers and Economic and Social

[53] AEC Treaty, art. 22. [54] AEC Treaty, preamble; arts. 1(c); 82(1); 98(1); and 99.

Commission of the OAU, respectively.[55] Membership of the AU is not coterminous with membership of the AEC; of the fifty-three AU member states, forty-nine have ratified the AEC Treaty.[56]

The OAU Charter has been replaced by the Constitutive Act of the African Union. In the Constitutive Act, member states affirmed their commitment to achieving the objectives of the AEC Treaty and promised to work to accelerate the establishment of the African Economic Community. No attempt was made to clarify the relationship between the AEC and the AU. The only provision that deals directly with the AEC is article 33(2). It provides that 'the provisions of this Act shall take precedence over and supersede any inconsistent or contrary provisions of the Treaty establishing the African Economic Community'. Undoubtedly, the AEC still constitutes an integral part of the AU; the AEC 'today forms the economic wing of the African Union'.[57] Accordingly, the functions of the AEC institutions have been taken over by the coordinate organs of the AU.[58] However, in this book, unless an express inconsistency exists, in which case the provisions of the Constitutive Act of the African Union will prevail, reference will be made to the organs as established under the AEC Treaty.

1.3.2 Economic Community of West African States

The ECOWAS currently operates under the Revised Treaty Establishing the Economic Community of West African States (ECOWAS Treaty). It has fifteen members: Benin, Burkina Faso, Cape Verde, Côte d'Ivoire, Gambia, Ghana, Guinea, Guinea Bissau, Liberia, Mali, Niger, Nigeria, Senegal, Sierra Leone and Togo. It began life under the Treaty Establishing the Economic Community of West African States, which came into force in June 1975.

Under article 3 of the ECOWAS Treaty, the aims of the community are to promote cooperation and integration, leading to the establishment of an economic union in West Africa to raise the living standards of the peoples, and to maintain and enhance economic stability, foster relations

[55] See also art. 21(1), which provides that the Secretariat shall be the General-Secretariat of the OAU.

[56] Djibouti, Eritrea, Madagascar and Somalia have not ratified the treaty.

[57] Kouassi (2007), p. 6.

[58] The organs of the AU are the: Assembly of the Union; Executive Council; Pan-African Parliament; Court of Justice; Commission; Permanent Representatives Committee; Specialized Technical Committees; Economic, Social and Cultural Council; and Financial Institutions.

among member states and contribute to the progress and development of the African Continent. In order to achieve these objectives, it is provided in article 3(2) of the treaty that the community shall ensure among other things: the harmonization and coordination of national policies and the promotion of integration programmes, projects and activities, particularly in food, agriculture and natural resources, industry, transport and communications, energy, trade, money and finance, taxation, economic reform policies, human resources, education, information, culture, science, technology, services, health, tourism and legal matters; the establishment of a common market and an economic union through the adoption of common policies in the economic, financial, social and cultural sectors, and the creation of a monetary union.

The principal institutions of ECOWAS are the: Authority of Heads of State and Government; Council of Ministers; Community Parliament; Economic and Social Council; Community Court of Justice; Executive Secretariat; Fund for Cooperation, Compensation and Development; and Specialized Technical Commissions.[59]

1.3.3 The Common Market for Eastern and Southern Africa

The Treaty establishing the Common Market for Eastern Southern Africa (COMESA Treaty) entered into force in 1994. COMESA currently has nineteen members: Burundi, Comoros, Democratic Republic of Congo, Djibouti, Egypt, Eritrea, Ethiopia, Kenya, Libya, Madagascar, Malawi, Mauritius, Rwanda, Seychelles, Sudan, Swaziland, Uganda, Zambia and Zimbabwe. COMESA began life under the 1982 Treaty for the Establishment of the Preferential Trade Area for Eastern and Southern African States.[60]

Under article 3 of the COMESA Treaty, the aims and objectives of COMESA are: to attain sustainable growth and development of the member states by promoting a more balanced and harmonious development of its production and marketing structures; to promote joint development in all fields of economic activity and the joint adoption of macro-economic policies and programmes to raise the standard of living of the people and to foster closer relations among its member states; to cooperate in the creation of an enabling environment for foreign, cross-border and domestic investment, including the joint

[59] ECOWAS Treaty, art. 6(1). [60] Gondwe (1998).

promotion of research and adoption of science and technology for development; to cooperate in the promotion of peace, security and stability among the member states to enhance economic development in the region; to cooperate in strengthening the relations between COMESA and the rest of the world and the adoption of common positions in international forums; and to contribute towards the establishment, progress and realization of the objectives of the African Economic Community. To these ends, in the field of trade liberalization, members have agreed to establish a customs union, abolish all non-tariff barriers to trade among themselves, establish a common external tariff and cooperate in customs procedures and activities. In 2009, the COMESA customs union was launched. There are plans for the formation of a common market and, by 2025, a monetary union.

The principal institutions of COMESA are the: Authority of Heads of State and Government; Council of Ministers; Court of Justice; Committee of Governors of Central Banks; Intergovernmental Committee; Technical Committees; Secretariat; and Consultative Committee.

1.3.4 *East African Community*

The Treaty of the East African Community,[61] which entered into force in 2001, established a community that consisted of Kenya, Uganda and Tanzania. In 2008, the community was expanded to include Burundi and Rwanda. The history of the EAC dates back to colonial times.[62] In its present form, the EAC is a resurrection of the East African Community established under the 1967 Treaty on East African Cooperation.

Under article 5 of the EAC Treaty, the objectives of the community shall be to develop policies and programmes aimed at widening and deepening cooperation among the member states, for their mutual benefit, in the political, economic, social and cultural fields, research and technology, defence, security and legal and judicial affairs. Pursuant to these objectives, the states have undertaken to establish among themselves a customs union, common market, monetary union and ultimately a political federation. In July 2010, the EAC common market was launched – a major feat for economic integration in Africa. That was about five years after the EAC customs union was launched.

[61] Kaahwa (1999); and Fitzke (1999).
[62] di Delupis (1970), pp. 19–50; Franck (1964); Sebalu (1972); and Bentil (1969).

The relatively faster pace at which the EAC is progressing can be attributed to a number of factors. These include its size, the fact that the founding members enjoy relatively stable and democratic political structures, and the strong bond that existed between the member states from colonial times and the days of the old East African Community.

The principal institutions of the EAC are the Summit of Heads of State and Government, Council of Ministers, Coordination Committee, Sectoral Committees, East African Court of Justice, East African Legislative Assembly and Secretariat.

1.3.5 Southern African Development Community

The SADC Treaty, which took effect in 1992, established a community consisting of Angola, Botswana, Democratic Republic of Congo, Lesotho, Madagascar, Malawi, Mauritius, Mozambique, Namibia, Seychelles, South Africa, Swaziland, Tanzania, Zambia and Zimbabwe. The SADC began its life as the Southern African Development Coordination Conference (SADCC), an 'organization' formed in 1980 with the principal objective of facilitating economic development in the member states and lessening dependence on South Africa. In August 1992, the SADCC was transformed into the SADC with the signing of the SADC Treaty.

Under article 5 of the SADC Treaty, the objectives of SADC include to: promote sustainable and equitable economic growth and socio-economic development that will ensure poverty alleviation with the ultimate objective of its eradication; enhance the standard and quality of life of the people of Southern Africa and support the socially disadvantaged through regional integration; promote common political values, systems and other shared values that are transmitted through institutions that are democratic, legitimate and effective; consolidate, defend and maintain democracy, peace, security and stability; promote self-sustaining development on the basis of collective self-reliance, and the interdependence of member states; achieve complementarity between national and regional strategies and programmes; promote and maximize productive employment and utilization of the region's resources; achieve sustainable utilization of natural resources and effective protection of the environment; and strengthen and consolidate the long-standing historical, social and cultural affinities and links among the people of the region. These objectives are broad and far-reaching.

Although economic integration is not specifically mentioned as an objective, it is significant that article 1 of the treaty defines 'community' – the Southern African Community – as 'the organisation for economic integration established by article 2 of this Treaty'. Indeed, in the preamble to the treaty, the member states expressed their conviction to mobilize resources to promote the implementation of national, inter-state and regional policies, programmes and projects within the framework for economic integration. Pursuant to this, the SADC became a Free Trade Area in 2008 and the plans were to have the area progress to a customs union in 2010.

Article 9 of the treaty establishes the following as the principal institutions of the community: Summit of Heads of State or Government; Organ on Politics, Defence and Security Cooperation; Council of Ministers; Integrated Committee of Ministers; Standing Committee of Officials; Secretariat; Tribunal; and SADC National Committees.

1.4 Socio-economic matrix of Africa's economic integration

A proper understanding of relational issues is enhanced with a background in the socio-economic and political context of Africa's economic integration. The socio-economic and political factors provide the *raison d'être* for Africa's regional economic integration and, sometimes, condition its progress and effectiveness. The RECs examined in this book comprise countries in Sub-Saharan Africa and, with the exception of COMESA, they consist of geographically contiguous countries. Geography is important to Africa's economic integration in another respect: many African countries are landlocked; they depend on their neighbours with coastlines for access to transportation for their exports and imports. This creates a natural bond of inter-dependency.[63] Geographical proximity is often combined with common colonial experience, such as with the EAC, where all the founding members – Kenya, Tanzania and Uganda – were British colonies. The association with former colonial powers could be a drain on African economic integration processes.[64]

From a legal perspective, the colonial experience often translates into a common legal infrastructure and can be an important complement to economic integration. Many of the member states of the communities adhere to the common law, Roman-Dutch law or civil law tradition because of their colonial associations with Britain, France and, to a lesser extent, Belgium, Portugal, Germany and the Netherlands. This colonial legacy can be meaningfully harnessed in addressing some of the challenges in

[63] Ndulu (2006). [64] Amuwo (1999).

integration, such as harmonization of laws. Admittedly, the colonial legal legacy sometimes constrains economic integration. While it has created a common legal infrastructure for a group of countries, it also implies that, within the same community, there are groups that adhere to different legal traditions and, concomitantly, have different substantive laws. Indeed, within the same group there may be differences in the substantive laws of states, which impose transaction costs on the undertaking of cross-border business.

The RECs share a common vision of promoting trade and economic development within their respective sub-regions. This vision is to be achieved via progress through the various stages of economic integration. To date, progress has been slow, especially for COMESA and ECOWAS, both of which have been in existence for decades. As noted above, COMESA became a customs union in 2009. ECOWAS is edging closer to creating a customs union and the EAC is already a customs union. The next stage for these communities would be to evolve into common markets. Indeed, the EAC is currently negotiating a common market protocol. The slow progress made by these communities can be attributed to a number of factors, including their size, internal political conflicts and multiple commitments of member states, which sometimes lead to legally irreconcilable duties. For example, progress towards a customs union between COMESA member states was delayed because some members were also parties to the EAC and SADC customs unions.

The economic conditions in most of the member states of the communities are nothing to write home about.[65] Some countries – such as Lesotho, Swaziland and Gambia – are so small that it is sometimes difficult to contemplate their economic survival as independent economic entities. Admittedly, the experiences of some 'small states', such as Luxembourg and Liechtenstein, indicate that size is not necessarily an obstacle to economic development. However, in Africa, this has not been the case. Indeed, the economic development of Lesotho and Swaziland is fostered by their close and long-standing economic integration arrangement with South Africa under the Southern African Customs Union. The levels of intra-African trade are generally low.[66] This is not because there are no reciprocal markets for each other's exports. Rather, it is due to numerous obstacles to trade. These include governments' unwillingness to surrender macro-economic policy-making to the dictates of the communities, fear of tariff-revenue loss, inadequate infrastructure,

[65] Bhattacharyya (2009). [66] But see Foroutan and Pritchett (1993).

cumbersome customs procedures, political instability and currency inconvertibility.[67] Recent studies have shown that regional integration has generated significant increases in trade among African countries. Indeed, a suggestion that the level of intra-African trade is low should be approached with caution. Official national trade statistics in Africa are often difficult to come by, and the level of unrecorded trans-border trade is estimated to be high, if not higher than recorded trade.[68]

A key to successful integration is political stability, democratic governance and the rule of law. Many African countries are struggling to consolidate the rule of law within their economies and remain strongly wed to their sovereignty. A number of member states of the communities have suffered from political instability, undemocratic regimes and abuse of power. Political instability, which sometimes translates into regional conflicts and frequent undemocratic changes in government, has been a drain on the progress of Africa's RECs. Their attentions have been directed more towards conflict resolution and prevention and diverted from promoting economic integration.[69] For more than a decade, ECOWAS, through the ECOWAS Monitoring Group (ECOMOG), struggled with conflicts in Liberia and Sierra Leone. The persistent conflict in the Democratic Republic of Congo has also been a trouble spot in the Southern African region. Arguably, political instability can provide a motivating force for and a boost to Africa's integration. It is difficult for economic allies to be at war with each other. Also, political instability suggests that governments committed to the course of integration may agree more readily to community policies to avert the risk of the rejection of those policies when there is a change in government. The revision of the 1975 ECOWAS Treaty to strengthen the community's institutions has been attributed in part to internal domestic strife, which threatened ECOWAS member states' ruling elites and called for strong intervention from ECOWAS.[70] Similarly, security considerations arising from threats posed by South Africa's Apartheid regime influenced the formation of the Southern African Development Coordination Conference, which is now the Southern African Development Community.

In addition to the above, there are other socio-economic and political factors that challenge economic integration and can undermine its effectiveness. These include the absence of mutual trust among the relevant member states, diversity in political ideology and political

[67] Geda and Kebret (2007). [68] Foroutan and Pritchett (1993), p. 98.
[69] Breytenbach (2008). [70] Kufuor (2006).

systems, lack of homogeneity in the level of economic development and the issue of how to distribute evenly the benefits of economic integration.

1.5 Conclusion

This chapter provided an introductory overview of economic integration in Africa and outlined the nature and scope of issues addressed in this book. Economic integration has been advocated as a path to economic development in Africa. Currently, it is being pursued at both the regional and continental levels, albeit within challenging socio-economic and political contexts. The goal is for the regional communities to progress on the various stages of economic integration and, ultimately, merge to form a continent-wide community, the African Economic Community. At present, all of the communities are progressing; the most advanced being the EAC, which is a common market. Without purporting to diminish the influence or importance of socio-political, cultural, historical and other factors, this book aims to put law at the forefront of discussions on economic integration in Africa. In that light, it is particularly noteworthy that all of the communities studied in the book have undergone some level of 'legal transformation'. Building on prior agreements, they now have constitutive treaties and laws which create more binding legal obligations and envisage greater legal integration between the legal systems of the communities they established and member states. The legal nature of the obligations created by the treaties and other community laws, issues surrounding the integration of community law into member states' legal systems, the relations between the states – as well as between the communities – form the subject matter of the rest of the book.

2

Legal framework for managing relational issues

2.1 Introduction

At present, the international community is witnessing a proliferation of RECs. They have become a predominant mode for organizing international trade.[1] As of July 2010, the World Trade Organization (WTO) had been notified about 474 regional trade agreements. Each regional trade agreement differs in its ultimate goal; it may create a free trade area, customs union, common market, economic union or complete economic integration. Whichever stage an REC is at, it is undeniable that economic integration results in a juxtaposition of states, laws, legal systems and institutions to achieve a common economic vision. This creates a complex web of relations in which the principal actors are the community, member states, individuals and other international organizations. Accordingly, a fundamental challenge in economic integration is that of structuring and managing the relations between and

[1] The following treaties have been consulted and some are often cited in this chapter: Consolidated Version of the Treaty on the Functioning of the European Union, 13 December 2007, [2010] OJ C83/47 (hereafter, EU Treaty); Marrakesh Agreement Establishing the World Trade Organization, 15 April 1994, 1867 UNTS I-31874, 33 ILM 1144 (hereafter, WTO Agreement); North American Free Trade Agreement between the United States of America, Canada and Mexico, 17 December 1992, 32 ILM 296 (hereafter, NAFTA); AEC Treaty); EAC Treaty; Treaty Establishing the Benelux Union, 3 February 1958, 381 UNTS 5471 (as revised by the Treaty Revising the Treaty Establishing the Benelux Economic Union, 17 June 2008) (hereafter, Benelux Treaty); Revised Treaty of Chaguaramas Establishing the Caribbean Community Including the CARICOM Single Market and Economy, 5 July 2001, 2259 UNTS I-40269 (hereafter, CARICOM Treaty); Agreement on the European Economic Area, 17 March 1993, 1793 UNTS I-31121 (hereafter, EEA Agreement); Treaty for the Establishment of a Common Market between the Argentine Republic, the Federative Republic of Brazil, the Republic of Paraguay and the Eastern Republic of Uruguay, 26 March 1991, 2140 UNTS I-37341 (hereafter, Asuncion Treaty); Agreement on the Foundation of the EURASIAN Economic Community, 10 October 2000, 2212 UNTS I-39321 (hereafter, EURASIAN Agreement); COMESA Treaty; ECOWAS Treaty; Southern African Customs Union Agreement, 21 October 2002, online: www.sacu.int/main.php?include=docs/legislation/2002-agreement/main.html (hereafter, SACU Agreement); and SADC Treaty.

among these actors. As noted in Chapter 1, relational issues are endemic in economic integration. The extent to which the issues are present in a community, how they are approached and the urgency with which they are addressed have a direct relationship with the stage of integration reached or envisaged. The further economic integration progresses, the more obvious these issues become – and the more immediate the need to address them.

This chapter argues that effective economic integration is the product of properly structuring and managing, within well-defined legal frameworks, vertical, horizontal and vertico-horizontal relations among states, legal systems, laws and institutions. In other words, a community must have well-structured and managed relations between itself and other legal systems as a necessary condition for its effectiveness. By structured relations, I am referring to a legal framework that: defines the relations between community and national laws; spells out the modalities for implementing community law in member states; defines the respective competences of the community and member states; and anticipates and provides rules for resolving conflicts of laws (i.e. conflict between legal systems), conflict of norms (i.e. conflict within a legal system) and conflict of jurisdictions. The object of such a legal framework should be to ensure the overall effectiveness of the community. The management of relational issues looks beyond the legal framework. Reciprocal trust and harmonious political coexistence among member states, education on community law and objectives, building up or nurturing constituencies with interest in the integration process, accessibility, the presence and free flow of information on community matters and a general sense of the need for cooperation are all important in this regard. A legal framework that allows individuals to rely on community law in member states will be useless unless it is complemented with education on and accessibility to community law. Furthermore, that framework must be utilized by constituencies to champion their individual causes and the cause of promoting integration. Similarly, a legal framework that gives national courts discretion to refer issues of interpretation of community law to a community court will be ineffective if there is no reciprocal trust or cooperation between both courts.

This chapter explores, comparatively, how communities all over the world have attempted to provide a legal framework that uses various principles and mechanisms of law to address relational issues. In general, these principles and mechanisms have their foundations in public and private international law. They are also influenced by domestic constitutional laws. I characterize them as relational principles of law for economic integration (relational principles). The chapter identifies and assesses relational principles used by communities to provide a legal framework for the relations between themselves and their member states, as well as among the member states. It is worth noting that the European Union (EU) has adopted and perfected most of the relational principles for the purpose of enhancing its economic integration processes. However, it would be wrong to assume or accept that the principles are the preserve of the EU – or that they have been utilized only by it. Many of the principles have roots in public and private international law. Without pretending that the list of relational principles identified is exhaustive, this chapter argues that they are a necessary part of the constitutional architecture of economic communities and should influence their design, especially as they progress through the stages of economic integration. However, using the principles is not a sufficient condition for ensuring an effective community. The chapter examines the social matrix within which the principles operate and argues that it often conditions their effectiveness.

2.2 Relational issues, public and private international law

For centuries, the relations between states and international organizations, as well as among states, have been addressed by public and private international law.[2] International organizations and states expect their laws, or at least some of them, will be given effect and observed in other states. This expectation is often limited, but the fact that international and national law have limited application externally does not affect their internal effectiveness, i.e. their effectiveness with the legal system of their origin. A state cannot expect that its laws will be automatically or wholly applied in a foreign court. Indeed, at common law, foreign revenue, penal and other public laws will not be applied in a national court, and the application of foreign law may be excluded on grounds of public policy. In addition, a state cannot expect that a foreign court will refer an issue of interpretation of its laws back to its courts for determination, or that its law will be accorded a status superior to the *lex fori.* In common law jurisdictions, foreign law is treated as a question of fact – when open

[2] On the use of private international law to regulate relations between laws of different legal systems, see generally Boggiano (2000), pp. 79–94; Siehr (2004); and Hay, Lando and Rotunda (1986).

to opposing interpretations, the court is entitled to make a choice as to which version is to be preferred and, when not satisfactorily proved, to apply the *lex fori*. From a dualist perspective, international law, especially treaty law, cannot claim to be directly part of, let alone superior to, national law. National courts can refuse to apply or put their own varying interpretations on international law. They are under no obligation to seek clarification either from the international organization that adopted the law or the institution that was established by it. Individuals cannot have any directly enforceable rights – or directly imposed duties – under international law, except those expressly created or imposed by national law. In other words, even though rights and responsibilities can be created for individuals at the international level, they remain ineffective at the national level unless they are so recognized under national law. Similarly, a right founded on foreign law is enforceable in another state only at the discretion of that state. In summary, within many states, foreign and international law enjoy no autonomous or privileged status. Surely, this state of affairs impacts on the effectiveness of international law and foreign states' laws in other states.

For international organizations, international lawyers have found ways of addressing this challenge to the national effectiveness of international law. In monism, they have argued that international and national law are part of one legal order. Compared with dualism, monism is not the dominant doctrine on the relationship between national and international law; however, even in dualist states, there are interpretive principles, such as the presumption of consistency, which work to enhance international law's national effectiveness. International lawyers have designated specialist norms, such as customary international law and *jus cogens* norms, with diverse effects. In countries that adhere to the doctrine of incorporation, customary international law is considered as automatically part of national law. *Jus cogens* norms add a sense of significance to international legal obligations. Furthermore, there are techniques within national legal systems that can facilitate the proper enforcement of *jus cogens* norms by directly or indirectly recognizing their effects.[3] Customary international law has been largely ignored in analyses of international economic law and, by extension, regional economic integration. The predominant view, which is right to a very large extent, is that international economic law is founded on treaties. However, as Zamora demonstrates, customary international law

[3] Orakhelashvili (2006), pp. 542–75.

has a role to play in international economic relations, especially in the political sphere.[4] It is indeed arguable that some of its fundamental tenets, such as the most-favoured nation treatment principle, have crystallized into rules of customary international law.[5]

International lawyers have also sought to elevate some organizations to a supranational status, with laws superior and directly applicable or effective in member states. Hay describes supranational organizations as organizations that 'possess both independence from and power over their constituent states to a degree which suggests the emergence of a new federal hierarchy and which goes beyond traditional intergovernmental cooperation in the form of international organizations'.[6] There are no accepted criteria of supranationalism. Independence of the organization from member states, the adoption of binding decisions by majority votes, the direct and binding effect of the organizations' laws on individuals in member states, financial autonomy, the impossibility of unilateral withdrawal from the organization, the power to enforce the organization's decisions even without the cooperation of governments, such as by using national courts, parliaments or other member states, and the transfer of sovereign powers to the organization have all been suggested as relevant criteria.[7] To Hay, the key to supranationalism is an appreciation of the relation of the organization and its laws to member states and the international community.[8]

Supranationalism is not a static feature of international organizations. It is dynamic in nature. It may evolve with an organization. It may be limited to specific areas of an organization's activities; in other words, supranationalism and intergovermentalism may coexist within the same organization, but on different issues or subject matters. Supranationalism inversely relates to the sovereignty of member states of a supranational organization. The greater the loss of sovereignty, the more supranational the organization is. As Hay has argued, 'with few exceptions . . . the criteria for loss of sovereignty coincide with those which much of the literature regards as the elements of supranationalism.

[4] Zamora (1989).

[5] The International Law Commission is working on the meaning and effect of most favoured nation clauses, especially in the field of investment. See International Law Commission (2007).

[6] Hay (1965), p. 733.

[7] Hay (1965), pp. 736–8; Schermers (1972), pp. 19–21; and Pescatore (1974), pp. 48–55.

[8] Hay (1965), p. 740.

Thus, the concept of transfer of sovereignty may be the legal-analytical counterpart of the political-descriptive notion of supranationalism'.[9]

Significantly, the international organizations that first demonstrated supranational characteristics were economic communities, namely the European Communities (now the EU) and, subsequently, the East African Community.[10] Indeed, the now defunct European Coal and Steel Community was expressly labelled 'supranational' in its founding treaty.[11] The work of some international organizations may not directly affect many internal policies of member states. In contrast, the activities of economic communities have a direct impact on policies in member states. Their effectiveness may require a transfer of sovereign powers to the community as regards those activities. The European Communities and East African Community were products of international law; they were all created by treaties.[12] However, it was realized that, regarding their legal relations with member states' laws, a legal framework very different from that hitherto existing between international organizations and member states would be required to ensure their effectiveness. In light of the legal framework it adopted, especially through the jurisprudence of the Court of Justice of the European Union (ECJ), the EU has often been characterized as *sui generis* – it is not an ordinary international organization. In his work on the subject, Weiler uses the concept of 'normative supranationalism' to describe an aspect of this legal framework. Normative supranationalism is 'concerned with the relationships and hierarchy which exist between community policies and legal measures on the one hand and competing policies and legal measures of the member states on the other'.[13] He provides three key elements or core attributes of the concept, namely direct effect, supremacy and pre-emption.[14]

Weiler's analysis of normative supranationalism is important. He provides a very useful analysis of the principles of direct effect and

9 Hay (1966), p. 69.

10 Schermers (1972), p. 21, where he characterizes the East African Community together with the European Communities as the most supranational organizations existing at the time.

11 Treaty Establishing the European Coal and Steel Community, 18 April 1951, 261 UNTS 140, Art. 9 paras. 5 and 6 (hereafter, ECSC Treaty).

12 ECSC Treaty; Treaty Establishing the European Economic Community, 25 March 1957, 298 UNTS 11 (hereafter, Treaty of Rome); Treaty Establishing the European Atomic Energy Community, 25 March 1957, 298 UNTS 140; and Treaty for East African Cooperation, 6 June 1967, 6 ILM 932.

13 Weiler (1981), p. 271; and Weiler (1991).

14 Weiler (1981), pp. 273–9.

supremacy, which are discussed below. However, to provide a more comprehensive and broader legal framework, it is helpful to look beyond 'legal measures' and focus on the broader notion of relations between legal systems, namely those of the community and member states, and international and regional systems. A robust legal framework for successful integration should not concentrate only on the relations between a community and its member states. It is equally important to provide a framework for the relations among member states of the community, as well as for the community's relations with legal systems outside its member states. Indeed, even as regards the relations between the community and member states, there are principles other than direct effect, supremacy and pre-emption, which are important.

As noted above, the rules of private international law, which regulate the status and effect of one state's laws in another state's legal system, sometimes impact on the domestic effectiveness of foreign laws. To overcome this, and for the purposes of ensuring effective integration, some communities, such as the EU, Southern Cone Common Market (MERCOSUR) and Organization of American States (OAS), have made reform of private international rules a key part of their agenda. The reforms provide supranational coordination for the principles of a subject which, despite its name, is part of municipal law. Within the EU, a very restricted meaning is given to public policy – a concept that is often used in traditional private international law to exclude the application of foreign laws or deny recognition of foreign judgments.[15] Certainly, an unrestricted invocation of public policy to deny the recognition of other member states' judgments, or the application of their laws, can restrict the free movement of persons, services and capital within the community.[16] Also, there is the principle of mutual recognition, which, like choice of law, determines whether and to what extent domestic effect should be given to another member state's laws.[17] Furthermore, the scope for the domestic application of other EU member states' laws is enhanced through definite and uniform choice of law rules on defined subject matters.

In summary, an effective legal framework to regulate community–state and interstate relations may have to depart from some traditional public and private international law principles. This should be borne in mind when creating a legal framework aimed at addressing the vertical, horizontal and vertico-horizontal relational issues arising in economic integration.

[15] Mills (2008). [16] Fumagalli (2004), p. 176. [17] Fallon and Meeusen (2002).

2.3 Economic community as a legal system

An economic community is not a state. However, an attribute it shares with states, which is important as far as its relations with member states and other entities is concerned, is that it constitutes a legal system with lawmaking and enforcement powers. The concept of a legal system is a difficult concept,[18] but four elements are generally considered necessary for the existence of such a system or legal order. Firstly, rules for conduct must be present. These rules regulate behaviour and activities within the legal system. Secondly, there must be defined entities to which the rules apply or relate. These are the subjects of the legal system. The legal system confers benefits and imposes burdens on the subjects. Thirdly, there must be a source from which one can identify the rules that form part of the legal system. It is not every norm that can claim a legitimate place within a legal system. Norms external to a legal system, such as international law and the laws of other states, are treated differently from norms internal to the legal system. Finally, there is the element of obligation to obey the norms of the legal system. This obligation is enforceable through both public and private means. Reliance on both mechanisms facilitates the effective enforcement of norms of a legal system. Exclusive reliance on public mechanisms, such as official state institutions, does not make for effective enforcement of norms; individuals have a crucial role to play. The subjects of a legal system must generally adhere to its rules. However, occasional infractions of specific rules do not necessarily negate the existence of the entire legal system. Hart captured these elements when he argued the following as the conditions for the existence of a legal system: the existence of a union of primary rules of obligation and secondary rules of change, adjudication and recognition; the acceptance by officials of the system that the rule of recognition provides the standards of official behaviour; and the existence of general compliance with the rules that are valid under the system's rule of recognition.[19]

These elements do not exhaust what may actually comprise a legal system. Dworkin has ably demonstrated the importance of principles and policies to the operation of a legal system. To him, an undue emphasis on rules provides an inadequate account of a legal system.[20] In addition, the obligation to obey the laws of the legal system may be attributed to the legal subjects' appreciation of the benefits that obedience brings, rather

[18] Raz (1970); and Harris (1979). [19] Hart (1994). [20] Dworkin (1967–8).

than any inherent force of the law or sanctions attached to it. In many instances, cooperation and compromise, rather than coercion, may be more effective methods for eliciting compliance with obligations imposed by the legal system.[21] These are important considerations, especially when one applies the concept of legal system to institutions that consist of sovereign states, such as economic communities. As Dowrick has observed in the context of the EU, one of its salient features is that 'for the most part it is essentially a co-operative, a consensual system, not a coercive order'.[22] Member states' commitment to a community and their preparedness to make it work, more than anything else, guarantees the success of a community through compliance with its laws. This is particularly true in Africa.

Although jurists differ on the characteristics of a legal system, there is near unanimity, at least among legal positivists, on the requirement of an ultimate and unrivalled source for the valid norms of the legal system. Norms from this source cannot be contradicted or made subordinate to any other norm, except where that source so decrees. Thus, not only is the source important, there must be clear rules on how norms emanating from it relate to other norms external to that source. Hart's rule of recognition helps identify rules that are a valid part of the legal system's set of norms.[23] The rule of recognition provides the criteria for the validity of norms within the legal system. John Austin wrote that a legal system must contain a determinate human superior, a 'sovereign', who will issue commands to his subjects.[24] Hans Kelsen also conceived of a legal system as a series of hierarchical norms that rest on the 'grundnorm', which is the ultimate source of authority.[25] The existence of an ultimate authority is not enough to constitute a legal system; however, its absence is fatal.

For an economic community, the fact that it should be the ultimate and unrivalled source of law on matters within its competence is particularly important. If member states exercise competences reserved for a community, or interpret and apply community law without uniformity, it can be inimical to a community's development. As will be discussed below, a number of relational principles, such as supremacy of community law, interpretive autonomy and a preliminary reference procedure, aim to ensure that a community remains the ultimate and unrivalled

[21] Chayes and Chayes (1995). [22] Dowrick (1983), p. 180.
[23] Hart (1994), pp. 94–5. [24] Austin (1995), pp. 212–13. [25] Kelsen (1991).

source of law. The above conceptualizations of a legal system offer useful insights into understanding how economic communities relate to member states' legal systems. Indeed, commentators have applied these conceptualizations to the study of economic communities and other trade regimes. Jones argues that Hart's theory of a legal system provides a model and framework of analysis that illustrates, explains and supports the ECJ's claim that there exists an autonomous EU legal system.[26] There is need for caution in treating economic communities as legal systems. The traditional conceptualizations of a legal system have often been made from the perspective of states and not the organizations that result from their coming together. Indeed, Kelsen conceived of only two legal systems – the many national legal systems and one international legal system. He did not extend the idea of a legal system to international organizations. Surely, a legal system derived from several states will look different from that of a single state. It will raise more complicated questions as to who its subjects are, and how it relates to them.

In summary, like a state's legal system, an economic community is norm-generating. It is endowed with institutions with ultimate powers granted by treaty to make laws and enforce them. Its subjects are the member states, institutions and individuals to whom its laws may be directed. The founding treaty of a community – its *grundnorm* – often provides for sanctions for non-compliance with its laws. But what is most important is member states' voluntary adherence to community law. Relational principles are adopted by communities with the aim of enhancing their lawmaking and enforcement powers.

2.4 Relational principles and mechanisms for economic integration

As noted above, economic integration progresses through various stages – free trade area, customs union, common market, economic union and complete economic integration. The stages are not watertight. Nor is progress through them necessarily sequential. A community may manifest features that straddle the various stages. The extent to which relational principles are significant and merit application within the legal framework governing community–state and interstate relations varies with the stage of integration attained. A community that is merely a free trade area or

[26] Jones (1984). See also Dowrick (1983); Palmeter (2000); Riesenfeld (1996–7); Weyland (2002); and Starr (1977).

customs union may apply a modest number of relational principles, but a common market or economic union is unlikely to be effective without utilizing many of them. This is because the further one progresses through the stages of integration, the deeper the level and scope of community-state and interstate legal interactions become; and the more immediate the need for a robust legal framework to regulate those interactions becomes. This section examines relational principles used by communities throughout the world to regulate those interactions. It exposes the inadequacies of traditional public and private international laws in dealing with the relational issues faced by communities. It assesses the contribution each relational principle makes to ensure that community–state and interstate relations enhance the effectiveness of a community.

2.4.1 Community autonomy as the foundation of relations

The autonomy of an international organization is a multifaceted concept. It covers a wide range of issues, including its separateness from member states, the independence of its institutions, finances and personnel, its ability to control the making, nature and effects of its law, and its ability to act using its own legal personality. As with some international organizations, the autonomy of some economic communities is expressly provided for in their founding treaties.[27] Such a treaty may confer a separate legal personality on a community to emphasize its separateness from member states.[28] It may provide for the neutrality and independence of personnel of specific institutions within the organization. It may also confer exclusive or final jurisdiction to its judicial institutions to interpret community laws.[29] Schilling characterizes this as 'interpretive autonomy', and defines it to mean that only the institutions of the particular legal order are

[27] NAFTA, Art. 103(2). See generally Sorensen (1983).

[28] EU Treaty, Art. 47; EAC Treaty, art. 138; Benelux Treaty, art. 95; CARICOM Treaty, art. 228; ECOWAS Treaty, art. 88; SACU Agreement, art. 4; and SADC Treaty, art. 3.

[29] EU Treaty, Art. 292; Benelux Treaty, art. 51(1); Treaty Creating the Court of Justice of the Cartagena Agreement, 28 May 1979, 18 ILM 1203 as revised by the Protocol Modifying the Treaty Creating the Court of Justice of the Cartagena Agreement, 28 May 1996, art. 42; Protocol of Tegucigalpa of Reforms to the Charter of the Organization of the Central American States, 13 December 1991, art. 35; and Agreement on the Statute of the Central American Court of Justice, 10 December 1992, 1821 UNTS I-31191; 34 ILM 921, art. 25 (hereafter, Statute of the Central American Court of Justice). A less absolute form of an exclusive jurisdiction clause is Art. 23 of the WTO Dispute Settlement Understanding. But in *United States: Sections 301–310 of the Trade Act of 1974* (1999), WT/DS/152/R at para. 7.43 (Panel Report), it was held that Art. 23(1) was an 'exclusive dispute resolution clause'.

competent to interpret its constitutional and legal rules.[30] Interpretive autonomy prevents institutions outside a community from interfering with the lawmaking and interpretation prerogatives of a community, and mitigates the concomitant prospect of inconsistencies in the interpretation and application of community law.[31]

More often than not, one has to infer a community's autonomy from its founding treaty by examining its lawmaking powers, legal status, modes of the application of its laws and the character of its dispute-settlement institutions. Seldom, if at all, will one find an express provision in a community's founding treaty that the community constitutes an autonomous and separate legal system.[32] Indeed, a community's autonomy must often be earned through the decisive work of its institutions and personnel. As Schermers once noted, supranationalism sometimes depends on 'the behaviour of men and groups of men'. It is contingent on 'the opinion of civil servants and governments about an organization, on how they see it. Their attitude may determine the influence of an organization more than the text of its constitution'.[33] A community's autonomy must also be supported by forces outside the community if it is to be sustained. In other words, attaining the status of an autonomous legal system will always involve legal and political contestation and, in that contest, individuals play an instrumental role.

Autonomy lies at the heart of any legal framework designed to regulate community–state relations. The relations between a community and its member states and, indeed, with other international organizations should be founded on the community's autonomy. Thus, it is a fundamental principle of EU law that the EU's external relations with other international organizations should not affect the autonomy of the

[30] Schilling (1996), pp. 389–90. But see Benelux Treaty, art. 50, which allows appeals to the International Court of Justice in the event that a member of the Union does not put into effect a judgment or conservatory measure of the Union's College of Arbitrators.

[31] Shany (2003), p. 182.

[32] The autonomy of the EU was the creation of the ECJ. *Van Gend en Loos* v. *Nederlandse Administratie der Belastingen*, Case 26/62, [1963] ECR 1, [1963] CMLR 105; *Flaminio Costa* v. *ENEL*, Case 6/64 [1964] ECR 585; *Yassin Abdullah Kadi and Al Barakaat International Foundation* v. *Council of the European Union and Commission of the European Communities*, Joined Cases C-402/05 and C-415/05, [2008] ECR I-6351; and Barents (2003). The MERCOSUR Tribunal has also affirmed the autonomy of MERCOSUR integration law. Piscitello and Schmidt (2007); and Albarrancin (1998). Compare US: Sections 301–310 of the Trade Act of 1974 (1999), WT/DS/152/R, para. 7.72. The panel held that 'the GATT/WTO did not create a new legal order the subjects of which comprise both contracting parties or Members and their nationals'.

[33] Schermers (1972), p. 23.

community's legal order.[34] Autonomy should be a key aspect of the supranational character of an economic community. It provides the foundation for adopting and applying relational principles, which ensure the effectiveness of community laws vis-à-vis their relations with the laws of other legal systems. For example, the ECJ derived two key principles from asserting the autonomy of the community legal order, namely that the validity of community law can be judged only in terms of community law, and that member states' constitutions cannot prejudice the supremacy of community law.

In summary, pragmatically and theoretically, autonomy is a *sine qua non* for the creation and effective existence of a community legal system. Accordingly, an economic community that aims to be effective should strive for autonomy. But its legal system should not be self-contained; it should not be sealed off from the legal systems of member states and the international community. Indeed, it must interact with them.[35] The very foundation of a community may be in international law or the community may have to comply with the requirements of international law. For example, the jurisprudence of a community's court should not be developed in 'clinical isolation' from the jurisprudence of other international courts or international law generally.[36] However, community–state relations and the relations between a community and other international organizations should have as their ultimate object the enhancement of the objectives of the community.

2.4.2 Direct applicability of community law

International law obliges parties to a treaty to perform their commitments in good faith.[37] However, in the absence of a specific treaty provision (and compelling practical imperatives) requiring the parties to give effect to the treaty within their national legal systems, there is no general obligation that a treaty must be incorporated into domestic law.

[34] Opinion 1/91, *Draft Agreement between the Community and the Countries of the European Free Trade Association relating to the Creation of the European Economic Area* [1991] ECR I–06079; and Opinion 1/00, *Proposed Agreement between the European Community and non-Member States on the establishment of a European Common Aviation Area* [2002] ECR I–03493. Eeckhout (2004), pp. 206–9.

[35] Hartley (2001), p. 1; and Bethlehem (1998).

[36] *United States – Standard for Reformulated and Conventional Gasoline* (1996), WT/DS2/AB/R at 17 (Appellate Body).

[37] Vienna Convention on the Law of Treaties, 23 May 1969, 1155 UNTS 331, 8 ILM 679, Art. 26.

Also, in the absence of a specific treaty provision, international law does not obligate states to grant individuals access to their national courts for the purpose of enforcing treaty provisions.[38] Thus, for international lawyers, a major problem with international law is implementation at the national level or becoming part of national law. In dualist countries, as opposed to monist countries, the solution lies in transformation; international law must be implemented nationally using national constitutional procedures or measures. This opens the way to a number of difficulties: states may not implement international law at all; they may delay in implementing it; or they may implement it incompletely or partially.

International and regional economic laws are no exception to the above principles and problems even though, by their very nature, domestic implementation is needed if they are to be effective. Regarding community law, some communities have found ways to bypass these difficulties through the principle of direct applicability.[39] It allows for the integration of community law into member states' legal systems without intervening national implementation procedures or measures. To the ECJ, direct applicability means the entry into force of community law is 'independent of any measure of reception into national law'.[40] This implies that direct applicability is concerned with how community law enters member states' legal systems; it is silent on the effect of community law once it so enters. It is worth noting that direct applicability does not deny the need to make community law known within member states. Often, there is the need for measures to bring community law to the attention of the public or other addressees of the law, but ensuring that aims to create awareness, not transform community law into a national law.

In community–state relations, direct applicability enhances community law in a number of ways. A community may consist of monist and dualist states. For such a community, direct applicability provides a uniform platform or procedure for the reception of community law into member states' legal systems. Community law takes effect in member

[38] Murphy (2009). Murphy argues that it is also possible for a right of access to be implied into the treaty (pp. 96–109).

[39] EU Treaty, art. 288; and EEA Agreement, art. 7(a). But others expressly deny the direct applicability of their laws in member states. See CARICOM Treaty, art. 240(1); EURASIAN Agreement, art. 14; COMESA Treaty, art. 5(2); ECOWAS Treaty, art. 5(2); EAC Treaty, art. 8(2); and SADC Treaty, art. 6(5).

[40] *Amsterdam Bulb* v. *Produktschap voor Siergewassen*, Case 50/76, [1976] ECR 137 at 146.

states at the same time and without potentially varying preconditions based on national laws. By using direct applicability, delay in implementation, non-implementation and partial implementation of community law are avoided. Direct applicability also maintains the specificity of community law in member states. It avoids a negative consequence of the dualist mode of nationally implementing international law, which is through an act of transformation, such as with an Act of Parliament, parliamentary resolution, or executive or legislative instrument. An Act of Parliament implementing international law is national law. Unless expressly stated, the Act does not enjoy any privileged status in national law. Accordingly, the Act is subject to national rules on the hierarchy of laws. Conflicts between the Act and another national law may be resolved by using conflict of norms rules, such as *lex posterior derogat priori*, *lex specialis derogat generali* or other presumptions of statutory interpretation. The same applies to using parliamentary resolutions, or executive or legislative instruments, to implement international law.

The application of presumptions of statutory interpretation, including the *lex posterior derogat priori* rule, to resolve conflicts between community and national laws can be inimical to vertical community–state relations. Direct applicability ensures that this does not happen. This is because even where community law conflicts with a national law, because each is of a different genus or, to borrow from Hart's theory of a legal system, each is subject to a different rule of recognition, it will be inappropriate to resolve the conflict using the *lex posterior derogat priori* rule.[41] Indeed, the use of conflict of norms rules to resolve a conflict between legal systems is often inappropriate.[42] Furthermore, by maintaining the distinct character of community law, direct applicability could enhance the prospect of using the preliminary reference procedure if the procedure is provided for in the community legal system. Issues involving community law become more visible as a result of the distinct nature of the community laws involved.

2.4.3 Direct effect of community law

It is insignificant if international law becomes part of national law but individuals cannot rely on it, or if reliance on it is contingent on preconditions that make such reliance largely illusory. An example of the former is section 102(c) of the United States' Uruguay Round

[41] Paulson (1983). [42] Michaels and Pauwelyn (2011); and Pauwelyn (2003).

Agreements Act.[43] Under section 101 of the Act, Congress approved the Uruguay Round Agreements, in other words, Congress gave the force of law to the Agreements in the United States. However, under section 102(c) of the Act:

> No person other than the United States shall have any cause of action or defense under any of the Uruguay Round Agreements or by virtue of congressional approval of such an agreement, or may challenge, in any action brought under any provision of law, any action or inaction by any department, agency, or other instrumentality of the United States, any State, or any political subdivision of a State on the ground that such action or inaction is inconsistent with such agreement.

Canada's World Trade Organization Agreement Implementation Act[44] illustrates the latter position. Arguably, section 8 of the Act gives that Agreement the force of law in Canada. However, under sections 5 and 6 of the Act:

> 5. No person has any cause of action and no proceedings of any kind shall be taken, without the consent of the Attorney General of Canada, to enforce or determine any right of obligation that is claimed or arises solely under or by virtue of Part I or any order made under Part I.
> 6. No person has any cause of action and no proceedings of any kind shall be taken, without the consent of the Attorney General of Canada, to enforce or determine any right or obligation that is claimed or arises solely under or by virtue of the Agreement.

The above means of giving effect to international law, in this instance WTO law, when extended to community law, renders it potentially ineffective, or subject to variable 'force' in member states. The principle of direct effect, which is adopted in some communities, overcomes this.[45] It has also been suggested as a mechanism for deepening or strengthening economic integration in a context where politicians are not open to solutions of a supranational character.[46] Direct effect enables individuals

[43] Uruguay Round Agreements Act, Pub. L. 103–465, 108 Stat. 4809, 19 USC 3501; North American Free Trade Agreement Implementation Act, s. 102(c); and Dunoff (2008).

[44] World Trade Organization Agreement Implementation Act, SC 1994, cl. 47; *Pfizer Inc.* v. *Canada (T.D.)* [1999] 4 FC 441, (1999) 2 CPR (4th) 298; and North American Free Trade Agreement Implementation Act, SC 1993, cl. 44, s. 6.

[45] *Van Gend en Loos* v. *Nederlandse Administratie der Belastingen*, Case 26/62, [1963] ECR 1, [1963] CMLR 105. Direct effect is denied by the founding treaties of some communities. See, e.g. NAFTA, Art. 2021; *US: Sections 301–310 of the Trade Act of 1974* (1999), WT/DS/152/R, para. 7.72; and de Mestral and Winter (2004).

[46] de Mestral and Winter (2004), p. 36.

to invoke community law before a national court.[47] It brings home to individuals rights created at the community level without subjecting the enforcement of those rights to varying nationally determined preconditions. It allows a national court to use community law as an independent, direct and autonomous basis of its decision. Direct effect integrates community law into member states' legal systems by turning national courts and individuals into enforcers of community law. With direct effect, the founding treaties of a community and laws made thereunder cease to be mere intergovernmental agreements. They attain the status of laws that have direct relevance for individuals; rights conferred by the laws can be directly enforced against governments by the individuals.

The principle of direct effect is most clearly developed in EU law, but it has national analogues, such as America's concept of 'self-executing treaty' and, as a legal concept, a much deeper historical root in public international law. Dating back to the nineteenth century, states have conferred powers on international organizations to make decisions that directly bind individuals within states in the same manner as decisions of national institutions would have done.[48] In the *Jurisdiction of the Courts of Danzig* case, the Permanent Court of International Justice noted the 'very object of an international agreement, according to the intention of the contracting parties, may be the adoption by the parties of some definite rules creating individual rights and obligations and enforceable by the national courts'.[49]

The principles of direct applicability and direct effect are different.[50] Direct applicability deals with the processes or means by which community law is implemented nationally. Direct effect deals with the legal enforceability of rights created by the laws that have become part of national law. Thus, although all directly effective laws are part of national law, not all directly applicable laws are directly effective; indeed, it is trite that not all laws are enforceable. A directly applicable law may be so vague, ambiguous, conditional or so targeted at a particular group or issue that a legally enforceable right cannot be founded on it. Surely, this does not mean that such a law is useless in a state. It might, for example, inform a court's interpretation of another national law, or be the basis for political agitation for reform and change.

[47] Craig (1992); and Dashwood (1977). [48] Jessup (1948), pp. 18–19.

[49] *Jurisdiction of the Courts of Danzig (Pecuniary Claims of Danzig Railway Officials who have Passed into the Polish Service, against the Polish Railways Administration)* PCIJ, Ser. B., No. 15, 1928 at 12.

[50] Winter (1972).

2.4.4 Supremacy of community law

Community–state relations extend beyond the issues of how community law becomes part of national law, and whether community law can be enforced in national courts. An equally important issue to consider in providing a legal framework to regulate community–state relations is the prospect of conflict between community and national laws. Regarding public international law, states often rely on ordinary rules of statutory interpretation, such as the *lex posterior derogat priori* and *lex specialis derogat generali* principles, which rely on the nature of the conflicting laws (for example, an Act of Parliament versus a subsidiary legislation) or constitutional provisions, which declare international law as superior or subordinate in cases of conflict. States vary in their approach to resolving such conflicts, and not all approaches are or will be favourable to maintaining vertical community–state relations. Indeed, as noted above, the use of conflict of norms principles to resolve conflicts between the laws of two legal systems is not entirely appropriate. This is especially so in the context of economic integration when one is dealing with conflict between national and community laws.

The principle of supremacy of community law overcomes this challenge to vertical community–state relations: it provides a uniform and community interest-oriented solution to conflicts between community and national law. Supremacy may be enshrined in a community's founding treaty. Article 8(4) of the EAC Treaty expressly provides that 'community organs, institutions and laws shall take precedence over similar national ones on matters pertaining to the implementation of this Treaty'.[51] Supremacy may also be judicially decreed through a teleological interpretation of the treaty.[52] The principle of supremacy enhances community law, in that it bypasses potentially inimical national conflict of norms rules. It affirms the autonomy of the community legal system, ensures that the community law is not overridden by national law and fosters a coherent community legal system.

To an extent, the principle of supremacy operates like choice of law rules in private international law; in cases of conflict, it mandates a choice of community law as the applicable law. However, unlike in private

[51] See also Treaty on the Harmonization of Business Law in Africa, 1 November 1997, Official Journal of OHADA No. 4, p. 1, art. 10 (hereafter, OHADA Treaty); and NAFTA, art. 103(2), on the supremacy of NAFTA over 'other agreements'.

[52] *Flaminio Costa* v. *ENEL*, Case 6/64, [1964] ECR 585. Alter also reports a decision of the Andean Community Tribunal which declared the supremacy of Andean Community law. Alter (2008b), p. 50, fn. 29. See generally Alter (2001).

international law, the mandate admits no exceptions or limitations. A national court cannot exclude or deny the application of community law on the grounds that it violates the forum's public policy, or that it is a penal or revenue law. The principle of supremacy is designed to enhance community law by moving beyond traditional private international law principles on the relations between the *lex fori* and *lex causae*.

The principle of supremacy should be distinguished from provisions often found in the founding treaties of communities that oblige member states to ensure the conformity of their laws with community law.[53] In theory, such provisions are not conflict of laws resolution provisions. They could be characterized as law-implementation provisions. They look to the executive and legislature rather than the judiciary for action. Their violation will often be a breach of an international obligation remediable at the international rather than national level. What the principle of supremacy declares is that where national law is not in conformity with community law, national courts should give preference to and apply community law.

2.4.5 Preliminary reference procedure

The application of law often entails issues of interpretation and the concomitant problem of who should be the ultimate interpreter of a particular law. In some states, the interpretation of the national constitution is reserved for the Supreme Court. A lower court faced with an issue of interpretation relating to the constitution must refer that issue to the Supreme Court. International law has no such ultimate interpreter: a national court is not barred from putting its own meaning on words in an international treaty that has been implemented domestically; it has no jurisdiction nor, indeed, standing to refer interpretive problems to the International Court of Justice; and the state in which the interpretive problem has arisen cannot, on its own, request an advisory opinion from the International Court of Justice.[54] Extending this state of affairs to community law will imply that, although national courts may give effect to community law, they can interpret it differently. This could lead to a situation in which community law will not be applied uniformly in member states.

[53] See, e.g. WTO Agreement, Art. XVI: 4.

[54] Statute of the International Court of Justice, 26 June 1945, 59 Stat. 1055, arts. 34 and 65. In 1929, Lauterpacht argued that the Permanent Court of International Justice be given jurisdiction to hear references from national courts. Lauterpacht (1929), pp. 94–5.

A preliminary reference procedure as part of the legal framework regulating community–state relations helps to overcome this challenge. In general, it is a procedure in the administration of justice that allows a lower court to seek interpretive guidance from a superior court on a point of law before making a final determination consistent with the superior court's ruling. In the context of economic integration, it unites community and national courts in an integrated system of judicial decision-making. In other words, it creates an organic or institutional link between community and national courts. The procedure provides a means through which the meaning of law is diffused into member states to be applied by their courts. It is a mechanism for ensuring unity and coherence in a community's legal system.

The efficacy of the procedure depends on whether or not it is mandatory, the willingness of national courts to find an interpretive problem and make a reference, the ability of a community court to influence national courts to make reference and whether the interpretation given by a community court is binding on all national courts within the community. Within the EU, the influence of the ECJ has been achieved largely through the use of this procedure. Indeed, de Richemont describes it as the 'keystone of the Community's legal structure'.[55] Foundational principles of EU law, such as direct effect, supremacy, pre-emption and implied powers, were all products of national court use of the preliminary reference procedure. More recently, the importance of the procedure has also been demonstrated in the Andean Community.[56] Because the procedure relates to the jurisdiction of a court, it has to be expressly provided for in community and national law. At present, the procedure is enshrined in the founding treaties of many economic communities.[57] National courts should also have a statutory mandate, at the national level, to make a reference to the community court.[58]

55 de Richemont (1978), p. 6. 56 Helfer, Alter and Guerzovich (2009).

57 EU Treaty, art. 267; COMESA Treaty, art. 30; EAC Treaty, art. 34; CARICOM Treaty, art. 214; Treaty Concerning the Establishment and Statute of the Benelux Court of Justice, 31 March 1965, 924 UNTS 13176, art. 6; Treaty Creating the Court of Justice of the Cartagena Agreement, 28 May 1979, 18 ILM 1203, art. 28–31; and Agreement between the EFTA States on the Establishment of a Surveillance Authority and a Court of Justice, [1994] OJ L344/3, art. 34 (hereafter, EFTA Court Agreement).

58 Within the EU, because art. 267 which enshrines the procedure is of direct effect, it has been suggested that many member states do not have legislation regulating the procedure. See generally Broberg and Fenger (2010); and UK: Civil Procedure Rules, Pt 68 and Practice Direction 68.

Although there is near unanimity on the utility of the procedure, there is some debate on why the procedure is used, and the conditions that make for its effective use. Studies have shown that among the factors that influence the use and effectiveness of the procedure are: the presence of national judges sympathetic to the use of the procedure and domestic actors or self-interested litigants who encourage its use; the work and jurisprudence of community judges; differences in national judicial structures and legal traditions; the level of transnational economic activity; and time.[59] Less obvious from these studies is the fact that there must be a considerable volume of substantive community law, implemented or applicable in member states, which potentially raises interpretive questions. Where there is a small body of substantive community law and a lack of national implementation of that law – as is the case with many African regional economic communities – the use of the procedure is likely to be minimal.

Another procedure for institutionalizing relations between community and national legal systems, akin to the preliminary reference procedure, is to allow national institutions to seek advisory opinion from community institutions, including their courts, on issues of community law. This procedure is reflected in article 2020 of the North American Free Trade Agreement.[60] It provides in part:

> If an issue of interpretation or application of this Agreement arises in any domestic judicial or administrative proceeding of a Party that any Party considers would merit its intervention, or if a court or administrative body solicits the views of a Party, that Party shall notify the other Parties and its Section of the Secretariat. The [Free Trade Commission] shall endeavor to agree on an appropriate response as expeditiously as possible. The Party in whose territory the court or administrative body is located shall submit any agreed interpretation of the Commission to the court or administrative body in accordance with the rules of that forum.

The Free Trade Commission consists of cabinet-level representatives of the Parties, or their designees. Its responsibilities include resolving disputes that may arise regarding the interpretation or application of the Agreement.[61] To date, the above procedure has not been invoked and it is arguable what the legal status of the 'agreed interpretation' of the Commission is before a national court. However, it is likely to be of only persuasive authority.

[59] Carrubba and Murrah (2005); and Helfer and Alter (2009).

[60] See also Broberg and Fenger (2010), pp. 17–25 on other ways in which national courts could seek guidance from EU institutions outside making a preliminary reference to the ECJ.

[61] NAFTA, art. 2001.

2.4.6 *Individuals' participation and standing*

Historically, individuals (both natural and legal persons) were not considered subjects of international law; only states were. Individuals did not have standing before international courts and could not participate on their own in international decision-making. Increasingly, this is ceasing to be so; individuals are now potential subjects of international law, they have standing before international courts and can participate, singularly or collectively, in the decision-making processes of many international organizations. For communities that aim to strengthen their relations with member states, individuals are a particularly important medium. Admittedly, a community that envisages its subjects as only member states may not necessarily be concerned with integrating individuals into its decision-making processes or activities. For such an 'inter-governmental' organization, there is no direct role for individuals. On the other hand, a community that envisages individuals as its subjects will have avenues to encourage and facilitate their participation. Through various means, such communities strive to enhance individuals' participation in their economic integration processes. For a community's legal system, this is important. A legal system thrives on its legitimacy. It must be legitimate in the eyes of its subjects to merit their adherence to its laws. In the context of economic integration, participation ensures the legitimacy of the community legal system. It is also a means by which the community and national legal systems interact with each other. The laws generated as a result of individuals' participation in the lawmaking processes of the community can in turn become a source of normative change within member states. A finding by a community court that national law is inconsistent with community law may lead to reform, review or abolition of that national law.

International organizations have seldom made use of legislative organs whose membership is drawn directly from parliaments of member states, or elected through universal suffrage from member states. However, increasingly, community parliaments, such as the European Parliament and East African Legislative Assembly, are being used by communities to ensure people's participation in community legislative processes. Both have full legislative powers, and members of the former are elected by universal suffrage. Other community parliaments, such as the Economic Community of West African States' Parliament and the Pan-African Parliament, have only advisory roles. Within the EU, a protocol has been recently concluded with a view to encouraging greater involvement of national parliaments in the activities of the EU and to enhance their ability to express their views on draft legislative acts of the EU.[62] The active involvement of national parliaments in a community's legislative processes provides an indirect means for individuals to influence the activities of the community.

A more direct means of participation increasingly used by communities is granting individuals standing before their respective community courts. Indeed, as a departure from the historical position in international law, a number of communities currently allow individuals to litigate directly against member states and the organizations' institutions before their community courts.[63] The communities vary in the preconditions to standing before the community courts, and also over what measures can be challenged. Some communities provide for unconditional and direct individual standing (for example, East African Court of Justice), others provide standing, but with the leave of the community court (for example, Caribbean Court of Justice) and some require the exhaustion of local remedies before an individual can have standing in the community court.[64]

These preconditions to standing sometimes pose difficulties for individuals. However, from the perspective of community–state relations, they could be important. The exhaustion of local remedies rule is illustrative of this. This rule of international procedural law provides that 'a state should be given the opportunity to redress an alleged wrong within the framework of its own domestic legal system before its international responsibility can be called into question at [the] international level'.[65] In other words, national mechanisms for the redress of alleged wrongs should be resorted to prior to invoking international avenues. In classical international law, the rule serves as a source of deference to states; it upholds and protects state sovereignty.[66]

[62] Protocol on the Role of National Parliaments in the European Union, 13 December 2007, [2010] OJ C83/203.

[63] COMESA Treaty, art. 26; EAC Treaty, art. 30; Agreement Establishing the Caribbean Court of Justice, 2001, online: www.caricom.org/jsp/secretariat/legal_instruments/agreement_ccj.pdf, art. XXIV (hereafter, Caribbean Court Agreement); and Statute of the Central American Court, art. 22(g). For a comprehensive list of these courts, see Alter (2009), pp. 266–8.

[64] See, e.g. COMESA Treaty, art. 26; and Protocol to the Southern African Development Community Tribunal and Rules Thereof, 7 August 2000, art. 15(2), online: www.sadc-tribunal.org/docs/Protocol_on_Tribunal_and_Rules_thereof.pdf (hereafter, SADC Tribunal Protocol).

[65] Trindade (1983), p. 1.

[66] Amerasinghe (2004), p. 62.

In economic integration, the rule creates relations between a community and member states. It regulates jurisdictional interactions between national and community courts. It allows national courts to have a 'first bite at the cherry' in cases involving community law before the community court has the last word. In the words of Amerasinghe, 'national courts perform functions as agents of the international legal order'.[67] Through this, national courts become engaged and familiar with community law; indeed, the rule sometimes performs an educational function. Also, national courts become validated and legitimized when their decisions are ultimately upheld by a community court. It has been argued that this encourages national courts to forge a stronger bond with the community legal system.[68] For community courts, the factual record created as a result of litigation before a national court can become the basis on which the former can make determinations as to whether a breach of community law has occurred. Given the limitations on the exhaustion of local remedies rule, it is not always the case that national courts will have a first take on disputes in which community laws are engaged. Sometimes, the circumstances render unjust a requirement to exhaust local remedies. For example, the Southern African Development Community Tribunal has recently held that, where an individual seeks an interim measure of protection pending the final determination of a dispute, the individual need not exhaust local remedies.[69] Indeed, the most robust and direct way to ensure that national courts engage with community courts is through the preliminary reference procedure.

2.4.7 *Inter-system jurisprudential communication*

Apart from relational principles, which integrate community law into the legal systems of member states through direct implementation, a legal framework on community–state relations should also emphasize indirect ways of exchanging norms. While the direct means of implementation, such as direct effect and direct applicability, are uni-dimensional (from community to member states), the indirect means of implementation emphasizes reciprocal exchange. An example of an indirect means of

[67] Amerasinghe (2004), p. 69.

[68] Helfer and Slaughter (1997). Another procedure, which looks more political than judicial, exists under chapter 11 of the Olivos Protocol for the Settlement of Disputes in MERCOSUR, 18 February 2002, 42 ILM 2.

[69] *Mike Campbell (Pvt) Ltd* v. *Republic of Zimbabwe*, Case No. SADCT 2/2007 (SADC Tribunal, 2007); and Amerasinghe (2004), pp. 200–15.

implementation is what I characterize as inter-system jurisprudential communication. This is a process by which law flows between legal systems. Civilizations thrive on borrowing; so do legal systems. In recent times, it has become increasingly popular, albeit controversial, for national courts to draw on each other's jurisprudence and also on principles of international law. Inter-system jurisprudential communication emphasizes comparativism and can take place at both legislative and judicial levels. Inter-system jurisprudential communication strengthens the bond between a community and member states; both become sensitive to each other's jurisprudence. This enhances the prospect that community law will fit into or be well received in member states.[70]

In making law, the community legislator or court may take as its starting point the laws of member states. It may also borrow from the jurisprudence of other communities or generally from public international law. Indeed, in some instances, community law expressly enjoins reliance on national law in the resolution of disputes before community institutions.[71] However, even in the absence of an express mandate, the use of extra-community laws may be legally supported. The founding treaties of some communities mandate their courts to ensure that, in the interpretation and application of the treaty, 'the law is observed',[72] or to 'ensure adherence to law'.[73] This suggests that there is a wider legal context within which the treaty and law made under it should operate. In other words, the treaty and laws made under it are the nucleus of a more extensive legal order.[74] Arguably, this legitimizes resorting to general principles of law, such as the principles of good faith, legal certainty, proportionality, *res judicata*, estoppel and respect for vested rights, as well as other legal principles developed in member states, other communities and international organizations.

Because of the importance of inter-system jurisprudential communication, a community should have institutional mechanisms designed to facilitate communication between it and member states. For example, the fact that judges of a community court are drawn from national courts, representatives in a community parliament are nominated from national parliaments and there are institutionalized workshops and seminars that bring together community legislators and judges, and their

[70] Lenaerts (2003), pp. 879–83.
[71] EU Treaty, art. 340; and SADC Tribunal Protocol, art. 21(a).
[72] Treaty on European Union, art. 19.
[73] COMESA Treaty, art. 19; and EAC Treaty, art. 23.
[74] Pescatore (1974), p. 74.

national counterparts, is important in this respect. In addition to communication between a community and its member states, member states should also communicate with each other. National legislators and judges may draw on jurisprudence from other states in making laws or deciding cases.[75] This will promote the harmonization of laws across the community. Communication between states is enhanced if they all adhere to the same legal tradition. However, the diversity of legal traditions should not necessarily hinder it. In summary, jurisprudential communication, and the mechanisms that enhance it, should be key components of a legal framework designed to regulate community–state and interstate relations.

2.4.8 *Interpretive and adjudicative relational principles*

Legal systems possess interpretive and adjudicative principles that allow them to take account of foreign laws in resolving disputes. Examples of these principles include consistent interpretation, choice of law, the doctrine of judicial notice and rules of evidence on foreign law. Considerations of justice, comity, effectiveness and efficiency in the administration of justice influence the use of these principles. These principles can be applied to community law to enhance its effectiveness in member states. The utility of these principles is that, compared with other modes of implementing community law, such as direct applicability, the relevant community law need not already be part of national law. In other words, even without direct applicability or a national statute implementing community law, it can still be used beneficially in member states.

The principle of consistent interpretation enjoins national courts to interpret national law in conformity with public international law to give effect to the latter.[76] There are national constitutions and statutes that endorse this principle. For example, article 233 of the Constitution of the Republic of South Africa 1996 provides that 'when interpreting any legislation, every court must prefer any reasonable interpretation of the legislation that is consistent with international law over any alternative interpretation that is inconsistent with international law'.[77] The absence

[75] Slaughter (2004). [76] Sawyer (2007); and Betlem and Nollkaemper (2003), p. 571.

[77] This provision was invoked to 'give effect' to Art. 11 of the WTO Agreement on Implementation of Article VI of the General Agreement on Tariffs and Trade, 1994 in *Progress Office Machines* v. *South African Revenue Services* 2008 (2) SA 13. See Eisenberg (1993–4).

of a constitutional or statutory endorsement of the principle is not fatal to its application. Indeed, it has been suggested that, on the whole, the application of the principle is only marginally influenced by constitutional provisions, and can be relied on by national courts in most instances.[78] Community law may also enjoin national courts to apply the principle of consistent interpretation.[79]

The principle of consistent interpretation enables courts to escape the strictures of the monist–dualist approaches to the relationship between international and national law. It can be applied by national courts under either tradition. Unlike other means for giving effect to community law, there is no justiciability test for the community law that is to be given effect under the principle. In other words, community law need not be of any specific quality; indeed, it is suggested that a court can look beyond 'the law' and take account of a community's goals and objectives. There are limitations on the use of the principle of consistent interpretation. Its application is contingent on the national text which is being interpreted; where there is no question of interpretation or where national law is not open to an interpretation that can be in conformity with community law, the principle cannot be applied.

National courts may take judicial notice of the existence of a community, its objectives and goals or particular community laws.[80] These may be treated as a fact that does not need to be proved. In other words, the failure of a party to plead them should not prevent courts from taking account of them and allowing them to influence the courts' decisions. Also, unlike the way in which common law courts treat foreign law, the meaning, effect and proof of community law can be deemed questions of law and, accordingly, a party need not prove it with expert evidence. This will reduce litigation costs and enhance the prospect of individuals relying on community law. Under English common law, which is arguably the position in common law African countries, the court may properly take judicial notice of international law. International law is not treated in the same way as foreign state law, which is a question of fact and must be pled and proved by expert evidence. In the words of Lord Justice Stephenson:

[78] Betlem and Nollkaemper (2003), p. 571.

[79] *Von Colson and Kamann* v. *Land Nordrhein-Westfalen*, Case 14/83, [1984] ECR 1891; COMESA Treaty, art. 5(1); CARICOM Treaty, art. 9; and ECOWAS Treaty, art. 5(1). See generally Drake (2005).

[80] UK: European Communities Act, 1972, cl. 68, s. 3.

> rules of international law, whether they be part of our law or a source of our law, must be in some sense 'proved,' and they are not proved in English courts by expert evidence like foreign law: they are 'proved' by taking judicial notice of 'international treaties and conventions, authoritative textbooks, practice and judicial decisions' of other courts in other countries.[81]

In public international law, national law is treated as a fact before international tribunals. Thus, contrary to what is being proposed here for national courts, an international tribunal will not take judicial notice of national law; it must be proved like any other fact.[82] It is suggested that where national courts take judicial notice of a community and its processes and relax their rules of proof of foreign law towards community law, or adopt the common law approach to prove international law, community courts should reciprocate. National law should not be treated as facts before a community court. However, this should not prevent a community court, in appropriate circumstances, from inviting expert evidence or detailed arguments from counsel on aspects of national law. In summary, what is being argued here is that a court can, subject to limitations imposed by national law, remedy the ignorance of counsel or a party about the possibilities that community law, goals and objectives offer to its case.

It is also possible for courts to apply community law as the applicable law if parties have so chosen. This presumes the existence of a body of substantive community law on the issue and a judicial philosophy that upholds party autonomy. In such an instance the relevant community law need not have been implemented in national law. With a view to enhancing intra-community trade, a community can adopt a set of principles on contract law or product liability that are not directly applicable, and which member states need not incorporate into their national laws. These principles can be chosen by individuals as the applicable law of their contracts, and this choice may be respected by the courts. The principles can also be directly incorporated into a contract, such that they become terms of the contract and binding on the parties to the contract. Admittedly, the utility of these possibilities may be constrained by the fact that national courts may view them – unfavourably – as an attempt to bypass national treaty incorporation procedures that are often constitutionally mandated.

81 *Trendtex Trading Corp.* v. *Central Bank of Nigeria* [1977] QB 529 at 569; and Hunter (1977–8).

82 Brownlie (2003), pp. 38–40; and Bhuiyan (2007), pp. 207–43.

2.4.9 Recognition and enforcement of foreign normative acts

The phrase 'normative act' is used here to cover judicial decisions, laws and administrative and executive acts that produce legal consequences. The recognition and enforcement of foreign normative acts, a key aspect of private international law, is a means through which legal systems interact. In economic integration, the recognition and enforcement of state and community normative acts facilitates their effective implementation and enhances cross-border economic transactions. Accordingly, a regime for the recognition and enforcement of foreign normative acts should be a key part of a community's legal framework on both community–state and interstate relations. Indeed, as Professor Casad has observed, 'an effective scheme for the mutual recognition and enforcement of civil judgments' is a feature of any economic integration initiative 'likely to achieve significant integration'.[83]

Already, many states have regimes that regulate the recognition and enforcement of foreign normative acts. These regimes are often imbued with discretionary elements, may be founded on reciprocity and may exclude certain normative acts from recognition and enforcement. In common law countries, the courts will not enforce foreign revenue, penal or other public laws. Also, aside from the many defences available to a judgment-debtor, there is no automatic right to have a foreign judgment recognized and enforced. Where statutes exist to regulate foreign judgment enforcement, they may be founded on reciprocity and only a few community member states may be designated. It is also important to note that state regimes on the recognition and enforcement of foreign normative acts have often been developed for normative acts emanating from other states. Accordingly, their extension to community normative acts, such as community court judgments, may be problematic. All of these can pose difficulty for the free circulation of normative acts within a community and, concomitantly, adversely affect economic transactions. Accordingly, a legal framework to regulate relational issues in integration should pay attention to the regimes for the recognition and enforcement of normative acts that exist in the member states. Some communities have developed or encouraged schemes[84] or principles

[83] Casad (1980–1).

[84] Council Regulation (EC) No. 44/2001 of 22 December 2000 on Jurisdiction and the Recognition and Enforcement of Judgments in Civil and Commercial Matters, [2001] OJ L12/1 (hereafter, Brussels I Regulation); CARICOM Treaty, art. 223; and EAA Agreement, art. 110.

aimed at ensuring the free circulation of normative acts, such as the principle of mutual recognition in EU law.

2.5 Relational principles – features and importance of context

In the preceding sections, it has been argued that a fundamental challenge for economic integration is structuring and managing relations between states, laws, legal systems and institutions. It has been suggested that, in managing these relations, a legal framework is needed. Various principles and mechanisms that should be part of this framework have been discussed. Admittedly, the principles and mechanisms discussed above are all legal in nature. This is not meant to deny or underplay the importance of 'non-legal' factors that serve to strengthen community–state and interstate relations. Examples of these factors are education and awareness creation about the work of a community, a commitment to common values, a state of affairs that necessitates mutual interdependence, and the degree of socio-cultural and ethnic homogeneity of a community's citizens. Ignorance and socio-cultural diversity engender a sense of alienation and indifference that can weaken community–state and interstate relations.[85] This section assesses the importance of the socio-cultural and political context within which relational principles operate. Before that, it examines the features of and relationship between the various principles.

A defining feature of relational principles is that they intrude into national legal systems and could potentially be construed as eroding sovereignty. The extent of intrusion will vary from country to country. A number of states, especially of the civil law tradition, have already made public international law part of their law, granted it precedence over conflicting national laws and allowed courts to apply it directly.[86] For such countries, direct applicability, direct effect and supremacy may not be entirely unfamiliar principles, at least in theory. In some common law countries, customary international law is often considered as being automatically part of national law. However, it must be admitted that community law will hardly ever qualify as customary international law. Many countries have procedures akin to the preliminary reference procedure that allows lower courts to seek interpretive guidance from superior courts on defined points of law. From a private international

[85] Inglehart (1970). [86] Nollkaemper (2002), pp. 166–9.

law perspective, the principles of direct applicability, direct effect and supremacy have some affinity with how foreign law is treated in states. Courts allow parties to found claims on foreign laws (direct effect). These laws need not be, indeed are not, implemented domestically (directly applicable) and, in some instances, the court may give effect to a foreign law even though it is inconsistent with a substantive law of the forum (supremacy). In other words, in almost all states within a community, there will be principles and procedures akin to some of the relational principles discussed above. The existence of these pre-existing national principles and procedures can be deployed as analogies in invoking relational principles in states.

A careful look at relational principles also reveals that some contain elements of deference to states. With direct effect, the enforcement of community laws begins and potentially ends at the national level. A state is not dragged, at the first instance, to a community forum for its breaches of community laws to be 'exposed'. The exhaustion of local remedies rule contains a similar deferential element. The same case can be made for the principle of supremacy of community law. Its effect is to compel the disapplication and not the abrogation of the national law to the issue at stake. The national law remains intact and could be applied to cases falling outside the scope of the relevant community law, as for example in cases involving non-member states of a community. A state may decide, in light of the conflict, to amend the affected law, but, in principle, the principle of supremacy of community law does not require that. Furthermore, direct effect and direct applicability need not be extended to all community laws; a community law may be in a form that allows member states to implement it in a manner appropriate to them without defeating community objectives. At the community level, the adoption of principles, such as supremacy and direct applicability, suggests the need for attention to detail and sensitivity in making the law. This is necessary to ensure the smooth integration of community law into national law. This is especially important in a community in which member states belong to different legal traditions. In other words, the intrusiveness of relational principles can be mitigated by attention to national exigencies in the community lawmaking creation processes. Inter-system jurisprudential communication and the participation of individuals in a community's lawmaking processes can be helpful in achieving this.

Another important feature of relational principles is their interconnectedness. Often, one cannot be effectively deployed without its complement. The principles of direct effect and supremacy are tightly connected.[87] The principles of direct applicability and supremacy create favourable conditions for the effective operation of direct effect. The enforcement of rights created by a community becomes illusory if a conflicting national law prevails. Similarly, direct effect and the preliminary reference procedure create a trilateral relationship among individuals, national courts and the community court for the effective enforcement of community law. Direct effect without a preliminary reference procedure leaves open the prospect of diverse interpretation of community law before national courts; uniformity in community law will be undermined and the coherence of the community legal system threatened. A legal framework to regulate community–state relations must pay attention to the interconnectedness of these principles.

The social matrix within which a legal system operates is as important as its substantive contents. Socio-cultural, economic and political conditions affect the extent to which relational principles can be effectively adopted or made to operate within a community and its member states. They condition the extent to which states will be receptive to community law and normative acts of other member states. Merely providing for relational principles in treaties – as has been done in the founding treaties of many communities, often with inspiration from Europe – will not guarantee their use or effectiveness. Indeed, to date, it appears that it is only within the EU that many of the relational principles operate most effectively. A recent study on the Andean Community by Helfer, Alter and Guerzovich suggests that while the overall experiment of economic integration may be judged unsuccessful, the use of some relational principles can enhance integration on specific subject matters.[88] The study demonstrates how, despite the difficult legal, political and economic conditions that prevail within the member states of the Andean Community, the Andean Court of Justice has effectively used the preliminary reference procedure to construct an effective intellectual property rights regime within the community. Arguably, apart from the EU, communities, including those in Africa, that have adopted relational principles in their founding treaties are at an early stage of development. For the African communities, an appreciable body of community law and case law has yet to emerge. Thus, it may be too early to make a detailed and objective assessment of the success, or otherwise, of the

[87] Koch (2005). [88] Helfer, Alter and Guerzovich (2009).

principles adopted by them. Indeed, the obstacles to their effective implementation are many. However, the Helfer, Alter and Guerzovich study suggests that relational principles, or at least some of them, can be made to work outside Europe.

The architecture of national legal systems, as well as domestic institutional and socio-cultural features, affects the extent to which community and national legal systems can be integrated. Neither the fact that relational principles contain elements of deference to states nor that they are complementary imply that they will be adopted wholesale or that their application will not meet resistance at the national level. A source of resistance could be in existing national laws, especially the constitutions – the supreme law of the land. Another source of resistance could be the result of existing socio-cultural and political conditions in member states. A country's legal system is part of its cultural heritage. It is an aspect of the state's social life and may be resistant to outside 'intrusions'. Studies have shown that, within the EU, the effective implementation of community law is inextricably linked with social and cultural processes within member states.[89] In the words of Wallace, 'legal culture constitutes a significant factor in the process of European integration'.[90]

More recently, Biukovic has demonstrated the importance of local practices and cultural norms in Japanese and Chinese compliance with WTO norms.[91] Indeed, legal culture – the assemblage of a society's attitudes, perceptions and ways of dealing with the law – may influence the extent to which states comply with community law or become legally integrated. A culture that favours respect for the rule of law and international law, emphasizes litigation and the proactive use of law as an instrument of change and development, is endowed with an activist and independent judiciary and lawyers with international perspectives, and possesses national actors and forces interested in the integration process, is more likely to favour the effective integration of community law into member states for the achievement of a community's objectives.[92]

2.6 Conclusion

Relational issues challenge economic integration. How they are approached affects the effectiveness of the integration process, especially

[89] Maher (1998); Maher (1996); and Wallace (1999). [90] Wallace (1999), p. 413.
[91] Biukovic (2008); and Biukovic (2006). [92] Alter (2009), pp. 63–91.

as regards the implementation of community law. There have been varying responses from communities to this challenge. In meeting the challenge, communities have deployed various relational principles. These principles often depart from the traditional private and public international law modes of giving effect to foreign and international law. At first sight, the principles appear very intrusive to national legal systems, but they also contain elements of deference to states. Their effective deployment demands constitutional accommodation in member states. It requires a rethink of existing national laws and procedures, and the legislature, judiciary and executive have a crucial role to play in this regard. In addition, there are various socio-cultural, economic and political factors that may affect the effective use of relational principles in regulating community–state relations. The remaining chapters examine Africa's economic integration processes through the lens of these principles.

3

The AU, AEC and regional economic communities

3.1 Introduction

Africa is awash with regional economic communities (RECs). Indeed, as far back as 1976, Ajomo picturesquely described the 'mercurial proliferation and disappearance' of regional economic institutions in Africa.[1] For political, economic and strategic reasons, many countries belong to more than one REC. The multiplicity of RECs and the concomitant multiple state memberships have created a complex patchwork that complicates decision-making for states, community officials, individuals and businesses. In what is, to date, the only detailed, continent-wide empirical study into the effect of the twin phenomena of many RECs and multiple memberships, the United Nations Economic Commission for Africa (UNECA) concluded that the phenomena impact negatively on the achievement of the goals of the African Economic Community (AEC).[2] In June 2009, some member states – Kenya and Uganda – could not join the newly formed COMESA customs union as they belonged to the EAC customs union. The phenomena also impact negatively on Africa's international trade relations. In the recent EU-led Economic Partnership Agreements negotiations, countries in Eastern and Southern Africa – the regions where the phenomena are most prevalent – had to form new regional groupings for the purposes of the negotiations.

A fundamental issue with Africa's economic integration is the relationship between the African Union (AU), RECs and AEC. This is a complex and unexplored question. Senghor's commentary on the processes leading to the formation of the AEC suggests that there were some discussions on this question. Indeed, he suggests that the relationship between the OAU and the AEC was a theme of special study by experts.[3]

[1] Ajomo (1976), p. 101. See generally Akintan (1977).

[2] United Nations Economic Commission for Africa (2006); and Jakobeit, Hartzenberg and Charalambides (2005).

[3] Senghor (1993); and Oppong (2009).

However, the existing legal framework does not suggest that the question was thoroughly addressed. Finding answers to it and clarifying the relationship are important for the success of economic integration in Africa. This is because the AU, AEC and the RECs are all working towards a common goal, albeit with different roles to play on the path to that goal.

The proliferation of RECs in Africa is part of a wider international phenomenon, the proliferation or increased density of international institutions. Against the background of this phenomenon, scholars have recently begun to discuss in great detail theories on 'regime complexes' or 'international regime complexity'.[4] A regime complex is an 'array of partially overlapping and non-hierarchical institutions governing a particular issue-area'.[5] The components of a regime complex are the elemental regimes. International regime complexity refers to the presence of nested, partially overlapping and parallel international regimes that are not hierarchically ordered.[6] International regime complexity empowers and disempowers.[7] It may work to the advantage of certain groups by providing opportunities for 'forum shopping' and arbitrage.[8] It may also disadvantage certain states or groups, such as on the basis of the sheer volume of information that has to be processed from the various regimes.

Studies on regime complexes help in understanding the relations between the many RECs in Africa. These RECs are non-hierarchical regimes with overlapping membership and jurisdiction. However, in terms of the focus of this chapter, there is one limitation in the studies; the existing studies have focused mainly on the evolution and interactions between rules or norms generated by elemental regimes of a regime complex. However, this chapter focuses principally on the institutional aspects of the coexistence of elemental regimes. In other words, the focus is mainly on institutions, not the norms generated by the institutions. Specifically, the chapter addresses the issue of how the RECs, as regional institutions, relate to each other and with the AU and AEC. The issues discussed in this chapter arise largely from the specific, and apparently unique, character of institutional density on economic integration in Africa. That is, the RECs ostensibly operate under an umbrella regime, the AEC, and their activities should be geared towards the realization of one objective – the creation of an African

[4] Raustiala and Victor (2004); and Alter and Meunier (2009).
[5] Raustiala and Victor (2004), p. 279. [6] Alter and Meunier (2009).
[7] Drezner (2009). [8] Raustiala and Victor (2004), pp. 280 and 299–300.

Economic Community. Thus, unlike other complex regimes, what exists in Africa is a complex regime on economic integration consisting of many elemental regimes (the RECs) and an umbrella regime (the AEC) – all working towards a common and singular treaty-mandated vision.

3.2 Existing regulatory legal framework

International regime complexity on many issues, such as intellectual property protection, human rights, international security and environment, does not have an overarching or umbrella regime that regulates the multiple regimes dealing with the particular issue. Arguably, regarding international trade in goods and services and regional trade agreements, an overarching regime apparently exists in the World Trade Organization (WTO). WTO law provides the legal foundation and a regulatory framework for regional trade agreements on goods and services.[9] The WTO has mechanisms for notifying such agreements, reviewing them and monitoring their compliance with WTO law. Such mechanisms do not affect the non-hierarchical nature of regional trade agreements. The mechanisms could have ensured a measure of coordination and harmonization among them through their compliance with a higher norm – WTO law. However, at present, the mechanisms are ill-equipped and ineffective, and the powers of enforcement and review have not been exercised rigorously.[10]

Unlike the situations with the WTO and regional trade agreements, international regime complexity on economic integration in Africa benefits from an umbrella regime, the AEC, and a modest regulatory framework under the Protocol on Relations between the African Union and the Regional Economic Communities (hereafter, Protocol on Relations).[11] The framework aims to harmonize and coordinate the

[9] General Agreement on Tariffs and Trade, 15 April 1994, Marrakesh Agreement Establishing the World Trade Organization, Annex 1A, 1867 UNTS 187, 33 ILM 1153, Art. XXIV; General Agreement on Trade in Services, WTO Agreement, Annex 1B, Art. V; Decision on Differential and more Favourable Treatment, Reciprocity and Fuller Participation of Developing Countries, 28 November 1979, GATT BISD (1980), 203, para. 2(c); and Lester and Mercurio (2009).

[10] Devuyst and Serdarevic (2007–8).

[11] Protocol on Relations between the African Union and the Regional Economic Communities, July 2007, online: www.afrimap.org/english/images/treaty/AU-RECs-Protocol.pdf (hereafter, Protocol on Relations). This protocol replaces the Protocol on Relations between the African Economic Community and the Regional Economic Communities, 25 February 1998, (1998) 10 Afr. J. Int'l & Comp. L. 157 (hereafter, Protocol on Relations – 1998).

activities of the RECs.[12] This is important since, unlike regional trade agreements established with the imprimatur of the WTO, the aim of Africa's RECs is to evolve and ultimately be absorbed into the African Economic Community.[13] The Protocol on Relations aims to formalize, consolidate and promote close cooperation among the RECs, and between them and the AU through the coordination and harmonization of their policies, measures, programmes and activities in all fields and sectors.[14] Another object of the protocol is to establish a framework for coordinating the activities of RECs in their contribution to the realization of the objectives of the Constitutive Act of the African Union and the AEC Treaty.[15]

To ensure the realization of these objectives, the parties to the protocol, namely the AU and the RECs, have undertaken to cooperate and coordinate the policies and programmes of the RECs with those of the AU.[16] Specifically, the RECs have undertaken to establish an organic link with the AU, with a view to strengthening their relations with the AU, and provide for their eventual absorption into the African Common Market as a prelude to the African Economic Community.[17] To enhance cooperation among the RECs, there are also provisions mandating or advocating entering into cooperation arrangements,[18] and participation in each other's meetings.[19] The RECs and the AU can attend and participate in, without voting rights, each other's meetings.[20] The Protocol of Relations establishes the Committee on Coordination and the Committee of Secretariat Officials as the institutions responsible for ensuring the coordination of policies and activities of the RECs and the implementation of the protocol.[21] The AU is also expected to open a liaison office at the headquarters of each REC.[22]

The regulatory framework under the Protocol on Relations is complemented by provisions in the founding treaties of the RECs dealing with their relations with other RECs and the AEC. The EAC Treaty provides that the member states 'shall foster co-operative arrangements with other regional and international organisations whose activities have a bearing on the objectives of the Community'.[23] The COMESA Treaty also allows the organization to 'enter into co-operation agreements with

[12] Protocol on Relations, art. 3(a)(b). [13] AEC Treaty, art. 88(1).
[14] Protocol on Relations, art. 3(a). [15] Ibid., art. 3(b).
[16] Ibid., art. 4(a). [17] Ibid., art. 5. [18] Ibid., art. 15(1).
[19] Ibid., art. 16(1). [20] Ibid., arts. 17 and 19. [21] Ibid., arts. 6–10.
[22] Ibid., art. 21. [23] EAC Treaty, art. 130(3).

other regional communities'.[24] A similarly worded provision is contained in the ECOWAS Treaty.[25] The SADC Treaty contains little detail on its relations with the AEC apart from a reference to the AEC in its preamble and a general reference to cooperation with regional and international organizations in article 24.[26] Obviously, these provisions are empowering, and some RECs have relied on them to establish cooperation arrangements with other RECs. The first and perhaps the most historic was the COMESA–EAC–SADC Tripartite Summit of Heads of State and Government held in Kampala, Uganda, in October 2008 under the theme: Deepening COMESA–EAC–SADC Integration. In a joint communiqué issued after the summit,[27] it was noted that the Heads of State and Government reviewed the activities of the three RECs, agreed on a programme of harmonization of their activities, and expressed their resolve to cooperate in the future. It was also resolved that the three RECs should immediately start working towards a merger into a single REC, with the objective of fast tracking the attainment of the African Economic Community. A taskforce was set up to design a roadmap for this merger.[28] The Heads of State and Government also approved the expeditious establishment of a free trade area encompassing the member states of the three RECs, with the ultimate aim of establishing a single customs union.[29] In line with a mandate from the Heads of State and Government, a Memorandum of Understanding on Interregional Cooperation and Integration has been signed by the three RECs.

Regarding relations with the AEC, the founding treaties of the RECs acknowledge the existence of the AEC and undertake to facilitate its goals.[30] However, they do not provide much detail on how and what form their relations with the AEC are or should be. The COMESA Treaty, the most detailed as far as this issue is concerned, affirms that its ultimate objective is to facilitate implementation of the AEC Treaty.[31] It enjoins member states to implement the provisions of the COMESA Treaty with due consideration to the provisions of the AEC Treaty,[32] and convert the organization, at a time to be agreed between it and the AEC, into an organic entity of the African Economic

[24] COMESA Treaty, art. 179(1). [25] ECOWAS Treaty, art. 79(1). [26] SADC Treaty.

[27] See Final Communiqué of the COMESA–EAC–SADC Tripartite Summit of Heads of State and Government, 22 October 2008, Kampala Uganda, online: www.tralac.org/cause_data/images/1694/FinalCommuniqueKampala_20081022.pdf.

[28] Ibid., at [13]. [29] Ibid., at [14].

[30] ECOWAS Treaty, art. 78; EAC Treaty, art. 130(2)(3); and COMESA Treaty, art. 3(f).

[31] COMESA Treaty, art. 178(1). [32] Ibid., art. 178(1)(b).

Community.[33] It enjoins the Secretary-General of the Community to coordinate the activities of COMESA with the AEC and report regularly to the Council of Ministers.[34] Indeed, in the preamble to the COMESA Treaty, the foundation of COMESA is traced to article 28(1) of the AEC Treaty, which calls for the strengthening and creation of RECs as the first stage in the evolution of the African Economic Community. Furthermore, 'the establishment, progress and the realisation of the objectives of the African Economic Community' are stated as the aims and objectives of COMESA.[35] These very generous provisions demonstrate a level of attention to problems of the relations between the AEC and COMESA. Admittedly, they still leave many difficult issues unresolved, but, compared with other RECs, they are advancements. In the EAC Treaty, the EAC is described as 'a step towards' the achievement of the objectives of the AEC Treaty.[36] In the ECOWAS Treaty, members undertake to facilitate 'the co-ordination and harmonization' of the community's policies and programmes with those of the AEC.[37] However, none of the treaties provides concrete details on its relations with the AEC. In other words, they do not address specific issues, such as: the legal nature of their relations with the AEC; whether they are bound by decisions of the AEC; and whether AEC law will prevail over their law in cases of conflict.

The above framework for regulating relations among the RECs, as well as their relations with the AEC, is short on detail and leaves many issues unaddressed. The next section discusses some of these issues and argues that, unless addressed, they could undermine the effectiveness of Africa's economic integration.

3.3 Inter-community relational issues

3.3.1 Legal status of AEC within the AU and RECs

Perhaps one of the greatest mysteries about Africa's economic integration is the legal status of the RECs within the AEC, and the AEC within the AU. The treaties do not shed much light on the issue and commentary on this is largely non-existent.[38] The starting point to unravelling this mystery, if it can be achieved at all, is the idea of legal personality.[39]

33 Ibid., art. 178(1)(b). 34 Ibid., art. 178(2). 35 Ibid., art. 3(f).
36 EAC Treaty, art. 130(2). 37 ECOWAS Treaty, art. 78. 38 Ajomo (1993), p. 40.
39 Amerasinghe (2005), pp. 66–104.

All of the RECs are endowed with legal personality in their founding treaties.[40] Although the AEC Treaty does not expressly say so, the legal personality of the AEC can be inferred from article 98(2), which provides that, in his capacity as the legal representative of the community, the Secretary-General may, on behalf of the community, enter into contracts and be a party to judicial and other legal proceedings. The Constitutive Act of the African Union (hereafter, Constitutive Act) is silent on the legal personality of the AU. This may, however, be explained by the fact that, under the General Convention on Privileges and Immunities of the Organization of African Union, the OAU (now the AU) possesses 'juridical personality'.[41]

With these provisions, the legal separateness of the RECs, AEC and AU is established in public international law. Accordingly, the legal status of one within the other should be defined by agreement to which both are parties, or, at least, in some definite and binding agreement. As regards the AEC and AU, the AEC Treaty is very clear that the AEC is an 'integral part' of the AU.[42] The Constitutive Act further provides that its provisions take precedence over and supersede any inconsistent or contrary provisions of the AEC Treaty.[43] Membership of the AEC is not coterminous with the AU. At present, there are four states – Djibouti, Eritrea, Madagascar and Somalia – all members of the AU that have either not signed or ratified the AEC Treaty. If one envisages the AU as a political and umbrella organization championing the cause of African unity – social, cultural, political and economic – then the AEC is that part of the AU solely devoted to the issue of economic integration. In other words, it is the economic leg of the AU. Comparatively, the relationship between the AEC and the AU is akin to – indeed might have been influenced by – that between the defunct European Community (EC) and the European Union (EU).[44] However, it must be admitted that even the relationship between the EC and EU was not without legal difficulty.

A difficult issue concerning the idea of the AEC as an integral part of the AU is how it appears to have been interpreted and applied. Like many words, 'integral' has multiple meanings. To the extent relevant

[40] COMESA Treaty, art. 186(1); EAC Treaty, art. 138(1); and ECOWAS Treaty, art. 88(1).

[41] General Convention on Privileges and Immunities of the Organization of African Unity, 25 October 1965, online: www.africa-union.org/root/au/Documents/Treaties/treaties.htm.

[42] AEC Treaty, art. 98(1). [43] Ibid., art. 33(2). [44] EU Treaty, art. 1.

here, the word describes component parts that, together, constitute a unity. It emphasizes divisibility, separateness and unity at the same time. As regards the relations been the AEC and the AU, it seems unity has been overemphasized, and this has led to the complete, or near-complete, loss of the separateness or distinct identity of the AEC. Laws and policies dealing with AEC-related issues are adopted by the AU instead of the AEC.[45] Furthermore, institutions of the AU have been co-opted to perform the functions of institutions of the AEC. However, there has neither been a clear separation of mandates nor examination of whether, as designed, the AU institutions are equipped to manage effectively the economic integration agenda.

An equally difficult issue is the legal status of the RECs within the AEC. Although the AEC Treaty contains more than twenty references to 'regional economic communities', and provides that the African Economic Community shall be established through the coordination, harmonization and progressive integration of the activities of the RECs, and imposes many duties with exact timelines on them, there is not a single provision on the status of the RECs within the AEC. Are they mere institutional observers within the AEC? Are they its organs, members, agents or subjects? Commentators on Africa's integration have assumed, and rightly so, that the RECs are the building blocks of the AEC. However, so far, none has investigated the important issue of what this means in legal terms, especially regarding the relations between the two organizations. The Protocol on Relations does not address this issue either.[46] It is an issue of both theoretical and practical importance. It is legally difficult to suggest that a REC is bound by decisions of the AEC[47] unless one is able to prove that the former is an organ, member, agent or subject of the latter.

The AEC Treaty does not set out a membership criterion, but it is implicit in article 2 that states that are parties to the treaty are the members of the AEC. There is no provision limiting membership of the AEC only to states. Indeed, there are international organizations, such as the Hague Conference on Private International Law, the WTO and the Food and Agriculture Organization which allow other

[45] See, e.g. Protocol on Relations (which should in principle have nothing to do with the AU, but is misleadingly titled as such and signed 'for the AU' not the AEC). Compare Protocol on Relations – 1998 (which was signed by the AEC).

[46] Articles 18 and 20 deal with the status of the RECs at AU meetings and the status of the AU at the RECs meetings respectively.

[47] AEC Treaty, arts. 10(2) and 13(2).

international organizations to become members. However, membership of an international organization cannot be inferred. The founding treaty of an international organization controls who can join it, under what conditions and by what procedure. There must be a conscious act on the part of a prospective member to become a member of an international organization, and an acceptance of its membership application by the organization.[48] In the absence of a definite agreement to that effect, it cannot be suggested that the RECs are members of the AEC. Nor can it be argued that the RECs are organs of the AEC; article 7 of the AEC Treaty clearly does not mention them. It is even more difficult to argue that the RECs are agents of the AEC. This is due to the absence of consent – express or implied – to such a relationship. International law places great emphasis on states and, by extension, international organizations, consenting to obligations to be imposed on them. The existence of an agency relationship between two international organizations with separate legal personalities cannot be presumed.[49]

It can, however, be argued, from a purposive reading of the AEC Treaty, to which the RECs are not parties and the Protocol on Relations, to which they are parties, that RECs are subjects of the AEC. They are subjects with a mandate to work towards the realization of the African Economic Community. To date, no REC has objected to the idea that it is evolving with an ultimate view to form the African Economic Community. Indeed, as noted above, provisions in some of the constitutive treaties of the RECs expressly proclaim this vision.

3.3.2 Future merger of the regional economic communities

The foundation of the AEC is the RECs; progress by the RECs is one step closer to the African Economic Community. This unique and hitherto unexplored approach to forming the African Economic Community raises numerous legal challenges. The size of the AEC makes the approach of using RECs as its building blocks almost inevitable. But this approach comes at a price. A recent UNECA study suggests that there is often tension between member states' commitment to the goals of the RECs and those of the AEC.[50] Also, concurrent membership of RECs creates tension among member states and between the RECs. The

48 Amerasinghe (2005), pp. 104–14; and Klabbers (2009), p. 93.
49 Sarooshi (2005), pp. 33–53.
50 United Nations Economic Commission for Africa (2006).

RECs are ultimately expected to merge or be 'absorbed'[51] to form the African Economic Community. Under article 88(1) of the AEC Treaty, the African Economic Community 'shall be established mainly through the co-ordination, harmonization and progressive integration of the activities of [RECs]'. Article 3 of the Constitutive Act of the African Union also underscores the need to 'coordinate and harmonize the policies between existing and future RECs for the gradual attainment of the objectives of the [African] Union'. Indeed, this is described as an 'objective' of the Union.

The simplicity of these provisions masks the complexity of the engagement of merging or absorbing international organizations such as RECs. Firstly, it is a unique and quite complicated approach to economic integration. It has not been experimented with anywhere else. Usually, countries form economic communities – free trade areas, customs unions or economic unions. To date, it appears that the only known case of a successful 'merger' of RECs has been the merger of the EC with the European Free Trade Area to form the European Economic Area.[52] A more recent attempt is the Union of South American Nations,[53] which is a continent-wide free-trade zone that unites the Common Market of the Southern Cone and the Andean Community. Secondly, the status of the RECs after the formation of the African Economic Community is not free from doubt. Whether they will disappear entirely or continue to operate as a mid-level legal system is not dealt with in the AEC Treaty or any protocol. Nor do the founding treaties of the RECs shed any brighter light on these issues. The UNECA conceives the future relationship between the AEC and the RECs in this way: after the RECs have achieved a customs union and a common market, they will merge to form the African Common Market, and the full-fledged African Economic Community intervention will follow. The African Economic Community will take the lead on dealing with member countries, and the functions and structures of the regional economic communities will be revised to serve as its implementation arms.[54]

The COMESA Treaty envisages the conversion of COMESA into an organic entity of the African Economic Community.[55] This suggests that

[51] Protocol on Relations, art. 5(1)(d). [52] Riechenberg (1995).

[53] It consists of Argentina, Bolivia, Brazil, Chile, Colombia, Ecuador, Guyana, Paraguay, Peru, Suriname, Uruguay and Venezuela. See Union of Southern American States Constitutive Treaty, 23 May 2008.

[54] United Nations Economic Commission for Africa (2006), p. 94.

[55] COMESA Treaty, art. 178(1)(c).

COMESA does not anticipate the formation of the African Economic Community as its demise. The treaty provides that the Authority of Heads of State and Government may, on the recommendation of the Council of Ministers, terminate the operations of the COMESA.[56] This suggests that a legal mandate exists for bringing COMESA to an end, if that is what is envisaged under the AEC Treaty after the formation of the African Economic Community. Neither the ECOWAS Treaty[57] nor the EAC Treaty[58] contains any provision directly relevant to their status after the formation of the African Economic Community. Indeed, the EAC Treaty is of perpetual duration.[59] Also, some of the RECs have and pursue objectives beyond economic integration, such as conflict prevention and political unification. Accordingly, it is difficult to suggest that the formation of the African Economic Community will represent the end of the RECs. The founding treaties of the RECs were drafted after the AEC Treaty. Therefore, one would have expected them to address the issue of their status after the formation of the African Economic Community more comprehensively and, perhaps, uniformly. As organizations created by treaties, the state parties retain an inherent right to terminate the treaties,[60] if that is what will be needed for them to merge and form the African Economic Community.

As the RECs are progressing through the stages of integration, the merger issue should engage the attention of the AEC. A merger protocol is needed. Indeed, it is suggested that negotiating a merger protocol should start now, given the complexity and size of the undertaking. Providing a model or draft legislation for such a protocol is beyond the scope of this work.[61] However, it is suggested that the protocol should address inter alia issues relating to: the post-merger legal status of the RECs; their assets and liabilities after the merger; whether the merger is compulsory or voluntary and, if compulsory, how that is going to be enforced; when the merger is to occur (simultaneously for all of the communities or incrementally after each reaches the necessary stage of

56 Ibid., art. 192(1).

57 Article 2(1) provides that the member states have decided that ECOWAS shall ultimately be the sole economic community in the region for the purpose of economic integration and the realization of the objectives of the African Economic Community.

58 In the preamble to the treaty, the member states affirmed their desire for a wider unity of Africa and regarded the Community as a step towards the achievement of the objectives of the Treaty Establishing the African Economic Community.

59 EAC Treaty, art. 144.

60 Vienna Convention on the Law of Treaties, 23 May 1969, 1155 UNTS 331, Art. 54(b).

61 Houben (1965–6); Linthorst (1965–6); and Riechenberg (1995).

integration); the status of their personnel and institutions, such as the various community courts; the institutional structure of the organization, which is to be formed after the merger; and the status of active RECs, such as the Southern African Customs Union, which is not an AU-recognized REC and, accordingly, will not, in my opinion, participate in the anticipated merger of the RECs.

The anticipated merger to form the African Economic Community raises other issues. Some RECs, like the EAC, are at an advanced stage of development. It is difficult to predict whether they will willingly merge with the AEC or with their less-progressive counterparts, such as the Inter-Governmental Authority on Development. Indeed, it can be argued that the longer the communities continue to evolve and develop on their separate paths, the further apart they will grow and the more difficult it will become to merge them. Furthermore, one may query whether the AU has the political will, legitimacy and wherewithal to impose its vision of an African Economic Community on the RECs. They are not parties to the AEC Treaty. Additionally, as discussed in Chapters 5 and 6, the treaty provisions of some of them on issues such as the jurisdiction of their community courts, *locus standi* for private parties, supremacy of community law, and the relations between community courts and national courts are superior to those of the AEC Treaty. Arguably, these advancements in community law and economic integration could be lost when they merge with the AEC if AEC law is not amended to incorporate those advances.

It is also debatable whether a merger of the RECs will be supported by interest groups within the RECs. Public choice theorists characterize international organizations as bureaucracies that are more responsive to the demands of organized interest groups, including their staff. As Vaubel notes, 'like all bureaucracies, international organizations fight for their survival and for more powers and resources. Thus, it is more difficult to abolish an international organization than to establish it, or to reduce its powers and resources than to increase them'.[62] Indeed, already, an overwhelming number of staff cases have appeared before the community courts.[63] This could be seen as evidence of people trying

[62] Vaubel (2003), p. 319.

[63] *Muleya* v. *Common Market for Eastern and Southern Africa (No. 3)* [2004] 1 East Afr. LR 173; *Muleya* v. *Common Market for Eastern and Southern Africa (No. 2)* [2003] 2 East Afr. LR 623; *Muleya* v. *Common Market for Eastern and Southern Africa* [2003] 1 East Afr. LR 173; *Ogang* v. *Eastern and Southern African Trade and Development Bank* [2003] 1 East Afr. LR 217; *Eastern and Southern African Trade and Development Bank* v. *Ogang* [2001] 1

to protect their 'turf'. The number of staff cases, and the tenacity with which they appear to have been litigated, lend some credence to Shams's thesis that economic integration has become a job-generating venture for Africa's educated elite,[64] and raise the prospect of obstructionist litigation before, during and, perhaps, after the merger. Additionally, the RECs are legal systems in their own right. Unlike the AEC, they are expressly endowed with a separate legal personality.[65] Thus, even before the merger, there is the need to structure and manage the relations between the AEC and RECs' legal systems, as well as among the RECs. The current legal framework on the relations between the AEC and the RECs – the Protocol on Relations – does not go very far in addressing these complicated issues.

3.3.3 *Conflict of laws and jurisdictions*

A central issue in the relations between the AEC and RECs' legal systems is the prospect of conflict of laws and jurisdictions. Alter and Meunier have observed that international regime complexity, such as that which exists in Africa on the issue of economic integration, reduces the clarity of legal obligations by introducing overlapping sets of legal rules and jurisdictions governing an issue.[66] To Raustiala and Victor, 'regime complexes are marked by the existence of several legal agreements that are created and maintained in distinct fora with participation of different sets of actors. The rules in . . . elemental regimes functionally overlap, yet, there is no agreed upon hierarchy for resolving conflicts between rules'.[67] In the area of international trade, especially against the

East Afr. LR 46; *Eastern and Southern African Trade and Development Bank* v. *Ogang (No. 2)* [2002] 1 East Afr. LR 54; *Tokunbo Lijadu Oyemade* v. *Executive Secretary of ECOWAS*, Suit No. ECW/CCJ/APP/01/04 (ECOWAS Court of Justice, 2006); *Executive Secretary of ECOWAS* v. *Tokunbo Lijadu Oyemade*, Suit No. ECW/CCJ/APP/01/05 (ECOWAS Court of Justice, 2006); *Executive Secretary of ECOWAS* v. *Tokunbo Lijadu Oyemade*, Suit No. ECW/CCJ/APP/04/06 (ECOWAS Court of Justice, 2006); *Tokunbo Lijadu Oyemade* v. *ECOWAS Council of Ministers*, Judgment No. ECW/CCJ/JUD/02/08 (ECOWAS Court of Justice, 2008); *Tokunbo Lijadu Oyemade* v. *Council of Ministers*, Suit No. ECW/CCJ/APP/02/08 (ECOWAS Court of Justice, 2009); and *Qudus Gbolanhan Folami* v. *Community Parliament (ECOWAS)*, Judgment No. ECW/CCJ/6/10/08 (ECOWAS Court of Justice, 2008).

[64] Shams (2005), pp. 6–7.

[65] COMESA Treaty, art. 186(1); EAC Treaty, art. 138(1); ECOWAS, art. 88(1); and SADC Treaty, art. 3(1).

[66] Alter and Meunier (2009), p. 16.

[67] Raustiala and Victor (2004), p. 279.

background of the proliferation of regional trade agreements, this is becoming a very prominent issue.[68]

The AEC appreciates the potential for these conflicts. The Protocol on Relations is meant to provide the institutional framework for coordinating and harmonizing relations between the AEC and the RECs. It emphasizes the coordination and harmonization of their activities. However, characteristic of the minimal significance given to relational issues in Africa's economic integration processes, there are no definitive provisions in the protocol addressing the issue of conflict of jurisdictions and laws. Does AEC law enjoy supremacy over conflicting laws of the RECs? Are the RECs also enjoined to 'observe the legal system'[69] of the AEC? Are there any areas where only the AEC can legislate? How are breaches of AEC decisions and directives to the RECs to be enforced?[70] Are the RECs competent before the AU Court of Justice? And can the AEC intervene in an action before a REC's community court where the interest of the AEC is affected? The answers to these important questions remain largely unknown.

The Protocol on Relations sheds dim light on some of these issues. It allows the AU to sanction RECs or member states that do not comply with its directives. It also includes a dispute-resolution mechanism, which gives RECs standing before the African Court of Justice and Human Rights. The Protocol's lack of attention to these complex relational issues is disheartening. It explicitly recognizes that external and internal policies of the RECs may conflict with the objectives of the AEC Treaty.[71] In this, we witness, yet again, another manifestation of inattention to relational issues; the possibility of conflict of jurisdictions and laws is acknowledged, but concrete steps have not been taken to address them.

3.3.4 *Multiple membership and inter-community relations*

An important issue for the RECs and AEC is the need to rationalize relations between the RECs in the light of the fact of their multiple memberships. It is arguable that this issue is short term: as the RECs progress along the stages of integration, a process of natural selection will take place. It will be difficult for a state to maintain membership of

[68] Graewert (2008); and Kwak and Marceau (2006). [69] AEC Treaty, art. 3(e).

[70] Ibid., art. 21. This article allows the Assembly or Council to give directives to the communities. Their decisions may include sanctions. A similar provision is in art. 22 of the Protocol on Relations.

[71] Protocol on Relations, art. 28(1).

two customs unions – applying two different external tariffs – unless the policies of the customs unions are harmonized. At that stage, each state will have to decide, taking into account political, economic and geographic considerations, which community it wants to be part of. Thus, some scholars speculate that if the Southern African Development Community's customs union succeeds, the Southern African Customs Union 'would fall away'.[72]

However, this vision is too optimistic. The trajectory of Africa's integration suggests that it is not only legal and economic considerations that dictate membership of RECs. A more dominant consideration is political; indeed, the UNECA has observed that 'countries seem to have barely analyzed the economic rationale of belonging to a particular group'.[73] The only case I know of REC demise is that of the first East African Community in 1977. Even with this, its demise was due mainly to political mistrust between the members. Therefore, it has to be accepted that unless there are structured mechanisms instituted and enforced to eliminate the problem of multiple memberships, the vision of some communities 'dying a natural death' will not materialize.

Effectively and boldly addressing the problems resulting from multiple memberships, and the troubling relational issues between the RECs and AEC, requires legal imagination, economic thought and strong institutional and political will. There is an urgent need for the AEC to rationalize actively the relations among the RECs, and between the RECs and itself. This is important for the development of the African Economic Community. The 2006 AU moratorium on the establishment and recognition of more RECs was an important first step.[74] So far, it has been heeded. Another important step is for the AEC to adopt a protocol founded on the principle of 'one country, one community' of the eight AU recognized RECs. With the help of national institutions and commissioned experts, countries should be guided to decide on predominately economic criteria, which REC best suits their needs, taking into account the fact that the ultimate realization of the vision of an African Economic Community may help to address some of the needs. This should be viewed not as an inappropriate infringement on state sovereignty, but as a measure needed to pool state sovereignty effectively for the common good. The legal foundation for this protocol can be found

[72] Draper, Halleson and Alves (2007), p. 20.
[73] United Nations Economic Commission for Africa (2006), p. 36.
[74] African Union, Decision on the Moratorium on the Recognition of Regional Economic Communities (Assembly/AU/ Dec.112 (VII), 2006).

in article 5(1) of the AEC Treaty. In it, member states undertook to 'create favourable conditions for the development of the Community and the attainment of its objectives, particularly by harmonising their strategies and policies', and to 'refrain from any unilateral action that may hinder the attainment of the said objectives'. I argue that the unilateral decision of AEC member states to be members of more than one REC creates unfavourable conditions for the development of the AEC.

Admittedly, getting support for and enforcing this protocol will be difficult. It will be the ultimate test, not only of the enforcement powers of the AEC, but also member states' commitment to the realization of its vision beyond their political rhetoric of support. It is suggested that non-complying states should be threatened with expulsion and, ultimately, expelled from the AEC and all but one of the RECs of which they are members. These countries can still maintain their membership of the AU, which is largely a political association of states. I dare say the vision of an African Economic Community should not be founded on the ideal of all African countries as members. The European Union does not consist of all the states in Europe. The North American Free Trade Agreement does not include all countries on the North American continent. And the World Trade Organization comprises fewer than all the countries of the world. There is no legitimate reason why an African Economic Community cannot consist of something less than all of Africa! For a continent consisting of fifty-three states, a few of them dysfunctional, collapsed or collapsing, and many with different levels of socio-economic, legal and political development, the pursuit of this ideal will delay, indeed thwart, the timely realization of a noble economic vision.

Writing in the context of the collapse of the OAU, Kufuor perceptively observed that 'unrestricted access in the form of virtually no entry requirements led to the tragedy of the regional commons, the degrading of the OAU as an organization of any value'.[75] Wouldn't the stature, integrity and effectiveness of the OAU/AU be enhanced if it consisted of, say, twenty democratic, human-rights-respecting, socially and economically developed states that extend the benefits of the organization to non-members on defined conditions? Like Kufuor, it is argued here that Africa's economic integration is being devalued, delayed and diluted due to the fact that countries are able to sign up at will without strict, previously defined and continuous commitments to implementation. An African Economic Community that consists of a few African states

[75] Kufuor (2005), p. 133.

can extend, through conditioned agreements, the benefits of integration to other countries that need not necessarily be members. The expansion of economic space need not be a concomitant of the expansion of institutional space.

The 'one country, one community' principle advocated above should be combined with full integration of the RECs into the legal framework of the AEC by making them members. It is unfortunate that neither the Protocol of Relations between the AEC and the RECs nor the new Protocol of Relations does this. For the RECs to become members of the AEC, it may demand an amendment to the AEC Treaty. Currently, the treaty does not have a membership provision or criterion, but it appears to assume that all African states are potential members. By becoming fully signed-up members of the AEC, the RECs will be bound by all AEC laws, including laws aimed at rationalizing and coordinating their activities. They will become subject to AEC-enforcement processes and active and interested participants in its decision-making processes. This will help to eliminate, or at least minimize, the potential for conflicting laws, policies and jurisdictions. When the RECs become members of the AEC, decisions being taken that are within the competence of the RECs should be taken by the RECs rather than the individual member states, who are also members of the AEC. In other words, regarding matters within the competence of the RECs, they should be the decision-makers during discussions at the AEC level.

The relationship between the EU and the WTO, and between the EU and the Hague Conference on Private International Law, is illustrative of what is being advocated here. The EU, together with all of its members, is a member of both organizations. In general, decisions on issues within the competence of the EU are taken by it, while those falling outside its competence are taken by member states.

The two steps advocated above, as a solution to the problem of multiple memberships and RECs, and the latter's relations with the AEC, differ in material respects from the five potential solutions advocated by the UNECA. These are: maintaining the status quo; rationalizing by merger and absorption; rationalizing around rooted communities; rationalizing through division of labour; and rationalizing by harmonizing policies and instruments.[76] Central to the two steps proposed here is the principle of 'one country, one community', the view that membership of RECs should be determined largely on the basis

[76] United Nations Economic Commission for Africa (2006), pp. 115–26.

of an economic criterion, and a call to abandon the ideal of an African Economic Community consisting of all African states. It should be emphasized that although the RECs have an independent legal personality, they exist because they have states as members. Therefore, any solution to the above problem should begin with the members, or at least pay very close and immediate attention to them. Although the two steps are radical and will demand much political will to be taken, it is the only sure and rapid path to achieving an African Economic Community using states and RECs that are genuinely committed to that object.

3.4 Conclusion

In this chapter, the complexity of the path to the formation of the African Economic Community has been discussed. The approach of using RECs as building blocks for the AEC is fraught with legal challenges, most of which have not been adequately addressed by the existing legal framework. The chapter has identified some of these challenges and provided a means for overcoming them. It has been suggested that the adoption of a merger protocol and a protocol redefining the membership of the AEC and RECs will help to address some of the challenges. More generally, this chapter shows that one of the ways to overcome the challenges posed by international regime complexity is to provide for an umbrella regime responsible for coordinating and harmonizing the activities of elemental regimes within the complex regime. However, providing for such a regime, if deemed necessary at all, is not easy: defining the legal status and mandate of the regime and ensuring the binding effect and compliance with its laws are potentially difficult issues. The AEC as an apparent umbrella regime for the elemental regimes of African RECs is a case in point. The next chapter focuses on community–state relations, the *locus* of most of the challenges in economic integration.

4

Community–state relations in Africa's economic integration

4.1 Introduction

From a legal perspective, and beyond issues on the relationship among the African Economic Community (AEC), African Union (AU) and Africa's Regional Economic Communities (RECs), the approach to economic integration adopted by the AEC raises other important issues, which are yet to be addressed in practice and in the discourse on Africa's integration.[1] These include the legal status of community institutions and law within member states' legal systems, the effectiveness of community institutions as enforcers of community law, the role of the community courts as arbiters of conflicts between and among the constituent legal systems, and the coordination and harmonization of the laws of member states. These issues form part of the more profound and broader problem that bedevils all economic integration processes: what are, or should be, the legal relations between the economic community and the member states? Economic integration results in a juxtaposition of legal systems. These legal systems include that of the organization responsible for the integration process (community), those of the member states and regional organizations, and the international legal system, which often provides the legal basis for the integration initiative. In addition to issues of management, organization and competition, this juxtaposition of legal systems creates legal problems and raises many questions: What is the relation between community and national legal systems? What is the status of national law in the community legal system and vice versa? What are the rules for resolving conflicts of laws between and among these legal systems? Which institution is responsible for resolving such conflicts?

These community–state issues are important for the effectiveness of economic integration and have received attention in the founding

[1] See generally Oppong (2006c).

treaties of some economic communities. That is largely not the case with the AEC. Indeed, in this regard, one cannot but notice the conspicuous absence in the AEC Treaty of an emphasis on legal issues in the integration process. In the sixty-five-page treaty, the word 'law' appears only three times.[2] None of these references relates to the laws of member states or to the impact of the AEC on their legal systems. Of the seven specialized technical committees established by the treaty,[3] none is specifically mandated to deal with the legal issues of integration, including the relational issues noted above.[4] It is possible that the specialized technical committees may deal separately with some of the issues identified above. However, such a fragmented approach may lead to unnecessary difficulties in the integration process. Generally, the treaty reveals a lack of appreciation of the need for a comprehensive legal framework for economic integration. Such a legal framework would set out the relevant jurisdictional parameters, define the legal relations between the community and member states, and pay attention to the broader international legal context within which economic integration operates.

It is difficult to fathom the minimal emphasis on legal issues in the AEC Treaty. Admittedly, not every issue can be anticipated and addressed in a treaty, but some issues are just too important to be left unattended to. Comparatively, the regional communities' treaties do not fare any better. The adoption of the AEC Treaty was not preceded by any form of wider consultation with interested parties, including lawyers or law associations in the member states.[5] This is ironic for a treaty that sets as one of its guiding principles 'popular participation in development'.[6] Kulusika's observation that lawyers' participation in drafting regional

[2] AEC Treaty, preamble, arts. 18(2) and 35(1)(a). Harmonization of law is only explicitly envisaged in the harmonization of the 'legal text' regulating existing stock exchanges. Ibid., art. 44(2)(d). The AEC Treaty may generally be criticized for its lack of detail and the relegation of detail to protocols with the attendant negotiating and ratification problems. Compare the Treaty of Rome, which made about twenty-five references to law, including, especially, the municipal laws of the member states.

[3] The committees are: the Committee on Rural Economy and Agricultural Matters; the Committee on Monetary and Financial Affairs; the Committee on Trade, Customs and Immigration Matters; the Committee on Industry, Science and Technology, Energy, Natural Resources and Environment; the Committee on Transport, Communications and Tourism; the Committee on Health, Labour and Social Affairs; and the Committee on Education, Culture and Human Resources.

[4] AEC Treaty, art. 25.

[5] This should be compared with the EAC Treaty, which was adopted after public consultations. See Mvungi (2002b); and Oluoch (2009).

[6] AEC Treaty, art. 3(h).

integration treaties and economic integration processes has been minimal may also explain the minimal emphasis on legal issues in the AEC Treaty.[7] This chapter discusses some of these unaddressed issues, including the legal status of the AEC and the relations between the AEC and its member states' laws. Although the chapter uses the AEC as its principal focus, the discussion is equally relevant for other RECs in Africa.

4.2 Legal status of the AEC

4.2.1 AEC as a legal system

The legal status of an international or regional organization is essential to gain a proper appreciation of its functions and competences. Regarding the AEC, its founding treaty does not expressly deal with this issue. It is provided that the AEC forms an integral part of the Organization of African Unity (OAU), which is now the African Union (AU).[8] The AU possesses legal personality and has capacity to enter into contracts and institute legal proceedings.[9] This leaves unanswered the question of whether, despite being an integral part of the AU, the AEC has its own legal personality.[10] Under the principles of international law, the lack of an express treaty provision on the legal personality of the AEC is not problematic. In the *Reparations* case,[11] the International Court of Justice held that the legal personality of an international organization can be inferred from the provisions of its constitutive treaty. Brownlie has identified the criteria for legal personality of organizations as: a permanent association of states with lawful objectives and equipped with organs; a distinction in terms of legal powers and purposes between the organization and its members; and the existence of legal powers exercisable on the international plane and not solely within the national legal systems of one or more states.[12] The AEC meets these criteria.

[7] Kulusika (2000). See generally Alter (2008a). [8] AEC Treaty, art. 98.

[9] General Convention on the Privileges and Immunities of the Organization of African Unity, 25 October 1965, art.1, online: www.africaunion.org/root/au/Documents/Treaties/treaties.htm.

[10] Ajomo (1993).

[11] *Reparation for Injuries Suffered in the Service of the United Nations, Advisory Opinion*: [1949] ICJ Reports 174.

[12] Brownlie (2003), p. 649.

Notwithstanding its silence on the legal personality of the organization, the AEC Treaty contains an innovative provision that is interesting from a legal perspective and relevant to an assessment of the legal status of the AEC. Article 3(e) enjoins member states to 'observe . . . the legal system of the Community'. This provision positively, albeit indirectly, affirms the AEC as a legal system and imposes an obligation on member states to promote its objectives. This provision is unique to the AEC Treaty; an examination of other economic integration treaties in Africa shows that the status of a legal system is not explicitly given to the communities. Indeed, even without this affirmation, the status of the AEC as a legal system could have been inferred from the treaty. The existence of rules and rule-making institutions is an essential component of any legal system. In my opinion, the AEC is a legal system, but, as will be shown below, this is not an assertion free from difficulty. Like any domestic legal system, the AEC has these institutions. Its lawmaking institutions are the Assembly of Heads of State or Government (hereafter, Assembly), the Council of Ministers (hereafter, Council) and the AEC Court of Justice, which is now the African Court of Justice and Human Rights (hereafter, African Court of Justice).[13] In addition to these institutions, one may add the Pan-African Parliament, which currently has only an advisory role in the AEC's legislative process, but is ultimately to have legislative powers. Aside the African Court of Justice, whose protocol is not yet in force, the remaining institutions are operating.

The AEC Treaty is silent on what the sources of law of the community will or should be. This is no idle omission. By failing to be explicit on its sources of law, one is left in doubt not only as to the sources, but also as to the relations between them. Undoubtedly, the AEC Treaty and protocols constitute the basic sources of law of the AEC. Decisions of the Assembly and regulations of the Council are also considered sources of law. The judgments of the African Court of Justice represent another source of community law. The general principles of law recognized by member states, as well as general principles of international law, may also be important sources of AEC law.

The Statute of the African Court of Justice remedies, in part, the omission on sources of law in the AEC Treaty. Article 31 of the statute

13 Protocol on the Statute of the African Court of Justice and Human Rights, 1 July 2008 (hereafter, Protocol on the African Court of Justice), and the Statute of the African Court of Justice and Human Rights (hereafter, Statute of the African Court of Justice), which is annexed to the Protocol, online: www.africa-union.org/root/au/Documents/Treaties/text/Protocol%20on%20the%20Merged%20Court%20-%20EN.pdf.

lists various sources of law to which the court 'shall have regard', but it is not clear on how the sources relate to each other as, for example, in situations of conflict. Ultimately, the African Court of Justice will have to lay down principles for resolving conflict of norms problems within the AEC legal system. In doing this, the court should be cautious in applying and, if possible, avoiding mechanical rules (for example, the last in time prevails rule) for resolving these problems. Rather, it should look at the substantive content of the laws in conflict and allow the law the substance of which best promotes the objectives of Africa's economic integration to prevail. Indeed, the promotion of integration should be the cornerstone of the court's interpretation and application of all laws.

Comparatively, it is worth recalling that, unlike the AEC Treaty, there was no express provision in the Treaty establishing the European Economic Community, 1957 (Treaty of Rome), declaring that the EC (now EU) was a legal system. The Court of Justice of the European Union (ECJ) inferred from the text and purpose of the Treaty of Rome that the EC exists as a distinct legal order. In *Van Gend en Loos* v. *Neder-Landse Tariefcommissie*,[14] the ECJ held that the EC 'constitutes a new legal order of international law, for whose benefit the States have limited their sovereign rights, albeit within limited fields, and the subjects of which comprise not only Member States but also their nationals'.[15] The court did this through a teleological interpretation of the Treaty of Rome. For the AEC, the judgment teaches that, even in the absence of an express treaty provision characterizing the AEC as a legal system, inferences can be drawn from the treaty to support a claim that it constitutes a new legal system with sovereign characteristics.

Whether through a treaty provision or judicial declaration, the existence of an international organization as a legal system has implications for and impact on member states' national legal systems. They should be conditioned – legally, socially and politically – for that impact to materialize and enhance the effectiveness of the organization. These conditions include: an activist and independent judiciary; a culture of respect for the rule of law; judicial decisions and international law; favourable constitutional laws; the presence of national constituencies, with interest to advance nationally the cause of the organization's legal system; and the political will to legislate to allow for the harmonious coexistence of both legal systems. These conditions are not wholly present in most African countries. But some

[14] Case 26/62, [1963] ECR 1; [1963] CMLR 105. [15] Ibid., at 129.

countries are making progress on these conditions; South Africa's judiciary is noted for its independence and the quality of its judgments. In 2008, Ghana democratically and peacefully changed government for the fifth time since 1992. Botswana, Namibia and Tanzania have been democratic, peaceful and stable for a very long time. Sadly, the success stories in Africa do not make it into the international media.[16] It must be remembered that the acceptance of the full implications of the ECJ declaration that the EC was a legal system was gradual in each member state. The same is likely to be the case in Africa.

The existence of the AEC as a legal system distinct from the legal systems of the member states can also be teleologically derived from the text of the AEC Treaty and its institutional arrangements. The preamble to the treaty acknowledges the need to secure the 'well-being' of the people. Article 14 establishes a Pan-African Parliament to ensure that the people of Africa are fully involved in the economic development and integration of the continent.[17] The treaty also establishes institutions to make decisions that are binding on and automatically enforceable in the member states. Presumably, and as discussed in Chapter 7, these decisions are enforceable without any national implementation measures, such as incorporation by an Act of Parliament. The institutions and their competence represent derogations from national sovereignty.

Indeed, the fact that AEC member states are expressly enjoined to observe 'the legal system of the Community' makes any claim that it does not have a distinct legal system untenable. Such a claim offends the text of the AEC Treaty. It fails to appreciate the unique place that community legal systems have in economic integration agreements. The existence of an economic community as a legal system has socio-economic and legal benefits. It constitutionalizes the community by granting it an identity with the autonomy and independence it needs to pursue its objectives. Having an independent existence reduces national governments' interference with the community. It also stabilizes the level of economic integration and reduces the risk and uncertainty associated with intra-community economic transactions. This is due to the fact that defined categories of economic activity within the community can be subject to only one legal regime that is independent of national legal systems. Even

[16] Posner and Young (2007).

[17] See also Protocol on the Pan-African Parliament. The East Africa Court of Justice's decision in *Mwatela* v. *East Africa Community* [2007] 1 East Afr. LR 237 reveals the crucial role played by community parliaments in economic integration.

on economic matters regulated by national regimes, the community may set out the parameters of the national rules or play a superintending role. This promotes economic interaction and development within the community. Socially, the fact that people live under one legal system may foster a sense of belonging and unity among the inhabitants of the community.

If these benefits are not to elude the AEC, the integrity of its legal system at the community level and its status within member states must be well defined and respected. However, so far, this has not been done. Without an appropriate legal framework on the relations between the AEC and national legal systems, the effectiveness of the AEC will be undermined. The goals enumerated in article 4 of the AEC Treaty require a strong degree of integration between the legal systems of the community and member states. This is facilitated by the surrender of state sovereignty to the AEC and its institutions. As one writer has noted, 'the depth of legislative coordination required to achieve these economic goals would appear to require the member states of a common market to cede large portions of sovereignty to an institutional structure capable of not only implementing such integration, but also policing whether member states follow through with their obligations'.[18]

4.2.2 AEC and member states' sovereignty

From a positivist perspective, a legal system is more than a set of laws. As discussed in Chapter 2, there must be an ultimate source the laws of which directly bind its subjects. Furthermore, these laws cannot be contradicted or subordinated, either by their subjects or any other external source. The absence of an ultimate source of law represents a serious challenge to the effectiveness of a legal system. Indeed, it calls its legal existence into question. It is in this regard that the AEC, as a community of sovereign states, faces an enormous challenge in the form of the sovereignty of the member states. Perhaps no concept defies definition more than sovereignty.[19] In this book, the term is used to connote the idea that a state's legal system is supreme and independent of other legal systems – it is sovereign – such that no norm outside of it can claim to be directly applicable, enforceable or effective within it, or override its norms.

[18] Taylor (1996–7), p. 867. [19] Jackson (2003b).

States have their own legal systems and enact laws that directly bind their subjects. As a sovereign state, these laws cannot be contradicted or subordinated by any other law, within or outside the national legal systems. States seldom surrender this sovereign power. Indeed, there are often constitutional provisions proclaiming the national constitution as the ultimate source of law and legality within the state's legal system. The idea of a foreign legal system, like the AEC legal system, existing independently of the state, yet having its norms directly binding on the state (and its subjects), being directly applicable and enforceable within the state's legal system or prevailing over contradictory national laws, is incompatible with this framework. It is only through a surrender of sovereignty at the international level, and the legitimization of that surrender at the national level, that such an idea can operate.[20]

A manifestation of the surrender of state sovereignty is to allow for the direct application and supremacy of laws generated by extra-state institutions. In other words, surrendering sovereignty is more than a mere delegation or abdication of decision-making powers to external institutions. Decisions made should become part of the delegating state's legal system and have binding effect within it. Sovereignty may be surrendered in whole or in part. A mere political association of states may exist without even a partial surrender of sovereignty, but no effective economic community may exist under such circumstances. It is impossible to envisage a common market or economic union in which member states have not partially ceded sovereignty and created a new legal order. Integrated economies like Australia, Canada, the EU, Nigeria and the United States exist because of the partial surrender of sovereignty by the member states.[21] In these economies, the laws made by the community (or federal government) in their areas of defined competence are generally directly applicable and supreme in the constituent states or provinces.

The AEC Treaty is silent on the issue of member states' sovereignty and how it relates to the AEC's legal system. As discussed in Chapter 7, neither does it appear that existing national constitutions have taken

[20] *Blackburn* v. *AG* [1971] 1 WLR 1073.

[21] In theory, it can be argued that because the federating 'states' in Canada, the United States and Nigeria were not sovereign states before the formation of their respective federations, this point does not apply to them. However, the reality is that they have ceded some powers to the federal government in a manner akin to the surrender of sovereignty to an external entity. In Canada, a more accurate description is that the constitution divides sovereignty.

notice of the potential impact of AEC law, and are prepared to treat it differently from ordinary international law. Indeed, the word 'sovereignty' is not used in the AEC Treaty, although 'sovereign equality' is affirmed as one of the governing principles of the AU under its Constitutive Act. Consequently, one can only draw inferences from the text of the AEC Treaty as to whether its member states have partially surrendered sovereignty to it. It can be argued that the fact that the treaty establishes institutions with powers to make decisions which are 'automatically enforceable in member states' suggests that the member states have ceded sovereignty to the organization. However, as will be shown in Chapter 7, one difficulty with this argument is that the concept of 'enforceable automatically' is not free from doubt. Indeed, its implications for member states are yet to be worked out.

The silence in the AEC Treaty should be contrasted with the ECOWAS Treaty, which explicitly acknowledges in its preamble that 'the integration of the Member States into a viable regional Community may demand the partial and gradual pooling of national sovereignties to the Community within the context of a collective political will'. Admittedly, it does not appear that the fact that the ECOWAS Treaty is more explicit on the question of sovereignty has placed ECOWAS law, compared with AEC law, in a better position within the member states. ECOWAS law still has minimal presence within member states and is seldom invoked before national courts. This suggests that while there may be significant provisions in international treaties, their true effect is often conditioned by social and political situations in states that are parties to them. Indeed, it can be argued that a formal declaration that states have surrendered sovereignty to the community is unnecessary, especially in the early stages of integration. States may find this politically unpalatable. An effective economic community necessarily eats into member states' sovereignty. In that sense, a gradual surrender of sovereignty, even if not expressly provided in a treaty, is inevitable.

Although the AEC Treaty is silent on the issue of sovereignty, it can be argued that AEC member states are required to cede sovereignty partially to it because they are enjoined to observe its legal system. As already noted, the presence of an ultimate source of authority is indispensable for an effective legal system. By affirming and declaring in article 3(e) of the AEC Treaty that they will observe the legal system of the community, therefore implicitly acknowledging that the legal system exists, member states have accepted the community as, at least, partially sovereign. The characteristics of such sovereignty include the ability to bind its subjects and to override 'private' laws. A state cannot be held to have observed the legal system of the community when community laws have no effect in its legal system or are overridden by its laws. Ultimately, the sovereignty issue will be presented to the African Court of Justice. Indeed, as discussed in Chapter 5, the relationship between state sovereignty and the goals of economic integration has already become an issue before the community courts in Africa.

Furthermore, some African states have recently realized the need sometimes to surrender sovereignty – partially to promote economic development through regionally coordinated policies. The EAC Treaty accords sovereignty to EAC institutions and organizations and elevates community laws above national laws. This development within the EAC, which represents a great leap towards the collective exercise of sovereignty through a distinct institution, is worth emulating in Africa. The OHADA Treaty represents another example of the willingness of African governments to surrender sovereignty, partially, to promote economic development. Under the treaty, OHADA member states have partially given up national sovereignty to establish a single regional regime of uniform business laws called Uniform Acts. Uniform Acts are directly applicable and overriding in the member states, notwithstanding any conflict they may give rise to in respect of previous or subsequent enactment of municipal laws.[22] In other words, they are automatically and immediately applicable in member states and abrogate contrary national laws.[23] The treaty also establishes the Common Court of Justice and Arbitration as the final authority on the interpretation and enforcement of the treaty, its regulations and the Uniform Acts.[24] The court hears appeals on referral from national courts or directly from aggrieved individuals.[25] The court's decisions are 'final and conclusive', and are entitled to enforcement and execution within member states.[26]

Given the appalling underdevelopment and economic marginalization of Africa, its governments should realize the urgency with which they must put aside their national and personal interests to forge a common course through the AEC. The threat of Communism and the devastations caused by World War II propelled Europe to integrate. So too should the tragic economic conditions in Africa motivate leaders to work together. Africa's underdevelopment and marginalization in the face of world prosperity should be enough, without any external force, to propel

[22] OHADA Treaty, art. 10.
[23] Dickerson (2005), p. 55.
[24] OHADA Treaty, art. 14.
[25] Ibid., art. 15.
[26] Ibid., art. 20.

African governments to unite and confer supranational decision-making powers to the AEC to pursue the common economic agenda laid out in the AEC Treaty. The benefits of economic integration in other regions of the world should encourage African leaders to approach the AEC integration initiative with zeal. Admittedly, success on this front will not come easily. But, with the necessary legal framework, institutional arrangements, political support and a favourable social, economic and political climate, it can be done.

To summarize, I have argued that the AEC is a legal system and, within its member states, should be the ultimate source of law in matters within its competence. The member states of the AEC are its primary subjects. Arguably, individuals are its secondary subjects. These subjects must observe its laws and institutions.

4.3 Supremacy of AEC law

Regional economic integration creates and operates within the context of vertical, vertico-horizontal and horizontal relations. Vertical relations exist between a community and its member states. Vertico-horizontal relations exist between a community, other communities and the international legal system. Horizontal relations exist among member states of a community. Establishing, defining and managing these relations are important for a community's effectiveness. This is especially so as the community progresses through the various stages of economic integration. Where these relations are not clearly defined, structured and managed, they can result in uncertainty, jurisdictional conflicts, non-uniform application of community law and, ultimately, destabilization of the community. Important issues in this regard are the status of community law in member states, and how to overcome the challenge posed to economic integration by differences in national laws. Conflicts between national and community laws occur in economic integration. From the perspective of community–state relations, such conflicts are part of the broader issue of the relations between national and international law. Accordingly, the rules developed in the latter context are useful in addressing the former. However, this should be done with caution. Automatic application of the traditional rules on the relationship between national and international law can work against a community's interests and development. Indeed, as I argue in Chapter 7, for Africa's economic processes to be effective there is the need to rethink existing constitutional laws, especially with regard to the methods for giving effect to international laws, rules on resolving conflicts between international and national laws, and the doctrines of sovereignty and supremacy of national constitutions.[27]

The relations between national and international law are often discussed from a monist–dualist perspective.[28] Monists view international and national law as part of a single legal system. To them, international law is directly applicable in national legal systems. In other words, there is no need for any domestic implementing legislation; international law automatically becomes part of the national legal system. Indeed, to monists, international law is superior to national law. Admittedly, not all monists adhere to such a conception of the relationship between national and international law. Although Hans Kelsen was an advocate of monism, he did not argue that international law was superior to national law. In his view, international law may be subjected to particular norms within national legal systems. In other words, to him, monism required that legal norms be part of a single system of law, but left open the question of the relationship between the norms.[29]

The dualists, on the other hand, view international and national law as separate legal systems, operating on different planes. International law does not, as such, form part of the national legal system. For international law to be applicable within the national legal system, it must be received through domestic legislative measures, which transforms the international rule into a national one. It is only after such a transformation that individuals may benefit from or rely on the international (now national) law. To dualists, international law cannot claim supremacy within states, although it is supreme in the international legal system.

It is difficult to categorize countries as strictly dualist or monist; the position often differs depending on which type of international law is at stake. The traditional view in many common law jurisdictions was that customary international law was automatically incorporated into national law, without the need for legislative intervention. However, it has recently been suggested that this view demands qualification. In *R.* v. *Jones (Margaret)*, Lord Bingham declined to 'accept the proposition in quite the unqualified terms in which it has often been stated' and suggested that 'there seems to be truth in Brierly's contention . . . that international law is not a part, but is one of the sources, of English law'.[30]

[27] Maluwa (1998); and Maluwa (1999), pp. 31–51.
[28] Nijman and Nollkaemper (2007). [29] Kelsen (1967), pp. 328–47.
[30] [2007] AC 136 at [11] citations omitted; and O'Keefe (2008), p. 85.

To Sales and Clement, 'the better view – and the view that accords with constitutional principle in modern conditions – is that domestic constitutional law operates as a filter governing the extent to which the domestic courts should recognise norms taken from [customary international law] and treat them as forming part of the common law and hence as directly enforceable in domestic law'. Some countries with written constitutions in which it is explicitly recognized that the reception of customary international law into domestic law is subject to the constitution, share this view.[31]

Indeed, the monist–dualist dichotomy is unsatisfactory in many respects. It focuses more on the source or pedigree of norms, and largely ignores the substance of the norms at issue. By creating a dichotomy between norms, on the basis of their source, it obscures attention to the substantive contents of the norms at issue. International law and national law have traditionally addressed relatively different issues, the former concentrating on the relationships among states, and the latter on relationships among persons within its jurisdiction. However, in recent times it cannot be denied that there is gradual convergence of interests, and the ultimate goal of both is – or at least includes – securing the well-being of individuals. Areas in which this common goal manifests itself include international economic law and human rights law. These are areas in which there is increasing interaction between the national and international. Thus, at present, international and national law share much in common, and an attempt to compartmentalize or isolate them would be analytically flawed and practically inapposite.

The theoretical problems with the monist–dualist paradigm aside, the relationship between international and national law has important practical implications for both systems and their subjects. It determines the extent to which individuals can rely on international law for the vindication of their rights within national legal systems; this has implications for the effectiveness of international law, which generally lacks effective enforcement mechanisms at the national level. As Professor Shaw has noted, 'it is precisely because of the inadequate enforcement facilities that lie at the disposal of international law that one must consider the relationship with municipal law as more than of marginal importance'.[32]

[31] See, e.g. Constitution of the Republic of South Africa, 1996, art. 232; Constitution of the Republic of Malawi, 1994, art. 211(3); and Constitution of Kenya, 2010, art. 2(5).

[32] Shaw (2003), p. 161.

The relationship between the two systems may also determine the extent to which there is cross-fertilization of norms generated in both systems. The extent to which international law can compel or induce reform in national law hinges on this relationship. The respect accorded to a legal system is enhanced when it is able to influence normative developments in other legal systems.

The AEC Treaty does not provide that community law enjoys supremacy over national laws. Indeed, of all the African economic integration treaties, only the Treaty establishing the East African Community (hereafter, EAC Treaty) contains such provision.[33] Some writers have attempted to infer the supremacy of AEC law over national laws by using the text, structure and objectives of the AEC Treaty.[34] The treaty requires the harmonization of policies. Conflicting national laws hinder the achievement of the AEC's objectives. Article 5 requires member states to refrain from acts that hinder the attainment of the AEC's objectives. Community decisions and regulations are also automatically enforceable in member states. These, together with the fact of the community's division of competence between itself and the member states, are cited as logically implying that community law is supreme. It is arguable whether such a claim to supremacy is sustainable under prevailing constitutional and political conditions. Surely, these inferences are easily made in academic circles; but, in the absence of an express treaty provision, it will take an activist African Court of Justice to assert the supremacy of AEC law, strong and supportive national judicial will and favourable constitutional laws to be internalized in member states, and a general political culture of respect for international law to sustain it. It is debatable whether these conditions are currently present in Africa, but there is certainly nothing to suggest that these conditions can never be present.

In this regard, the experience of the EU merits examination.[35] The Treaty of Rome, like the AEC Treaty, was not explicit on whether EC law enjoyed supremacy over member states' laws. Nonetheless, the ECJ was able to constitutionalize the Treaty of Rome and elevate it above national

[33] EAC Treaty, art. 8(4). Article 8(5) envisaged that the member states would make the necessary laws to confer precedence on community organs, institutions and laws over similar national ones. So far, no such laws have been enacted. The national statutes incorporating the EAC Treaty are silent on the issue. Tanzania – Treaty for the Establishment of East African Community Act, 2001; Kenya – Treaty for the Establishment of East African Community Act, 2000; and Uganda – East African Community Act, 2002.

[34] Naldi and Magliveras (1999), pp. 620–1. [35] Alter (2001).

laws. In *Van Gend en Loos*,[36] the ECJ held that the EC constituted a new legal order that was separate and distinct from its members' legal order. But it was in *Flaminio Costa* v. *ENEL*[37] that the court, relying on teleological interpretation, elevated EC law above national laws. It held that 'the law stemming from the Treaty, an independent source of law, could not, because of its special and original nature, be overridden by domestic legal provisions, however framed, without being deprived of its character as Community law, and without the legal basis of the Community itself being called into question'.[38]

At present, the doctrine of supremacy of EU law is firmly entrenched; not even a fundamental rule of national constitutional law can be invoked to challenge an EU law.[39] In the sobering words of Weatherill: 'Even the most minor piece of technical Community legislation ranks above the most cherished national constitutional norm.'[40] However, it took some time before EU member states accepted the supremacy of EU law. It was resisted on the grounds that it challenged national sovereignty and rested on 'weak' textual arguments.[41] National courts initially provided mixed responses.[42] Even though now well accepted and entrenched in member states, courts have often explained their acceptance in terms of the national legal framework instead of any inherent superior power attributed to EU law by the ECJ. Indeed, to this day, there are still occasional judicial dicta from English courts suggesting that they may uphold an Act of Parliament that expressly overrides EU law.[43]

The idea of a supreme AEC law would be good for Africa's economic integration. It would ensure that community law is consistently applied across member states. This will be important for the stability of the AEC, and will create a secure and certain legal framework for business decision-making. It will also ensure the equal treatment of all people affected by AEC law. It remains to be seen, when an opportunity is

[36] *Van Gend en Loos* v. *Neder-Landse Tariefcommissie*, Case 26/62, [1963] ECR 1, [1963] CMLR 105 at 129.

[37] *Flaminio Costa* v. *ENEL*, Case 6/64, [1964] ECR 585 at 592–3.

[38] Ibid., at 592–3.

[39] *Amministrazione delle Finanze dello Stato* v. *Simmenthal SpA*, Case 106/77, [1978] ECR 629, 3 CMLR 263.

[40] Weatherill (1995), p. 106. [41] Craig and de Búrca (2003), p. 279.

[42] Craig and de Búrca (2003), pp. 285–314; and Cappelletti and Golay (1986), pp. 261, 311–15.

[43] *Macarthys Ltd* v. *Smith* [1979] ICR 785 at 789; *Macarthys Ltd* v. *Smith* [1981] QB 180 at 200; and *Thoburn* v. *Sunderland CC* [2003] QB 151 at 184–5.

presented, if the African Court of Justice will adopt a teleological approach to interpreting the AEC Treaty and assert the supremacy of AEC law over national laws. Since the court is yet to be operational, we have no cases from it from which we can infer its jurisprudential vision for community law. However, the East African Court of Justice has considered the issue. In *Anyang' Nyongo* v. *AG of the Republic of Kenya*, one issue on which it had to decide concerned the legal position when an EAC Treaty provision conflicts with national law.[44] The court held, in apparent disregard of article 8(4) of the EAC Treaty, that the treaty did not provide an explicit solution for such conflicts! Rather, it looked at basic principles of international law and the persuasive jurisprudence of the ECJ for answers. The court rightly came to the conclusion that the treaty prevailed in the event of conflict with national law.[45] However, its apparent disregard of the clear words of article 8(4) is troubling. There is no stronger foundation for a judicial decision than a legislative provision.

4.3.1 *Response of national courts*

It is uncertain how national courts will respond to an assertion by the African Court of Justice that AEC law is supreme over national laws. The effectiveness of such an assertion will depend, in part, on their responses. The existing national jurisprudence reveals two approaches, both of which appear inimical to the supremacy of community law within national legal systems. The first outrightly rejects the supremacy of community law. The second, a refined version of the first, suggests a rigid separation of community and national legal systems. For this approach, community law is supreme only at the community level. It cannot override domestic laws, and remedies for breaches of community laws must be sought at the community level. Both approaches reflect the dualist school's perspective on the relations between

44 *Anyang' Nyong'o* v. *AG of the Republic of Kenya* [2008] 3 KLR 397. The ECOWAS court's judgments also contain dicta that one may interpret as supporting the supremacy of community law. In *Frank Ukor* v. *Alinnor*, Suit No. ECW/CCJ/APP/01/04 (ECOWAS Court of Justice, 2005) at [21], the court held that the treaty is 'the supreme law of the ECOWAS, and it may be called its Constitution'. In *Jerry Ugokwe* v. *The Federal Republic of Nigeria*, Case No. ECW/CCJ/APP/02/05 (ECOWAS Court of Justice, 2005) at [32], it held that the distinctive feature of the community legal order of ECOWAS is that it sets forth a judicial monism of first and last resort in community law.

45 *Anyang' Nyong'o* v. *AG of the Republic of Kenya* [2008] 3 KLR 397 at 430–1.

international and national laws – a perspective prevalent in the former British colonies in Africa.

Kenya v. *Okunda*[46] illustrates the first approach. At issue was the supremacy of EAC law over Kenyan law. Two individuals were prosecuted under the EAC's Official Secrets Act of 1968 without the consent of the counsel for the EAC. Under section 8(1) of the Act the consent was necessary. The issue was whether the Attorney General of Kenya could institute the proceeding without that consent. Resolving this issue involved examining the relationship between EAC law and section 26(8) of the Kenyan Constitution, which provides that, in the performance of his duty, 'the Attorney-General shall not be subject to the direction or control of any other person'.[47] Counsel for the EAC submitted that the conflict between the two provisions should be resolved in favour of community law. He argued that under the Treaty for East African Cooperation, members agreed to take all steps within their power to pass legislation to give effect to the treaty, and to confer the force of law upon acts of the community within their territory. Furthermore, under article 4 of the treaty, the members were enjoined to 'make every effort to plan and direct their policies, with a view to creating conditions favourable for the development of the Common Market and the achievement of the aims of the Community'.[48] Counsel argued that, by these provisions, member states agreed to 'surrender part of their sovereignty'.[49]

The court held that Kenya did nothing to breach these obligations and that the laws of the community are, under the Kenyan Constitution, part of the laws of Kenya. In the event of conflict, EAC laws are void to the extent that they are inconsistent with the national constitution.[50] The constitution is the supreme law of the land. An appeal from this decision was dismissed by the Court of Appeal for East Africa.[51] The court

[46] *Kenya* v. *Okunda* (1969) 91 ILM 556 (hereafter, *Okunda*). [47] Ibid., at 556–7.

[48] Ibid., at 557 (citing Treaty for East African Cooperation, 1 December 1967, 6 ILM 932, art. 4).

[49] For comparative purposes, it is revealing how these arguments of counsel mimic, without making reference to them, similar teleological and textual arguments used by the ECJ in *Flamino Costa* to assert the supremacy of EU law above the national laws of member states. In an article in the East African Law Journal some few years before the *Okunda* decision, the author made reference to the *Flamino Costa* decision, but did not comparatively discuss its implications for East African Community law. Njenga (1968), p. 151.

[50] *Kenya* v. *Okunda* (1969) 91 ILM 556 at 558.

[51] *East African Community* v. *Republic of Kenya* (1970) 9 ILM 561.

recognized that the case raised an issue of fundamental importance. It held that 'the Constitution of Kenya is paramount and any law, whether it is of Kenya, of the Community or any other country which has been applied in Kenya, which is in conflict with the Constitution, is void to the extent of the conflict'.[52] This decision of the Court of Appeal can be criticized, but one may rationalize it with an argument that the court heard appeals from decisions of national courts on issues designated by national law.[53] The power to interpret and apply the treaty was entrusted to the Common Market Tribunal.[54] Accordingly, the Court of Appeal did not necessarily have to take account of the promotion of the objectives of economic integration in deciding cases. Like a national court, domestic legal considerations were paramount, even if such an outlook on issues in which community law was engaged was detrimental to the objective of effective economic integration.

Another case that affirmed the supremacy of Kenyan law was *In the Matter of an Application by Evan Maina*.[55] It arose under the East African Customs and Transfer Management Act, a community legislation, which defined a number of offences. Section 174 provided that, if the Commissioner of Customs was satisfied that any person has committed an offence against the Act in respect of which a fine was provided, he may compound the offence and summarily order him to pay a sum not exceeding 200 shillings. The section was held inconsistent with section 77(1) of the Kenyan Constitution; which provides: 'if any person is charged with a criminal offence, then, unless the charge is withdrawn, the case shall be afforded a fair hearing, within a reasonable time, by an independent and impartial court established by law'. The court rejected the contention for the customs' authorities that the offence under consideration was a 'customs' rather than a 'criminal' offence and, therefore, section 77 of the Constitution had no bearing on the case. Other subsections of section 77 required the trial to proceed only in the presence of the accused, unless he agreed otherwise, or his conduct made it difficult. Also, the accused had to be provided with an opportunity to defend himself, either in person or by a legal representative of his choice. Both provisions were held to be inconsistent with section 174. Moreover, the Commissioner of Customs was not a 'court' within the meaning of

[52] Ibid., at 565–6. [53] Treaty for East African Cooperation, art. 81.
[54] Ibid., art. 32; and Ross (1972).
[55] Case no. 7/1969. I have been unable to access a copy of this case. The account here relies on a summary of it in Ghai (1976), pp. 34–5; Ghai (1969), pp. 76–8.

section 77 of the Constitution. There was, therefore, a clear clash between section 174 of the Community Act and section 77 of Kenya's Constitution. The court held that community law could not be upheld, since the Constitution provides that 'if any law is inconsistent with this Constitution, this Constitution shall prevail and the other law shall to the extent of inconsistency be void'.

It was, perhaps, to avoid similar judgments in future that article 8(4) of the EAC Treaty was introduced. However, so far, this provision appears to have gone unnoticed by courts within the EAC.[56] In *Peter Anyang' Nyong'o* v. *AG*,[57] the High Court of Kenya again held that if a treaty is in conflict with the Constitution, the municipal court's first duty is to uphold the supremacy of the Constitution.[58] Given that the EAC Treaty has the 'force of law' in Kenya[59] and article 8(4) does not exclude national constitutions from the scope of its supremacy provision, this holding by the High Court of Kenya is arguably a breach of EAC law.

The second approach, which suggests a rigid separation between community and national legal systems, is also reflected in the Kenyan case of *Peter Anyang' Nyong'o* v. *AG*.[60] The central issue was whether amendments to the EAC Treaty should follow the procedure laid down in the Kenyan Constitution or that set out in the EAC Treaty. A peripheral issue was whether the applicant could bring a suit relying on provisions of the EAC Treaty. The court held that individuals could not enforce any rights under the treaty because the state was not their agent or trustee; remedies for alleged breaches of EAC law should be sought at the community level. This was so notwithstanding the fact that the treaty had been incorporated into Kenyan law and, as the court rightly recognized, the municipal Act was to provide 'an enabling climate for the objectives of the Treaty to be implemented'. According to the court, incorporation did not make the treaty lose its independent existence at the international level, such that it should be amended in accordance with municipal law. Indeed, the court described the applicant's description of the Treaty as a subsidiary legislation as

[56] In *Shah* v. *Manurama Ltd* [2003] 1 East Afr. LR 294, the Ugandan court cited the provision as one of the reasons why a resident of the community need no longer pay security for costs when litigating before national courts.

[57] [2007] eKLR (Kenya High Court, 19 March 2007). [58] Ibid., at 13.

[59] Treaty for the Establishment of the East African Community Act 2000.

[60] [2007] eKLR (Kenya High Court, 19 March 2007).

'a horrendous view'. Certainly, this interpretation is right. However, the reasoning of the court should be approached with caution. A rigid separation of community and national legal systems in an economic integration process can undermine the effectiveness of community law. It will lead to instances in which community laws are not given effect in member states. In general, the above judgments reflect inattention to the interconnectedness of community and national legal systems in economic integration.

At present, it appears that only the Kenyan courts and the East African Court of Justice have dealt with the issues of supremacy and conflict between community and national laws, including national constitutions. Generally, their responses do not portend well for establishing a proper nexus between community and national laws with a view to strengthening economic integration in Africa. Their approaches suggest that community law is treated as another kind of international law. The traditional judicial approaches to the place of international law in states have been automatically extended to community law. I argue that this is wrong. As far back as 1974, Pescatore cautioned against the 'tendency to transfer in rather too facile a manner to community law the solutions – good or bad – which had previously been worked out in relation to the domestic application of international law'.[61] It is a caution that African courts should take notice of when dealing with community law.

To an extent, it is difficult to criticize the Kenyan courts on their decisions in *Okunda*, *Maina* and *Anyang' Nyong'o*. Indeed, in all three cases, the courts' task was not made any easier by the fact that the cases involved conflicts between community law and the national constitution – the highest law of the land. National courts' reception of community law will be influenced and constrained by domestic constitutional imperatives. This appears to have been a paramount consideration in the Kenyan cases. In those countries where the constitution is declared as the supreme law of the land and any other law found to be inconsistent with it is void, it will take a great deal of judicial imagination to accept the supremacy of community law. It is possible that the three decisions might have been different had the conflicts involved 'ordinary' domestic legislation. Apart from *Okunda*, it also does not appear that the specific demands made by EAC law on Kenya's legal systems were argued in court. If community law is to assume a paramount and superior place in states, lawyers have a crucial role to play.

[61] Pescatore (1974), p. 96.

This raises a broader issue: the extent to which African lawyers and judges are aware of Africa's economic integration treaties and their implications for national legal systems. The development of community consciousness in these professionals is essential to ensure that community law occupies a superior place in member states. In this regard, it is a commendable and welcome development that law societies of EAC member states successfully challenged a decision of the community and member states before the East African Court of Justice.[62] The litigation evidences an awareness of the existence and importance of the EAC and demonstrates a willingness to defend its values. Many more legal challenges are needed to advance Africa's economic integration.

It is inappropriate to suggest that other African courts will follow the Kenyan courts on the issue of conflicts between community and national law. It must be admitted, however, that the prospect does not look good for community law unless national courts appreciate its unique character and do not treat it as just another type of international law. Indeed, making AEC law take precedence over national law implicates national sovereignty, and this is likely to be resisted by national institutions. Intensive judicial and legal education is needed on the distinct nature of community law (as opposed to public international law), its appropriate relations with national laws and the role expected of judges and lawyers in their approach to community law issues. In this regard, national seminars, conferences, workshops and the inclusion of the legal aspects of economic integration in the curriculum of law schools are important. This education will definitely take time to bear fruit. However, one can be cautiously optimistic, especially if the benefits of economic integration are felt directly in people's lives and industry.

4.3.2 Political reaction

Apart from national judicial response to an assertion by the African Court of Justice that AEC law supersedes national laws, the domestic socio-political climate is also important. The issue is whether there is a general political culture of respect for international law to sustain this assertion and, especially, its full legal implications for national legal systems. In Europe, Alter has demonstrated how socio-political forces shaped and enhanced the influence exercised by the ECJ over the EC's

[62] *East African Law Society* v. *AG of Kenya* [2008] 1 East Afr. LR 95.

integration process through its jurisprudence.[63] Her work with Helfer on the Andean Community Tribunal also reveals how 'the environment' of that community constrains the Tribunal's jurisprudence.[64]

An investigation into political reactions to international law and judicial decisions can provide some guidance on the future role of the African Court of Justice in Africa's economic integration. There has been occasional resistance to international law in some African countries. Maluwa discusses an amendment to the Constitution of Zimbabwe that was introduced ostensibly to prevent judges from relying on international law.[65] More recently, an unfavourable decision from the East African Court of Justice[66] was met with amendments to the EAC Treaty.[67] The amendments were subsequently found by the court to have been effected in a manner inconsistent with the procedures laid down in the EAC Treaty.[68] In August 2010, the SADC Summit of Heads of State and Government decided that a review of the role, functions and terms of reference of the SADC Tribunal should be undertaken. This was apparently a response to perceived hostile decisions given against Zimbabwe by the Tribunal. This political reaction towards community law is inimical and should be condemned. There are indications, from the perspective of national constitutions and international treaties, that Africa is becoming more 'international law-friendly',[69] even if that remains largely on paper. Indeed, in the unadopted Proposed

[63] Alter (2009). [64] Alter and Helfer (2010). [65] Maluwa (1998), p. 64.

[66] *Anyang' Nyong'o* v. *AG of the Republic of Kenya* [2008] 3 KLR 397.

[67] The amendments were to: restructure the court into two divisions, i.e. a First Instance Division and an Appellate Division; expand the grounds for removing a judge of the court from office; provide for suspension of a judge who is under investigation for removal or is charged with such offence; limit the court's jurisdiction so as not to apply to jurisdiction conferred by the treaty on organs of member states; provide a time limit within which a reference to the court by legal and natural persons may be instituted; provide grounds on which appeal may be made; and deem past decisions of the court and existing judges to be decisions and judges of the First Instance Division respectively. The court accepted the argument that some of these amendments were meant to intimidate the judges.

[68] *East African Law Society* v. *AG of Kenya* [2008] 1 East Afr. LR 95. The court reasoned that the failure to carry out consultation on the amendments outside the community institutions was inconsistent with the principle of promoting people's participation in the activities of the EAC as envisaged in various provisions of the treaty. However, the court declined to invalidate the amendments. It declared that its holding on the requirement of involvement of people in the treaty amendment process should have prospective application. This anticlimax to an otherwise bold decision left the question of the future status of the amendments to the political will of member states, who unsurprisingly have implemented the amendments.

[69] Oppong (2007a).

Constitution of Kenya, 2005, EAC law was listed as part of the laws of Kenya.[70] This provision could have had profound impact on the status of EAC law in Kenya's legal system.

It must be admitted that the real political reaction to international law, especially decisions of international courts, such as the African Court of Justice, is difficult to assess. So far, there does not appear to have been a systematic study on the level of African states' compliance with decisions of international courts. However, a recent study on compliance with decisions of the African Commission on Human and People's Rights offers useful insights. The study reports that between 1994 and mid-2003 the African Commission for Human Rights found violations of the African Charter for Human and People's Rights in respect of forty-three communications (complaints). As of 31 December 2004, only six had been complied with fully and in a timely fashion; states clearly had failed to comply in thirteen cases and had only partly complied in fourteen cases. In the words of the authors, there was 'clearly an overall lack of state compliance with the recommendations of the African Commission'.[71] In countries such as Botswana, Namibia and South Africa, where international law occupies a respected place in their legal systems,[72] it is likely that community law and an assertion that community law supersedes national law may be well received. Recently, a South African court demonstrated its respect for community law by agreeing to register a Southern African Development Community Tribunal judgment that was given against the Zimbabwean Government.[73] This was so despite the fact, to date, that the Treaty of the Southern African Development Community has not been incorporated into South African law.

In countries where democracy and the rule of law are absent, the reaction may be hostile. A recent decision of the SADC Tribunal – which has been registered by the South African High Court – declared Zimbabwe's policy of seizing farms of the applicants as a breach of the Southern African Development Community Treaty.[74] In a reaction to

[70] Proposed New Constitution of Kenya (2005), Kenya Gazette Supplement No. 63, art. 3. However, in the newly adopted Constitution of Kenya, 2010, this provision has been omitted.

[71] Viljoen and Louw (2007). [72] Tshosa (2007); and Tshosa (2010).

[73] *Fick* v. *Government of the Republic of Zimbabwe*, Case No. 77881/2009 (North Gauteng High Court, South Africa, 2010). Earlier in *Gramara (Pvt) Ltd* v. *Government of the Republic of Zimbabwe*, HC 33/09 (Zimbabwe, High Court, 2010), the court refused to enforce the judgment on grounds of public policy.

[74] *Mike Campbell (Pvt) Ltd & Others* v. *The Republic of Zimbabwe*, SADC (T) Case No. 2/2007 (SADC Tribunal, 2008).

the decision, President Mugabe declared that the Tribunal had no right to intervene on the farmers' behalf. In his words: 'Some farmers went to the SADC, but that's nonsense, absolute nonsense, no-one will follow that. We have courts here in this country that can determine the rights of people. Our land issues are not subject to the SADC tribunal.'[75] International law resisted by politicians often takes the form of international human rights laws, which act as constraints on state action. Community laws need not always be of such character. The fact that supremacy of community law does not imply the abrogation of the national law, but rather its disapplication in the specific issue at stake, should make it a little easier to accommodate.

It remains to be seen, when the African Court of Justice becomes operational and the opportunity presents itself, if the court will assert the supremacy of AEC law. If it does, the next challenge will be the national judicial and political reaction. The responses may vary from country to country. Indeed, it may take considerable time for all to be in favour of the supremacy of AEC law. In the meantime, there is a need for the AEC and the RECs to conduct studies on their members to ascertain how their legal systems relate to those of the communities and what should be done by member states to ensure the harmonious coexistence of national and community law, including the supremacy of community law. There is a need for amendments of national constitutions to define or clarify the status of community law within their respective legal systems.[76] An interesting example is section 102(1) of Zimbabwe's Customs and Excise Act, which provides that trade agreements concluded by the President under the provisions of the Act 'shall have force and effect notwithstanding anything inconsistent therewith contained elsewhere in this Act or in any other law or instrument having effect by virtue of any law'. It is proposed that member states of economic communities in Africa should consider introducing the following provision into their national constitutions to enhance the effectiveness of community law:

[75] BBC News, 'Mugabe Vows to Seize more Farms', 28 February 2009, online: http://news.bbc.co.uk/2/hi/africa/7916312.stm. In June 2009, the SADC Tribunal held that Zimbabwe and its agents had failed to comply with the decision of the Tribunal and, pursuant to article 32 (5) of the Protocol on the Tribunal, reported its findings to the Summit of Heads of State and Government for the latter to take appropriate action. *William Michael Campbell* v. *The Republic of Zimbabwe*, Case No. SADC (T) 03/2009 (SADC Tribunal, 2009).

[76] Within the EU, some member countries had to amend their constitutions to meet the demands of community law. See Bebr (1971), pp. 485–7 for a survey of these amendments. Some countries recently admitted into the EU have had to effect similar amendments.

> This Constitution shall be the supreme law of [*insert name of state*], and any other law found to be inconsistent with any provision of this Constitution shall to the extent of inconsistency be void.
>
> Without prejudice to the above, no provision of this Constitution invalidates laws enacted, acts done or measures taken by the State in line with its obligations as a member of the [*insert name of Community*] or prevents laws enacted, acts done or measures taken by the [*insert name of Community*], or its institutions, or by bodies competent under the [*insert name of treaty establishing the Community*], from having the force of law in the State.
>
> For the avoidance of doubt, laws made by the [*insert name of Community*] shall have the force of law in [*insert name of state*]. Such laws are supreme and shall prevail in case of inconsistency with any law enacted by the Parliament of [*insert name of state*] or deriving its authority from any such law enacted by Parliament.

4.4 Harmonization of law

4.4.1 Differences in national laws

A key interstate relational issue in economic integration is how to overcome the challenges posed by differences in national legal traditions and laws. These differences, which exist in substantive and procedural laws, may even extend to legal culture and mode of legal thought. In Africa, differences in national laws are attributable to the diversity of legal traditions, namely common law, civil law, Roman Dutch law, customary law and Islamic law. The legal traditions of the former colonizers of Africa still prevail in their former colonies. The extent to which laws vary from country to country in Africa should not be exaggerated. Geographical proximity, common colonial experience and the legislative draftsman's penchant to copy legislation from neighbouring countries have led to a situation where, as between countries adhering to the same legal tradition, their laws are very similar. A Ghanaian lawyer who moves to Nigeria will not be bewildered by the principles of the Nigerian legal system. Nor will a Namibian lawyer who moves to South Africa. The same cannot be said of a Ghanaian lawyer who moves to South Africa. This presents advantages and challenges for Africa's economic integration. Differences in national laws are manifest in many areas of law. For example, in the field of private international law, as regards jurisdiction in international claims relating to money, the Roman–Dutch law countries[77] have attachment as the basis of jurisdiction. The common law states[78] have service as the foundation of jurisdiction. Similarly, the use of jurisdiction agreements to confer jurisdiction on national courts is much more constrained in the Roman–Dutch law countries than in common law states. These differences in national laws will become more significant as economic integration progresses and cross-border economic activities increase.

Differences in national laws complicate business decision-making. Persons transacting in many countries may have to seek legal advice on different legal regimes. It may mean that they will have to adhere to different national standards. These add to the cost of doing business. Differences in national laws may lead to the concentration of investments in countries with well-developed legal systems or favourable rules to the detriment of other members of an economic community. In the Roman–Dutch law countries, an investor's assets can be attached to found jurisdiction and he will be unable to deal with the assets until the end of the litigation. This could be a relevant consideration when investing in those countries, especially if the country is plagued by delays in trials as is the case with many African states. In common law countries, the assets will still be available for the investor's use during the litigation unless specifically prevented from dealing with them through the granting of a pre-trial Mareva injunction. Unlike attachment, the injunction is relief *in personam* and does not operate as an attachment on property. Accordingly, it allows the defendant to deal with the property in a limited number of cases. It is no happenstance that the powerhouses of Africa's RECs – South Africa, Kenya and Nigeria – have relatively developed legal systems compared with their neighbours. Concentration of investments in specific countries in an economic community could breed jealousy and domestic resentment. This can lead to the disintegration of the community, especially if there is no community fund available to offset any losses states may incur from membership of the community. The collapse of the old East African Community is often cited as an example of this prospect.[79] Differences in national laws also do not afford equal legal

[77] Botswana, Lesotho, Namibia, South Africa, Swaziland and Zimbabwe.

[78] Gambia, Ghana, Kenya, Malawi, Nigeria, Sierra Leone, Tanzania, Uganda and Zambia. One should also add Liberia, which, although not a British colony, has laws influenced by English law. This is because of its historical association with the United States of America.

[79] Fitzke (1999); and Orloff (1968).

protection to citizens of a community, since legal rights on the same issue may vary between states.

Harmonization or unification of national laws within an economic community overcomes the above problems. Harmonization involves synchronizing the laws in the member countries. It reduces differences in laws to the barest minimum, but it does not eliminate them. Harmonization allows countries to take account of their diverse national needs when implementing the harmonized laws. Unification, on the other hand, provides a single and uniform body of law for the participating countries. In my opinion, with fifty-three countries of diverse legal traditions and laws, harmonization of laws should be the path for African countries.

Harmonization (indeed some may argue unification) of laws is an important part of the legal infrastructure of integrated economies. This is reflected in the constitutive treaties and laws of some communities.[80] Indeed, a degree of harmonization of laws is inherent in all economic integration arrangements, in the form of common internal tariffs and, depending on the stage of integration, common external tariffs. Harmonization promotes certainty by subjecting trans-boundary transactions to the same, or similar, substantive or procedural laws. It engenders equality of legal treatment, and potentially reduces transaction costs. If law is the cement of society, then it is also arguable that people living under a harmonized system of law will feel more interconnected. Thus, harmonization provides an avenue for social integration, and can be an important complement to political and economic integration. It is, therefore, little wonder that harmonization of laws has been suggested as being essential to Africa's economic integration processes. Differences in national laws are seen as an obstacle to economic integration.[81]

As early as 1965, and just two years after the formation of the OAU, Professor Allott concluded that the international harmonization of laws in Africa was a key aspect of the 'pan-African spirit in action'.[82] He anticipated that the rebuilding of regional institutions, such as the East African Community, would make 'a limited contribution to harmonization of laws' in areas that affect trade, taxation and the movement of

[80] See, e.g. CARICOM Treaty, art. 74(2); Protocol on the Establishment of the East African Community Common Market, 20 November 2009, arts. 12 and 47; and EU Treaty, art. 114.

[81] Thompson (1990), pp. 99–100; Thompson and Mukisa (1994), p. 1454; and Omorogbe (1993), pp. 364–5.

[82] Allott (1965), p. 374.

people.[83] However, this has not happened, even though article 2(j) of the Treaty for East African Cooperation, 1967, called for the approximation of the commercial laws of the member states. In recent times, numerous calls, within and outside the context of economic integration, have been made for the harmonization of laws in Africa.[84]

The AEC Treaty is not explicit on the importance of states harmonizing their laws. The importance of this issue appears not to have attracted the attention of the drafters of the AEC Treaty. However, the treaty contains references to harmonization of policies.[85] It is suggested that 'policy' should be broadly interpreted to encompass law. Unlike the AEC Treaty, other African economic integration treaties contain provisions that enjoin member states to harmonize various aspects of their laws.[86] However, to date no significant efforts with concrete results have been made in that direction. In August 2009, the Investment Climate Facility for Africa announced a project in partnership with the member states of the East African Community (EAC) to harmonize commercial laws within the region. The project will be implemented in two phases over a period of twelve to fifteen months, with the end goal of establishing a common legal system across Burundi, Kenya, Rwanda, Tanzania and Uganda. The project will focus on harmonizing key commercial laws in the region. It will focus on the following nine areas of commercial law: banking laws; business transaction laws; finance and fiscal legislation; insurance and re-insurance legislation; investments; procurement and disposal of assets legislation; monetary legislation; standardization, quality assurance and metrology legislations; and trading law.[87]

There is currently one laudable initiative towards the harmonization of substantive laws among some sixteen countries,[88] and it has produced

83 Allott (1968a), p. 85.

84 Ndulo (1993b); Ndulo (1993a); Ndulo (1996); Yakubu (1999); Bamodu (1994); and Ovrawah (1994).

85 AEC Treaty, arts. 3(c), 4(1)(d), 5(1) and 77.

86 ECOWAS Treaty, art. 57; COMESA Treaty, art. 4(6)(b); EAC Treaty, art. 126; and Protocol on the Establishment of the East African Community Common Market, 20 November 2009, online: www.eac.int/advisory-opinions/cat_view/68-eac-common-market.html, art. 47.

87 www.icfafrica.org/en/news-resources.php.

88 Benin, Burkina Faso, Cameroon, the Central African Republic, the Comoros, Congo-Brazzaville, Côte d'Ivoire, Gabon, Guinea, Guinea Bissau, Equatorial Guinea, Mali, Niger, Senegal, Chad and Togo. Liberia, Angola, and the Democratic Republic of Congo are on record as having expressed interest in becoming members. Martor, Pilkington, Sellers and Thouvenot (2007); Dickerson (2005); Enonchong (2007); Mancuso (2007); and Fagbayibo (2009).

some concrete results. The initiative is being pursued under the aegis of the Organisation for the Harmonization of Business Laws in Africa (OHADA), which is not an economic integration organization. Most of the members of OHADA are francophone states in West Africa, and they all share a civil law tradition. The objective of the OHADA Treaty is to harmonize the business laws in the contracting states through the elaboration and adoption of simple, modern and common rules adapted to their economies.[89] The states' willingness to abandon their disparate national laws in favour of harmonized rules represents a triumph for international cooperation in Africa. However, so far, it is an isolated example.

From the perspective of using legal harmonization as a means of defining the relations between laws in different legal systems, two principal areas of law for harmonization are recommended for African countries to consider. These are the harmonization of substantive rules and the harmonization of private international law rules. Harmonization of substantive law involves ensuring a degree of similarity in the substantive laws of the countries concerned. Harmonizing private international law rules implies that the substantive laws of the states remain intact, but harmonized choice-of-law, jurisdiction and foreign judgment enforcement rules are provided to ensure that parties transacting across national boundaries can be well informed of the governing law and the court(s) with jurisdiction in case of disputes.

Harmonizing either area has merits and faults. Substantive harmonization of laws brings certainty because people transacting across national boundaries will be subject to the same substantive law. Indeed, to some, substantive harmonization is preferred to the harmonization, or unification, of private international law rules.[90] Although substantive harmonization of law reduces the scope for private international law problems, it requires great effort to achieve. Even when successful, 'private international law will remain of considerable importance in the resolution of cross border disputes'.[91] Accordingly, it is important that both areas are addressed. Harmonizing private international law rules generally entails only a minimal disturbance in national legal systems, as private international law addresses only matters involving foreign elements. Consequently, it is more likely to appeal to the

[89] OHADA Treaty, art. 1.
[90] Hay, Lando and Rotunda (1986), p. 256.
[91] Goode (2005), p. 541.

politician with an eye for preserving his country's unique or perceived superior legal system. The process is considered simpler because a whole branch of substantive law may be covered by a few choice-of-law clauses.[92]

Given that no attempt has been made towards continent-wide harmonization of substantive laws, private international law may be the place to start. This is especially so in the area of commercial law, which is of immediate importance to the promotion of regional economic activity in Africa, and for which national values may not be too diverse. As Allott has perceptively observed, in Africa it is those areas of law with 'less peculiar local content' that are more likely to be susceptible to transnational harmonization.[93] The Institute for Private International Law in Africa, which is part of the University of Johannesburg, could be given a role to play as regards harmonization of private international law. Furthermore, the efforts of OHADA to harmonize substantive law can be adopted by the AEC and made a continent-wide initiative. This would be consistent with, albeit an extension of, the philosophy of using regional economic communities as building blocks of the AEC. Indeed, it is reported that the AU has taken interest in the OHADA initiative, and is studying the approximation of OHADA law and the common law.

Harmonization of either substantive or private international law requires a choice as to the character of the legal instruments to be used. The OHADA approach, which relies on hard law instruments that are binding and directly applicable, could be used by the AEC. An alternative to hard law instruments is model laws that will subsequently be adopted with adaptations by national parliaments. At these formative stages of the development of the AEC, model laws may be particularly apposite. Model laws allow for legislation to be made while taking into account specific national demands. A limited, albeit useful, addition will be for the AEC to encourage member states to be more active in international initiatives on the unification of private law, and for them to be parties to instruments generated from the initiatives.

4.4.2 *Paths to harmonization of laws*

A path to harmonizing laws in Africa would be organizing them along legal traditions under what could be characterized as a pyramid scheme

[92] Hay, Lando and Rotunda (1986), pp. 170–4. [93] Allot (1968a), p. 86.

for harmonization. This scheme takes as its foundation the idea or assumption that the legal principles of countries with the same legal tradition are very similar. Accordingly, harmonization should begin among countries belonging to the same legal tradition. With the appropriate institutional support and enthusiastic legal personnel, this should proceed fairly quickly and easily. The scheme should end with the harmonization of the outcomes of the intra-legal traditions harmonization process. This stage should also move fairly quickly, since it will entail dealing with small numbers of legal instruments.

Applying the pyramid scheme to the ECOWAS, Gambia, Ghana, Liberia, Nigeria and Sierra Leone should constitute one group (common law group). Benin, Burkina Faso, Cape Verde, Côte d'Ivoire, Guinea, Guinea Bissau, Mali, Niger, Senegal and Togo would constitute another group (civil law group). A similar grouping of countries can be pursued under COMESA, EAC and SADC. To avoid unnecessary duplication and conflicts resulting from the fact that states are often members of more than one regional community, it is suggested that under the scheme a country participates in only one community of its choice. An advantage with starting the harmonization process within the RECs is that, even if an instrument covering all the communities does not materialize, or there is delay in achieving it, each grouping within a community will have one harmonized law on the chosen subject. This will reduce the burden of investigating different national laws when engaging in cross-border transactions within the community.

Table 2 provides a procedural outline for a harmonized law on jurisdiction and the recognition and enforcement of foreign judgments for members of COMESA, EAC, ECOWAS and SADC using the scheme. Countries that are members of more than one community have been placed into only one community. The process covers almost all Sub-Saharan African countries.

It is suggested, using the pyramid scheme as a model, that the AEC should immediately embark upon the task of promoting the harmonization of both substantive and private international laws in Africa. In this regard, it is significant that the Pan-African Parliament is currently seeking an expansion of its purely advisory role to that of a legislative role with a view to, inter alia, aiding the harmonization of national laws across Africa. It is recommended that the Assembly of Heads of State and Government, in exercising powers conferred on it by article 25(2) of the AEC Treaty, should establish a specialized technical committee to look into legal issues involved in integration. This committee should have a

Table 2 *COMESA, EAC, ECOWAS and SADC: pyramid harmonization for convention on jurisdiction and the recognition and enforcement of foreign judgments*

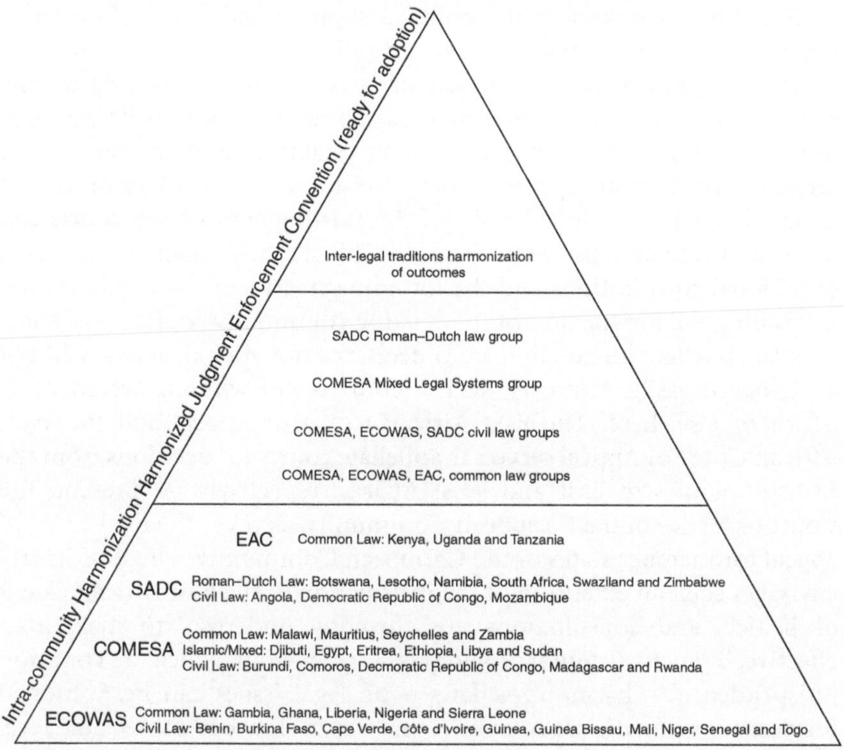

specific mandate to look into the implications of the issues discussed in this book, including the harmonization of law for the success of the AEC. Additionally, one of the principal responsibilities of the Committee on Coordination is the coordination and harmonization of 'integration legislation'. This Committee was established by the Protocol on the Relations between the African Union and the Regional Economic Communities. It is suggested that the Committee should interpret this responsibility broadly to include not only legislation, but also the impact of existing legal regimes in member states on the success of the AEC. The newly established African Union Commission on International Law could be another forum for dealing with the issue of harmonization of laws in Africa.[94] Its mandate is broad enough to encompass the myriad of legal issues that bedevils Africa's economic integration processes. In summary, the requisite institutions exist – at least on paper – with the mandate to engage in work relevant to the harmonization of laws in Africa. What is lacking is the political support and financial commitment to translate the mandate into tangible and beneficial outcomes.

Another path to harmonization of laws in Africa is to rely on the courts. This could be characterized as the judicial path to harmonization. A radical step on this path is to establish regional courts with jurisdiction to hear appeals from decisions, civil and criminal, of national courts. The jurisdiction of the existing community courts can be expanded to accommodate this role. This step will entail amendments of national constitutions and the founding treaties of the communities. Expanding the jurisdiction of the existing community courts, to encompass an appellate jurisdiction from decisions of national courts, will not be achieved easily. However, such a court is not without precedent in Africa or elsewhere. The East African Court of Appeal and the West African Court of Appeal served as appellate courts for decisions from the British colonies in East and West Africa, respectively. At present, the Court of Justice of the Caribbean Community serves as the final court of appeal for member states of the Caribbean Community. The EAC Treaty envisages such an extension of the jurisdiction of the East African Court of Justice, and consultations are currently underway to make that effective.[95] Such a court provides a forum from which a 'common jurisprudence' – harmonized laws – on legal issues can be fashioned for decisions of national courts. In this way, a slow but appreciable level of harmonization can be achieved within the communities.

A strong case exists, even outside the harmonization context, for a community court with appellate jurisdiction. Given the character of its jurisdiction – hearing appeals from decisions of national courts – the court is bound to be active. The existence of such a court can boost people's and investors' confidence in the communities. It would provide investors with a forum outside the ordinary state judicial structure, in which disputes could ultimately be settled. This confidence can materialize only if the independence of the community courts and their

[94] Statute of African Union Commission on International Law, 4 February 2009, www.africa-union.org/root/au/Documents/Treaties/text/STATUTE%20OF%20THE%20AUCIL-Adopted%20-%20Feb%202009.pdf.

[95] EAC Treaty, art. 27(2); and Draft Protocol to Operationalise the Extended Jurisdiction of the East African Court of Justice (EAC Secretariat, 2005).

processes are guaranteed. A community court with appellate jurisdiction should be impervious to local or national pressures.

A less ambitious step on the judicial path to harmonization is through jurisprudential communication. National courts should be more attentive to the jurisprudence of each other in deciding cases with a view to achieving uniformity of outcomes. The potential for jurisprudential communication as a path to harmonization is currently evident within the Roman–Dutch law jurisdictions of Southern Africa. South Africa serves as the 'unofficial' parent jurisdiction, and its jurisprudence is of considerable persuasive force within the other countries.

4.5 Conclusion

The initiative to integrate the economies of African states through the AEC is laudable and must be encouraged. It is one of the surest paths to economic development of Africa. The success of the AEC will depend on its ability to overcome the demands and challenges of integration, be they economic, political, social or legal. The absence of legalism at community, regional and national levels remains an important problem for Africa's integration. A key issue identified in this chapter is community–state relations. Unfortunately, there is a lack of attention in the AEC Treaty and related instruments to this issue. Unless strong community–state relations are established, the stability of the AEC will be endangered and its effectiveness undermined. Such relations can develop only with strong community institutions, including an active judicial branch, supportive national courts, a bureaucracy committed to the goals of integration, the existence of political will favourable to integration and an active role for individuals in regional economic integration processes.

This chapter recommends that a committee be established by the Assembly of Heads of State and Government to look into community–state relations and their impact on Africa's economic integration processes. The committee should be charged with the responsibility of examining, amongst others things: the status of AEC law within member states; areas where there is potential for conflict between community and national law; how these conflicts may be addressed; and how community law will impact and relate to the legal systems of member states. At the present stage in the development of the AEC, the difficulties arising from the lack of attention to these issues have not been very prominent, but this by no means suggests that they will not arise. The opportunity exists for them to be addressed before they become stumbling blocks on the path to a stable and effective African Economic Community. Indeed, some of these community–state issues have already arisen in the RECs. The next chapter examines how their respective community courts are addressing them.

5

Relational issues before the community courts

5.1 Introduction

Relational issues in economic integration take various forms and arise in different forums. A vehicle for addressing them is the founding treaty of an economic integration process. However, given the complexity and continuing character of economic integration, these issues, and the problems resulting from them, may continue to haunt the process. Community courts are legal guardians of an economic integration process, enforcers of the benefits it brings, agents who decide when a breach has occurred and the remedy for it, and arbiters of the institutional tensions inherent in it. They are often called upon to solve these problems. As Shany has observed, 'economic integration/trade liberalization courts . . . have been created primarily in order to help sustain a very delicate equilibrium between the states parties and other stakeholders participating in a special legal regime, and between the states and other stakeholders and the regime's institutions'.[1] In addition to dispute settlement, community courts are responsible for norm-advancement and regime maintenance. Implicit in these observations is the idea that the functions of a community court go beyond what one would ordinarily expect of a national court. A community court has both judicial and 'political' functions. Compared with national courts, their role resembles more of a constitutional court than other lower courts.

This chapter assesses how community courts in Africa, confronted with relational issues, have performed both functions. The chapter uses the founding treaties of the Common Market for Eastern and Southern Africa (COMESA),[2] the Economic Community of West African States (ECOWAS),[3] the East African Community (EAC)[4] and the Southern African Development Community (SADC),[5] plus the community courts established by them, as the focus. A key to a community court's ability to

[1] Shany (2009), p. 82. See generally Alter (2008a); and Mann (1972).
[2] COMESA Treaty. [3] ECOWAS Treaty. [4] EAC Treaty. [5] SADC Treaty.

address the challenges of economic integration effectively is its jurisdiction and institutional set-up. Accordingly, this chapter begins with a comparative survey of the institutional structures of the COMESA, ECOWAS, EAC and SADC courts. This is followed by a descriptive account of some decided cases, in which relational issues, and the problems resulting from them, were articulated or addressed. The cases selected raise interesting issues relating to the organizational structure of the communities, the status of individuals within them and power relations between the communities and member states.

5.2 Organization and jurisdiction

Courts are important in economic integration. In a complex regime, such as that generated by economic integration, the presence of a robust court to monitor aspects of the regime through dispute settlement is essential.[6] Dispute settlement is an essential aspect of governance in economic integration. It improves the chances of state compliance with their treaty obligations and instils business confidence. However, as observed by Smith, the potential for courts to use their jurisprudence to restrict governmental discretion, especially regarding domestic policy, conditions the extent of powers entrusted to them by states.[7] Schneider has categorized, into four groups, the dispute-settlement regimes used by international trade organizations.[8] These are the negotiation, investor arbitration, international adjudication and supranational court regimes. She distinguishes these regimes using the criteria of direct effect, supremacy of the institution's law over domestic law, *locus standi*, transparency and enforcement. The choice of regime in a given organization is influenced by a number of socio-economic, political and legal considerations. These include the level of integration desired, political systems in the member states, degree of control they want to exercise over the dispute-settlement process and legal culture.[9] Smith also classifies dispute settlement institutions along a spectrum that flows from the diplomatic to the legalistic. The latter is characterized by automatic third-party rulings and review, directly binding and effective decisions, permanent tribunals and standing for individuals, states and institutions of the organization.[10]

[6] Keck and Schropp (2008); Taylor (1996–7); and Nyman-Metcalf and Papageorgiou (2005).

[7] Smith (2000). [8] Schneider (1998–9). [9] Ibid., pp. 727–52.

[10] Smith (2000), pp. 139–43.

The institutional structure of the community courts under review can be characterized as supranational and legalistic. The founding treaties contain provisions that allow 'the tribunals to interact directly with the principal players in national legal systems'.[11] This is remarkable for a continent that is traditionally perceived as having no litigation culture and with a fetishist attachment to state sovereignty. It is explainable on the grounds that the levels of economic integration envisaged by the communities demand a supranational and legalistic court regime. As Smith has observed, the more ambitious the level of proposed integration – and such is the case in Africa – the more willing political leaders should be to endorse legalistic dispute settlement.[12]

Institutional design is one thing. Whether the institution actually functions as envisaged is another issue. The simple provision of supranational jurisdiction is not a guarantee of effective adjudication. It is possible for states to design a supranational court on paper, while at the same time being conscious of the fact that existing (but changeable) socio-economic, political and cultural conditions may prevent it from operating as such. These conditions may include overt and covert political interference with the court's work, underfunding of its work, the prohibitive cost of international litigation, the absence of a supportive domestic constituency and the absence of a litigation culture. Thus, it is important to look beyond the balance between the quest for treaty compliance and the desire for autonomy in domestic policy-making when one tries to account for the choice of a particular regime for dispute settlement in economic integration.

5.2.1 *Structure of the community courts*

The COMESA, ECOWAS, EAC and SADC treaties establish courts of justice as one of their principal institutions.[13] Each court is charged with ensuring adherence to law in the interpretation and application of the

[11] Helfer and Slaughter (1997), p. 277. [12] Smith (2000), p. 148.

[13] COMESA Treaty, art. 7; ECOWAS Treaty, art. 6(e); and EAC Treaty, art. 9. The detailed provisions on the ECOWAS and SADC courts are contained in protocols. See Protocol A/P.1/7/91 on the Community Court of Justice of the High Contracting Parties as amended by Supplementary Protocol A/SP/.1/01/05 Amending the Protocol Relating to the Community Court of Justice (hereafter, ECOWAS Court Protocol); and SADC Tribunal Protocol. See generally Ruppel and Bangamwabo (2008).

treaty.[14] The COMESA court became fully operational in 1998. It is located in Lusaka, Zambia, but, ultimately, it will have a permanent seat in Khartoum, Sudan. The ECOWAS court was inaugurated in 2001 and sits in Abuja, Nigeria. The EAC court was inaugurated in 2001 and sits in Arusha, Tanzania. The SADC Tribunal was inaugurated in 2005 and is located at Windhoek, Namibia. These courts are fully operational with an appreciable caseload. Indeed, compared with other newly established community courts, the African community courts are doing relatively better in terms of caseload.[15]

The COMESA and ECOWAS courts consist of seven judges each.[16] The SADC Tribunal consists of not less than ten members, but only five are designated as regular members.[17] The East African court has two divisions – a First Instance Division and an Appellate Division. The EAC court is composed of a maximum of fifteen judges of whom not more than ten shall be appointed to the First Instance Division and not more than five to the Appellate Division.[18] Judges for the COMESA, ECOWAS and SADC courts hold office for five years and are eligible for reappointment once.[19] Judges for the EAC court hold office for a maximum of seven years.[20] The judges are appointed from among persons recommended by the community institution consisting of Heads of State and Government.[21] This process of appointing judges raises questions as to their independence, and how insulated they are from the influence of their appointing authority.[22]

Some economic communities outside Africa have explored alternative modes of appointing judges with a view to guaranteeing their independence.[23] To insulate community judges from governmental influence, it is suggested that the appointment of judges to the community courts

[14] COMESA Treaty, art. 19; ECOWAS Court Protocol, art. 9(1); EAC Treaty, art. 23; and SADC Treaty, art. 16(1).

[15] The Caribbean Court of Justice, established in 2001, heard its first case which invoked its original jurisdiction (jurisdiction relating to the interpretation and application of the CARICOM Treaty) in 2008. *Trinidad Cement Ltd* v. *The Co-operative Republic of Guyana* [2008] CCJ 1 (OJ) (*Trinidad Cement I*); and *Trinidad Cement Ltd* v. *The State of the Co-operative Republic of Guyana* [2009] CCJ 1 (OJ).

[16] COMESA Treaty, art. 20(1); and ECOWAS Court Protocol, art. 3(2).

[17] SADC Tribunal Protocol, art. 3(1)(2).

[18] EAC Treaty, art. 24(2).

[19] COMESA Treaty, art. 21(1); ECOWAS Court Protocol, art. 4(1); and SADC Tribunal Protocol, art. 6(1).

[20] EAC Treaty, art. 25(1).

[21] COMESA Treaty, art. 20(1); ECOWAS Court Protocol, art. 3(1); EAC Treaty, art. 24(1); and SADC Tribunal Protocol, art. 4(4).

[22] Mackenzie and Sands (2004).

[23] Caribbean Court Agreement.

should be entrusted to an independent body composed of people who do not represent the member states. This is possible only through an amendment of the treaties and protocols regulating the courts. Membership of the appointing body can be drawn from the respective Bar Associations, Judicial Councils, Law Faculties, Chambers of Commerce and civil society organizations. Admittedly, this suggestion will be difficult to market. Executive and political domination of the economic integration processes and their institutions is the norm in Africa. As in other parts of the world, the appointment of international judges is an executive privilege.[24] However, independence is a key to ensuring that community courts are able to perform effectively their judicial function in economic integration – something which Africa's integration processes need.

Under the treaties, judges must be persons of proven integrity, impartiality and independence. They must fulfil the conditions required in their own countries to hold high judicial office or they must be jurists of recognized competence.[25] In practice, judges of the community courts are appointed from serving judges of national courts. This provides a linkage between the national and community legal systems. However, the approach of appointing community court judges from national courts has its dangers; it could undermine the independence of community judges. This is especially so in instances where, on appointment to a community court, one's employment as a national judge is not terminated. Governments dissatisfied with rulings of a community judge could seek 'revenge' at the national level. An issue that arose in East Africa was whether a national judge appointed to the EAC court could continue to sit on the latter after he had been suspended from the former pending a corruption investigation. The issue was dealt with by a treaty amendment that allows for the simultaneous suspension of the judge at the community level pending the outcome of the national investigation.[26] Within the SADC, the possibility of such a scenario is avoided as full-time members of the Tribunal are not permitted to hold any other office or employment.[27]

It is also significant that among the persons qualified to be appointed to the ECOWAS court are 'jurisconsults of recognized competence in international law'.[28] This lays a foundation for forging a relationship between the ECOWAS and international legal systems. A judge who has an

[24] Voeten (2007).
[25] COMESA Treaty, art. 20(2); ECOWAS Court Protocol, art. 3(1); EAC Treaty, art. 24(1); and SADC Tribunal Protocol, art. 3(1).
[26] EAC Treaty, arts. 2, 2A and 2B. [27] SADC Tribunal Protocol, art. 6(3).
[28] ECOWAS Court Protocol, art. 3(1).

international law background is more likely to bring the norms of the international legal system to bear on his or her decisions. Indeed, article 20 of the ECOWAS Court Protocol, unlike the COMESA and EAC treaties, specifically enjoins the court to have regard to the body of laws contained in Article 38 of the Statutes of the International Court of Justice in its decision-making.[29] Article 21(1) of the SADC Tribunal Protocol also enjoins the Tribunal to 'develop its own Community jurisprudence having regard to applicable treaties, general principles and rules of public international law, and any rules and principles of the law of States'. The importance of these provisions is borne out in the jurisprudence of the courts, in which reliance is often placed on international law.[30] The absence of such a provision in the COMESA and EAC treaties has, however, not prevented their respective courts from relying on international law.

Judges of the COMESA, EAC and ECOWAS courts may be removed by the appointing authority for misconduct or inability to perform the functions of their office due to infirmity of mind or body.[31] The ECOWAS Court Protocol and the EAC Treaty have built in mechanisms to ensure the process of removing judges is not arbitrary. Under the EAC Treaty, a judge's removal should occur only after an ad hoc independent tribunal, set up for the purpose and consisting of three eminent judges drawn from within the Commonwealth of Nations, has recommended it.[32] Under the ECOWAS Court Protocol, the court must assess, in a plenary session, the grounds of removal and make a recommendation to the Assembly of Heads of State and Government. This provision allows for the removal process to be monitored and controlled by a body composed of the judge's peers. This is essential to ensuring the independence and impartiality of judges.[33] The COMESA

[29] Ajulo (2001); and Ajulo (1989).

[30] See, e.g. *Frank Ukor* v. *Alinnor*, Suit No. ECW/CCJ/APP/01/04 (ECOWAS Court of Justice, 2005); *Jerry Ugokwe* v. *The Federal Republic of Nigeria*, Case No. ECW/CCJ/APP/02/05 (ECOWAS Court of Justice, 2005); *Tokumbo Lijadu-Oyemade* v. *Executive Secretary of ECOWAS*, Suit No. ECW/CCJ/APP/01/05 (ECOWAS Court of Justice, 2005); and *Mike Campbell (Pvt) Ltd* v. *The Republic of Zimbabwe*, SADC (T) Case No. 2/2007 (SADC Tribunal, 2008).

[31] EAC Treaty, art. 26; ECOWAS Court Protocol, art. 4; and COMESA Treaty, art. 22.

[32] EAC Treaty, art. 26(1)(3).

[33] There have been two decided cases where allegations of bias (unrelated to governmental influence) have been levelled against judges of the COMESA and EAC courts. In both cases, the courts rejected the allegation. *Eastern and Southern African Trade and Development Bank* v. *Ogang (No. 2)* [2002] 1 East Afr. LR 54; and *AG of the Republic of Kenya* v. *Anyang' Nyong'o*, Application No. 5 of 2007 (East Africa Court of Justice, 2007).

Treaty provides less protection for the judges of the COMESA court. Under article 22(1) of the treaty, they can be removed by the Authority of Heads of State and Government for stated misbehaviour or inability to perform the functions of their offices, due to infirmity of mind or body, or due to any other specified cause. The treaty is silent on how the Authority should arrive at its determination. Compared with the ECOWAS Court Protocol and EAC Treaty's provisions, the COMESA provision represents a threat to the independence of the court and needs to be revisited. The provision of the SADC Tribunal Protocol on the removal of members of the Tribunal is quite terse; it offers little guidance. It simply provides that no member may be dismissed unless in accordance with the rules, but an examination of the relevant rules does not yield much insight.

One factor that contributes to judicial independence and, indeed, the integrity of a court as an institution, is financial security. Under article 29 of the ECOWAS Court Protocol, the remuneration, allowances and other benefits of the court's judges are determined by the Assembly of Heads of State and Government.[34] The salary and other conditions of service of the EAC court's judges are determined by the Summit of Heads of State and Governments on the recommendation of the Council of Ministers.[35] The COMESA Treaty is silent on this important issue. It only provides that the terms and conditions of service of the Registrar, and other staff of the court, shall be determined by the Council of Ministers on the recommendation of the court.[36] Under article 11 of the SADC Tribunal Protocol, the terms and conditions of service, salaries and benefits of the members are determined by the Council of Ministers.

There are two worrying aspects of these financial provisions. Firstly, it is uncertain whether the salary and other conditions of service of the judges can be varied to their disadvantage while they are in office. In some African countries, judges are constitutionally protected from adverse variations in their conditions of service.[37] A similar approach in the communities will enhance the independence of the community

[34] The budget of the ECOWAS court is subject to the approval of the Council of Ministers. ECOWAS Court Protocol, art. 30; and ECOWAS Treaty, art. 69.

[35] EAC Treaty, art. 25(5). The budget of the EAC court is subject to the approval of the Council of Ministers. EAC Treaty, art. 132.

[36] COMESA Treaty, art. 41(3).

[37] Constitution of the Republic of Ghana, 1992, art. 127(5); and Constitution of the Republic of Malawi, 1994, art. 114(2).

judges. There is no legitimate reason why judges of the community courts should be less protected than their counterparts in national courts. Secondly, the fact that the budget of the courts is tied to the communities' budgets and subject to the approval of political institutions can undermine the courts' independence. Preferably, a separate fund, independently managed and financed, from which their expenditure is charged, would be more appropriate.[38]

5.2.2 *Subject-matter jurisdiction*

A community court's jurisdiction influences its ability to guide an economic integration process and to arbitrate tensions inherent in the relations that result from it. It is impossible to assess the role played in an economic integration arrangement by a dispute-settlement mechanism without review of its jurisdiction. There is considerable convergence between the treaties on the community courts' jurisdiction. However, there are also some notable differences. The jurisdiction of the courts falls into four broad categories. Firstly, there is the jurisdiction over the interpretation and application of the treaty. The interpretive jurisdiction of the EAC court is subject to the proviso that it 'shall not include the application of any such interpretation to jurisdiction conferred by the Treaty on organs of Partner States'.[39] Secondly, there is the jurisdiction to hear and determine disputes between the community and its employees.[40] Thirdly, they have jurisdiction to determine cases referred to them as a result of parties – be they the community, its institutions or natural and legal persons – choosing any of them as a forum for the arbitration of disputes.[41] Finally, it is envisaged that the jurisdiction of the EAC court will be extended to include original, appellate, human

[38] Revised Agreement Establishing the Caribbean Court of Justice Trust Fund, online: www.caribbeancourtofjustice.org/legislation.html.

[39] EAC Treaty, art. 27(1); COMESA Treaty, art. 19; ECOWAS Court Protocol, art. 9(1)(a); and SADC Tribunal Protocol, art. 14.

[40] EAC Treaty, art. 31; COMESA Treaty, art. 27; ECOWAS Court Protocol, art. 9(1)(f), 10(e); and SADC Tribunal Protocol, art. 19. In *Eastern and Southern African Trade and Development Bank* v. *Nyagamukenga*, Reference No. 3 of 2006 (COMESA Court of Justice, 2009), the court held that it has jurisdiction in an application which sought to vary or set aside an arbitration award between the bank – a COMESA institution – and the respondent, a former employee. On the substantive issue, the court dismissed the application.

[41] EAC Treaty, art. 32; and COMESA Treaty, art. 28. ECOWAS Treaty, art. 16; and ECOWAS Court Protocol, art. 9(5). The SADC Tribunal has no arbitral jurisdiction.

rights and other jurisdictions, as will be determined by the Council of Ministers at a suitable future date.[42]

For the purposes of pushing forward economic integration through law, and allowing individuals to be active participants in the integration processes, this arbitral jurisdiction of the community courts is welcomed. It allows individuals to access the courts for the determination of their disputes through arbitration. The subject matter may even be a commercial contract that does not engage community law or community interest in any way. In general, the community courts can be viable forums for individuals who seek neutral forums for dispute settlement. Indeed, their arbitral jurisdiction over commercial contracts could be used to develop the courts into forums for the resolution of international commercial disputes in Africa. However, the jurisdiction raises a number of issues, which will be explored in Chapter 8. These include the law that governs such arbitration, especially where the parties do not specify a governing law, and enforceability of awards made by the community courts.

The member states of the EAC are expected to conclude a protocol to extend the court's jurisdiction to include original, appellate and human rights issues. So far, no such protocol has been concluded, but consultations are under way regarding original jurisdiction. Regarding jurisdiction over human rights matters, the EAC court has held that, while it will not assume jurisdiction to adjudicate on human rights disputes, it will not abdicate from exercising its jurisdiction of interpretation under article 27(1) merely because the case before it includes allegations of human rights violations.[43] This offers an indirect route by which human rights issues may be brought before the court. For example, article 6(d) of the EAC Treaty stipulates 'good governance including adherence to the principles of democracy, the rule of law, accountability,

[42] EAC Treaty, art. 27(2). No such provision is found in the COMESA Treaty. Article 9(4) of the ECOWAS Court Protocol grants the court jurisdiction over violations of human rights in member states. A majority of the cases decided by the ECOWAS Court are human rights orientated. See, e.g. *Jerry Ugokwe* v. *The Federal Republic of Nigeria*, Case No. ECW/CCJ/APP/02/05 (ECOWAS Court of Justice, 2005); *Etim Moses Essien* v. *Republic of Gambia*, Case No. ECW/CCJ/APP/05/07 (ECOWAS Court of Justice, 2007); *Frank Ukor* v. *Alinnor*, Suit No. ECW/CCJ/APP/01/04 (ECOWAS Court of Justice, 2005); and *Alhaji Hammani Tidjani* v. *Federal Republic of Nigeria*, Suit No. ECW/CCJ/APP/01/06 (ECOWAS Court of Justice, 2007).

[43] *James Katabazi* v. *Secretary General of the East African Community*, Reference No. 1 of 2007 (East African Court of Justice, 2007); and *Mike Campbell (Pvt) Ltd* v. *The Republic of Zimbabwe*, SADC (T) Case No. 2/2007 (SADC Tribunal, 2008).

transparency, social justice, equal opportunities, gender equality, as well as the recognition, promotion and protection of human and peoples' rights' as fundamental principles of the community. An action alleging a breach of article 6(d) – which is within the jurisdiction of the court – will in many instances qualify as an action alleging a violation of human rights, which in theory is outside the court's jurisdiction.

It is important that, until its jurisdiction is extended to include human rights claims, the court exercises caution in admitting, indirectly, human rights claims. Too many human rights claims are likely to burden the court and distract it from the economic integration agenda. It is also likely to breed tension between the court and already established forums for vindicating human rights, such as national courts, which should be allies of the court in promoting economic integration. Indeed, the 'transformation' of the community courts – either through legislation or judicial activism – into 'human rights courts' is an unnecessary move and should be avoided. National courts, national human rights commissions, the African Commission on Human and Peoples' Rights and the African Court of Justice and Human Rights have jurisdiction over human rights violations. Aggrieved individuals can resort to one of these forums. To be sure, it is not suggested here that the community courts should not take into account human rights in deciding cases. Rather, the claim is that the community courts should not become centres for human rights litigation.

An issue on which there is significant variation in the approaches of the community treaties relates to actions for damages against the communities. Under the ECOWAS Court Protocol and SADC Tribunal Protocol, the community courts have exclusive jurisdiction to determine any non-contractual and, arguably, contractual liability of the communities.[44] The COMESA and EAC treaties are silent on this issue. However, it appears their provisions that disputes to which the community is party should not, on that ground alone, be excluded from the jurisdiction of national courts will allow for tortious actions and contractual claims against the community to be instituted before national courts.[45] Both provisions appear to have been borrowed from article 274 of the EU Treaty. However, unlike the EU Treaty, which, in article 268, confers jurisdiction in non-contractual matters on the Court of Justice of

[44] ECOWAS Court Protocol, arts. 9(1)(g) and 9(2); and SADC Tribunal Protocol, art. 18.
[45] COMESA Treaty, art. 29(1); and EAC Treaty, art. 33(1).

the European Union, no such provision exists in the COMESA and EAC treaties. The danger of 'incomplete borrowing' is evident here: the combined effect of articles 268 and 274 is in procedural terms; it is not possible for EU non-contractual liability to be decided by national courts.[46] But the effect of article 274 standing alone – and that is what the COMESA and EAC treaties borrowed – is that it is possible for non-contractual liability of both communities to be decided by their respective national courts.

From a private and public international law perspective, this prospect raises difficult issues. Firstly, in non-contractual or contractual litigation before the ECOWAS and SADC courts, what will be the applicable law? Will it be the national laws of the member states, which, owing to the many legal traditions they embrace, are likely to vary? Or, will it be a yet-to-be-developed ECOWAS or SADC law on contractual and non-contractual liability? The closest one comes to finding a solution to this problem is the reference in article 20 of the ECOWAS Court Protocol to Article 38 of the Statute of the International Court of Justice as a potential source of law for decisions of the court. However, it is arguable that, given the international character of the sources listed in Article 38, that they cannot provide the corpus needed to resolve contractual and non-contractual claims. Ultimately, the court will have to fall back on a careful synthesis of national laws. In this regard, the SADC Tribunal protocol fares better in that the Tribunal is enjoined to develop its own community jurisprudence, taking into account the laws of the member states.[47]

Secondly, if contractual and non-contractual disputes involving the communities are litigated before national courts, as envisaged under the COMESA and EAC treaties, will the communities automatically lose their immunity? Both under national legislation and, where no such legislation exists, arguably, at common law, the communities enjoy immunity from the civil processes of their member states.[48] If immunity

[46] Craig and de Búrca (2003), pp. 571–2; and Oliver (1997), pp. 285–309.

[47] Compare EU Treaty, art. 340.

[48] Kenya – Treaty for the Establishment of the East African Community Act, 2000, art. 7; Tanzania – Treaty for the Establishment of the East African Community Act, 2001, art. 7; Uganda – East African Community Act, 2002, art. 8; *J.H. Rayner (Mincing Lane) Ltd* v. *Department of Trade and Industry* [1989] Ch. 72 at 199–203, 252–3; and *J.H. Rayner (Mincing Lane) Ltd* v. *Department of Trade and Industry* [1990] 2 AC 418 at 516. Southern African Development Community Protocol on Immunities and Privileges, online: www.sadc-tribunal.org/docs/ImmunitiesAndPrevileges.pdf.

is successfully claimed, in which forum will an individual be able to seek remedy? This question has practical implications for those transacting within the communities, or with the communities, whose transactions are likely to be affected by the work of the communities. From a relational perspective, one may also question the propriety of subjecting a community to what could, potentially, be the application of national law before a national court. Decisions relating to the liability of the community for its activities may, in some instances, entail passing judgment on the community's policies. It is open to question whether national courts should be entrusted with such a role. Furthermore, subjecting the community to the jurisdiction of national courts and national law may not engender uniformity on issues of community liability. It is suggested that the COMESA and EAC should consider introducing a treaty amendment that grants their community courts exclusive jurisdiction regarding the contractual and non-contractual liability of the communities.

5.2.3 *Standing and preconditions*

Access to the community courts is granted to member states, specific community institutions, legal and natural persons, and national courts. A member state may make a reference to the courts alleging breach of an obligation arising under the treaty or an infringement of its provisions.[49] The secretaries of the COMESA, ECOWAS and EAC may also make a similar reference to the courts.[50] Actions by member states and community secretaries are unlikely to be a major source of cases before the courts. Indeed, to date, the judgments of the courts reveal very few instances in which states or community institutions have sued each other.

All of the community courts allow for natural and legal persons' (individuals') access.[51] In other words, individuals can bring claims before the courts. In economic integration, direct individual access to community courts is important for a number of reasons: it increases the number of persons that may potentially bring cases; it provides a means for overcoming the traditional reluctance of states to sue each other;

49 EAC Treaty, art. 28; COMESA Treaty, art. 25; and SADC Tribunal Protocol, art. 17.
50 COMESA Treaty, art. 25; ECOWAS Court Protocol, art. 10; and EAC Treaty, art. 29.
51 COMESA Treaty, art. 26; EAC Treaty, art. 30; ECOWAS Court Protocol, art. 10; and SADC Tribunal Protocol, art. 15.

it performs the constitutional function of limiting the power of governments to decide which disputes warrant litigation; it minimizes governments' control over which claims can be brought; and it potentially guarantees greater governmental compliance with community law, since governments are aware that breaches will not go uncontested. In other words, individual access provides a layer of private enforcement to complement public enforcement mechanisms, such as states' periodic reporting on compliance or enforcement actions by community institutions. Individual access also enhances the legitimacy of the communities' legal systems. It grants them a stake in the evolution of community law and creates a national constituency for community law. Through litigation on issues of community law, they can effect legal change both domestically and at the community level. Also, by sometimes beginning the process of litigation in national courts while exhausting local remedies, they help create a nexus between national and community legal systems. Through this means, community courts become an 'appellate' forum for judgments of national courts. Generally, individual access provides a mechanism for bridging the disjunction between community and national legal systems.

Although all of the community courts allow for individual access, they vary as to the conditions precedent to access. Similar variations exist as regards to what, who or which community institution can be challenged in the courts in actions by individuals. Article 30 of the EAC Treaty provides that 'any person who is resident in a Partner State may refer for determination by the Court, the legality of any Act, regulation, directive, decision or action of a Partner State or an institution of the Community on the grounds that such Act, regulation, directive, decision or action is unlawful or is an infringement of the provisions of this Treaty'. Article 26 of the COMESA Treaty has a similar provision, but limits challenges to acts, regulations directives or decisions of 'the Council or of a Member State'. Prima facie, this excludes actions of a number of important community institutions from individual challenges. Article 26 severely constrains the scope of actions amenable to challenge by individuals.[52] It insulates from individual challenge the decisions of the Authority of Heads of State and Government, the highest decision-making organ of the COMESA. Additionally, under the COMESA Treaty and SADC

[52] The ECOWAS Court Protocol has a more limiting provision. Under art. 10(c) individuals can only bring an action for the determination of whether 'an act or inaction of a community official' violates their rights.

Tribunal Protocol, where the challenge relates to a member state's action, the individual must first exhaust the local remedies of its national courts or tribunals.[53]

Exhausting local remedies before litigating at the international level poses significant problems for individuals. In *Republic of Kenya* v. *Coastal Aquaculture*,[54] the applicant, for over eight years, had been unsuccessful in completing the domestic legal processes for challenging or seeking compensation for the compulsory acquisition of his land. The COMESA court 'sympathized' with his plight, but held that he had not exhausted local remedies and lacked *locus standi*. This was an unfortunate outcome for the applicant. Even if the court concluded that the applicant had *locus standi*, it would still have been debatable whether it had jurisdiction to grant an injunction restraining the Kenyan Government from compulsorily acquiring the applicant's land, or how that injunction would be enforced. Within the context of economic integration, exhausting local remedies can be an important avenue for linking national and community legal systems. Individual actions before national courts on matters involving community law are likely to raise questions of treaty or community law interpretation. This raises the prospect of a reference to the community courts for a preliminary ruling. Requests for preliminary rulings will facilitate closer cooperation between national courts and the community courts. It will ensure that national courts become active players and knowledgeable in community law, and reduce the workload of the community courts. References to the community courts can also become a source of legitimacy for national courts and their decisions, as the latter are 'validated' at community level.

A significant aspect of individual standing under the COMESA and EAC treaties is that individuals do not have to show any personal interest affected by the action being challenged. This has subsequently been confirmed in decisions of the EAC court.[55] On this, the ECOWAS Court Protocol parts company with them. Article 10 of the protocol allows individuals and corporate bodies to access the court, but only for the

[53] COMESA Treaty, art. 26; SADC Tribunal Protocol, art. 15(2); *United Republic of Tanzania* v. *Cimexpan (Mauritius) Ltd*, Case No. SADC (T) 01/2009 (SADC Tribunal, 2010); and *Bach's Transport (Pty) Ltd* v. *The Democratic Republic of Congo*, Case No. SADC (T) 14/2008 (SADC Tribunal, 2010). Exhaustion of local remedies is not a prerequisite for actions before the ECOWAS court. *Mme Hadijatou Mani Koraou* v. *The Republic of Niger*, Suit No. ECW/CCJ/JUD/06/08 (ECOWAS Court of Justice, 2008) at [36]–[53].

[54] *Republic of Kenya* v. *Coastal Aquaculture* [2003] 1 East Afr. LR 271.

[55] *East African Law Society* v. *AG of Kenya* [2008] 1 East Afr. LR 95.

acts or omissions of community officials that violate their rights. This provision prevents what, potentially, could have been public interest litigation by corporations, Non-Governmental Organizations (NGOs) and other legal persons. Public interest litigation can boost economic integration.[56] It is hoped that corporations and NGOs will explore alternative means of indirectly accessing the court. They can actively recruit and sponsor people who have standing or lobby governments to bring actions relevant to their causes. So far, this has not happened within the ECOWAS. Almost all of the cases decided by the ECOWAS court have been brought by natural persons. NGOs have been actively behind a couple of human rights cases.[57]

National courts may seek preliminary rulings from the community courts on questions relating to the interpretation or application of their respective community treaties, or the validity of community regulations, directives or decisions.[58] National courts within the EAC and ECOWAS have discretion in seeking such rulings. Under the COMESA Treaty and SADC Tribunal Protocol, national courts or tribunals, from whose judgment there is no judicial remedy under national law, must seek such a ruling when issues as to the interpretation or validity of community acts are raised.[59] So far, no national court has requested a preliminary ruling from any of the community courts, although some have faced issues that merited a reference.[60]

The Summit or Authority of Heads of State and Government, the Council of Ministers or a member state may also request an advisory opinion regarding a question of law arising under their community treaty from their respective community courts.[61] Under the ECOWAS Court Protocol, the Executive Secretary, or any other community institution, can also request an advisory opinion.[62] So far, only one advisory

[56] Cichowski (2007).
[57] *Chief Ebrimah Manneh* v. *The Gambia*, Suit No. ECW/CCJ/JUD/03/08 (ECOWAS Court of Justice, 2008); and *Mme Hadijatou Mani Koraou* v. *The Republic of Niger*, Suit No. ECW/CCJ/JUD/06/08 (ECOWAS Court of Justice, 2008). See generally Shaffer (2003).
[58] COMESA Treaty, art. 30; ECOWAS Court Protocol, art. 10(f); EAC Treaty, art. 34; and SADC Tribunal Protocol, art. 16.
[59] COMESA Treaty, art. 30(2); and SADC Tribunal Protocol, r. 75.
[60] See, e.g. *Peter Anyang' Nyong'o* v. *AG* [2007] eKLR (Kenya High Court, 2007). The issue was whether an amendment to the EAC Treaty should be made in accordance with national or community law.
[61] COMESA Treaty, art. 32; EAC Treaty, art. 36; and SADC Tribunal Protocol, art. 20.
[62] ECOWAS Court Protocol, art. 11.

opinion has been given. In the *Matter of a Request by the Council of Minister of the East African Community for an Advisory Opinion*,[63] an advisory opinion was sought by the Council on two central issues: namely, whether the principle of variable geometry is in harmony with the requirement for consensus in decision-making; and whether the requirement for consensus in decision-making implies unanimity of the member states. Variable geometry is enshrined in article 7(1)(e) of the EAC Treaty as an operational principle of the community. It is defined in article 1 as the principle of flexibility that allows for progression in cooperation among a sub-group of members in a larger integration scheme in a variety of areas and at different speeds. Under the treaty, consensus lies at the heart of decision-making in the Summit and the Council. Regarding the first issue, the court held that variable geometry was in harmony with the requirement for consensus in decision-making if appropriately applied. In the court's view, consensus related to the decision-making in the relevant institutions, while variable geometry was a strategy for implementation. In other words, the fact that a decision has been taken by consensus does not mean that it has to be implemented in the same way and with the same speed. The states may agree on implementation at different speeds due to different national readiness levels or priorities, but such an approach to implementation must also be agreed to by the states by consensus. Put differently, where states have agreed on a particular course of action, no one state can unilaterally decide to implement it differently, asynchronously, or not implement it at all. Such a decision must be approved by the other states by consensus. Indeed, the court advised that variable geometry should be resorted to as an exception and, in doing so, regard must be had to the experiences of other communities, such as the European Union. On the second issue, the court held that consensus does not imply and should not be construed as synonymous with unanimity. The court acknowledged that the concept of consensus was not defined in the EAC Treaty and, without providing any further guidance, advocated a treaty amendment to address the issue.

In summary, the ECOWAS, COMESA, EAC and SADC treaties have been attentive to important legal issues in designing their courts. They have addressed, often in a similar manner, issues such as the courts' jurisdiction, their relations with national courts, their sources of law and whether and how individuals can access the courts. The COMESA, EAC,

[63] Application No. 1 of 2008 (East African Court of Justice, 2009).

ECOWAS and SADC courts have been designed as supranational and legalistic court regimes. Whether they have actually operated and will operate as such is difficult to judge. There have been instances where decisions affecting member states have been complied with. Other decisions have been met with resistance. What is certain is that the courts appreciate their role in economic integration, and they have responded to the challenges through their jurisprudence.

5.3 Emerging jurisprudence

A sizeable proportion of the cases decided in the community courts, especially the ECOWAS and COMESA courts, have either been staff cases or cases alleging violations of human rights.[64] However, there have been a few cases that have direct bearing on, and are of significance to, economic integration. The jurisprudence of the COMESA, ECOWAS, EAC and SADC courts in these cases reflects the myriad of legal problems associated with economic integration. This section provides a descriptive account of a selection of them. The cases address issues that include the potential place of community law in member states and its impact on national policies, the proper role of national courts in giving meaning to community law, the relations between community institutions and the important, albeit sometimes constrained, role of community courts as guardians of community law and legality.

[64] See, e.g. *Muleya* v. *Common Market for Eastern and Southern Africa (No. 3)* [2004] 1 East Afr. LR 173; *Muleya* v. *Common Market for Eastern and Southern Africa (No. 2)* [2003] 2 East Afr. LR 623; *Muleya* v. *Common Market for Eastern and Southern Africa* [2003] 1 East Afr. LR 173; *Ogang* v. *Eastern and Southern African Trade and Development Bank* [2003] 1 East Afr. LR 217; *Eastern and Southern African Trade and Development Bank* v. *Ogang* [2001] 1 East Afr. LR 46; *Eastern and Southern African Trade and Development Bank* v. *Ogang (No. 2)* [2002] 1 East Afr. LR 54; *Eastern and Southern African Trade and Development Bank* v. *Nyagamukenga*, Reference No. 3 of 2006 (COMESA Court of Justice, 2009); *Tokunbo Lijadu Oyemade* v. *Executive Secretary of ECOWAS*, Suit No. ECW/CCJ/APP/01/04 (ECOWAS Court of Justice, 2006); *Executive Secretary of ECOWAS* v. *Tokunbo Lijadu Oyemade*, Suit No. ECW/CCJ/APP/01/05 (ECOWAS Court of Justice, 2006); *Executive Secretary of ECOWAS* v. *Tokunbo Lijadu Oyemade*, Suit No. ECW/CCJ/APP/04/06 (ECOWAS Court of Justice, 2006); *Djoy Bayi* v. *Federal Republic of Nigeria*, Suit No. ECW/CCJ/APP/10/06 (ECOWAS Court of Justice, 2009); *Chief Ebrimah Manneh* v. *The Gambia*, Suit No. ECW/CCJ/JUD/03/08 (ECOWAS Court of Justice, 2008); *Mme Hadijatou Mani Koraou* v. *The Republic of Niger*, Suit No. ECW/CCJ/JUD/06/08 (ECOWAS Court of Justice, 2008); and *Ernest Francis Mtingwi* v. *The SADC Secretariat*, SADC (T) Case No. 1/2007 (SADC Tribunal, 2008). For a commentary on the human rights related jurisprudence of the courts, see Ebobrah (2007); Ebobrah (2009); and Duffy (2009).

5.3.1 Mwatela *v.* East Africa Community

The EAC court's decision in *Mwatela* v. *East Africa Community*[65] was a reference under article 30 of the EAC Treaty by three members of the East African Legislative Assembly (EALA). The applicants challenged the validity of a meeting of the Sectoral Council on Legal and Judicial Affairs (hereafter, the Sectoral Council)[66] held on 13 to 16 September 2005, and the decision taken at the meeting to withdraw four private member bills that were pending before the EALA.[67] The Council of Ministers (hereafter, the Council), acting on the Sectoral Council's report and in the light of its earlier decision,[68] decided that protocols rather than legislation enacted by the EALA were more appropriate for two of the bills, and that they should accordingly be withdrawn.[69] For the remaining bills, a request was made using a Ministerial Statement for a stay of their consideration by the EALA to enable consultation with the member states. The applicants sought an order declaring that the report of the Sectoral Council upon which these decisions were made was void *ab initio*, and that all decisions, directives and actions taken under it were similarly void. The court considered three issues, namely: (i) the establishment of the Sectoral Council and its meeting; (ii) the status of the contentious bills; and (iii) the relations between the Council and the EALA as regards legislation.

The court held that the Sectoral Council had not been properly constituted from its inception, in that it comprised people not qualified under the treaty. Under the treaty, the Council was to establish sectoral councils from among its members. But the Sectoral Council at issue consisted of the partner states' Attorneys General, who were not qualified members of the Council. Consequently, the meeting and the

[65] [2007] 1 East Afr. LR 237.

[66] The council was established by the Council of Ministers from among its members under art. 14 of the EAC Treaty to deal with specific issues. The Sectoral Council on Legal and Judicial Affairs was created at a meeting of the Council of Ministers in 2001.

[67] Private member bills are allowed under art. 59 of the EAC Treaty. The bills were the East African Community Trade Negotiations Bill, the East Africa Community Budget Bill, the East African Immunities and Privilege Bill, and the Inter-University Council for East Africa Bill.

[68] In November 2004, the Council decided that policy-oriented bills, such as those with implications for the member states' sovereign interests and on the budgetary aspects of the community, ought to be submitted to the EALA by the Council under art. 14(3)(b) of the EAC Treaty as opposed to being submitted as private members bills under art. 59 of the treaty.

[69] These bills were the East African Immunities and Privilege Bill and the Inter-University Council for East Africa Bill.

decisions taken were unlawful. However, the court applied the doctrine of prospective annulment and saved the decisions, which the Sectoral Council had taken from its inception.

It was further held that a Ministerial Statement was an ineffective means of withdrawing the bills from the EALA. At the time of the statement, the bills had become the EALA's property and could be withdrawn only by a motion under the EALA's rules. Although the decision to withdraw the bills was ultimately a Council decision (in some instances, decisions of the Council bind the EALA), the court held, under the treaty, regarding matters in the Assembly's area of jurisdiction,[70] the decisions of the Council had no precedence. According to the court, 'the Assembly is a representative organ in the Community set up to enhance a people-centred co-operation' and therefore its independence should be preserved.[71] The court reaffirmed the rights of private members to introduce bills subject to limits defined in the treaty. In this instance, the character of the limitations meant that to determine whether the bills fell outside the limitations would have required the court to delve into their provisions in great detail. Given that the bills were pending before the EALA, the court deemed it unwise to undertake such an exercise for fear of encroaching on the EALA's jurisdiction.

5.3.2 Anyang' Nyong'o *v.* AG of the Republic of Kenya (I and II)

In *Peter Anyang' Nyong'o* v. *AG of the Republic of Kenya*,[72] the applicants contended that the process by which Kenya's representatives to the EALA were nominated contravened article 50 of the EAC Treaty because no elections were held to elect the representatives. They sought inter alia an interpretation of article 50 and a declaration that the Treaty for the Establishment of the East African Community (Election of Members of the Assembly) Rules, 2001 (hereafter, Kenyan election rules) applied by the Kenya National Assembly, contravened article 50 and, hence, that they should be declared void. Pending the determination of the substantive issues, they sought an injunction restraining the respondents from recognizing and inducting the representatives into office. The respondents raised preliminary objections to the court's jurisdiction. They argued that the court's jurisdiction, under article 27(1) of the treaty,

[70] EAC Treaty, arts. 14 and 16.
[71] *Mwatela* v. *East Africa Community* [2007] 1 East Afr. LR 237 at 249.
[72] [2008] 3 KLR 397. See generally van der Mei (2009).

was restricted to the interpretation and application of the treaty. It did not extend to determining questions arising from the election of EALA members. In their view, that jurisdiction was reserved under article 52(1) of the treaty for an appropriate national institution, in this instance, the Kenya National Assembly and, in cases of dispute, the High Court of Kenya. To the respondent, it was in the High Court that the applicant should have sought remedy, at least in the first instance.

The court swiftly rejected the objections. It held that the combined effect of articles 27 and 30 of the treaty was that the court had jurisdiction to determine the legality of any act, regulation, directive, decision or action of a partner state or community institution on the grounds that it infringed a provision of the treaty. Accordingly, since the applicants were challenging the validity of the Kenyan election rules in the light of the provisions of the treaty, the matter fell squarely within its jurisdiction.[73] The court granted the injunction. It reasoned that there was a prima facie case with a probability of success, and the current state of the law was such that, unless restrained from taking office, the alleged illegality was likely to continue even after a favourable decision for the applicants was made. Such a state of affairs would cause irreparable damage to the applicants, the EALA and the Community.

The substantive determination of the case came in March 2007. In *Anyang' Nyongo* v. *AG of the Republic of Kenya* (*Anyang II*),[74] the court identified three issues for determination. These were: (1) Does the complaint disclose any cause of action within the meaning of article 30 of the EAC Treaty? (2) Was an election undertaken within the meaning of article 50 of the treaty? (3) Do the Kenyan election rules comply with article 50 of the treaty? The court held that article 30 of the treaty conferred jurisdiction on it. Additionally, although article 33(2) also envisaged interpretation of treaty provisions by national courts, this jurisdiction should only be incidental to the determination of cases before them. Thus, contrary to the respondent's position, an individual could not directly refer a question of treaty interpretation to national courts. This decision is important from a relational perspective. Treaty interpretation by national courts is likely to result in varying national interpretations and thus undermine the unity of community law and its

[73] This decision has been reversed by an amendment to the treaty. The amendment provides that the court's jurisdiction to interpret the treaty under art. 27(1) 'shall not include the application of any such interpretation to jurisdiction conferred by the Treaty on organs of Partner States'.

[74] [2008] 3 KLR 397.

meaning. The court further held that article 30 created a special cause of action that did not require the claimant to show a right or interest that was infringed, damaged or suffered as a result of the matter complained of; an allegation of infringement was enough. Article 30 granted the individual the right of direct access to the court. There was no requirement to exhaust local remedies; there was no such remedy to exhaust.

Finally, the court held that elections under article 50 of the treaty should involve a voting procedure. This might be accomplished through secret ballot, show of hands or acclamation. It may also involve campaigns, primaries and/or nominations. But, ultimately, the decision to elect should be that of the national assemblies of the partner states. In this instance, the court held that the circumstances surrounding the sending of the list of Kenya's representatives was not an election within the meaning of article 50 of the treaty. The court held that the purpose of article 50 was to constitute each national assembly into an electoral college as a deliberate step to ensure the constitution of an EALA comprising the peoples' representatives. The national assemblies, as institutions of peoples' representatives, were, second to the peoples, the next best alternative for electing representatives to the EALA. To the court, such an approach to electing representatives was consistent with the fundamental principle of good governance, including adherence to the principle of democracy that underlies the treaty.[75] The court concluded that Kenya's election rules infringed article 50 of the treaty, since they did not provide that the National Assembly should elect members to the EALA. Rather, it provided that a list of nominated candidates should be submitted to the House Business Committee. The committee ensured that the requirements of article 50 were fulfilled and then tabled the names of the nominees before the National Assembly. The nominees so tabled were 'deemed elected' to the EALA. According to the court, this legal fiction circumvented the express provisions of article 50. Kenya has amended its election rules to bring them into line with the court's ruling.[76] Kenya's expeditious compliance with the decision of the court is commendable.

[75] EAC Treaty, art. 6(d).

[76] Treaty for the Establishment of the East African Community (Election of Members of the Assembly) Rules, 2007. Under the new rules, nine representatives were elected to the EALA. See Treaty for the Establishment of the East African Community (Election of Members of the Assembly) Rules, 2007: Election of Members of the East African Legislative Assembly, 30 May 2007, Kenya Government Gazette Notice No. 4873.

5.3.3 Eastern and Southern African Trade and Development Bank *v.* Ogang

In *Eastern and Southern African Trade and Development Bank* v. *Ogang*,[77] the COMESA court affirmed its role as the guardian of the limits of institutional competence under the COMESA Treaty. The respondent, an employee of the Preferential Trade Area Bank, sought, in an application, an order suspending a decision of the bank's board of directors. The bank raised a preliminary objection against the application on the grounds that the court had no jurisdiction over it. The bank was established under the 1982 Treaty, which established the Preferential Trade Area for Eastern and Southern African States, and it continued in existence under article 174 of the COMESA Treaty. To the bank, it was an autonomous institution, not an organ of COMESA, and, hence, not answerable to COMESA's laws and regulations.

The court rejected this argument. It held that under article 174 of the COMESA Treaty, the bank was one of the institutions of COMESA. The court was entrusted with the function of ensuring that the organs and institutions of COMESA adhered to law in the interpretation and application of the treaty. Accordingly, as the bank was an organ of COMESA, the court had jurisdiction over it. The court further held that article 7(4) of the COMESA Treaty, which provides that the organs of the COMESA shall perform their functions and act within the limits of the powers conferred on them by or under the treaty, would be superfluous without the superintending jurisdiction of the court or national courts.[78] The courts define and enforce the limits of those powers. It is significant that a supervisory role for national courts is envisaged by the COMESA court as a possibility, even on an issue as delicate as superintending the conduct of community organs. However, to maintain the vertical relations between community and national legal systems, this supervisory jurisdiction should be exercised with great care.

5.3.4 Olajide Afolabi *v.* Federal Republic of Nigeria

In *Olajide Afolabi* v. *Federal Republic of Nigeria*,[79] the applicant, a Nigerian businessman, was to purchase and take delivery of some goods in the Republic of Benin. He was prevented from doing so due to the closure of the Nigeria–Benin border by the Nigerian

[77] [2001] East Afr. LR 46. [78] [2001] East Afr. LR 46 at 51. [79] [2005] 52 WRN 1.

Government. He alleged that he had suffered loss as a result of the border closure. He brought an application before the ECOWAS court for declarations that the unilateral closing of the border breached articles 3(2)(d)(iii) and 4(g) of the ECOWAS Treaty, and violated the fundamental rights to freedom of movement of persons and goods guaranteed by the Treaty and the African Charter on Human and Peoples' Rights.

The respondent successfully raised a preliminary objection to the applicant's standing. The respondent argued under article 9 of the protocol on the ECOWAS court that only states can be parties before the court.[80] The court rejected counsel for the applicant's argument that it should emulate the activist judicial approach of the European Court of Justice (ECJ) and admit claims by individuals. The court reasoned that the ECJ's approach of filling gaps in the EU Treaty has attracted criticism and it 'do[es] not want to toe the same line'.[81] In this case, the court was right in declining to go down the route advocated by counsel for the applicant. The jurisdiction of a court, especially an international court, must be conferred by legislation. However, the court's dictum should be confined to the facts of the case. An important function for the community courts will be to fill the gaps in the treaties and other community laws. This function derives from their jurisdiction over the interpretation and application of the treaties. It will ill-serve the cause of economic integration in Africa if, for fear of being criticized, the courts backtrack from this role.

5.3.5 Mike Campbell *v.* Republic of Zimbabwe

Of all the cases decided in the community courts in Africa, the *Mike Campbell* litigation represents the best instance of a community court confronted with a major national policy: in this instance, Zimbabwe's controversial land-reform policy. The applicants challenged the compulsory acquisition of their agricultural lands in Zimbabwe by the respondent. The acquisitions were effected under legislation that also ousted the jurisdiction of the Zimbabwe courts to hear claims related to such acquisitions.[82] The applicants alleged that the acquisitions were inconsistent with articles 4(c) and 6(2) of the SADC Treaty. These articles

[80] This provision has been amended to give individuals standing before the ECOWAS court.

[81] *Olajide Afolabi* v. *Federal Republic of Nigeria* [2005] 52 WRN 1 at [56].

[82] Constitution of Zimbabwe (Amendment No. 17, 2005), s. 16B.

obliged member states to act in accordance with 'human rights, democracy and the rule of law', and prohibited them from discriminating against any person on grounds of 'race'.

Pending the final determination of the application, the applicants sought an order for the status quo on the lands to be preserved. After satisfying itself that this was ligation between natural and legal persons and a state,[83] it involved a question of interpretation of the treaty[84] and the Tribunal had jurisdiction to grant interim relief,[85] the Tribunal examined whether the applicants had, as required by the SADC Tribunal Protocol,[86] exhausted local remedies. It was argued by the respondent's counsel that the same matter involving the applicants was pending before the Supreme Court of Zimbabwe. The Tribunal, without providing detailed reasoning or authority, held that the issue of exhaustion of local remedies could not be raised in the present interlocutory application, in which the applicants were seeking an interim measure of protection. However, it could be and in fact was raised in the substantive case.

Prior to deciding the substantive case, the Tribunal granted more than seventy applicants the right to intervene in the proceedings. It granted them interim relief pending the substantive determination of the case.[87] The Tribunal also reported to the Summit of Heads of State and Government the respondent's failure to adhere to the interim measures granted earlier to the applicants.

In the substantive case,[88] the Tribunal identified four issues for determination. These were whether: it had jurisdiction to entertain the application; the applicants had been denied access to the Zimbabwean courts; the applicants had been discriminated against on the basis of race; and compensation was payable for the lands compulsorily acquired from the applicants.

The Tribunal held that individuals were expected to exhaust local remedies before instituting action at the Tribunal. However, where municipal law did not offer any remedy, or the remedy that was

[83] SADC Tribunal Protocol, art. 15(1). The tribunal has no jurisdiction in action between natural and legal persons. *Nixon Chirinda* v. *Mike Campbell (Pvt) Ltd*, SADC (T) Case No. 09/08 (SADC Tribunal, 2008); and *Albert Fungai Mutize* v. *Mike Campbell (Pvt) Ltd*, SADC (T) Case No. 8/08 (SADC Tribunal, 2008).

[84] Ibid., art. 14. [85] Ibid., art. 28. [86] Ibid., art. 15(2).

[87] *Gideon Stephanus Theron* v. *The Republic of Zimbabwe*, SADC (T) Case No. 2/08; 3/08; 4/08; 6/08 (SADC Tribunal, 2008).

[88] *Mike Campbell (Pvt) Ltd* v. *The Republic of Zimbabwe*, SADC (T) Case No. 2/2007 (SADC Tribunal, 2008).

offered was ineffective, an individual was not required to exhaust local remedies. In the instant case, the court observed that Amendment No. 17 ousted the jurisdiction of the Zimbabwean courts – a position previously affirmed by the Zimbabwean Supreme Court.[89] Whether the substantive issues in the application fell within the subject-matter jurisdiction of the Tribunal, it was held that, given the terms of article 4(c) of the SADC Treaty, the Tribunal had jurisdiction in respect of any dispute concerning human rights, democracy and the rule of law, which were the very issues raised in the application. After a detailed examination of the law – national and international – and the facts, the Tribunal held that the applicants had established that they were deprived of their lands without the right of access to the courts and the right to a fair hearing. To the Tribunal, these amounted to breaches of article 4(c) of the SADC Treaty. The Tribunal also held that although Amendment 17 did not explicitly refer to 'white' farmers, its implementation affected white farmers only and consequently constituted indirect discrimination. To the Tribunal, the respondent had discriminated against the applicants on the basis of race and, accordingly, violated its obligation under article 6(2) of the SADC Treaty. It was also held that, in accordance with international law, fair compensation was due and payable to the applicants by the respondent – the respondent argued that it should be paid by the United Kingdom, the former colonizing power – in respect of the expropriated lands.

The Tribunal directed the respondent to take all necessary measures to protect the possession, occupation and ownership of the applicants' lands, and to take all appropriate measures to ensure that no action is taken, pursuant to Amendment 17, to evict from, or interfere with, the peaceful residence on and of those farms by the applicants. It also directed the respondent to pay fair compensation to three of the applicants. In Zimbabwe, political and judicial reactions to the decision have been hostile and unfavourable; it was condemned by the executive, including the President and Attorney General, and the High Court declined to enforce it.[90] In two separate rulings – the second given after non-compliance with the first – the Tribunal, in accordance

[89] *Mike Campbell (Pvt) Ltd* v. *Minister of National Security Responsible for Land, Land Reform and Resettlement*, Judgment No. SC 49/07 (Zimbabwe Supreme Court, 2008).

[90] *Gramara (Pvt) Ltd* v. *Government of the Republic of Zimbabwe*, HC 33/09 (Zimbabwe, High Court, 2010).

with article 32(5) of the SADC Treaty, reported its findings of non-compliance to the Summit for it to take 'appropriate action'.[91] To date, no such action has been taken.

5.4 Community courts' jurisprudence and economic integration

The jurisprudence of the community courts, which is reflected in their judgments, represents important first steps as they fulfil their mandates and define their roles in Africa's economic integration processes.[92] It is a novel engagement for them; there are no precedents in Africa for their roles. Comparatively, the African community courts are not alone in dealing with the challenges thrown at them by economic integration.[93] Happily, they have the rich experiences of other courts working on issues of regional and international economic law, such as the ECJ, WTO panels and Appellate Body, to draw on. However, they should always be mindful of their own unique regional contexts.

For any court, its initial jurisprudence sets the stage or tone for its future work, and provides a glimpse into its approaches, goals and challenges. The publications of its officers provide additional insight, but, so far, unlike judges of other international courts, the African judges have largely not taken advantage of publishing in books and journals their vision of the communities and their roles. As the first 'active' community courts in Africa operating on economic integration issues, their jurisprudence can also provide a source of comparative law for the African Court of Justice. It is in this light that the courts' jurisprudence is important. They address difficult, sometimes politically sensitive, issues in Africa's economic integration processes, but they still leave unanswered potentially troubling questions.

5.4.1 *Role of individuals*

Individuals have a crucial role to play in economic integration. Indeed, there can be no economic community or successful regional trade without involving them. They are the vessels through which trade is

[91] *William Michael Campbell* v. *The Republic of Zimbabwe*, Case No. SADC (T) 03/2009 (SADC Tribunal, 2009); and *Fick* v. *The Republic of Zimbabwe*, Case No. SADC (T) 01/2010 (SADC Tribunal, 2010).

[92] Jackson (2003–4).

[93] *Trinidad Cement Ltd* v. *The Co-operative Republic of Guyana* [2008] CCJ 1 (OJ) at [1]–[2]; and O'Brien (2009).

pursued and economic integration enhanced. As liberal international relations theorists suggest, individuals influence states' choices, and their voices and actions can condition the extent to which a state becomes actively involved in economic integration.[94] They are the human medium that links the multiple legal systems operating in the context of economic integration. An economic integration process pursued by politicians, without their active involvement, suffers from inertia. It becomes an institutional edifice without meaningful impact on their lives, save, perhaps, those employed by community institutions. A key to enhancing individuals' roles in economic integration is to grant them direct or indirect access to community institutions, including the courts.

Historically, individuals have not been granted access to community courts under Africa's economic integration treaties. They have also seldom relied on community law before national courts. Generally, Africa's early attempts at economic integration did not make provision for judicial institutions,[95] or the tribunals provided were never established.[96] As noted above, the recent wave of economic integration treaties, including the COMESA, ECOWAS, EAC and SADC treaties, remedy this defect. There is also an emerging body of national cases, albeit mainly in East and Southern Africa, in which individuals have actively relied on community law or national courts have made use of community law.

The wisdom of providing for individual access is revealed in the community courts' judgments. Almost all of their judgments resulted from actions instituted by individuals alleging breaches of community law. Only one of the cases examined involved interstate litigation. In *Eritrea* v. *Ethiopia*,[97] Ethiopia sought from the Government of Eritrea the release of goods belonging to Ethiopians, which had been detained at the Eritrean Ports of Assab and Massawa, and damages arising from the detention. Ethiopia argued that the detention was contrary to the provisions of the COMESA Treaty, but the case was settled out of court.

[94] Moravcsik (1997).
[95] ECOWAS Treaty 1975; Treaty Establishing a Central African Economic and Customs Union, 8 December 1964, 4 ILM 699; and Charter of the Organization of African Unity, 25 May 1963, 2 ILM 766.
[96] Treaty for East African Cooperation, 6 June 1963, 6 ILM 932; and Treaty for the Establishment of the Preferential Trade Area for Eastern and South African States, 21 December 1981, 21 ILM 479.
[97] [1999] LawAfr. LR 6.

Another case involved inter-institutional litigation.[98] Indeed, counsel's arguments in some of the cases indicated that, left to the affected governments, the actions would not have been instituted. The Attorney General of Kenya's argument that the issues involved in the *Anyang* cases were of public interest and, therefore, should have been instituted by the Attorney General as guardian of the public interest is an instance of this. The Attorney General's discretion to institute actions is seldom reviewable. Accordingly, a great blow would have been dealt to economic integration in East Africa had this argument prevailed. The community courts' judgments represent a triumph for individual rights in Africa's economic integration, and a vindication of the treaty drafters' wisdom.

Individual access to community courts affects inter-institutional relations, the balance of power within communities and community–state legal relations. It also provides an avenue through which a community court can effect normative change in member states. The combination of a proactive court with individuals willing to enforce rights inuring to them under community law is a fundamental challenge to executive and legislative powers. In theory, this combination gives a court the final word. It makes it a powerful 'political' actor in the sense that, although absent from the decision-making table, its jurisprudence exerts a subtle influence on outcomes. States and community institutions bargain in the shadow of the court's jurisprudence. In Africa's economic integration processes, this judicial power could be an important complement to the work of the communities' secretariats, which have been relegated to performing mainly administrative functions with few enforcement powers. In other words, the community courts could provide a counterbalance to executive domination of the economic integration processes and complement the weak (mainly advisory) legislative organs. They could also complement the minimal enforcement powers of the administrative branches. To be able to do this, their independence should be guaranteed in community law, and respected in practice by other community institutions and the member states.

The community courts' judgments reflect the above prospects. The EAC court has upheld individual right of action, but has not clearly articulated any limitations on such a right. This shifts the balance of power within the EAC heavily in the court's favour. As long as individuals are prepared to litigate, member states and other community

[98] *Parliament of ECOWAS* v. *Council of Ministers*, Suit No. ECW/CCJ/APP/03/05 (ECOWAS Court of Justice, 2005).

institutions will no longer have the final say – the court will. The fact that under article 30 of the EAC Treaty, as confirmed by the court, individuals do not have to exhaust local remedies, or show any personal interest affected by the challenged action,[99] makes for a frightening prospect for member states and other community institutions. Quite unsurprisingly, the political reaction to this judgment – which came in the form of amendments to the treaty – was swift and, arguably, aimed in part at curtailing the court's powers. The ECOWAS court has also held that exhaustion of local remedies has no relationship to the procedures for accessing it.[100] By holding in *Anyang II* that Kenya's election rules did not comply with EAC Treaty provisions, the EAC court provided the foundation for developing a new national rule, or regime, for elections in Kenya. Through the judgment, the court became a messenger calling for electoral law reform within Kenya's legal systems. As noted above, Kenya subsequently amended its legislation to bring it in line with the judgment.

A worrying aspect of the EAC court's jurisprudence, as far as individual access is concerned, relates to standing. The extremely liberal standing rules could pose fundamental challenges for the court. It may potentially be overwhelmed by cases in a manner that will tax its administrative capabilities. The two-month limitation period, imposed under article 30(2) of the EAC Treaty on individual actions that seek to challenge the legality of any Act, regulation, directive, decision or action of a member state or an institution of the Community – evidence of states' unease with individual actions – may help to reduce the court's caseload. Additionally, where individuals bypass national courts and run to the EAC court to invoke article 30, it is likely to antagonize national courts, which should be its close allies. Tensions between national and community courts may impact negatively on community–state relations. Admittedly, in the initial stages of integration, liberal standing for individuals should be encouraged to ensure people's involvement in the integration processes and for the courts also to be engaged.

Already, the possibility of tension between national and community courts is reflected in some cases. But, so far, the latter have been careful not to collide with the former. The COMESA court resisted a potential source of tension when it rejected an application that sought to reverse a

[99] Compare *Odafe Oserada* v. *ECOWAS Council of Ministers*, Judgment No. ECW/CCJ/JUD/01/08 (ECOWAS Court of Justice, 2008).

[100] *Etim Moses Essien* v. *Republic of Gambia*, Case No. ECW/CCJ/APP/05/07 (ECOWAS Court of Justice, 2007) at 13.

decision of the Kenya Court of Appeal.[101] In *Alhaji Hammani Tidjani* v. *Federal Republic of Nigeria*,[102] the ECOWAS court held that it had no power to act as an appeal court for decisions of national courts, nor would it embark on such a venture in breach of judicial comity. Also, in an action seeking a declaration that two persons were improperly elected to the EALA, and that they were not members of Tanzania's parliament, the EAC court held that the matter was within the remit of the High Court of Tanzania.[103] In *Jerry Ugokwe*,[104] the ECOWAS court declined jurisdiction in a Nigeria electoral dispute that had already been judicially determined by the Nigerian Court of Appeal.

Given the conditions for individual standing in the community courts, they will increasingly be faced with cases that require great sensitivity to the jurisdiction of national courts. In instances of potential tension, the community courts may have to show deference to national courts, with a view to strengthening their relations with them. This is especially important in these initial stages of the development of the community courts. National courts should be their allies, not competitors. However, the community courts should always be mindful of their duty as guardians of the community treaties and laws.

It is important for the EAC court (and for the COMESA, ECOWAS and SADC courts in dealing with standing) to define the limits of article 30 in a manner that balances the competing interests of member states, national courts, individuals, the court and the ultimate goals of the community. This is a delicate task, for which the comparative experiences of other international courts will be useful. The legitimacy of the community courts' role will depend on the political sensitivity they show in the face of the multiple, and often conflicting, interests of the member states, national institutions, communities, community institutions and individuals.

The majority of the cases decided to date have involved natural persons. What has been absent, both at national and community levels, are actions instituted by legal persons (for example, companies) and interest groups to champion the cause of economic integration.[105] In 2009, in the first

[101] *Standard Chartered Financial Services, A.D. Gregory and COMESA. Cahill* v. *Court of Appeal for the Republic of Kenya*, Reference No. 4/2002 (COMESA Court of Justice, 2002).

[102] Suit No. ECW/CCJ/APP/01/06 (ECOWAS Court of Justice, 2007) at 14.

[103] *Christopher Mtikila* v. *AG of the United Republic of Tanzania*, Application No. 8 of 2007 (East African Court of Justice, 2007).

[104] *Jerry Ugokwe* v. *The Federal Republic of Nigeria*, Case No. ECW/CCJ/APP/02/05 (ECOWAS Court of Justice, 2005).

[105] But see *East African Law Society* v. *AG of the Republic of Kenya* [2007] 1 East Afr. LR 5; and *East African Law Society* v. *AG of Kenya* [2008] 1 East Afr. LR 95.

action of its kind within the EAC, a company unsuccessfully brought an application before the EAC court against the Kenya Ports Authority for damages for losses incurred by the applicant as a result of the respondent's delay in clearing the applicant's containers of fruit juices and mineral water. The court dismissed the application for lack of jurisdiction. It reasoned that the Kenya Ports Authority was neither a member of the EAC nor one of its institutions.[106]

Generally, interest groups' participation in and influence on Africa's economic integration has been minimal,[107] especially when it comes to using litigation to promote economic integration. Happily, the community treaties define 'person' as any natural or legal person, and also envisage a role for civil society. As already noted, in litigating before the EAC court, a person does not have to show personal interest affected by an alleged breach of the treaty. This opens up the prospect that, under article 30 of the EAC Treaty, legal persons who are resident in the EAC can bring actions directly before the EAC court without facing very restrictive standing rules. The huge cost of international litigation may prevent natural persons from directly litigating before the community courts. However, so far, there has been no study suggesting that this is the case. Legal persons, especially companies and businesses, can benefit greatly from the community courts' jurisprudence and the realization of the goals of economic integration in the form of improved market access, a favourable trade environment and expanded investment opportunities. It is suggested that they should become more actively involved in the economic integration processes, including making use of the standing granted to them by the community treaties. They should challenge national measures that hinder intra-community trade before the community courts.

Apart from direct litigation, another avenue for legal persons and interest groups' participation is through the submission of *amicus curiae* briefs. Through these briefs, they can shape the community courts' jurisprudence. In this regard, it is significant that the East African Law Society appeared as *amicus curiae* in major cases before the EAC court, including *Anyang* and the *Request for Advisory Opinion.* Indeed, article 40 of the EAC Treaty allows, with the leave of the court, a resident of a member state to intervene in a case before the court. However, the

[106] *Modern Holdings (EA) Ltd* v. *Kenya Ports Authority*, Reference No. 1 of 2008 (East African Court of Justice, 2009).

[107] Deen-Swarray and Schade (2006).

submission of an intervening party should be limited to evidence supporting or opposing the arguments of a party to the case. Regrettably, law societies in the other communities have not taken advantage of this opportunity to influence the course of economic integration within the respective sub-regions.

The above discussion, while extolling the virtues of litigation as a means of pushing forward economic integration through law, does not deny the importance of using existing political channels effectively, such as negotiating with or lobbying national governments and the communities for policies conducive to business and regional trade. It is the combination of reliance on litigation and the political channels that will lead to strong and effective communities.

The minimal participation of interest groups in Africa's economic integration processes is troubling. They have devoted considerable attention to human rights issues and litigation in Africa, but they have spent little time on the economic integration agenda. In part, this is so because, while the importance of human rights and good governance have been 'sold' to domestic and foreign donors and attract huge funding for interest groups, Africa's economic integration has not been similarly marketed. Nor does economic integration appear to be a priority for donor funds. A recent audit adjudged the EU's support for regional integration in East and West Africa as 'only partially effective'.[108]

Even where interest groups have paid attention to economic integration issues, they have emphasized mainly the human rights dimensions. Their involvement in advocating an amendment to the protocol of the ECOWAS court to allow for individual standing was motivated largely by a desire to litigate, in the court, states' violations of human rights. A similar movement is underway to extend the EAC court's jurisdiction to cover human rights issues. The vigour and passion with which interest groups have championed the human rights cause in Africa should equally be made available to that of economic integration. The links between economic development and human rights are too obvious to merit discussing. Indeed, there is a human right to development. Successful economic integration and the concomitant prosperity it brings may be the panacea to many of Africa's human rights ills.

[108] European Court of Auditors (2010), p. 33.

5.4.2 Role of national courts

Like individuals, national courts have a crucial role to play in Africa's economic integration.[109] They provide an institutional medium through which community norms can be translated into domestic benefits for individuals. They are an essential complement to the communities' law enforcement mechanisms. Historically, national courts' role in economic integration has not been recognized in Africa's economic integration treaties. At present, this is being remedied. As noted above, the COMESA, ECOWAS, EAC and SADC treaties envisage a role for national courts. They can seek preliminary rulings from the community courts on questions of interpretation or application of the treaties, or the validity of community regulations, directives or decisions. To date, no national court has made use of the preliminary rulings procedure. However, the fact that the procedure exists represents a remarkable shift in approach to economic integration in Africa.

Bebr has identified some factors in the European context that made national courts initially reluctant to seek preliminary rulings.[110] They included uncertainty as to the legal nature of the ECJ, especially regarding its place in the hierarchy of national judicial structures, the novelty of the procedure, and the lack of a national equivalent. These reasons are equally relevant in Africa. In the African context, it should be added that there is an absence of a substantial volume of community laws, and a lack of legislation implementing those laws within member states. Procedures akin to preliminary reference exist in some African states, especially on issues of constitutional interpretation.[111] However, the procedure of reference to a court outside the ordinary national judicial structure is unknown. The power of a court to refer a matter to another court – national, regional or international – for decision is a question of jurisdiction; it must be expressly provided for by statute. Accordingly, for the preliminary reference procedure enshrined in the treaties to work, the jurisdiction of national courts should be statutorily extended to encompass it. So far, I am unaware of any state that has done this. This implies that the national legal infrastructure for the community-decreed procedure to 'take off' is non-existent.

It is inevitable that, as part of exercising jurisdiction, national courts may have to address issues that engage community law. As the body of

[109] See generally Hilf (1997). [110] Bebr (1977), pp. 241–3.

[111] See, e.g. Constitution of the Republic of Ghana, 1992, art. 130(2); and Constitution of the Republic of Sierra Leone, 1991, art. 124(2).

community law expands and individuals become more aware of it, people will seek to rely on it before national courts and these issues will increase. There may be parallels between this anticipated development and the current resolve of individuals to invoke international human rights norms in domestic claims. Individuals will lay claim to and enforce a law, whatever its source, which confers a personal advantage on them as long as they are aware of it and the legal system allows effect to be given to that law.

Indeed, there are, currently, emerging cases in which individuals have relied, sometimes unsuccessfully, on community law before national courts. In *Movement for Democratic Change* v. *President of the Republic of Zimbabwe*,[112] the applicant sought a declaration that Zimbabwe's Electoral Commission Act and the Electoral Act did not incorporate sections of the SADC Principles and Guidelines adopted in Mauritius in 2004. Furthermore, sections of the Public Order and Security Act, Access to Information and Protection of Privacy Act and Broadcasting Act were incompatible with the provisions of the SADC Principles and Guidelines. In dismissing the application, the court held that the applicant appeared to have elevated the SADC Principles and Guidelines to law and placed that law in a position superior to domestic law. To the court, there was no legal principle that made a regional instrument in the nature of the SADC Principles and Guidelines binding on member states. They were model rules with no binding force. In addition, the Principles and Guidelines had not been incorporated into domestic law and were, accordingly, not enforceable by the court. To the court, the Principles and Guidelines were not a source of domestic law. Although these pronouncements are legally correct, they are nonetheless remarkable. Earlier in the judgment, the court found that subsequent to and following the summit at which the principles were adopted and signed by the Zimbabwean Government, the government initiated, and piloted through Parliament, two specific pieces of legislation aimed at regulating the conduct of elections in Zimbabwe in accordance with the Principles and Guidelines. These were the Zimbabwe Electoral Commission Act and the Electoral Act, the very legislation at issue in the case. The case demonstrates the importance of national laws and institutions for the effective implementation of community law; it is not enough to adopt community law if national legal systems have not been conditioned for its reception.

[112] HC 1291/05 (Zimbabwe High Court, 2007).

In the Kenyan case of *Republic* v. *Kenya Revenue Authority, ex parte Aberdare Freight Services Ltd*,[113] the applicant argued that the respondent's decision to detain its sugar consignment was illegal and contrary to the COMESA Free Trade Area Rules and COMESA Treaty, to which Kenya is party. The consignment had been detained with a view to imposing duties that the applicant wanted to avoid. The court had to determine whether section 27 of Kenya's Sugar Act, No. 10/2001, which vested power in the Kenya Sugar Board to control imports in order to safeguard national interests concerning the importation of sugar, was consistent with the COMESA Treaty. The court held that the treaty applied to the quota that had been imposed on the applicant's import. It considered the relevant treaty provisions, namely articles 3(a), 45, 49(1) and (2) and 61 and held that the Sugar Act did not contravene them. The court reasoned that the measures taken by the respondent were an articulation of the national interest in the allocation of quota for sugar imports, and were safeguards aimed at protecting local industry. In the court's opinion, such measures did not violate the COMESA Treaty.[114]

The Ugandan case of *Shah* v. *Manurama Ltd*[115] also illustrates concretely the instrumental role that national courts can play in securing the benefits of community law for individuals and, at the same time, act as a medium through which community law influences national legal systems. In *Shah*, the defendant brought an application seeking an order requiring the plaintiff to pay security for the defendant's costs. The plaintiff was a resident in Kenya, and thus outside of the jurisdiction of the Uganda High Court. The defendant argued that the plaintiff was resident abroad and this was 'a *prima facie* ground for ordering payment of costs'.[116] The defendant relied on well-established domestic common law principles to support this claim. In reply, the plaintiff argued that, given the re-establishment of the EAC and the legal regime it had created, the question of residence, for the purpose of ordering security for costs, should be re-examined.[117] The court denied the application. It held that in East Africa, 'there can no longer be an automatic and inflexible presumption for the courts to order payment of security for costs with regard to a plaintiff who is a resident in the East African Community'.[118] The court stated that the establishment of the EAC 'beg[ged] for a fresh re-evaluation of our judicial thinking' as regards

113 [2004] 2 KLR 530 at 539–40. 114 Ibid., at 543. 115 [2003] 1 East Afr. LR 294.
116 Ibid., at 296. 117 Ibid. 118 Ibid., at 298.

the law requiring plaintiffs to pay security for costs.[119] Among the factors that influenced the court in its decision were the following:

- All three countries – Uganda, Kenya and Tanzania – are partner states in the EAC.
- The EAC Treaty (like the European Community Treaty) seeks to establish a customs union, common market and monetary union – as integral pillars of the community – and, ultimately, a political union among the partner states. In particular, the EAC Treaty makes express provision for the unification and harmonization of the laws of the partner states, including the 'standardization of the judgments of courts within the community' (article 126) and establishment of a common bar (cross-border legal practice).
- The underlying objective of undertaking all of the initiatives described above – and many more not discussed in this ruling – are stated in article 5 of the EAC Treaty as being the need to develop policies and programmes aimed at widening and deepening cooperation among the partner states in political, economic, social and cultural fields, research and technology, defence, security and legal and judicial affairs, for their mutual benefit.
- Article 104 of the EAC Treaty provides for the free movement of persons, labour, services, and the right of establishment and residence. The partner states are under an obligation to ensure the enjoyment of these rights by their citizens within the community. In this regard, the court is mindful of the fact that the East African Community Treaty has the force of law in each partner state (article 8(2)(b)), and that this treaty law has precedence over national law (article 8(5)).[120]

This case demonstrates an appreciation of the importance of community law and its impact on national law. It shows how national courts can become a medium for giving effect to community law and the community's objectives.[121] The case also provides a refreshing example of how individuals can, domestically, enforce their right to the benefits of community law. The existence and objectives of the communities elicit a re-evaluation of national judicial thinking with regard to matters in

[119] Ibid., at 297. [120] Ibid., at 298.

[121] The Kenyan case of *Healthwise Pharmaceuticals Ltd* v. *Smithkline Beecham Consumer Healthcare Ltd* [2001] LawAfr. LR 1279 adopted a different approach. In *Healthwise*, the Kenyan court rejected the applicant's argument that it was a resident of the EAC and therefore the defendant would have no difficulties in recovering any costs that may be awarded in the suit.

which community law and community objectives may be involved. *Shah* shows that even in the absence of substantive community law on an issue, national courts can draw on a community's goals and broad principles and advance them through their judgments. In cases where community issues are engaged, national courts should interpret statutes in light of community principles and goals. This may entail interpreting domestic law to promote, rather than undermine, community goals, affording remedies that enhance or facilitate rights envisaged by community objectives, such as the free movement of persons, goods and services and refraining from actions that may hinder the community's objectives.

The reliance on community law within member states by individuals is a welcome development. Admittedly, the response of national courts has been varied and, indeed, sometimes unfavourable. Nevertheless, it is important that this development is encouraged with a view to strengthening economic integration in Africa through the integration of community law into member states' laws. National courts are forums through which individuals can seek the benefits of integration and community laws. The reliance on community law in states offers the prospect of a preliminary reference to the community courts. The ability of the community courts to forge links with national courts will be essential to the former's development. The cases also demonstrate a level of awareness of the potentially beneficial impact of community law. However, one cannot be over-enthusiastic about their numbers. They are relatively few compared with the number of years economic integration has been going on in Africa, and the significant (albeit still relatively small) volume of laws the communities have produced. These laws cover a wide range of issues, including the free movement of persons, goods and enterprises. It is troubling that after years of economic integration, many more of the benefits it brings and the challenges it poses have not found their way into national courts. The potential cost of litigation, a lack of awareness of the economic integration processes and the rights existing as a result, low intra-African trade, the fact that lawyers have neither integrated community law into their practice nor developed it as a specialized area of practice, and a perceived absence of a litigation culture in Africa may collectively account for this. In addition, member states have not provided the legal infrastructure necessary for individuals to rely on and give legal effect to community laws.

In this regard, and as discussed in Chapter 7, there are formidable constraints on individuals' reliance on community law before African national courts. The constraints can affect the participation of both individuals and national courts in the economic integration processes. At the community level, the constraints take the form of the absence of direct effect and direct applicability provisions in the community treaties. At the national level, they take the form of inimical constitutional provisions and unfavourable judicial precedents. If proper community–state relations are to exist, and domestic effect is given to community law, it will demand a rethink of the existing constitutional laws and jurisprudence of national courts.

An interesting aspect of the community courts' judgments is the fair amount of jurisprudential borrowing and judicial dialogue between community and national courts. The ECOWAS court has held that it can rely on decisions from 'member states' courts and regional courts when deciding cases.[122] The community courts' judgments contain references to numerous decisions of national courts. This provides another avenue for forging mutually beneficial reciprocal relations. The reputation of a court depends in part on the reach of its jurisprudence and the respect accorded to it by other courts. As community courts use national courts' decisions, the latter's positions within their national legal systems are enhanced through the community affirmation of the quality of their jurisprudence. National courts may reciprocate by drawing on the jurisprudence of the community courts and giving effect to their judgments. However, it is imperative that jurisprudential borrowing is done with circumspection. Where it is possible, community courts should draw on cases from all member states and not only a few. For example, judgments of the ECOWAS court contain copious references to decisions of Nigerian courts, but little or nothing from courts of other member states. Unless jurisprudential borrowing is approached with care, the community courts risk alienating some national courts – and being perceived as extensions of other member states' courts. The fact that judges of the community courts are drawn from member states, and must be persons who fulfil the conditions required in their own countries to hold high judicial office, may facilitate judicial dialogue and jurisprudential borrowing between community and national courts.

The community courts have also found useful the jurisprudence of other more experienced international and regional courts outside Africa. Given the novelty of the mandate entrusted to them, it is right that they

[122] *Executive Secretary of ECOWAS* v. *Tokunbo Lijadu Oyemade*, Suit No. ECW/CCJ/APP/01/05 (ECOWAS Court of Justice, 2006) at [3.03].

seek the benefit of the decades-long experiences of these courts. The jurisprudence of the ECJ has been a fertile source of persuasive authority for the community courts. In *Muleya* v. *Common Market for Eastern and Southern Africa*,[123] Justice Ogoola sought guidance from 'the rich jurisprudence' of the ECJ on an ambiguous point on pleadings. He noted that decisions of the ECJ did not bind the COMESA court, but are nonetheless of 'enormous persuasive value'.[124] With its rich experience on issues of economic integration, the jurisprudence of the ECJ can be highly relevant in the settlement of disputes before the community courts.

Regrettably, it appears that the community courts have been unaware of each other's jurisprudence or, at least, have not been borrowing from each other's jurisprudence.[125] Their judgments do not contain references to decisions of other African community courts, or legal developments or laws in other communities. This is unfortunate. Attention to each other's judgments would have enriched some of the judgments, even if it might not have changed their outcome. In *Afolabi*,[126] the ECOWAS court could have used other African economic integration treaties to demonstrate how ECOWAS stood alone on the question of individual access to community courts, and how, given that the communities were the building blocks of the AEC, such an isolationist stance was unacceptable. Indeed, since the communities are building blocks of the AEC, one expects judicial dialogue among their courts to be an important part of 'building' the AEC. Furthermore, the fact that there are considerable similarities across the communities' constitutive treaties and objectives should encourage more dialogue. As Mistry has observed, 'it appears as if the drafting of all these arrangements across Africa was done from the same template'.[127] At present, the difficulty of accessing each other's judgments owing to the absence of systematic law reporting may account for the lack of judicial dialogue among the community courts. It is suggested that jurisprudential borrowing among them should be encouraged to facilitate the gradual development of a continental jurisprudence on economic integration.

This can be done by facilitating access to their judgments and fostering regular interactions between their officers. It is recommended that each court should approach councils for law reporting in member states about officially publishing judgments. Publication of the judgments

[123] [2003] 1 East Afr. LR 173. [124] Ibid., at 175.
[125] Miller (2002); and Pirker (2011).
[126] *Olajide Afolabi* v. *Federal Republic of Nigeria* [2005] 52 WRN 1.
[127] Mistry (2000), pp. 564–5.

should be considered a public good, aimed at promoting economic integration in Africa and enhancing the effectiveness of the courts. Publication of judgments extends the international and domestic visibility of the community courts. With limited access to judgments, it is little wonder that some writers perceive the courts as existing 'mostly on paper'.[128] Kenya's National Council for Law Reporting has published a judgments of the EAC court. It would also be possible for an academic institution to take up this task on a continental scale. It is unlikely that, at this stage, and given the volume of cases, a law report devoted solely to the community courts' judgments will be commercially viable such that it can attract a private commercial publisher. A continental jurisprudence on economic integration will immensely benefit Africa.

5.4.3 *Role of public international law*

Regional economic integration processes operate within the context of an overarching international legal system. The foundation of regional economic integration processes and the source of their validity are in international law. It is therefore not surprising that international law is often deployed in the settlement of disputes by judicial institutions working in the field of international economic law; a field of learning, which, although epistemologically distinct, still maintains its international law foundations. The WTO's Appellate Body has held that the WTO agreements cannot be read in clinical isolation from public international law.[129] Reliance on international law in adjudication before the WTO panels and Appellate Body has been contentious. However, it is generally recognized that it is beneficial.[130] Within the EU, the interaction between EU law and international law remains a source of controversy in the jurisprudence of the ECJ.[131] When a community court relies on international law, either as a persuasive authority or as the legal basis of its decision, it makes the community and international legal systems interact.

As noted above, of the community treaties under review, only the ECOWAS Treaty and the SADC Tribunal Protocol make a direct

[128] Alter (2008b), p. 57.

[129] *United States – Standards for Reformulated and Conventional Gasoline* (1996), WTO Doc. WT/DS2/AB/R at 17 (Appellate Body Report).

[130] McMahon and Young (2007); Hu (2004); and Cameron and Gray (2001).

[131] de Búrca (2010).

reference to international law as a source of law for the court.[132] And one of the principal qualifications for appointment to the ECOWAS court is to be a jurisconsult of recognized competence in international law. It was suggested that this offers a greater prospect that international law would be brought to bear on the court's decisions. The judgments of the ECOWAS court, with their constant reference to the decisions of the international courts, provide evidence that this may be true. Unlike the ECOWAS Treaty, there is only one reference to international law in the EAC Treaty. It is in the preamble, and provides that the countries resolve to adhere to the principles of international law governing relationships between sovereign states. Notwithstanding this absence of an express reference to international law as a source of law, both applicants and respondents in the *Anyang* case relied on it in their arguments, and so did the court in its judgment. Indeed, a recent judgment of the EAC court on the consistency of amendments to the treaty with the procedures for amendment laid down in the treaty reveals, once again, the court's heavy reliance on international law.[133]

To date, reliance on international law by the community courts appears uncontested. However, with time, more fundamental questions as to the relations between international law, international law commitments of member states and the community treaties will become issues for determination. One problematic issue will be conflicts between the obligations of member states under the community treaties and their obligations under the WTO agreements or other trade agreements. Admittedly, a state may not invoke its internal law as justification for the non-fulfilment of its international treaty obligation.[134] However, it is arguable whether it can invoke before a community court its international obligations as an excuse for the non-fulfilment of its regional treaty obligations or, before an international court, its regional obligations as a justification for not fulfilling its international obligations.[135] Regarding WTO law, the response to this question before a community court will, in part, depend on the extent to which WTO law will be considered to be an applicable

[132] See also Protocol on the Establishment of the East African Customs Union, art. 39(1)(f), which provides that the customs law of the community shall consist of 'relevant principles of international law'.

[133] *East African Law Society* v. *AG of Kenya* [2008] 1 East Afr. LR 95.

[134] Vienna Convention on the Law of Treaties, 23 May 1969, 1155 UNTS 331, Art. 27.

[135] *Brazil – Measures Affecting the Importation of Retreaded Tyres* (2007), WT/DS332/AB/R at [213]–[234] (Appellate Body Report).

law in disputes before the community courts. No such issue has arisen before the community courts in Africa, but in some national courts the relevance of WTO law has become evident.[136]

The present reliance on international law by the community courts has not been contested. This is in part because international law has been invoked mainly as a guide to interpretation, and not as the direct foundation of the community courts' decisions. However, it is still important to caution against unthinking invocation of international law in the interpretation of the community treaties. An instance of this is the EAC court's ruling in *Anyang II* that the EAC Treaty did not provide an explicit solution to the issue of conflicts between community treaty provisions and national laws.[137] This ruling was given without regard to the clear provisions of article 8(4) of the treaty, which provides that 'community organs, institutions and laws shall take precedence over similar national ones on matters pertaining to the implementation of this Treaty'. This provision obviously implies that, in cases of such conflicts, community law should prevail over national law. Thus, contrary to the court's suggestion, the solution did not lie in a basic principle of international law, or the persuasive jurisprudence of the ECJ. The solution lay in article 8(4) of the EAC Treaty! The fact that the court glossed over this important provision is particularly troubling, given that the article appears to have been introduced[138] as a direct reaction to previous judicial decisions, such as *Okunda* v. *Republic*,[139] which rejected the subordination of national law to community law. The EAC court and, indeed, the national courts within the EAC must recognize the revolutionary nature of this supremacy provision, and use it to strengthen community law.

Another issue the community courts will ultimately have to address is the problem of overlapping jurisdictions among themselves and, internationally, with the WTO dispute-settlement bodies or other dispute-settlement systems in which member states are parties. Multiple-state membership of communities is a key feature of Africa's economic integration processes. Countries are often members of more than one community in addition to being members of the WTO. For example,

136 *Progress Office Machines* v. *South African Revenue Services* 2008 (2) SA 13; and *International Trade Administration Commission* v. *SCAW South Africa (Pty) Ltd* [2010] ZACC 6.

137 *Peter Anyang' Nyong'o* v. *AG of the Republic of Kenya* [2008] 3 KLR 397.

138 No such provision existed in its predecessor, the Treaty for East African Cooperation, 6 June 1967, 6 ILM 932.

139 [1970] East Afr. LR 453; and [1970] East Afr. LR 457.

Burundi, Kenya, Uganda and Rwanda, all members of the EAC, are also members of COMESA and the WTO. What happens if, in a hypothetical scenario, Kenya sues Uganda before the EAC court, Uganda sues Kenya before the COMESA court, and Egypt petitions for a WTO panel to be set up over what is, essentially, the same dispute? Currently, and unlike other agreements outside Africa,[140] there are no community treaty provisions for resolving the issue of conflicting jurisdictions and forum shopping. As will be discussed in Chapter 8, in the absence of such provisions, the community courts will have to work out doctrines and rules to regulate the issue of conflicting jurisdictions.

5.4.4 *Sovereignty and inter-institutional relational problems*

In the formative stages of the development of an international organization, its institutions try to define their roles within it and protect their prerogatives. Accordingly, inter-institutional problems are prominent at these formative stages: what are the competences of the various institutions; what are the limits of those competences; which institution monitors the boundaries, and so on. A classic illustration of this problem is the case of *Parliament of ECOWAS* v. *Council of Ministers of ECOWAS*,[141] in which the applicant unsuccessfully challenged decisions of the Council of Ministers, which, according to the applicant, violated the independence and financial autonomy it enjoyed. A less direct instance is the *Mwatela* case, which, although not instituted by the EALA, was aimed in part at maintaining its right to have a voice in the EAC's law-making process. Concomitant with inter-institutional problems, when member states begin to experience the practical national impact of what they have agreed, their enthusiasm in joining the international organization becomes tempered by a growing unwillingness to surrender sovereignty to it. This reluctance is particularly strong where decisions made by the organization have significant national impacts. Accordingly, a defining challenge for the court of the organization is how to mediate the relational problems between the organization's institutions, as well as between member states and the organization. The community courts have become the arbiter of inter-institutional problems and moderators of the relations between the communities and the member states.

140 e.g. NAFTA, art. 2005.

141 *Parliament of ECOWAS* v. *Council of Ministers*, Suit No. ECW/CCJ/APP/03/05 (ECOWAS Court of Justice, 2005).

The judgments of the courts reveal an attempt to address some of these problems identified above. The proper resolution of these problems is important for the effective development of the communities. A number of inter-institutional relational problems are revealed in the community courts' judgments. We have already noted how the liberal individual *locus standi* rules affect the balance of power within the communities and can be potentially problematic. Another example was the issue of the sufficiency or otherwise of protocols as the legislative medium for the purposes that the private members' bills sought to achieve in *Calist.*[142] Also worth recalling is the bank's argument in *Ogang*[143] that the COMESA court lacked jurisdiction over it because it was an autonomous institution, not an organ of COMESA, and, accordingly, not answerable to COMESA laws. All of these are manifestations of inter-institutional problems. They are very weighty problems that merit careful scrutiny. These problems often ensue when one institution attempts to bolster its interests at the expense of other institutions' interests.

The issue of the appropriate legislative instrument in the *Mwatela* case was not an insignificant one. At its heart was the question of which community institutions may participate in the EAC's law-making processes. As in states, the choice of legal instrument (for example, executive instrument, constitutional instrument, Act, Order, etc.) often dictates the law-making procedure and the participating institutions. Protocols and Acts are the two main modes of legislating within the EAC. Protocols supplement, amend or qualify the EAC Treaty.[144] They are legislation pursuant to the treaty. The member states conclude protocols as may be necessary in each area of cooperation and spell out the objectives and scope of institutional mechanisms for cooperation and integration. They are approved by the Summit of Heads of States and Government on the recommendation of the Council of Ministers.[145] Unlike Acts of the community,[146] the EALA is clearly excluded from the negotiation and adoption of protocols.

142 *Mwatela* v. *East Africa Community* [2007] 1 East Afr. LR 237.
143 *Eastern and Southern African Trade and Development Bank* v. *Ogang* [2001] 1 East Afr. LR 46.
144 EAC Treaty, art. 1. 145 Ibid., art. 152.
146 Article 62(1) provides that the enactment of legislation of the Community shall be effected by means of bills passed by the Assembly and assented to by the Heads of State, and every bill that has been duly passed and assented to shall be styled an Act of the Community.

Thus, beneath the argument that protocols were best suited for the purposes for which the private members' bills in *Calist* were directed, there was a careful and subtle attempt to exclude the EALA altogether from the issues addressed in the bills. This attempt reflects the culture of executive domination of Africa's economic integration processes. While the EAC Treaty stipulates a number of defined areas where a protocol must be adopted, it does not set those areas as the limit. Thus, theoretically, the scope of matters over which protocols can be adopted is undefined. The thought that the EALA, which consists of the people's representatives, can be excluded from participating in community law-making simply through the use of protocols represents a frightening prospect for good governance within the EAC, an ideal which is espoused as a fundamental principle of the organization.[147]

One troubling aspect of this prospect is that under the EAC Treaty, and unlike other organs of the community, the EALA is not one of the institutions that can challenge other institutions before the EAC court.[148] The member states[149] and individuals[150] may sue the EALA as a community institution. However, there is no equivalent power in the EAC Treaty for the EALA to sue a member state or other community institution to protect its prerogatives in areas such as law-making[151] and control over the community budget.[152] Unless this limitation is circumvented or remedied, the possibility of the EALA being consigned to irrelevance in the face of unbridled 'protocolism' is real. The ability of individual members of the EALA to bring actions to challenge other institutions before the court, as happened in *Mwatela*, is one, albeit inadequate, means of addressing this limitation. In this area, the interpretive approaches of the court will be crucial in protecting the prerogatives and competence of the EALA.[153] Whether the EAC court will be able to do this or we will have to wait for a treaty amendment remains to be seen.

The doctrine of prospective annulment has become an important tool for balancing the competing interests of the community and member states before the EAC court. It has been used authoritatively to state the

[147] Ibid., art. 6(d).

[148] But see ECOWAS Court Protocol, art. 10(b). It grants the ECOWAS Parliament standing to challenge 'the legality of an action in relation to any Community text'.

[149] EAC Treaty, art. 28.

[150] Ibid., art. 30.

[151] Ibid., art. 49(1).

[152] Ibid., art. 49(2)(b).

[153] For comparative purposes, it is worth noting that, historically, the European Parliament did not have standing to bring actions before the ECJ for annulment of EC laws. However, the court remedied this defect after a period of hesitance. See *Parliament* v. *Council* (C-302/87) [1988] ECR 5616; and *Parliament* v. *Council* (C-70/88) [1990] ECR I-2041.

law to guide future decisions and, at the same time, ensure that past unlawful decisions of community institutions and member states are not sanctioned in a manner that adversely affects the community's work. In two instances, the court invoked the doctrine to save decisions that would otherwise have been void *ab initio.*[154] The COMESA court has also been using the exhaustion of local remedies requirement to balance the competing interests of individuals and member states. But it is arguable that its tendency to dismiss individual actions for lack of exhaustion of local remedies has not struck the right balance.[155] These balancing tools are important in maintaining harmonious inter-institutional and community–state relations in the formative stages of the communities' development. However, community courts must be more circumspect in invoking and applying them, otherwise they could send the wrong signal to community institutions and member states that breaches of community law would be 'condoned' by the courts.

A significant source of the problems between member states and the communities was the scope of national prerogatives in economic integration; what can states continue to do and what are they prevented from doing as a result of becoming parties to the community treaties? In *Anyang II*, the EAC court characterizes this as the hurdle of 'balancing individual state sovereignty with integration'.[156] It is a hurdle that all economic integration processes struggle with. Indeed, as previously discussed, state sovereignty challenges the very idea and existence of a community legal system. In Africa, striking the right balance is likely to be more challenging since the community treaties do not clearly lay out the communities' competences vis-à-vis those of member states: What matters, if any, are within the exclusive competence of the communities? What matters are within the exclusive competence of member states? Are there any areas of shared competence? In case there is a dispute, who decides whether a community or member state is competent as regards a defined issue? The ability of the community courts to strike the right balance in overcoming this hurdle will be fundamental to the success of Africa's economic integration processes.

Sovereignty-based arguments are used by states in their attempts to constrain the decision-making powers of community courts. Such

[154] See *Mwatela* v. *East Africa Community* [2007] 1 East Afr. LR 237; and *East African Law Society* v. *Att-Gen of Kenya* [2008] 1 East Afr. LR 95.

[155] *Intelsomac* v. *Rwanda Civil Aviation Authority*, Reference No. 1 of 2009 (COMESA Court of Justice, 2010).

[156] *Anyang' Nyong'o* v. *Att-Gen of the Republic of Kenya* [2008] 3 KLR 397 at 432.

arguments aim at shaping a court's jurisprudence in a manner perceived to be more in line with states' interests, and cutting back the extent of a community's competences. However, as the EAC court held in *Anyang II*, 'while the [EAC Treaty] upholds the principle of sovereign equality . . . by the very nature of the objectives they set out to achieve, each partner state is expected to cede some amount of sovereignty to the Community and its organs albeit in limited areas to enable them to play their role'.[157] In *Mwatela*, the court had earlier noted that 'the competence of the Community is restricted to matters which are within its jurisdiction. Any matter which is still under the exclusive sovereignty of the Partner States is beyond the legislative competence of the Community'.[158] Definitely, this will not be the last time the sovereignty argument will be put before the community courts. The ultimate test for them is how, tactfully, to push back the threats of sovereignty and, at the same time, maintain the member states' trust and confidence in the economic integration processes and the jurisprudence of the courts.

Inter-institutional and community–state relational problems should be appreciated as part of the evolutionary process in the growth of an international organization. The responses to these problems should be measured and well thought through to ensure they do not generate more problems or lead to institutional paralysis. It is in this regard that the amendment to the EAC Treaty, ostensibly a response to the EAC court's 'anti-government' jurisprudence, is worrying. The amendments have: restructured the court into two divisions, i.e. a First Instance Division and an Appellate Division; expanded the grounds for removing judges from office; provided for suspension of a judge who is under investigation for removal or is charged with an offence; limited the court's jurisdiction not to apply to jurisdiction conferred by the treaty on institutions of member states; provided time limits within which a reference to the court by individuals may be instituted; provided grounds on which appeal may be made; and deemed past decisions of the court and existing judges to be decisions and judges of the First Instance Division, respectively. Equally troubling is the decision of the SADC Summit of Heads of State and Government to review the role and functions of the SADC Tribunal after a series of decisions given by the latter against the Zimbabwean Government. The power to make community laws remains the privilege of the communities' executive and legislative institutions. But it should not be used in a manner that undermines or constrains the work of the judicial

[157] Ibid. [158] *Mwatela* v. *East Africa Community* [2007] 1 East Afr. LR 237 at 251.

institutions. Experience elsewhere indicates that the judicial branch can be a driving force in economic integration. It will help the cause of Africa's integration if this fact is appreciated.

5.5 Conclusion

Strong judicial institutions have an important role to play in economic integration. They act as guardians of the processes and arbiters of inter-institutional and community–state relational problems inherent in them. The character of a community court reflects the depth of integration desired and how much of a role is given to law in the integration process. A limited role for courts reflects an unwillingness to relinquish sovereignty, and may hamper the attainment of deeper integration. The community courts in Africa have a crucial role to play in advancing economic integration through law. They have to evolve their own jurisprudence that ensures compliance with treaty obligations, checks excesses on the part of community institutions, engenders investor confidence and nurtures a sense of judicial discipline and legitimacy among national courts.[159] Indeed, an activist community court with broad subject matter and personal jurisdiction can sometimes push forward integration in the face of political inertia. Nowhere has this been truer than within the EU. The jurisprudence of the ECJ has been critical to the community's development. The COMESA, EAC, ECOWAS and SADC courts have a crucial role in managing inter-institutional and community–state relations in their respective sub-regions.

However, without the active support of national courts and individuals, they cannot perform this role effectively. A trilateral relation among individual litigants, national courts and community courts is important to ensure the effectiveness of Africa's economic integration processes. The jurisprudence of the COMESA, EAC, ECOWAS and SADC courts points to the importance of this trilateral relationship. Their jurisprudence offers useful lessons to the African Court of Justice when it becomes operational. However, it is doubtful whether the African Court of Justice is equipped to address, effectively, the issues faced by the community courts. As discussed in the next chapter, there are provisions in the Protocol on the Statute to the African Court of Justice and Human Rights that require amendment before the court can truly develop this trilateral relationship, which will enable it to perform effectively its role in Africa's economic integration.

[159] Kiplagat (1995), pp. 449–50.

6

AU/AEC institutions and the enforcement of community law

6.1 Introduction

An integral part of any legal system, and a key to its effectiveness, are the enforcement mechanisms provided to ensure compliance with its laws. In the context of economic integration, enforcement mechanisms are avenues through which community and national legal systems are linked. Enforcement of community law strengthens a community's legal system, at both community and national levels. It allows individuals to benefit from the integration process. This enhances the legitimacy of the community legal system, creates a national constituency with interest in community law and provides a focal point of interaction between national and community legal systems. Enforcement of community law occurs at both national and community levels. Indeed, unless there is effective enforcement at both levels, and a high level of coordination between them, community law will become ineffective. Put differently, a disjunction will be created between community and national legal systems, and the effectiveness of the community will be undermined. An essential feature of an enforcement mechanism that is likely to ensure the effective implementation of community law is its ability to take advantage of pre-existing law-enforcement regimes in member states. As Shaw has observed, 'it is precisely because of the inadequate enforcement facilities that lie at the disposal of international law [community law] that one must consider the relationship with municipal law as more than of marginal importance'.[1] Accordingly, proper relations between a community and pre-existing national law-enforcement institutions or mechanisms are important for community law's effectiveness. In the preceding chapter, we discussed how trilateral relations between individuals and courts at the national level and community courts can enhance

[1] Shaw (2003), p. 161.

the work of the latter. This chapter examines the extent to which this idea is reflected in the design of institutions responsible for the enforcement of the laws of the African Economic Community.

6.2 Institutions for the enforcement of AEC law

6.2.1 Executive institutions

Under the AEC Treaty, the Assembly of Heads of State and Government (Assembly) is the supreme institution of the community.[2] It is responsible for implementing the community's objectives.[3] At present, the Assembly of Heads of State and Government of the African Union performs the functions of the AEC Assembly; there is no separate and distinct Assembly specifically devoted to matters arising under the AEC Treaty. From the perspective of making available to the AEC the enforcement mechanisms existing in member states, entrusting this function to the Assembly appears to be a good approach. As heads of the executive in their respective states, they may be able to invoke easily the mandate of national institutions – such as the police, customs and immigration – to enforce community law, or propose the enactment of laws giving effect to community law. However, there are disadvantages in this approach.

Regarding decision-making at the community level, because the Assembly is composed of politicians who represent individual member states' interests, it is probable that political considerations, rather than the ultimate goals of the AEC, will be paramount in their deliberations. This is especially so since achieving the goals of the AEC may lie in adopting domestically unpalatable decisions, which must be enforced in member states. A similar arrangement under the Treaty for East African Cooperation, 1967,[4] was described as 'negative' since it defeated the aim of achieving a 'vigorous Community'.[5] The Treaty Establishing the East African Authority was the 'principal executive authority of the Community'. It was responsible for, and had the general direction and control of, the performance of the executive functions of the Community. Under the current Treaty Establishing the East African Community, the Summit of Heads of State and Government is responsible for giving 'general directions and impetus to the development and

[2] AEC Treaty, art. 8(1). [3] Ibid., art. 8(2).
[4] Treaty for East African Cooperation, 6 June 1967, 6 ILM 932.
[5] Ghai (1976), p. 24.

achievement of the objectives of the Community'.[6] In contrast, the powers of the Authority of Heads of State and Government, declared to be the 'supreme' institution responsible for the 'general direction and control' of the Community under the COMESA and ECOWAS treaties, are more extensive.[7] However, these subtle variations in the powers of these executive institutions may exist only on paper. In practice, the dominance of the institutions consisting of heads of state and government in African economic integration processes cannot be underestimated.

An assembly of politicians may seek political compromises rather than the strict enforcement of laws. With their heavy national and international schedules, and numerous domestic socio-economic and political problems, it is unlikely that heads of state and government can forcefully implement the AEC's objectives. This ultimately dilutes or slows down the economic integration process.[8] Indeed, the current state of inertia in the development of the AEC is palpable evidence of this. At the national level, political pressure from domestic constituencies, coupled with a personal motivation to maintain political power, may undercut the willingness or ability of the executive to implement community law. There have been instances where governments have bowed to domestic pressure and closed their national borders or expelled foreigners, thus hindering trade and free movement of persons as agreed under various ECOWAS protocols.[9] In 2008, Ghana closed its border with Togo two days prior to the country's presidential and parliamentary elections. This decision, which was roundly condemned by the ECOWAS as a potential violation of ECOWAS protocols on the free movement of persons, goods and right of establishment,[10] appeared to have been directed at preventing non-nationals from voting in the Volta region, which is traditionally an opposition (now government in power) stronghold.

Also, an overbearing Assembly may dominate the agenda of other community institutions, such as the council of ministers and the secretariat. As far back as 1972, Sundström noted that 'in most African organisations the conference of heads of state dominates to the extent that ministerial committees often may be reduced to acting as

[6] Ibid., art. 11(1). [7] ECOWAS Treaty, art. 7; and COMESA Treaty, art. 8.
[8] Kufour (1994). [9] Brown (1989).
[10] See Ghana News Agency, 'ECOWAS Regrets Closure of Ghana's Borders', 27 December 2008, online: http://news.myjoyonline.com/news/200812/24368.asp.

preparatory bodies'.[11] This is especially likely as, apart from the Court of Justice, none of the major decision-making institutions is guaranteed independence under the AEC Treaty. The Council of Ministers is responsible for the 'functioning and development of the Community'.[12] It is composed of ministers of state who hold their positions at the pleasure of their respective president, prime minister or king. Although the Secretary General and the staff of the Secretariat are 'accountable only to the Community', the Secretariat is not a decision-making institution, and cannot push the economic integration agenda on its own.[13]

The absence of an independent institution, with expert personnel, to push the agenda of economic integration leaves the process entirely in the hands of politicians. This may delay the integration process, especially given the history of politics in Africa. Both the Assembly and the Council are composed of members who lack the expertise and security of tenure needed to take or propose bold measures. Although great advances are being made, politics in Africa is still characterized by the personalization of power, abrupt changes in government, personal and ideological differences among leaders, and decisions made on the bases of immediate and short-term objectives. These adversely affect the rigorousness of decision-making and the stability in governance that the AEC needs to progress.

Within the EU, the European Commission has been described as the 'single most important political force for integration, ever seeking to press forward to attain the [Union's] objectives'.[14] It is the EU's motor of integration. It is able to do this not only because it consists of technocrats, but also because members are required to be persons whose 'independence is beyond doubt', and who neither 'seek nor take instructions from any government or other institution, body, office or entity'.[15] It is the European Commission's sole responsibility to 'promote the general interest of the Union and take appropriate initiatives to that end. It shall ensure the application of the Treaties, and of measures adopted by the institutions pursuant to them. It shall oversee the application of Union law under the control of the Court of Justice of the European Union'.[16] It can be argued that its decision-making powers are minimal compared with the EU's Council of Ministers. But that understates the European Commission's role in shaping and developing the EU. The executive, legislative, judicial and administrative functions

[11] Sundström (1972), p. 229. See also Sohn (1972), p. 217.
[12] AEC Treaty, art. 11. [13] Ibid., art. 24. [14] Craig and de Búrca (2003), p. 64.
[15] EU Treaty, art. 17(3). [16] Ibid., art. 17(1).

of the European Commission are not matched by any of the AEC's institutions and, indeed, those of the other communities in Africa. In contrast to the approach under the AEC Treaty, the European Council, which consists of the EU member states' Heads of State and Government, is responsible for providing the EU with 'the necessary impetus for its development and shall define the general political directions and priorities' of the EU.[17] It exercises no legislative functions. It is ultimately the members of the Council of Ministers that commit their governments to decisions taken within the EU, and the European Commission that sees to the implementation of those decisions. The effective combination of independent technocrats, with wide enforcement powers, and politicians partly accounts for the EU's success. The technocrats have wide powers to propose policies and enforce decisions taken on those proposals by the Council of Ministers and the European Parliament.

In addition to the need for sound economic policies, political stability, good governance and respect for fundamental rights,[18] the roles played by strong institutions in ensuring effective economic integration should not be underestimated. The absence of strong, independent institutions to counterbalance political inertia is, no doubt, a major reason behind the slow pace of economic integration in Africa. The dominance of Heads of State and Government in the institutional make-up of Africa's economic integration organizations has hindered their development. Personal differences between leaders of the East African Community led to a situation whereby there was no meeting of the East African Authority, the supreme organ of the community, between 1971 and 1977. The collapse of the former East African Community has, in part, been attributed to this institutional paralysis. As far back as 1991, Johnson suggested that for the success of economic integration in Africa, 'major operational decisions of a union should not be taken by organs that contain the top political leadership of the member-states'.[19] A move in that direction is long overdue.

6.2.2 *Pan-African Parliament*

Legislative institutions are not often thought of as principal agents when it comes to the enforcement of law; they make law, and its implementation resides with the executive. But they can have a crucial role in law enforcement, or at least influence it. An emerging feature of Africa's

[17] Ibid., art. 15. [18] Olowu (2003). [19] Johnson (1991), p. 12.

economic integration processes is the use of community parliamentary institutions. In addition to the Pan-African Parliament, there are currently operating the East African Legislative Assembly, Economic Community of West African States Parliament, Network of Parliamentarians of the Economic Community of Central African States, Parliament de l'Union Économique et Monétaire Ouest Africaine, and Southern African Development Community Parliamentary Forum. The Inter-Parliamentary Union of the Intergovernmental Authority on Development is not yet operational.[20] Community parliaments offer two channels that aid implementation of community law. Firstly, they can ensure people's participation in their legislative processes. This enhances the legitimacy of laws enacted and improves the prospects of compliance. A key feature of Africa's economic integration processes is the lack of integration of individuals into the lawmaking processes of the communities. Community parliaments, the membership of which is often drawn from national parliaments, can bridge this gap. Secondly, they can engage with national parliaments, which may be the ultimate decision-makers on the issue of nationally implementing community law.

The Pan-African Parliament was envisaged under article 14 of the AEC Treaty and, subsequently, under article 17 of the Constitutive Act of the African Union. However, the full details on the Parliament are contained in the Protocol to the Treaty establishing the African Economic Community Relating to the Pan-African Parliament.[21] The Pan-African Parliament, inaugurated in 2004, is fully operational. Its seat is in South Africa. It is currently an advisory and consultative body.[22] Members are drawn from national parliaments.[23] It is, ultimately, to evolve into an institution with full legislative powers. Members will be elected through universal adult suffrage. The fact that Pan-African parliamentarians are drawn from national parliaments provides an opportunity to create a relationship between the AEC and member states. Indeed, the Pan-African Parliament is enjoined to work in 'close cooperation' with national parliaments.[24] The knowledge held by Pan-African parliamentarians about the AEC and its legislative processes may be used to influence their national colleagues when it comes to implementing AEC law at the national level.

The absence of universal adult suffrage limits the extent to which the Pan-African Parliament engages with Africans. However, one of the

[20] Karuuombe (2008). [21] Protocol on the Pan-African Parliament.
[22] Ibid., art. 2(3)(i). [23] Ibid., arts. 4 and 5. [24] Ibid., art. 18.

objectives of the Pan-African Parliament is to familiarize Africans with the objectives and policies aimed at integrating the African continent.[25] This can be done through educational campaigns, workshops, lectures and seminars. The presence of a domestic constituency with interest in Africa's economic integration is one of the surest ways of ensuring the implementation and effectiveness of community law. Interested individuals, including businesses, can lobby governments to implement community law, report breaches to community institutions and try to remedy those breaches through litigation at both the national and community levels. It is important that in the Pan-African Parliament's engagement with Africans, these roles are stressed. This is consistent with its objective to facilitate the implementation of the policies and objectives of the AEC.[26]

6.2.3 African Court of Justice

The Court of Justice of the AEC is an important institution for the enforcement of AEC law.[27] It is independent of all other community institutions. Its mandate is to 'ensure the adherence to law in the interpretation and application of [the AEC Treaty] and . . . decide on disputes submitted thereto pursuant to [the AEC Treaty]'.[28] It is provided in article 20 of the AEC Treaty that a protocol should be adopted to regulate the work of that court. To date, no such protocol has been adopted. Rather, what has been adopted recently – but is not yet in force – is the Protocol on the Statute of the African Court of Justice and Human Rights (hereafter, Protocol on the African Court of Justice).[29] This protocol aims to merge two courts established under the Protocol to the African Charter on Human and Peoples' Rights on the Establishment of an African Court on Human and Peoples' Rights[30] and the Protocol of the Court of Justice of the African Union.[31] The former protocol entered into force on 25 January 2004. The latter entered into force on 11 February 2009. The court established under the Protocol of the Court of Justice of the African Union has never been operational;

25 Ibid., art. 3(4). 26 Ibid., art. 3(1).
27 Obilade (1993), p. 312. 28 AEC Treaty, art. 18(2).
29 Annexed to the Protocol is the Statute of the African Court of Justice.
30 Protocol to the African Charter on Human and Peoples' Rights on the Establishment of an African Court on Human and Peoples' Rights, 10 June 1998, online: www.africa-union.org/root/au/Documents/Treaties/Text/africancourt-humanrights.pdf.
31 Protocol of the Court of Justice of the African Union, 11 July 2003, (2005) 13 Afr. J. Int'l & Comp. L. 115 (hereafter, AU Court Protocol).

indeed, judges of the court have not been appointed. The inaugural judges for the African Court on Human and Peoples' Rights, which is located in Arusha, Tanzania, were sworn in on 2 June 2006 and its first judgment was delivered in December 2009.[32]

There is some uncertainty as to whether the court established under the Protocol on the Statute of the African Court of Justice and Human Rights, the African Court of Justice and Human Rights (hereafter, the African Court of Justice), will assume the jurisdiction of the court of justice envisaged under article 18 of the AEC Treaty. The Protocol is silent on this issue. However, it is almost certain that the African Court of Justice will exercise the jurisdiction of the court of justice envisaged under article 18 of the AEC Treaty. There are constitutional and pragmatic reasons for this. The AEC is an integral part of the AU. Thus, in the absence of express provisions in the Protocol, the African Court of Justice, which has jurisdiction over the Constitutive Act of the AU, has jurisdiction over the AEC Treaty. The jurisdiction of the African Court of Justice, which covers the interpretation, application or validity of Union treaties and all subsidiary legislation adopted within the framework of the Union or Organization of African Unity, is wide enough to encompass the jurisdiction of the court envisaged under article 18 of the AEC Treaty. Unless this is the case, difficult questions of jurisdiction, including conflict of jurisdictions between the two courts, will arise. Pragmatically, the adoption of the Protocol on the African Court of Justice evinces a desire to have a single, multi-purpose court that also reduces cost. It is recommended that the African Court of Justice utilizes the provisions of article 17, which divides the court into a General Affairs Section and a Human Rights Section, and article 19, which allows for these sections to be constituted into chambers to set up a special chamber to deal with cases relating to the AEC Treaty and other AEC laws.

The African Court of Justice is composed of sixteen judges, who must all be nationals of states that are parties to the Protocol on the African Court of Justice.[33] One of the qualifying criteria to be a judge of the court is to 'possess the qualifications required in their respective countries for appointment to the highest judicial office'.[34] The structure, independence and jurisdiction of courts are significant factors in enhancing their ability to meet the challenges of economic integration.

[32] *In the Matter of Michelot Yogogombaye* v. *Republic of Senegal*, Application No. 001/2008 (African Court of Human and Peoples' Rights, 2009). Mujuzi (2010).

[33] Statute of the African Court of Justice, art. 3(1). [34] Ibid., art. 4.

There are provisions in the Protocol on the African Court of Justice that seek to secure the independence and effectiveness of the court. Under article 12 of the Statute of the African Court of Justice, the independence of judges shall be fully ensured, in accordance with international law. Judges are enjoined to act impartially, fairly and justly, and they are not subject to the direction or control of any person in the performance of their duties.

Judges are elected by the Council of Ministers from a list of nominees submitted by state parties to the Protocol on the African Court of Justice,[35] and appointed by the Assembly of Heads of State and Government for a period of six years.[36] A judge cannot be removed from office except by a two-thirds majority decision of the judges of the court that the affected judge no longer fulfils the requisite conditions of the position.[37] The Assembly gives final approval to any recommendation to remove a judge.[38] Judges enjoy diplomatic immunity in accordance with international law.[39] They are immune from legal proceedings, both during and after their term of service, for acts performed in the discharge of their judicial functions.[40]

The Assembly determines the salaries, allowances and compensation of judges on the recommendation of the Council of Ministers.[41] These payments cannot be decreased during a judge's terms of office.[42] The court prepares its own budget and submits it to the Assembly through the Council of Ministers.[43] The court's budget is borne by the African Union.[44] The Protocol on the Court of Justice is silent on whether the Assembly can reduce the court's budget.

The Assembly's control over the court's budget is a potential threat to the independence of the court. Indeed, it is open to question whether the above provisions on the appointment, removal, independence and remuneration of judges are adequate to guarantee a strong and independent court that will be strong enough to face up to the challenges of promoting economic integration in Africa. These provisions are very similar to those relating to the COMESA, EAC, ECOWAS and SADC courts. To an extent, and without purporting to diminish the importance of constitutional guarantees of independence, the strength of

[35] Ibid., art. 7(1). [36] Ibid., art. 8(1).

[37] Ibid., art. 9(2). Under art. 11(2) of the earlier AU Court Protocol, a unanimous recommendation from the judges was required before a judge could be removed.

[38] Ibid., art. 9(4). [39] Ibid., art. 15(1). [40] Ibid., art. 15(2)(3).

[41] Ibid., art. 23(3). [42] Ibid., art. 23(1). [43] Ibid., art. 26(1).

[44] Ibid., art. 26(2).

a court depends on the character and intellectual strength of its judges.[45] Chapter 5 notes a number of decisions from the EAC court of justice that demonstrated remarkable independence of judgment, and an ability tactfully to balance competing interests in their jurisprudence. Whether the African Court of Justice will follow a similar trajectory remains to be seen.

The Caribbean Court of Justice, established under the Caribbean Court Agreement,[46] provides an interesting comparative alternative on how to structure an international court with a view to facilitating its work and guaranteeing its independence. The appointment of the court's judges and the determination of their remuneration are entrusted to the Regional Judicial and Legal Services Commission (hereafter, Regional Commission) and not member states.[47] To insulate the Regional Commission from government interference, no government representative is a member, and the members of the commission are not appointed by governments. Rather, the Regional Commission consists of representatives of the bar, Judicial Services Commission, Public Service Commission, civil society and specified faculties of law.[48] The commission is also responsible for exercising 'disciplinary control over Judges of the Court'.[49]

Additionally, the Revised Agreement Establishing the Caribbean Court of Justice Trust Fund[50] has created a trust fund to insulate the court from political interference or manipulation of its finances. The purpose of the fund is to provide the resources necessary to finance the Court's capital and operating budget and the Regional Commission in perpetuity.[51] The fund is financed by contributions of member states, income accruing to the fund and third-party contributions.[52] It is expressly provided that third-party contributions should not prejudice the independence or integrity of the court.[53] Also, the fund may not solicit or accept any grant, gift or other material benefit from any source except with the consent of all of the member states.[54] A board of trustees, on which there are no government representatives, manages the fund.[55] This Caribbean model is still progressing; the court is still at an early stage in its development. However, it represents

45 Helfer and Slaughter (1997), pp. 318–23. 46 McDonald (2004), pp. 970–1015.
47 Caribbean Court Agreement, art. 4(7). 48 Ibid., art. 5. 49 Ibid., art. 5(3)(2).
50 Revised Agreement Establishing the Caribbean Court of Justice Trust Fund, 12 January 2004, online: www.caribbeancourtofjustice.org/legislation.html.
51 Ibid., art. 3. 52 Ibid., art. (4)(1). 53 Ibid., art. (4)(1)(c).
54 Ibid., art. 4(2). 55 Ibid., arts. 5–8.

a unique and interesting innovation in structuring international courts. The model merits close study by the AEC. It provides novel solutions to the problems of interference and underfunding, which are perennial challenges to African courts.

The jurisdiction of the African Court of Justice is broad. In theory, it covers, potentially, any international dispute arising between states that are parties to the Protocol on the African Court of Justice. Under article 28 of the Statute of the African Court of Justice:

> The Court shall have jurisdiction over all cases and all legal disputes submitted to it in accordance with the present Statute which relate to: (a) the interpretation and application of the Constitutive Act; (b) the interpretation, application or validity of other Union Treaties and all subsidiary legal instruments adopted within the framework of the Union or the Organization of African Unity; (c) the interpretation and the application of the African Charter, the Charter on the Rights and Welfare of the Child, the Protocol to the African Charter on Human and Peoples' Rights on the Rights of Women in Africa, or any other legal instrument relating to human rights, ratified by the States Parties concerned; (d) any question of international law; (e) all acts, decisions, regulations and directives of the organs of the Union; (f) all matters specifically provided for in any other agreements that States Parties may conclude among themselves, or with the Union and which confer jurisdiction on the Court; (g) the existence of any fact which, if established, would constitute a breach of an obligation owed to a State Party or to the Union; (h) the nature or extent of the reparation to be made for the breach of an international obligation.

The scope of article 28 brings within the jurisdiction of the African Court of Justice the AEC Treaty and any laws adopted under it. In carrying out its functions, the court is enjoined to have regard to: the Constitutive Act of the African Union; international treaties, which have been ratified by the contesting states; international custom, as evidence of a general practice accepted as law; the general principles of law recognized universally or by African States; judicial decisions and writings of the most highly qualified publicists of various nations, as well as the regulations, directives and decisions of the African Union, as subsidiary means for the determination of the rules of law; and any other law relevant to the determination of the case.[56] If the parties agree, the court may also decide a case *ex aequo et bono*.[57]

[56] Statute of the African Court of Justice, art. 31. [57] Ibid., art. 31(2).

An issue arising from the list of applicable laws in article 31 is the status of the court's judgments. In other words, what is the precedential value of the court's judgments to the court itself? Do judicial decisions in article 31(e) include decisions of the court? In discussing this issue, one must distinguish between judgment as remedy and judgment as principle. The former is the redress provided for the parties, such as an injunction, damages or a declaration. The latter is the legal foundation of the remedy. If there is internal coherence in the jurisprudence of the African Court of Justice, this will definitely serve the AEC legal system well, by providing certainty and predictability in outcomes. This partly results from following previous decisions, albeit not slavishly. Other international courts, faced with similar provisions, have not found it limiting. International courts strive towards achieving an internally coherent body of jurisprudence by following previous case law. But, perhaps, the Protocol on the African Court of Justice could have been more explicit on the precedential value of the court's judgments.[58]

In this respect, it is significant that an earlier provision in the Protocol on the Court of Justice of the African Union that 'judgments of the Court shall be binding on the parties and in respect of that particular case' was dropped in the Statute of the African Court. The provision appears to have been borrowed from article 59 of the Statute of the International Court of Justice (ICJ), which provides: 'the decision of the Court has no binding force except as between the parties and in respect of that particular case'. The ICJ has held that 'the object of [Article 59] is simply to prevent legal principles accepted by the Court in a particular case from being binding on other States or in other disputes'.[59] Admittedly, in practice, the ICJ has not applied strictly this understanding of article 59; it was unlikely that the Court of Justice of the African Union would have done so.

The strength of a court depends not only on its independence, but also on the scope of its subject matter and personal jurisdiction. Under article 29 of the Statute of the African Court of Justice, the following entities are entitled to submit cases to the court on 'any issue or dispute'[60] provided for in article 28: states that are parties to the

[58] Compare Caribbean Court Agreement, art. 22. It provides that the judgments of the Court of Justice, CARICOM, shall be legally binding precedents for parties in proceedings before the court.

[59] *German Interests in Polish Upper Silesia* (Permanent Court of International Justice, 1926), cited in Brownlie (2003), pp. 20–1.

[60] On human-rights-related disputes, the list of entities that can bring actions before the African Court of Justice includes: the African Commission on Human and Peoples' Rights; the African Committee of Experts on the Rights and Welfare of the Child; African

Protocol on the African Court of Justice; the Assembly; the Parliament and other organs of the AU authorized by the Assembly; and a staff member of the AU. A state that is not party to the protocol may not submit a case to the African Court of Justice;[61] the court has no jurisdiction to hear a dispute involving such a party.

The fact that the court has no jurisdiction over states that are not parties to the protocol, even though they may be parties to the AEC Treaty, poses a challenge to judicial enforcement of the treaty.[62] Surely, in international law, states, as an attribute of their sovereignty, cannot be dragged to an international tribunal without their consent.[63] However, in the context of economic integration,[64] this jurisdictional gap will not aid the uniform application and enforcement of community law in member states. This gap is a reflection of a lack of attention to the importance of relational issues in integration. A foundation for instability is laid where uneven obligations, in terms of the enforcement and enforceability of community law, are imposed on member states. It is difficult to conceive of a stable community where community law is not uniformly applicable within and enforceable against member states. Indeed, the very essence of integration is defeated: 'uniformity in the meaning of law is part of the constitutional glue that holds the Community together'.[65]

In Chapter 5, we discussed the importance of individuals as a medium through which community and national legal systems interact. We saw that the COMESA, EAC, ECOWAS and SADC treaties provide fairly liberal rules on individuals' participation in the communities' judicial processes. Individuals have been responsible for almost all of the disputes settled by the courts to date. The Statute of the African Court of Justice adopts a radically different approach. Except for human rights

Intergovernmental Organizations accredited to the Union or its organs; African National Human Rights Institutions; and, for states that specifically agree to this, individuals or relevant NGOs accredited to the African Union or to its organs. Statute of the African Court of Justice, art. 30.

61 Ibid., art. 18. 62 Smith (2000). 63 Romano (2007).

64 Such a jurisdictional gap might work in a purely political context. For example, except with their express consent, the ICJ has no jurisdiction over states which do not consent to its jurisdiction although they are members of the United Nations and, *ipso facto*, parties to the Statute of the International Court of Justice. The case of the African Court of Justice represents an inappropriate extension of an approach developed and workable in a purely political context to economic integration.

65 Weatherill (1995), p. 135.

claims, individuals have no standing before the African Court of Justice. On matters relating to the interpretation, enforcement and validity of AEC laws, individuals cannot bring an action in the African Court of Justice. A provision in the earlier Protocol on the Court of Justice of the African Union,[66] which allowed individuals to access the court under conditions determined by the Assembly and with the consent of the state concerned, has been omitted from the Statute on the African Court of Justice. With this approach, the African Court of Justice resembles the international adjudication regime category in Schneider's typology of dispute-settlement systems.[67] Such a regime is ill-suited to the level of integration envisaged under the AEC Treaty, although it may adequately serve the needs of the AU – the political organization.[68]

This absence of *locus standi* for individuals restricts the number of potential disputes that may be brought before the African Court of Justice. It makes the dispute settlement process unavailable to some of the most important players in the integration process – including consumers, traders, corporate bodies, investors and interest groups. It fails to utilize a principal medium through which the community–state relationship is strengthened in economic integration. A plausible alternative, which is still more restrictive compared with the standing rules of the COMESA, EAC, ECOWAS and SADC courts, would be to allow individuals to litigate before the African Court of Justice with special leave of the court,[69] or after exhausting local remedies. Another alternative is to create a reference procedure between national courts and the African Court of Justice. This alternative would provide individuals with indirect access to the African Court of Justice.

Admittedly, no legal system grants individuals unlimited access to its courts. However, every advanced legal system recognizes the important role played by private litigation, not only in sustaining the system, but also in its development. Legal systems have two principal means of enforcing norms. These are public enforcement through the state and its institutions, and private enforcement by individuals. The combination of these two enforcement mechanisms ensures a legal system's

[66] AU Court Protocol, art. 18. [67] Schneider (1998–9).

[68] Ibid., p. 761, where she notes that the international adjudicatory regime 'is best used when the goals of integration are limited'.

[69] CARICOM Treaty, art. 222. *Trinidad Cement Ltd* v. *The State of the Co-operative Republic of Guyana* [2009] CCJ 1 (OJ); and *Trinidad Cement Ltd* v. *The Caribbean Community* [2009] CCJ 2 (OJ).

effectiveness. In economic integration, private enforcement complements public enforcement by community institutions. However, it appears that under the Statute on the African Court of Justice this complementing role is constrained by the unduly restrictive standing rules for individuals. The above should not be read to mean that the African Court of Justice will be useless because it does not provide for individual standing. What is being suggested here is that, to the extent that the court is expected to perform a role that will aid economic integration in Africa, its ability to do that will be constrained by the lack of standing for individuals who could have been its principal source of cases. Surely there are international courts, such as the ICJ, before which individuals have no standing. However, it is important to note that the ICJ is not superintending the enforcement of an economic integration treaty, and its work and jurisprudence are not meant to facilitate an economic integration process.

In general, governments are reluctant to submit to binding interstate dispute-resolution processes.[70] In the absence of a private right of action, the African Court of Justice might be underused and may be consigned to 'abject inactivity and irrelevance'.[71] One can only imagine what would have happened to the COMESA, ECOWAS, EAC and SADC courts if there were no individual standing rights before them. Granting private right of action will ensure the use of the African Court of Justice, and prevent its descent into inactivity and irrelevance.

Arguably, the absence of individual rights of action reflects a desire of states to dominate the African Court of Justice, even if only indirectly, and cut it off from any relations with those most affected by the economic integration process. It may also be an indirect attempt to shape the court's jurisprudence and reduce its potential role as a legislator of community norms: 'control over litigation entails a degree of control over the type of law that is made'.[72] States can do this by shaping the type of arguments that come before the court to suit particular ends. The absence of individual rights of action is inconsistent with the position in other African regional economic treaties and defies recommendations of scholars.[73] It is recommended that any revisions of the Statute of the African Court of Justice should provide for individual rights of action, either directly, through special leave of the court

70 Guzman (2002). 71 Maluwa (1989), p. 307.
72 Trachtman and Moremen (2003), p. 223.
73 See, e.g. COMESA Treaty, art. 26; EAC Treaty, art. 30; and Udombana (2002–3a), p. 842.

or after exhausting local remedies, or indirectly, through reference from national courts.

Another medium for enhancing community–state relations is national courts. As discussed in Chapter 7, they provide an avenue for giving domestic effect to community law apart from executive and parliamentary acts, such as ratification, publication of community instruments and administrative action. Using national courts to enforce community law has advantages. It is cheaper for litigants, as they are more widely and easily accessible than community courts. As forums of first resort, their work could also reduce significantly the workload of community courts. In Chapter 5, we noted that they have been given a significant role to play under the COMESA, EAC, ECOWAS and SADC treaties through the procedure of preliminary reference. National courts also have a role in the enforcement of judgments of the COMESA, EAC, ECOWAS and SADC courts. This is not the case with the African Court of Justice; there is no express provision in the AEC Treaty or the Statute of the African Court of Justice for relations between national courts and the African Court of Justice. There is no provision for preliminary reference procedure, and it is not provided that national courts should aid the enforcement of judgments of the African Court of Justice. This disjunction between both courts may seriously hamper the effectiveness of the African Court of Justice.

The absence of some form of relations between the African Court of Justice and national courts is particularly ironic since, as already noted, a number of African regional economic integration treaties envisage a role for national courts. One would have expected that the drafters of the Protocol on the African Court of Justice would have been inspired by these treaties. The communities created by these treaties are the building blocks of the African Economic Community. As the AEC develops and community law expands into member states, national courts will definitely be faced with cases that engage aspects of community law, and for which a reference to the African Court of Justice for interpretation would be helpful. The fact that it is not provided that national courts will aid the enforcement of judgments of the African Court of Justice is explainable on the grounds of individuals' very limited rights of access to the court. In the absence of cases from individuals, it is unlikely that many judgments will be for pecuniary compensation, the kind of judgments national courts are best suited to enforce. Judgments given in interstate litigation are more likely to be enforced through diplomatic means.

The absence of relations between national courts and the African Court of Justice will pose a challenge for the uniform application of AEC law, and hence its effectiveness. Through incorporation, treaties become part of member states' laws. National courts may resort to them in adjudication, and private parties may rely on them in litigation. The absence of relations between the African Court of Justice and national courts implies that there may not be uniform interpretation of AEC laws in member states. Nothing could be more destabilizing for the AEC's legal system than varied application of its laws in member states. The goals of free movement of persons, capital and services, the right of establishment, taxation, transport and communication, which are envisaged by the AEC Treaty, are intrinsically bound to national legal systems. The absence of defined relations between the African Court of Justice and national courts may undermine the realization of these goals.

Even more destabilizing will be the fact that the African Court of Justice's judgments do not appear to be binding on national courts.[74] This creates the prospect of conflicting judgments between national courts and the African Court of Justice. It also opens up the possibility that governments will avoid, at the national level, their international obligations. Developments surrounding recent judgments of the Southern African Development Community Tribunal and the Supreme Court of Zimbabwe illustrate this prospect. In *Mike Campbell (Pvt) Ltd* v. *Republic of Zimbabwe*,[75] the SADC Tribunal restrained the Zimbabwean Government from compulsorily acquiring the agricultural land of the applicant. At the time of this decision, an action relating to the same land was pending before the Supreme Court of Zimbabwe. The Supreme Court, in apparent disregard of the SADC Tribunal's injunction, ruled in favour of the government,[76] and the government declared its intention to go ahead with the seizure of the applicant's land – and, in fact, seized the land. While Zimbabwe will incur responsibility at the community level (for the seizure), this offers no hope at the national level for the applicant whose right was vindicated at the community level.

[74] See Statute of the African Court of Justice, art. 46(1). It provides that 'the decisions of the Court shall be binding on the parties'.

[75] SADC Tribunal Case No. SADCT: 2/07 (SADC Tribunal, 2007). For the judgment on the substantive issues in this case, see *Mike Campbell (Pvt) Ltd* v. *The Republic of Zimbabwe*, Case No. SADC (T) 2/2007 (SADC Tribunal, 2008).

[76] *Mike Campbell (Private) Ltd* v. *Minister of National Security Responsible for Land, Land Reform and Resettlement*, Judgment No. SC 49/07 (Zimbabwe Supreme Court, 2008).

It is recommended that a role for national courts, including a procedure of reference for preliminary rulings, be adopted by the AEC. In the absence of individuals' standing rights before the African Court of Justice, allowing national courts to seek preliminary rulings will provide a substitute. Individuals can litigate at the national level in the hope that community law issues arising from their action may be resolved at the community level. This system of reference should be matched by appropriate restrictions on the type of courts that can make a reference, to reduce the judicial workload. For the AEC, this limitation would be important, due to its size and the fact that resolving human rights disputes is part of the African Court of Justice's competence.

In addition to formal procedures, it is also important that the African Court of Justice cultivates healthy 'personal' relations with national courts through consultations and workshops to help national judges familiarize themselves with community law. The fact that judges of the African Court of Justice may, potentially, be drawn from national courts should provide an important means for forging relations with national judges. As has been the case with the community courts, the African Court of Justice can also draw on the jurisprudence of member states' courts. International courts often make use of general principles of law developed in national courts. It is significant that the Statute of the African Court of Justice lists general principles of law recognized universally or by African states, as well as judicial decisions as sources of law for the court.[77] A cautious reliance on general principles of law and decisions of national courts may encourage national courts to 'reciprocate' by borrowing from or applying the jurisprudence of the African Court of Justice. Admittedly, the adjudicatory approach of relying on decisions of foreign courts as persuasive authority, especially prevalent in common law countries, is ordinarily not extended to international courts given their unique character and often specific mandates. It is not often that a national court will make reference to a decision of an international court.

However, it is increasingly advocated that there must be interaction, dialogue or transjudicial communication between national and international courts.[78] Indeed, already, some African national courts demonstrate a willingness to rely on decisions of international courts in

[77] Statute of the African Court of Justice, art. 31(d)(e).
[78] Martinez (2003–4).

deciding cases, but to date, there appears to be no reliance on decisions of African international courts. The absence of a reliance on African international tribunal decisions is disheartening. The community courts in Africa have provided some instructive jurisprudence, especially on human rights and public international law. Hopefully, national courts will begin to pay attention to the jurisprudence of the community courts and, when it becomes operational, decisions of the African Court of Justice. This will provide an indirect means of enforcing community law.[79] A court expands its authority by expanding the reach of its jurisprudence; national courts' reliance on decisions of the African Court of Justice will enhance the latter's effectiveness. If Africa's economic integration processes are to succeed, then there is a need for more engagement among the communities, national courts and individuals. The AEC Treaty and the Statute of the African Court fail to satisfy this need.

6.3 AU institutions doubling as AEC institutions

The above exposition raises a fundamental question: why have African states created and adopted institutions to address the challenges of economic integration in a manner which ill-equips them for the challenges? It is suggested that this is because there has been a convolution of the economic integration agenda with a political integration agenda under a nebulous idea variously described as 'African Union', 'African Unity', 'Union Government for Africa' and 'United States of Africa'. The process of integrating the economies of African states has not been clearly divorced from the objective of creating a 'united' African continent.

Political integration has been defined as 'the process whereby political actors in several distinct national settings are persuaded to shift their loyalties, expectations and political activities toward a new centre, whose institutions possess or demand jurisdiction over the pre-existing national states. The end result of a process of political integration is a new political community, superimposed over the pre-existing ones'.[80] Economic integration, on the other hand, is the process of removing obstacles to transnational economic activities in the fields of trade, movement of labour, services and the flow of capital. So defined, the

[79] *Von Abo* v. *Government of the Republic of South Africa* 2010 (3) SA 269, in which the court noted that the respondents could have taken advantage of an SADC Tribunal as fortification for effective diplomatic intervention on behalf of the applicant.

[80] Hass (1958), p. 16. See also Lindberg (1963), p. 6.

two are very distinct processes. Admittedly, there are close relations between economic and political integration. Some advocates of economic integration may not see it as an end in itself, but a means to greater political and social cooperation. Indeed, as Hass perceptively observed, economic integration 'may be based on political motives and frequently begets political consequences'.[81] But the fact they are related does not suggest that they are the same or, indeed, should be pursued alongside each other.

For the AEC, the problem fusing 'the economic' with 'the political' began when its founding treaty, the AEC Treaty, declared in article 98(1) that 'the Community shall form an integral part of the [Organisation of African Unity]'. Article 99 went on to declare that the treaty and protocols adopted under it shall form an integral part of the OAU Charter. With these provisions, it appears that the drafters thought it unnecessary expressly to give the AEC a separate legal personality; accordingly, the treaty is silent on this issue. The immediate understanding and effect of these provisions was that the institutions of the OAU were co-opted to perform the functions of the AEC's institutions. There appears to have been no careful thought as to whether, as then structured, the OAU institutions suited the needs of economic integration. The Constitutive Act of the African Union did not remedy this problem. After passing references to the African Economic Community in the preamble, it simply provided that the 'Act shall take precedence over and supersede any inconsistent or contrary provisions of the Treaty establishing the African Economic Community'.[82]

The African Court of Justice is, perhaps, the best example of the inappropriateness of the convolution of institutional roles. As a court for the political organization, the African Union, it is unproblematic; its structure and jurisdiction closely resembles those of the International Court of Justice of the United Nations Organization. However, as a court that also has jurisdiction over economic integration issues, its structure and jurisdiction are highly inadequate. It appears to be the only court with jurisdiction over an economic integration treaty whose jurisdiction is not compulsory; a party to the AEC Treaty that has not ratified the Protocol of the African Court of Justice is not subject to the jurisdiction of the court.[83] As discussed above, this will seriously affect the application and enforcement of AEC law.

81 Hass (1958), p. 12.
82 Constitutive Act, art. 33(2).
83 Statute of the African Court of Justice, art. 29(2).

Historically and comparatively, it is worth recalling that the Treaty for East African Cooperation,[84] which established the East African Community, had 'as an integral part of the Community'[85] the East African Common Market. However, unlike the situation with the AEC, the Treaty for East African Cooperation established at least two institutions devoted specifically to the East African Common Market, namely the Common Market Council and Common Market Tribunal.[86] More recently, Asante decried the use of the organs of the OAU (now AU) as the AEC's basic organs.[87] These organs are ill-equipped to meet the challenges of integration. The effect has been the loss of the AEC's identity. Indeed, as Asante graphically puts it, the AEC has no 'letterhead of its own', it 'has, in fact, become just a division, albeit an important one, of a continental political institution'.[88] In his view, which I endorse, 'the AEC surely requires distinct and separate institutional arrangements',[89] or, at worst, there should be clear institutional role splitting.

6.4 Looking beyond institutions

In seeking to enhance community–state relations with a view to ensuring a community's effectiveness, there is a need to complement law and legal approaches with other non-law mechanisms.[90] There is a need for greater coordination between national institutions, such as parliaments, the ministries of trade and foreign affairs, and AEC institutions. The AEC must build strong relations with these institutions by ensuring a mutual flow of information between them. An important first step is to identify these institutions. They may vary, not only from country to country, but also with regard to particular policies or issues. Already, in some countries, there are ministries or government departments the specific mandates of which relate to economic integration. Many more of these national executive institutions will be needed to ensure the effective implementation of the AEC's goals. The presence of community consciousness and an awareness of community law on the part of these institutions can further the implementation of community law.

Community consciousness must also exist among residents of the AEC. Individuals are the direct beneficiaries of community law. They serve as an effective means for monitoring compliance with community

[84] Treaty for East African Cooperation, 6 June 1967, 6 ILM 932.
[85] Ibid., art. 1(1). [86] Ibid., arts. 3, 30–1 and 32–42. [87] Asante *et al.* (2001).
[88] Asante *et al.* (2001), pp. 8–9. [89] Asante *et al.* (2001), p. 16.
[90] Van den Bossche (1996).

law through their vigilance and reporting of breaches. Education on the AEC's role and creating an accessible means for filing complaints will strengthen their monitoring role. In the absence of individual rights to bring actions before the African Court of Justice, the AEC can establish a well-designed, publicized and accessible complaint procedure. The Secretariat of the African Union, which serves as the Secretariat of the AEC, could be the forum for this procedure. Implementation of community law will also be greatly enhanced when community law is accessible, comprehensible, clear and coherent. Complex rules create difficulties for implementation and raise difficult questions of interpretation. This may result in non-compliance or varied application of community law. To ensure the effectiveness of the AEC, it is important that it engages actively the people who are the beneficiaries of its activities.

An important means to foster community consciousness among individuals is to enhance and ensure access to information on the community. At present, it is very difficult to access information on the AEC and, indeed, other African economic communities. While the founding treaties are easily accessible online, other community laws and court judgments are not. In this present age, the effective deployment of modern technology, including use of the internet, should be part of the communities' information dissemination arsenal.

6.5 Conclusion

Institutions matter for effective economic integration. The extent to which they are able to facilitate economic integration depends in part on how they relate to institutions in member states. The extent to which the framers of the AEC Treaty and other laws made under it appreciated this is open to debate. The institutional links between the Assembly of the AEC, the executive in member states, the Pan-African Parliament and national parliaments are useful. However, they could also have an adverse impact on decision-making at the community level and decision implementation at the national level. An independent institution with powers to propose policies, and ultimately implement the AEC's decisions, would have been preferable. The African Court of Justice is even less equipped for the challenges of integration. The fact that its jurisdiction is not compulsory, individuals have no standing before it as far as economic integration issues are concerned and it has no formal relations with national courts are profound shortfalls in its structure. Successful economic integration of Africa will surely demand a restructuring of the court.

In general, there is the need to isolate clearly Africa's economic integration processes from the political integration agenda (not the same as politics). With Africa's fifty-three sovereign states, the political integration agenda is manifestly unachievable; sovereign states break up, they seldom join up to form another state. The record of pre-existing internationally recognized sovereign states voluntarily coming together to form a political union is almost non-existent. The (re)unification of West Germany and East Germany to form the Federal Republic of Germany and the unification of North Yemen and South Yemen to form the Republic of Yemen are the closet examples. But compared with politically integrating fifty-three countries, both were very small-scale exercises indeed. When the economic integration processes are isolated from the political integration agenda, Africans will be better able to focus on the former and achieve remarkable success.

7

Implementing community law in African states

7.1 Introduction

The effectiveness of economic integration depends largely on how it is received and implemented within member states. It is through implementation that the divide between the community and national legal systems is bridged. In economic integration, 'the relationship between the rules that shall govern its activities and the domestic laws of the member states is quite crucial to its development'.[1] Residents in a community and national institutions should be receptive to the objectives of economic integration – and prepared to champion them. Thus, a principal challenge in economic integration is ensuring the implementation of community law in member states. How economic integration and especially community law is received nationally depends on a number of factors, of which the legal infrastructure is just one.[2] Legal infrastructure, which conditions how effectively community law is implemented in member states, includes constitutional laws, judicial philosophy and legal culture. With these elements, various mechanisms exist that render non-domestic laws – in this instance community law – enforceable or applicable within states. These mechanisms include

1 Akiwumi (1972), p. 79.

2 Another important aspect which is not investigated in this chapter is the existence and capacity of national executive institutions responsible for integration matters. Except for ECOWAS, there does not appear to be community-wide studies on this issue. See Senghor (2007). Senghor's paper draws on a more comprehensive study, *Study on National Focal Points for ECOWAS and NEPAD Programmes* (ECOWAS Secretariat, 2004). Its overall observation is that the state of affairs in many of the member countries is unsatisfactory: under-staffing, lack of expert staff, inadequate training, frequent personnel movements, inadequate funding and resources – these have all been noted as issues of concern. Some countries have full-fledged ministries on integration; others have departments or units within ministries; and yet in some, like Gambia, 'ECOWAS is more of a dossier'. Ibid., p. 162. The paper also suggests that the interface or relations between the national units responsible for ECOWAS matters and the ECOWAS Secretariat is very poor: indeed, it appears 'not to be of the highest priority' within the Secretariat. Ibid., p. 170. See also Agu (2009).

national incorporation of international law, the use of foreign laws as aids to construction, the use of foreign laws as the applicable law under the rules of private international law, and taking judicial notice of foreign laws. The use of these mechanisms to implement community law aims to enhance the effectiveness of the economic integration process. They decentralize a community's law enforcement machinery and make it accessible to residents in the community. Administratively, these mechanisms reduce the burden on the institutions set up to monitor and seek remedy for violations of community law. The absence or under-utilization of these mechanisms to implement community law leads to a disjunction between community and member states and the alienation of individuals from the economic integration process. In general, it undermines a community's effectiveness.

This chapter examines, from constitutional and case-law perspectives, how the challenge of implementing community law is addressed in Africa's economic integration processes. It draws on materials from East, Southern and West African countries, and the founding treaties of the Economic Community of West African States (ECOWAS), the Common Market of Eastern and Southern Africa (COMESA), the East African Community (EAC) and the Southern African Development Community (SADC). It examines how the founding treaties of these communities, as well as national constitutions and judicial philosophy, address the issue of the relations between community and national laws. On the whole, the community treaties, national constitutions and case law are not conducive to facilitating the implementation of community law in member states. However, a number of actions can be taken to ensure the implementation of community law at the national level. These include amendments to national constitutions and laws, and adopting judicial philosophies or approaches conducive to enhancing the status of community law within national legal systems.

7.2 Community treaties and community law implementation

The founding treaties of regional economic communities often contain provisions that define the relations between community and national law, and how the former can be made effective in member states. In the absence of these provisions, one must look for answers in national constitutions and the jurisprudence of the courts. Indeed, even where these provisions exist, one still has to look to national constitutional laws and jurisprudence of the courts to determine whether the approach adopted by the treaty can be accommodated by member states. This is because states are sovereign and, for the 'intrusion' of foreign laws into their legal systems to be accommodated, it must have the imprimatur of the sovereign state. For example, a provision in a community's treaty that individuals have rights under it cannot be effective nationally unless national laws and judicial decisions allow for the enforcement of such internationally created rights.

7.2.1 Direct applicability of community law

As discussed in Chapter 2, the principle of direct applicability of community law enables community law to become part of national law without intervening national implementation measures. Direct applicability is defined by the European Court of Justice (ECJ) as the entry into force of community law being 'independent of any measure of reception into national law'.[3] The measure of reception can be a resolution or Act of parliament, or an executive act, such as cabinet approval.[4] The character of the measure of reception often determines the domestic application or enforceability of the relevant international law. In general, and especially in common law countries, an Act of Parliament is required before international treaties become enforceable in a state;[5] mere ratification by parliament does not suffice.[6] Customary international law is often treated differently. Subject to the proof that it exists, it is automatically considered part of national law.[7] Community law is principally treaty-based. Therefore, it is unlikely to benefit from this treatment of customary international law.

Direct applicability maintains the specificity of community laws within member states. This renders issues involving community

3 *Amsterdam Bulb* v. *Produktschap voor Siergewassen* (50/76) [1976] ECR 137 at 146.

4 See, e.g. Uganda: Ratification of Treaties Act 1998, Chapter 204, s. 2(a). It allows the cabinet to ratify defined treaties without resort to parliament. Constitution of the Republic of South Africa 1996, art. 231(3) (hereafter, South Africa Constitution).

5 South Africa Constitution, art. 231(4). It provides that 'any international agreement becomes law in the Republic when it is enacted into law by national legislation; but a self-executing provision of an agreement that has been approved by Parliament is law in the Republic unless it is inconsistent with the Constitution or an Act of Parliament'.

6 Malawi Constitution, art. 211(1). It provides that 'any international agreement ratified by an Act of Parliament shall form part of the law of the Republic if so provided for in the Act of Parliament ratifying the agreement'. Constitution of Kenya 2010, art. 2(6) (hereafter, Kenya Constitution).

7 South Africa Constitution, art. 232; Constitution of the Republic of Malawi 1994, art. 211 (3) (hereafter, Malawi Constitution); Constitution of the Republic of Namibia 1990, art. 144 (Namibia Constitution); and Kenya Constitution, art. 2(5).

law more visible. It is not uncommon for a state to integrate provisions of an international convention into statute without explicitly saying so, such that, to someone unfamiliar with the international convention, the international character of the national provision is 'lost'. The legislative draftsman is not always explicit about his sources. The prospect of community law losing its specificity when it is not directly applicable and the subsequent dangers are illustrated in the South African case of *Moolla Group Ltd* v. *Commissioner, South African Revenue Service.*[8] The case involved a conflict between a South African statute incorporating a bilateral trade agreement between South Africa and Malawi, and the bilateral agreement itself. It was held that, in cases of such conflict, the national legislation should prevail. In the words of the court, 'if there were to be an apparent conflict between general provisions of the statute and particular provisions of an agreement, difficulties of interpretation might indeed arise. The Act must, of course, prevail in such a case: the agreement once promulgated is by definition part of the Act'.[9] The dictum seems to suggest wrongly that, by incorporation, international law loses its independent existence.[10] It reveals a danger inherent in 'nationalizing' international agreements.

Direct applicability also circumvents a consequence of the traditional international law modes for giving effect to international law in states, which is, subjecting international law to the national hierarchy of laws. Within a state's legal system, conflict of norms is resolved using national rules, such as invalidity ('this source – i.e. the constitution – trumps all others'), *lex specialis derogat lex generalis,* and *lex posterior derogat priori.* The application of these rules to community law could upset the vertical relations between a community and its member states, hinder the uniform application of community law and generally cause community law to be ineffective. For example, the *lex posterior derogat priori* rule implies that a subsequent Act of Parliament can render ineffective a community law that has been incorporated into national law by a prior Act, while that community law remains in force in other member states. Article 39(2) of the Protocol on the establishment of the East African Customs Union, which provides that 'the customs law of the Community shall apply uniformly in the Customs Union', is unlikely to be

[8] 2003 (6) SA 244; and Erasmus (2003). [9] *Moolla Group* at [15].

[10] Compare *Peter Anyang' Nyong'o* v. *AG* [2007] eKLR (19 March 2007) at 9, where the Kenyan court held that the fact that the Treaty establishing the East African Community Act gives the force of law to the Treaty establishing the EAC does not make the treaty lose its 'independent existence'.

effective when conflicts between an 'incorporated customs law' and national laws are resolved using the *lex posterior derogat priori* rule.[11] Happily, unlike the COMESA,[12] ECOWAS[13] and SADC treaties, the EAC Treaty provides for the principle of supremacy of community laws.[14] This principle should be applied to prioritize an 'incorporated customs law' when it conflicts with a national law.

Some economic integration treaties provide for direct applicability of community law,[15] but none of the African communities provides for it. This does not imply that the concept is unknown or that the importance of the principle is not appreciated in Africa. Indeed, in his commentary on the draft treaty establishing the EAC, Mvungi advocated the introduction of a provision for the 'direct application of community law and decisions in the domestic jurisdiction of the Partner States'.[16] Unfortunately, this call was not heeded by drafters of the EAC Treaty. Instead, provisions allowed member states to resort to their respective constitutional procedures to give effect to community law.[17] For example, under article 5(2) of the COMESA Treaty, 'each Member State shall take steps to secure the enactment of and the continuation of such legislation to give effect to this Treaty and in particular: . . . (b) to confer upon the regulations of the Council the force of law and the necessary legal effect within its territory'. This provision, without a defined time frame for enacting the legislation or a sanction for non-compliance, is susceptible to breach.[18] Only within the EAC have all the founding member states enacted legislation giving 'the force of law' to 'the provisions of any Act of the Community . . . from the date of the publication of the Act in the Gazette'.[19] Indeed, although the principle of direct applicability is not expressly provided for in the EAC Treaty, it appears that it was adopted in implementing the EAC Customs and Management Act 2004. This Act, a community Act, together with the EAC Treaty and the EAC Customs

[11] See also the SADC Treaty. It provides that 'member states shall take all steps necessary to ensure the uniform application of this Treaty'.

[12] COMESA Treaty. [13] ECOWAS Treaty. [14] EAC Treaty, art. 8(4).

[15] EU Treaty, art. 288. EEA Agreement, art. 7(a). [16] Mvungi (2002a).

[17] See EAC Treaty, art. 8(2); COMESA Treaty, art. 5(2); ECOWAS Treaty, art. 5(2); and SADC Treaty, art. 6(5).

[18] Compare EAC Treaty, art. 8(2), which set a twelve-month deadline for enacting the relevant national legislation.

[19] See Kenya – Treaty for the Establishment of East African Community Act 2000, art. 8(1); Uganda – East African Community Act 2002; and Tanzania – Treaty for the Establishment of East African Community Act 2001.

Union Protocol, forms the legal framework for the East African Customs Union. The Act applies to all member states[20] and commenced on 1 January 2005, a date appointed by the Council of Ministers.[21] Consistent with article 8(4) of the EAC Treaty, article 253 of the Act provides that it 'shall take precedence over the Partner States' laws with respect to any matter to which its provisions relate'.

The community treaties include some provisions that may be interpreted as implying the direct applicability of community law. Article 9 (6) of the ECOWAS Treaty provides that decisions of the Authority of Heads of State and Government 'shall automatically enter into force sixty days after the date of their publication in the Official Journal of the Community'.[22] Almost identical provisions are contained in the EAC and COMESA treaties.[23] In light of the fact that the treaties already envisage the use of national constitutional measures to give the 'force of law' to community law, it can hardly be argued that these provisions were meant to enshrine the principle of direct applicability.[24] In other words, these provisions give the force of law to community law at the international – not the national – level. This view is supported by the fact that publication of the relevant law is envisaged at the community level – in the Official Journal or Gazette – and not the national level. Indeed, a cursory reading of article 10 of the COMESA Treaty, which was obviously borrowed from article 249 of the Treaty Establishing the European Community (now article 288 of the EU Treaty), reveals that the phrase 'directly applicable' was deliberately omitted by drafters.[25]

In general, member states of the other communities have been remarkably coy about implementing or giving the force of law to community laws. Bethlehem has noted that 'in most instances, the trade, financial and economic agreements to which South Africa is a party have not been enacted into municipal law'.[26] Within ECOWAS, of the five

[20] East African Community Customs and Management Act 2004, art. 1(2).
[21] Ibid., art. 1(3).
[22] The same rule applies to regulations adopted by the council of ministers. See ECOWAS Treaty, art. 12(4).
[23] EAC Treaty, art. 14(5); and COMESA Treaty, art. 12(1).
[24] COMESA Treaty, art. 5(2)(b); EAC Treaty, art. 8(2)(b); and ECOWAS Treaty, art. 5(2).
[25] Article 288 of the EU Treaty provides that 'a regulation shall have general application. It shall be binding in its entirety and directly applicable in all Member States'. But art. 10(2) of the COMESA Treaty provides that 'a regulation shall be binding on all the Member States in its entirety'. The other paragraphs in the two articles on directives, decisions, recommendations and opinions are similarly worded.
[26] Bethlehem (2005).

protocols on free movement of persons, residence and establishment,[27] only one, which provides for a visa-free entry for up to ninety days for citizens of member states, has been completely implemented in all member states. The reliance on national constitutional measures to give effect to community law is a principal reason for the ineffectiveness of Africa's economic integration process, at least to the extent that community law is not immediately implemented at the national level. The provisions that mandate reliance on national constitutional measures are too broad and do not discriminate between various types of community laws. For the reason discussed below, it is appropriate to subject the communities' founding treaties to national constitutional procedures. However, there is no reason why some defined laws emanating from duly constituted community institutions which have followed the laid-down legislative procedures should not be immediately or directly applicable in member states. This is especially so if the states have already given legal effect to the founding treaty – the legal foundation of subsequent community laws. This approach is worth exploring by the communities to overcome the perennial problem of member states not giving, or delaying giving, effect to community law.

Relying on national constitutional measures to implement community law is not wholly disadvantageous. It can be used to boost Africa's integration if extensive national debates and people's involvement are made key aspects of the process. Economic integration has serious national implications. Accordingly, membership in a community and the implementation of some community laws should not be sanctioned casually in parliament or by the executive. People should be involved in the process through organized debates and, perhaps, referenda. Indeed, it is arguable that some constitutions demand a referendum before treaties – such as economic integration treaties, which involve a transfer

[27] 1979 Protocol A/P.1/5/79 relating to Free Movement of Persons, Residence and Establishment; 1985 Supplementary Protocol A/SP.1/7/85 on the Code of Conduct for the implementation of the Protocol on Free Movement of Persons, the Right of Residence and Establishment; 1986 Supplementary Protocol A/SP.1/7/86 on the Second Phase (Right of Residence) of the Protocol on Free Movement of Persons, the Right of Residence and Establishment; 1989 Supplementary Protocol A/SP.1/6/89 amending and complementing the provisions of Article 7 of the Protocol on Free Movement, Right of Residence and Establishment; and 1990 Supplementary Protocol A/SP.2/5/90 on the implementation of the Third Phase (Right of Establishment) of the Protocol on Free Movement of Persons, Right of Residence and Establishment. These protocols are reproduced in ECOWAS Secretariat, *An ECOWAS Compendium on Free Movement, Right of Residence and Establishment* (Abuja, ECOWAS Secretariat, 1999).

or surrender of national sovereignty – can be implemented nationally.[28] However, so far, no referendum on the community treaties has been held in any African country. Involving people directly in matters relating to economic integration is important for its legitimacy and ultimate success.

7.2.2 *Direct effect of community law*

As discussed in Chapter 2, the principle of direct effect enables individuals to invoke community law before national courts. It allows national courts to use community law as an independent, direct and autonomous basis for decisions. It turns national courts and individuals into private enforcers of community law. In summary, direct effect 'nationalizes' rights created at the community level. The COMESA, EAC, ECOWAS and SADC treaties are silent on the issue of whether they or laws generated under them have direct effect. This is despite the fact that they all envisage, through various mechanisms or principles, a role for individuals in their economic integration processes. An example is the preliminary reference procedure, which allows national courts to refer questions of community law to the community courts for binding answers.[29] Implicit in this procedure is an assumption that issues of community law can arise before national courts through means which include the direct invocation of community law by parties to a dispute. Indeed, if the interpretation sought by a national court from a community court under the preliminary reference procedure is not to be the direct and autonomous basis of the national court's subsequent decision, it is difficult to appreciate why the procedure was adopted.

To date, the jurisprudence of the community courts has not dealt with the issue of direct effect of community laws. However, unlike in other trade agreements,[30] direct effect of community law is not explicitly denied in the African treaties. Accordingly, if the community courts adopt a teleological or purposive approach to interpreting the community treaties, they can make direct effect part of their respective

[28] Constitution of the Central African Republic 2004, art. 70 (hereafter, Central Africa Constitution); and Constitution of Republic of the Gambia, 1997, art. 79(2) (hereafter, the Gambia Constitution).

[29] COMESA Treaty, art. 30; EAC Treaty, art. 34; ECOWAS Court Protocol, art. 10(f); and SADC Tribunal Protocol, art. 16.

[30] NAFTA, art. 2021. In US-Section 301–310 of the Trade Act of 1974, WT/DS/152, (Panel Report) at [7.72], it was held that 'neither the GATT nor the WTO has so far been interpreted by GATT/WTO institutions as a legal order producing direct effect'.

community's legal system. This will be realized if the courts' interpretation of the treaties is informed by the goal of facilitating national implementation of community law. At present, the purposive approach is the dominant approach to interpretation in national courts, the source from which most community court judges are usually drawn.[31] Hopefully, the judges will bring to bear on their work the purposive approach when interpreting the community treaties. Indeed, Article 31 of the Vienna Convention on the Law of Treaties,[32] which has already been invoked by some community courts, enjoins this approach to interpretation. As the EAC court observed: '. . . we think that we have to interpret the terms of the Treaty not only in accordance with their ordinary meaning but also in their context and in light of their objective and purpose. Primarily, we have to take objective of the Treaty as a whole, but without losing sight of the objective or purpose of a particular provision'.[33]

Another means for direct effect to be given to community law is for member states to legislate that a cause of action can be directly based on community law. An example of this – albeit, providing a very constrained right – is the Uganda Law Reform Commission's proposed WTO (Implementation) Agreement Bill.[34] Article 12 of the bill allows for private actions on WTO agreements with the consent of the Attorney General.[35]

7.2.3 *'Automatically enforceable' community law*

The AEC Treaty contains a unique provision on automatic enforceability. With a view to ensuring the effective implementation of community law at the national level, the provision may be interpreted as entailing both direct applicability and direct effect. Article 10 of the treaty provides that decisions of the Assembly of Heads of State and Government are 'automatically enforceable' thirty days after they are signed by the Chairman of the Assembly. Similarly, article 13 provides that regulations of the Council of Ministers must be approved by the

[31] Asare (2006).
[32] Vienna Convention on the Law of Treaties, 23 May 1969, 1155 UNTS 331, 8 ILM 679 (hereafter, Vienna Convention).
[33] *East African Law Society* v. *AG of the Republic of Kenya* [2008] 1 East Afr. LR 95.
[34] Uganda Law Reform Commission (2004).
[35] Compare Canada: World Trade Organization Agreement Implementation Act, SC 1994, C. 47, ss. 5 and 6.

Assembly and are also 'enforceable automatically' thirty days after they are signed by the Chairman of the Council.

The concept of 'automatically enforceable' is unique to the AEC Treaty. The COMESA, SADC, EAC and ECOWAS treaties, all of which were adopted after the AEC treaty, contain provisions akin to articles 10 and 13 of the AEC Treaty, but it appears that they consciously avoided the phrase 'automatically enforceable'.[36] The AEC Treaty is silent on where the enforceability is envisaged. Is it at the community level or within member states? The treaty is also silent on who can implement the relevant decision or regulation at the locus of enforcement. Is it only the community, its institutions and states, or does it include individuals? A purposive interpretation of the provisions suggests that automatic enforceability should not be limited to enforcement at the community level. Decisions and regulations of the Assembly and Council are likely to be of national significance or have impact on member states. Decisions or regulations that are enforceable only at the community level, and not within member states, will run counter to member states' duty to 'observe the legal system of the community'[37] and potentially undermine the effectiveness of community law. Accordingly, it is argued here that automatic enforceability envisages enforcement at both the community and national levels.

This still leaves unanswered the question as to what automatic enforceability of regulations and decisions entails at the national level. The concept of automatic enforceability could mean directly applicable, that is, no national implementing or incorporating measures are necessary to implement the decision or regulation at the national level. It could also mean directly effective, that is, the decision or regulation creates rights that individuals can invoke in national courts. This uncertainty surrounding the concept is reinforced by the fact that, under article 5(2) of the AEC Treaty, member states are obliged to take all necessary measures to ensure the enactment and dissemination of such legislation as may be necessary for the implementation of the AEC Treaty provisions. Enacting legislation to implement a decision or regulation is inconsistent with the principle of direct applicability.

At present, there is no community jurisprudence on the meaning and effect of the concept of automatic enforceability. I argue for an interpretation that entails both direct effect and direct applicability of

[36] The ECOWAS Treaty uses the phrase 'automatically enter into force'. The COMESA and EAC treaties adopt the phrase 'come into force'.

[37] AEC Treaty, art. 3(e).

decisions and regulations of the AEC. The treaty uses the concepts of 'automatic' and 'enforceable'. If the drafters intended to limit it only to incorporation, they could definitely have used a more limiting concept, such as 'automatically incorporated'. Enforceability suggests that rights can accrue under the relevant decision or regulation. No individual rights accrue under an international law at the national level unless it becomes (in this instance automatically) part of state law. I argue that, by using automatic enforceability, the drafters sought to achieve the two ends of direct effect and direct applicability.

This view is strengthened by what could be considered an elaboration on the full meaning of articles 10 and 13 of the AEC Treaty in the Rules of Procedure of the Assembly of the African Union (AU),[38] and the Rules of Procedure of the Executive Council.[39] As subsequent agreements by parties to the AEC Treaty, which were adopted under the aegis of the African Union, of which the AEC is an integral part, they could shed light on the meaning of the AEC Treaty.[40] Under rule 33 of the Assembly Rules, Assembly decisions can be in the form of Regulations, Directives, Recommendations, Declarations, Resolutions and Opinions. Regulations are applicable in all member states that take all necessary measures to implement them.[41] Directives are addressed to any or all member states, to undertakings or individuals. They bind member states to the objectives to be achieved, while giving national authorities the power to determine the form and means to be used for their implementation.[42] Recommendations, Declarations, Resolutions and Opinions are not binding and are intended to guide and harmonize the viewpoints of member states.[43] Regulations and Directives are automatically enforceable thirty days after the date of publication in the Official Journal of the African Union or as specified in the decision.[44] Regulations and Directives are binding on member states, RECs and organs of the AU.[45] All of these provisions are also contained in the Executive Council Rules. However, there is one significant clarification or addition: not only are Regulations of the Executive Council 'binding and applicable in all Member States', but also 'national laws shall, where appropriate, be aligned accordingly'.[46] From these provisions, it is evident that

[38] (2005) 13 Afr. J. Int'l & Comp. L. 41 (hereafter, Assembly Rules).
[39] (2005) 13 Afr. J. Int'l & Comp. L. 55 (hereafter, Executive Council Rules).
[40] Vienna Convention, Art. 31. [41] Assembly Rules, r. 33(1)(a).
[42] Ibid., r. 33(1)(b). [43] Ibid., r. 33(1)(c). [44] Ibid., r. 34(1)(a).
[45] Ibid., r. 34(b). [46] Executive Council Rules, r. 34(1)(a).

community law will be applied in member states, and may create rights and obligations for individuals.

From the perspective of enabling the implementation of community law in member states, these forms of AU decisions are useful, especially the Regulations and Directives. However, an examination of Assembly and Executive Council decisions between 2002 and 2009 does not reveal any attention to these categories of decisions.[47] Decisions taken by the Assembly and Executive Council are still labelled '"decision" on . . .'. There is no attempt to distinguish between decisions using the stipulated categories. Occasionally, there are Declarations and Resolutions, but, so far, there appear to be no Directives or Regulations, or, at least, they have not been so described. Surely, this is worrying: this casts real doubt on whether these forms of decisions are meant to have a meaningful legal impact on the mode of implementing the AU's decisions.

Apart from this worrying trend, it must be admitted that the above view on the meaning of automatically enforceable will be difficult to sell to member states of the AEC. Automatic enforceability, if interpreted and applied as advocated here, will represent a serious limitation on member states' sovereignty. The idea of a legal system existing independently of a state, yet having its norms directly applicable and effective within the state's legal system, is a radical departure from the traditional legal approach in many states to the implementation of international law. As discussed below, African states have varying constitutional procedures for implementing international law. In some states, before the suggested interpretation of automatic enforceability can be applied, a constitutional amendment will be needed.

From a comparative perspective, the principle of automatic enforceability captures the essence of the principles of direct applicability and direct effect in EU law, and the concept of self-executing treaties used in the United States of America and other states.[48] A self-executing treaty does not require specific implementing legislation. It may create rights inuring directly to individuals without implementing legislation. In other words, no legislation is needed to give the treaty the force of law within the state. In this regard, it can be argued that, if direct effect and direct applicability are European doctrines, and self-execution is an American doctrine, then automatic enforceability is Africa's

[47] These decisions are available at www.africa-union.org/root/au/Documents/Decisions/decisions.htm.

[48] South Africa Constitution, art. 231(3)(4); and Ngolele (2006).

contribution to the perennial problem of how to bridge the gap between international and national law.

The experience of Europe and America with direct effect, direct applicability and self-execution indicates that their effectiveness depends on the complementing role of national courts and, in Europe, the procedure of preliminary reference to the ECJ. Under the AEC Treaty and the Protocol on African Court of Justice,[49] these complementing factors are absent. Neither the treaty nor the protocol envisages any direct role for national courts, and there is no procedure for reference from national courts to the African Court of Justice. Accordingly, the concept of automatic enforceability, which could have provided a versatile means for implementing decisions and regulations of the AEC in member states, is likely to be ineffective. Ultimately, it will be left to the African Court of Justice to work out the full meaning and effect of automatic enforceability. It also remains to be seen whether and how national courts will accommodate automatic enforceability in light of the fact that they are given no express role in the enforcement of community law under the AEC Treaty or the Protocol on the African Court of Justice. Unless there is a direct or indirect means for individuals to access the African Court of Justice,[50] and national courts are involved in the enforcement of AEC law, an otherwise potent concept for enforcing AEC law in member states may be rendered useless.

7.2.4 Protecting implemented community laws

An economic community has an interest in ensuring and facilitating the implementation of its laws in member states. This interest should be matched by mechanisms and principles aimed at protecting nationally implemented community laws from inimical treatment, which may render them ineffective. As noted above, the ECOWAS, COMESA, EAC and SADC treaties have adopted what is arguably a less effective, but perhaps politically expedient, means for implementing community laws in member states. Their founding treaties rely on national constitutional procedures instead of the principle of direct applicability. The treaties are also silent on the issue of direct effect of community law and, accordingly, have rendered uncertain the issue of whether an individual

[49] Annexed to the protocol is the Statute of the African Court of Justice.

[50] Under art. 30 of the Statute on the African Court of Justice, individuals or relevant NGOs accredited to the AU or to its organs can bring cases to the court on human-rights-related matters.

can invoke community law before a national court and argue that the law creates enforceable rights.

Notwithstanding the above, the treaties contain principles and mechanisms that can be characterized as aiming to protect implemented community laws from inimical treatment in member states. Firstly, the principle of supremacy of community law, which is enshrined only in the EAC Treaty, envisages that conflicts between community and national law will be resolved in favour of the former. Secondly, the preliminary reference procedure anticipates that, ultimately, questions of community law arising before national courts will be authoritatively decided at the community level. Through this, the community's interests will be protected and conflicting national interpretations will be avoided. The preliminary reference procedure is a means for diffusing into member states a uniform understanding of community law. However, this can be achieved only when national courts are prepared to make references to the community courts. The procedure is mandatory under the COMESA and EAC treaties for designated courts, but a national court first has to make a determination regarding whether a ruling from the community court on the issue at stake is 'necessary to enable it to give judgment'.[51] Unless national courts approach this condition liberally, the utility of the reference procedure will be hampered. Finally, individuals' direct access to the community courts will ensure that breaches of community law occurring within member states are brought to the communities' attention for remedy. Without this, some breaches might escape the attention of the communities whose institutional presence within member states is minimal.

These mechanisms and principles would be useful elements to examine when the community courts are faced with issues relating to the member states' implementation of community law, especially the extent to which the treaties envisage the integration of community law into member states' legal systems. These mechanisms and principles envisage a stronger place for community law in member states than the treaties prima facie suggest. With the active involvement and cooperation of national courts, such a vision can be realized.

A mechanism for protecting a community's interests in ensuring adherence to and proper interpretation of its laws will be to grant it the right to join, intervene or appear as *amicus curiae* in national judicial proceedings in which community law becomes an issue. Put

[51] COMESA Treaty, art. 30; and EAC Treaty, art. 34.

differently, instead of making a preliminary reference to a community court, a national court can, on its own motion or at the request of a party, notify the community of the issue and invite submissions from it. This procedure will be important where national courts are reluctant to make references to the community courts. It is also important because, at present, no national legislation gives national courts the jurisdiction to seek preliminary rulings from the community courts. The community treaties endow the communities with international legal personality. The COMESA and EAC treaties also provide that 'disputes to which the Community is a party shall not, on that ground alone, be excluded from the jurisdiction of the national courts'.[52] Thus, the treaties anticipate that the communities may become parties to national judicial proceedings.

As with the jurisdiction to seek preliminary rulings, the right to join, intervene or appear as *amicus curiae* should be provided for in the laws of member states. Some African courts have held that where artificial legal personality is conferred on or denied to an entity by a foreign legal system, it will be recognized for the purposes of deciding whether that entity should be allowed to sue in an action before the court.[53] These decisions imply that the legal personality conferred on the communities by their founding treaties will be recognized nationally, to allow them to sue, be sued, join or intervene in proceedings.[54] Currently, the law in some countries allows a person to intervene in defined proceedings to protect that person's interests.[55] To be able to intervene, one must have a direct and substantial interest in the judgment.[56] At any stage in

[52] EAC Treaty, art. 33(1); and COMESA Treaty, art. 29(1). These provisions which, in principle, operate as a waiver of immunity, will allow individuals to bring claims against the community in matters such as contractual disputes over which the community courts lack jurisdiction. For a commentary on a similar provision in the EC Treaty, see de la Torre (2005).

[53] *Shah* v. *Aperit Investment SA* [2002] KLR 1; *Bank of Baroda* v. *Iyalabani Co. Ltd* [2002] 40 WRN 13; and *Edicomesa International Inc.* v. *Citec International Estates Ltd* [2006] 4 NWLR 114.

[54] Reinisch (2000), pp. 37–70 on the recognition of the legal personality of international organizations by national courts.

[55] Sierra Leone – High Court Civil Procedure Rules 2007, Order 12 r. 13, Order 55 r. 11 and Order 56 r. 17; and Ghana – High Court (Civil Procedure) Rules 2004, Order 66 r. 34 and Order 62 r. 14.

[56] *United Watch & Diamond Co. (Pty) Ltd* v. *Disa Hotels Ltd* 1972 (4) SA 409 at 415–17; and *Burdock Investment* v. *Time Bank of Zimbabwe Ltd*, HH 194/03 HC 9038/02 (High Court, Zimbabwe, 2003).

proceedings in Ghana, the court, on its own motion, can order any person 'whose presence before the Court is necessary to ensure that all matters in dispute in the proceedings are effectively and completely determined and adjudicated upon to be added as a party'.[57] Similar rules exist in other countries.[58] All of these suggest that the legal infrastructure already exists in member states for the procedure advocated here.

What is left is to attune the existing national rules and procedures to the specific demands of community law. Among the issues that must be addressed are: the procedure to be followed by a community; the time frames within which a community must act; whether the original parties to the action can oppose the joinder, intervention or admission of a community's *amicus curiae* brief; and the effect of the judgment given in the case for the intervening community and other member states, especially regarding the court's interpretation of the relevant community law. In terms of protecting community law from diverse interpretation and application in member states, the right to intervene or submit an *amicus curiae* brief is the second-best option to the preliminary reference procedure. It is unlikely to lead to the uniform interpretation of community law. However, it is an important procedure capable of complementing the preliminary reference procedure. The communities should work with member states in designing this procedure, which, as far as possible, should be uniform in all member states.

7.3 National laws and community law implementation

7.3.1 National constitutions and community law

Implementation of community law in member states is greatly influenced by national constitutions and the judicial philosophy on the relations between international and national law.[59] Because states are sovereign, giving effect to or enforcing a non-domestic law should often have the state's express or tacit approval. Where the judiciary enforces or relies on foreign laws without this approval, it can be accused of inappropriate judicial activism and blurring the lines between executive, judicial and legislative functions. This is especially the case where foreign

[57] High Court (Civil Procedure) Rules 2004, Order 4 r. 5(2)(b).

[58] Sierra Leone – High Court Civil Procedure Rules 2007, Order 18 r. 6(2)(b)(i); Uganda – Civil Procedure Rules 1964, Order 1 r. 10(2); Tanzania – Civil Procedure Code 1966, Order 1 r. 10(2); and Kenya – Civil Procedure Rules 2009, Cap. 21, Order 1 r. 10(2).

[59] Hilf and Petersmann (1993); and Jyranki (1999).

laws are used to create rights that were hitherto non-existent in member states or, given the state of the existing law, would not have been available to the person claiming those rights.

A discussion on how African constitutions may influence the implementation of community law should begin with an examination of the extent to which they acknowledge the existence of the regional economic communities. In some constitutions, there are passing references to the communities (here one should include the Organization of African Unity, the African Union) and a constitutional commitment to abide by their principles, or work towards the achievement of their goals. Article 40 of the Constitution of the Republic of Ghana provides that 'in its dealings with other nations, the Government shall adhere to the principles enshrined in or, as the case may be, the aims and ideals of . . . (ii) the Charter of the Organisation of African Unity; . . . (iv) the Treaty of the Economic Community of West African States'.[60] Other constitutions include foreign policy objectives, such as 'promoting sub-regional, regional and inter-African co-operation and unity',[61] 'promotion of African integration and support for African unity'[62] and 'respect for international law and treaty obligations'.[63]

[60] See also Constitution of the Kingdom of Swaziland 2005, art. 236(1)(d) (hereafter, Swaziland Constitution). It provides that 'in its dealing with other nations, Swaziland shall . . . (d) endeavour to uphold the principles, aims and ideals of . . . the African Union, the Southern African Development Community'. In the preamble to the Constitution of the Republic of Burundi 2004 (hereafter, Burundi Constitution), the people expressed their 'commitment to the cause of African unity in accordance with the Constitutive Act of the African Union of May 25, 2002'. The preamble to the Constitution of the Republic of Chad 1996 (hereafter, Chad Constitution) proclaims their 'attachment to the cause of African unity and our commitment to work in every way toward the realization of sub-regional and regional integration'. It is worth remembering that the AEC is an integral part of the AU. See the Constitution of the Republic of Niger 1999 (hereafter, Niger Constitution) preamble, in which they proclaim their 'attachment to African Unity and undertake to do all that is possible to perform regional and sub-regional integration'.

[61] Constitution of the Republic of Sierra Leone 1991, art. 10(b) (hereafter, Sierra Leone Constitution). The preamble to the Constitution of the Republic of Côte d'Ivoire 2000 (hereafter, Côte d'Ivoire Constitution) expresses the peoples' 'commitment to the promotion of regional and sub-regional integration, in view of the constitution of African unity'.

[62] Constitution of the Federal Republic of Nigeria 1999, art. 19(b) (hereafter, Nigeria Constitution); Constitution of the Republic of Angola 1975, art. 14 (hereafter, Angola Constitution); and Interim National Constitution of the Republic of Sudan 2005, art. 17 (b) (hereafter, Sudan Constitution).

[63] Namibia Constitution, art. 96(d).

Although very superficial, these provisions are significant. They demonstrate sensitivity to the existence and ideals of African economic integration processes. However, as channels for integrating community law into member states' laws, they are of limited use. They mainly relate to the conduct of interstate relations, a view reflected by the fact that they are often contained in the 'foreign policy' provisions of the constitutions. They do not purport to make community law part of national law. It will take a great deal of stressful legal arguments and convoluted judicial reasoning before effect can be given to community law on the basis of these provisions. In other words, they are unlikely to be bases on which individuals can claim, before national courts, the enforcement of community laws that have not been made part of national law using the laid-down constitutional procedures. Notwithstanding these observations, courts can have regard to the provisions in the interpretation and enforcement of national law vis-à-vis community law.

The fact that the constitutions acknowledge the existence of the communities and the objectives of economic integration is important. However, even more salient is the constitutions' vision of the relations between national and international law.[64] This vision directly affects the implementation of community law in member states. Traditionally, the relationship between national and international law is discussed from monist–dualist perspectives.[65] Monism has its roots in natural law theories, which see all laws as the product of reason. It envisages international law as automatically being part of national legal systems. The foundation of dualism is in legal positivism. It speculates that international and national laws operate on separate legal planes: international law governs relations between states; and national law regulates relations between individuals and the state. Under dualism, international law can play no role in the national legal systems, except insofar as it has been received or adopted by them. The monist–dualist paradigm has been a target for trenchant academic criticism, but it is still useful for understanding how states implement international law, especially treaties. This is especially so if, in approaching the paradigm, we appreciate that what really matters is not the doctrinal debate, but rather the actual practices of states.

[64] Ginsburg, Chernykh and Zachary (2008).
[65] Nijman and Nollkaemper (2007); Brownlie (2003), pp. 31–53; and Aust (2007), pp. 178–99.

African constitutions reflect the monist–dualist perspectives.[66] Other constitutional provisions appear to merge aspects of both perspectives.[67] Generally, the former British colonies have provisions that tend towards dualism; international law does not have the force of law in the Commonwealth countries unless it has been expressly given that force by a national measure, usually an Act of Parliament.[68] Many other African countries, most of them former French colonies, have constitutional provisions that adopt the monist perspective. Their provisions are modelled on article 55 of the French Constitution of 1958. In general, they provide that treaties or agreements duly ratified or approved shall, upon their publication, have an authority superior to that of domestic legislation, subject, for each agreement or treaty, to application by the other party.[69] These provisions give the force of law to international law, and also determine its status within the national hierarchy of laws. Under these provisions, as soon as an international treaty or agreement is signed, it has precedence over national laws, subject to implementation

[66] Oppong (2007d); Maluwa (1998); Adede (1999); Tshosa (2007); Tshosa (2010); and Gonidec (1998).

[67] Burundi Constitution, art. 292; Constitution of the Republic of Cape Verde 1992, art. 11 (hereafter, Cape Verde Constitution); Constitution of the Federal Democratic Republic of Ethiopia 1995, art. 9(4) (hereafter, Ethiopia Constitution); Constitution of the Republic of Gabon 1991, art. 114 (hereafter, Gabon Constitution); and Namibia Constitution, art. 144.

[68] Constitution of the Republic of Ghana 1992, art. 75 (hereafter, Ghana Constitution); South Africa Constitution, art. 231; Malawi Constitution, art. 211; Constitution of the Republic of Uganda 1995, art. 123 (hereafter, Uganda Constitution); Nigeria Constitution, art. 12; Constitution of the Republic of Zimbabwe 1979, art. 111B (hereafter, Zimbabwe Constitution); Swaziland Constitution, art. 238(4); Namibia Constitution, arts. 32(3)(e) and 63(2)(e); and Constitution of the Republic of Seychelles 1993, art. 64 (3)(4)(5) (hereafter, Seychelles Constitution).

[69] Constitution of Burkina Faso 1991, art. 151 (hereafter, Burkina Faso Constitution); Constitution of Cameroon 1996, art. 45 (hereafter, Cameroon Constitution); Constitution of Mali 1992, art. 116 (hereafter, Mali Constitution); Constitution of the Republic of Benin, art. 147 (hereafter, Benin Constitution); Constitution of the Republic of Algeria, art. 132 (hereafter, Algeria Constitution); Central African Republic Constitution 2004, art. 72; Chad Constitution 1996, art. 222; Constitution of the Federal Islamic Republic of the Comoros 1996, art. 18 (hereafter, Comoros Constitution); Constitution of the Democratic Republic of the Congo 2005, art. 215 (hereafter, DR Congo Constitution); Constitution of the Republic of the Congo 2002, art. 185; Côte d'Ivoire Constitution, art. 87; Constitution of the Republic of Guinea 1990, art. 79; Constitution of Republic of Madagascar 1998, art. 82.3(VIII) (hereafter, Madagascar Constitution); Constitution of the Islamic Republic of Mauritania 1991, art. 80; Niger Constitution, art. 132; Constitution of the Republic of Senegal 2001, art. 98 (hereafter, Senegal Constitution); and Constitution of the Republic of Rwanda 2003, art. 190 (hereafter, Rwanda Constitution).

by the other parties to the treaty or agreement. The international treaty becomes applicable as law in those monist states as soon as it is ratified. It may be invoked directly in national courts.

Although the constitutional provisions in the francophone countries make treaties superior to domestic law, conditions must be satisfied for this to happen.[70] Firstly, the agreement has to be duly ratified or approved, and published. Due ratification usually entails ensuring legislative, and sometimes judicial, approval or participation.[71] This contrasts with the approach in the Commonwealth countries, where the executive negotiates and concludes treaties that must subsequently be approved by the legislature; the judiciary rarely has a role in the treaty-making process.[72] The second requirement is that of reciprocity in the application of the treaty.[73] This requirement does not exist for the common law jurisdictions. Indeed, in the context of economic integration, making the domestic application of community law contingent on its reciprocal application by other member states can be inimical to the coherent development of a community's legal system.[74]

The implementation of community law in member states, using the constitutional provisions above, still leaves unanswered the question of the status of community law and the community itself within member states' legal systems. This is especially the case in the dualist countries. What is the position of community law within national hierarchies of laws? Will community law trump national law in case of conflict? Will all national courts have jurisdiction to adjudicate matters in which community law or a community is engaged? These are weighty issues and, for answers, one must look again at existing national constitutions.

Many African constitutions, especially those of the Commonwealth countries, contain provisions that self-proclaim the constitution as the supreme law of the land.[75] Article 1(2) of the Constitution of the

70 Kronenberger (2000).

71 Madagascar Constitution, art. 82.3(VII). It provides that 'prior to any ratification, treaties shall be submitted by the President of the Republic to the Constitutional Court'.

72 Ghana Constitution, art. 75; and South Africa Constitution, art. 231.

73 For a critique of the reciprocity requirement, see Cassese (1985), pp. 405–8.

74 In this respect, it is significant that one of the principal arguments used for denying direct effect to WTO law is that other countries do not provide for it. Eisenberg (1993–4); and Schlemmer (2004).

75 The Constitution of the Republic of Botswana, 1966 (hereafter, Botswana Constitution) appears to be an exception to this. There is no express provision in the constitution proclaiming it as the supreme law of the land, although it cannot be denied that it is indeed the supreme law.

Republic of Ghana captures this feature. It provides that 'this Constitution shall be the supreme law of Ghana and any other law found to be inconsistent with any provision of this Constitution shall, to the extent of the inconsistency, be void'.[76] Other constitutions are less flamboyant; they shy away from spelling out the consequence of the constitution being supreme. Article 1(6) of the Constitution of the Republic of Namibia, 1990, tersely provides that 'this Constitution shall be the Supreme Law of Namibia'. Whatever the phraseology adopted, the import is the same: the constitution is the *grundnorm* of the legal system from which all laws derive their legal validity.

The effective implementation of community law within states demands that the *grundnorm* validates community law. Also, the *grundnorm* should, in some instances, allow itself or a national law to be displaced by community law. Given the current structure of the constitutions, these will not be possible without a constitutional amendment. Making room for these may be politically unpalatable; it may be deemed as surrendering sovereignty, a key component of statehood. However, unbridled adherence to sovereignty is an obstacle to effective economic integration. In this respect, it is noteworthy that in the preamble to the ECOWAS Treaty, member states were 'convinced that the integration of the Member States into a viable regional Community may demand the partial and gradual pooling of national sovereignties to the Community within the context of a collective political will'. It is suggested that an additional demand is for member states to create a favourable constitutional climate for the implementation of community law.

In the absence of a constitutional amendment allowing for community law to prevail over conflicting national constitutional provisions, domestic courts may have no choice other than to obey the dictates of the constitution. As Peters has observed, the position of many international courts is that international law takes precedence over all national laws, including the constitution. However, national courts have not come to this conclusion, especially regarding relations between

[76] See also Malawi Constitution, art. 1(5); Sierra Leone Constitution, art. 171(15); South Africa Constitution, art. 2; Nigeria Constitution, art. 1(3); Gambia Constitution, art. 4; Constitution of the Republic of Zambia 1991, art. 1(3); Constitution of Republic of Kenya 2010, art. 2(1)(4); Uganda Constitution, art. 2(2); Constitution of the United Republic of Tanzania 1977, art. 64(5); Zimbabwe Constitution, art. 3; Constitution of the Republic of Lesotho 1993, art. 2; Swaziland Constitution, art. 2(1); Constitution of the Republic of Eritrea 1997, art. 2(3); Ethiopia Constitution 1995, art. 9(1); Constitution of the Republic of Mauritius 1968, art. 1(2); Seychelles Constitution, art. 5; Rwanda Constitution 2003, art. 200; Sudan Constitution, art. 3; and Benin Constitution, art. 3.

international law and the constitution.[77] Thus, in *Sikunda* v. *Government of the Republic of Namibia*, the Namibian High Court held that a UN Security Council resolution, even if part of Namibia's domestic law, 'would still be subservient to the Constitution, which is the supreme law of this country'.[78] This judicial stance reflects the fact that the court's jurisdiction is constrained by specific constitutional provisions, such as those declaring the constitution as the supreme law, as well as broader principles, such as separation of powers, which allocate the functions of national institutions in treaty making and implementation.

So far, it appears that African governments have not appreciated that economic integration makes constitutional demands and, on some issues, requires a rethink or amendment of existing constitutional or legislative provisions to accommodate community law and the community itself within their respective states. The fact that there appear to be no national laws that address the many challenges created by economic integration is testament to the lack of appreciation of the legal demands for successful integration. This non-appreciation is in part attributable to the fact that the rates of ratification and national implementation of community laws have been slow. This hinders integration at the community level and minimizes the interaction between community and national law. It is such interaction that generates many of the constitutional challenges or questions. This is borne out by the fact that, within the EAC, where the EAC Treaty has been given the force of law in member states and a number of community laws have been implemented, a body of case law is emerging on issues related to the interaction between community and national law at the national level. However, even within the EAC, the ratification and national implementation of community laws have not been perfect. At its September 2008 meeting, the Council of Ministers noted five protocols concluded in 2006 and 2007 that had not yet been ratified by member states, and suggested that the belated ratification hampers 'the enactment of legislation based on them'.[79] A similar problem of non-ratification of protocols and non-implementation at the domestic level exists within the SADC.[80]

Comparatively, many European countries have effected significant constitutional amendments in response to the legal demands of European

[77] Peters (2007), pp. 259–69. [78] 2001 NR 86 at 95.
[79] East African Community, Report of 16th Meeting of the Council of Ministers, Ref. EAC/CM 16/2008 (AICC, Arusha, Tanzania, 2008), pp. 28–9.
[80] Cronje (2010).

integration.[81] In the words of Vereshchetin, 'European integration had a serious impact on several Western European constitutions . . . [and] required the adoption of special constitutional provisions in a number of States'.[82] Article 148 of the Constitution of Romania, which recently became an EU member, is an example in this respect. It provides:

> (1) Romania's accession to the constituent treaties of the European Union, with a view to transferring certain powers to community institutions, as well as to exercising in common with the other member states the abilities stipulated in such treaties, shall be carried out by means of a law adopted in the joint sitting of the Chamber of Deputies and the Senate, with a majority of two thirds of the number of deputies and senators.
> (2) As a result of the accession, the provisions of the constituent treaties of the European Union, as well as the other mandatory community regulations shall take precedence over the opposite provisions of the national laws, in compliance with the provisions of the accession act.
> (3) The provisions of paragraphs (1) and (2) shall also apply accordingly for the accession to the acts revising the constituent treaties of the European Union.
> (4) The Parliament, the President of Romania, the Government, and the judicial authority shall guarantee that the obligations resulting from the accession act and the provisions of paragraph (2) are implemented.

Presently, this level of constitutional accommodation, which definitely facilitates the implementation of community law, has no parallels in the constitutions of African states. In article 3 of the Proposed New Constitution of Kenya 2005, it was provided that the EAC laws will form part of the Kenyan laws. But for the rejection of this constitution in a referendum in November 2005, this provision would have transformed the place of EAC law in Kenya's legal system. It would have been the most significant provision in an African constitution on the status of community law within a national legal system. The 2010 Constitution of Kenya does not contain this provision. However, because article 2(6) of the constitution makes treaties or conventions ratified by Kenya 'part of the

[81] See, e.g. Basic Law for the Federal Republic of Germany, art. 23; Constitution of Belgium, art. 34; Constitution of Luxembourg, art. 49*bis*; Constitution of the Netherlands, art. 92–4; United Kingdom, European Communities Act 1972; and Constitution of Poland, art. 91(3). See generally Pernice (1998).

[82] Vereshchetin (1996), p. 31.

law of Kenya', many EAC laws – including the EAC Treaty – are now part of Kenya's legal system.

Admittedly, the current stage of the EU's development makes constitutional demands on member states very different from those that apply at the present stage in Africa's economic integration processes. Indeed, in Europe, the interactions between EU law and national constitutions did not become a dominant issue until the period immediately before the Maastricht Treaty in 1992.[83] At present, given the existing EU law on the interaction between community and member states' laws, it is impossible to become an EU member without the prospective member taking a critical look at its constitution and making substantive amendments to it. Notwithstanding the fact that Africa's economic integration processes are still in the early stages of development, it is undeniable that African constitutions have remained largely ambivalent towards community law. After decades of a professed commitment to economic integration, one would have expected significant provisions in national constitutions on the subject.

Historically, there existed in Africa constitutional provisions that anticipated the strengthening of integration, and that were prepared to accommodate that. The immediate post-independence constitutions were imbued with preambles that extolled the virtues of African unity and Africans uniting. They also contained specific and legally binding provisions that envisaged the ultimate surrender of national sovereignty to aid African unity. In article 13 of the Constitution of the Republic of Ghana 1960, it was provided that 'the independence of Ghana should not be surrendered or diminished on any ground other than the furtherance of African unity'. In article 2, 'in the confident expectation of an early surrender of sovereignty to a union of African states and territories', Ghanaians conferred on Parliament 'the power to provide for the surrender of the whole or any part of the sovereignty of Ghana'. Article 34 of the Constitution of the Republic of Guinea 1958 had earlier provided that 'the Republic may conclude with any African State agreements providing for association or the establishment of a community and involving partial or total relinquishment of sovereignty with a view to the achievement of African Unity'. Similar provisions in other African countries have been chronicled by Schwelb.[84] The speed with which the OAU was formed is a

[83] Maus (1999), pp. 47–9. [84] Schwelb (1960), pp. 640–2.

testament to the importance of these constitutional provisions that encapsulated a consciousness favourable to uniting Africa.

However, it is ironic that, contrary to these provisions, when the Charter of the Organization of African Unity[85] was drafted and the organization was formed in 1963, 'sovereign equality of all Member States', 'non-interference in the internal affairs of States' and 'respect for the sovereignty and territorial integrity of each State and for its inalienable right to independent existence' were entrenched as cardinal guiding (ultimately, debilitating) principles.[86] The OAU never purported to be an economic integration organization or, at least, did not set out a clear economic integration agenda. Accordingly, the effect that the post-independence constitutional provisions could have had on any economic integration process and, especially, on the implementation of community law in member states remains uncertain. What is certain is that these constitutional provisions did not make their way into subsequent constitutional revisions in many states. However, a few countries, all non-anglophone, still retain constitutional provisions that envisage relinquishing national sovereignty to promote African unity.[87] Article 133 of the Constitution of the Republic of Niger 1999 is perhaps the most detailed on this subject. It provides that:

> The Republic of Niger may conclude with any African State agreements of association or community bringing partial or total abandonment of sovereignty with the view to realizing African unity.
>
> The Republic of Niger may conclude agreements of cooperation and of association with other States on the basis of reciprocal and advantageous rights.
>
> It accepts to create with these State intergovernmental organisms of common management, of coordination and of free cooperation.
>
> These organisms may in particular have as objectives: the harmonization of economic, finance and monetary policy; the establishment of union endeavoured to the economic integration through promotion of production and exchanges; the cooperation in judicial matters.

The fact that such constitutional provisions have largely disappeared from African constitutions says much about the commitment of African

85 Charter of the Organization of Africa Unity, 25 May 1963, 2 ILM 766.
86 Ibid., art. III(1)(2)(3).
87 Central Africa Republic Constitution, art. 70; Burkina Faso Constitution, art. 146; DR Congo Constitution, art. 217; Mali Constitution, art. 117; Senegal Constitution, art. 96; and Benin Constitution, art. 149.

states to Africa's economic integration processes. Indeed, one recent constitution severely constrains the possibility of the state surrendering sovereignty – a key requisite for integration – to aid economic integration.[88] It is worth noting that these constitutions, which seem to pay very little attention to the legal demands of economic integration, were promulgated after the signing of the Treaty establishing the AEC in 1991.

The interaction between community and national law is not unidimensional. As community law is implemented at the national level, so must a community take account of existing national laws when making community law. The latter is important for the effective implementation of community law at the national level. It also reflects the fact that membership of a community entails only a partial surrender of sovereignty. In making laws, a community should not lose sight of the areas still within the competence of member states. Through a number of provisions, the community treaties acknowledge the existence of national constitutions, adopt conclusions legitimized by them or utilize their procedures for the implementation of community law.[89] One area where this is visible is that of giving effect to the treaties or other community laws. Under article 5(2) of the ECOWAS Treaty, 'each Member State shall, in accordance with its constitutional procedures, take all necessary measures to ensure the enactment and dissemination of such legislative and statutory texts as may be necessary for the implementation of the provisions of this Treaty'. Although the COMESA and EAC treaties do not make reference to constitutional procedures, this can be inferred from reading the relevant provisions.[90]

Community institutions also draw on existing national institutions for their make-up. The composition of the Assembly of Heads of State and Government, Council of Ministers and community parliaments is contingent on national institutions. Indeed, article 1 of the EAC Treaty defines a Head of State and Head of Government as 'a person designated as such by a Partner State's Constitution'. Similarly, under article 50(2)(b), a person shall be qualified to be elected a member of the Assembly of the EAC by the National Assembly of a partner state if such a person is,

[88] Gambia Constitution, art. 79(2).

[89] In one provision, the community treaty seems to dictate to national constitutions. Article 145 of the EAC Treaty provides that 'a Partner State may withdraw from the Community provided: (a) the National Assembly of the Partner State so resolves by resolution supported by not less than two-thirds majority of all the members entitled to vote'. Member states of the EAC have their own constitutional provisions which dictate the number of votes needed on any particular issue.

[90] EAC Treaty, art. 8(2); and COMESA Treaty, art. 5(2).

amongst other things, 'qualified to be elected a member of the National Assembly of that Partner State under its Constitution'.

Community law also sometimes reflects values already entrenched in national constitutions. This is so on issues such as human rights, the rule of law and democracy. At first sight, this may appear superfluous when these values are already entrenched, at least on paper, at the national level. However, that is not so. Firstly, compliance with these provisions within member states creates the necessary democratic and rule-of-law-oriented environment in which economic integration thrives. Secondly, community law becomes an added layer of legality by which the conduct of national governments may be tested. This becomes important in instances where governments act in violation of their own national constitutional values. For example, in the Ugandan case of *Katabazi* v. *AG of Uganda*,[91] the applicants, who were being tried for treason, were granted bail by the High Court of Uganda. However, armed security agents surrounded the court premises and prevented the execution of bail. They re-arrested the applicants, re-incarcerated them and re-charged them to appear before a court martial. They were not released even after the Constitutional Court of Uganda so ordered. This conduct was held to be a violation of the rule of law enshrined in article 6(d) of the EAC Treaty. It is worth remembering that the Constitution of the Republic of Uganda contains a bill of rights.

It is evident from the above that relations between community law and national constitutions go beyond issues bordering on giving effect to community law or resolving conflicts between community law and national law.[92] Community law may influence national constitutional values on issues such as democracy, good governance, the rule of law and human rights. Indeed, the community treaties contain provisions stipulating democracy, respect for the rule of law and human rights as guiding principles.[93] These principles can inform constitutional design and interpretation at the national level. There is a strong positive correlation between constitutionalism at the national level and the effectiveness of economic integration.[94] The community treaty provisions can also be useful in adjudicating, at the community level, the legality of conduct at the national level.

[91] Reference No. 1 of 2007 (East African Court of Justice, 2007).

[92] Wouters (2000), pp. 25–7.

[93] ECOWAS Treaty, art. 4(g)(j); EAC Treaty, art. 3(3)(b), 6(d), 7(2); and COMESA Treaty, art. 6(e)(g)(h).

[94] Adewoye (1997).

The interactions between community and national law go beyond national constitutions. The constitutions provide only the initial platform for receiving community law. Equally important are the existing statutory laws. Often, community law defers to national law on certain matters, or allows member states to escape from the full breadth of their community obligations. The EAC Customs Management Act 2004 contains more than fifteen direct references to the law in force in member states. Deference to national law is important; it recognizes state sovereignty and allows law to be adapted to local circumstances. However, it could sometimes hinder the effective implementation of community law. Under article 4 of the ECOWAS Protocol Relating to the Free Movement of Persons, Residence and Establishment 1979, member states reserved the right to 'refuse admission into their territory any Community citizen who comes within the category of inadmissible immigrants under its laws'. Studies on national laws, most of which predate the protocol, suggest that they often conflict with the letter and spirit of the protocol and its supplements, and have been used to exclude community citizens without explanation or process for review.[95] To overcome the challenge deference to national law poses for the effective implementation of community law, the communities must be attentive to national laws in their legislative processes. They should also keep abreast of changes to national laws on an ongoing basis through mechanisms such as annual reporting. These will help to avoid potential conflicts between community and national laws, and also ensure that exceptions provided by community law do not become a national refuge for denying effect to it.

7.3.2 *National judicial philosophy and community law*

It was discussed in Chapter 5 that, as an institution, national courts are important for economic integration. Equally important is the judicial philosophy that informs their decisions, especially regarding disputes in which community law is involved. Judicial philosophy has a direct impact on the implementation of community law. This is especially so in instances where community law has not been incorporated into national law or is not directly applicable. Judicial philosophy that is attuned to the goals and demands of economic integration, but is nonetheless sensitive to national constitutional limits on the exercise of judicial power, especially on issues of foreign policy, is important for

[95] Adepoju, Boulton and Levin (2007), p. 11.

ensuring the effectiveness of community law in member states. A state's external economic relations or policies may fall into the domain of foreign policy. Courts should act with restraint in intervening or judicially reviewing the direction of such relations or policies. This is not to deny that the judiciary has a crucial role to play in trade policy.[96] Indeed, in appropriate cases, especially where individual rights are involved, judicial intervention, including a criticism of the direction of such relations or policies, may be appropriate.[97] Apart from criticizing government policies inimical to economic integration, judicial philosophy, which takes account of the goals of economic integration, can be relevant in courts' approaches to the principle of consistent interpretation, general reliance on foreign laws, taking of judicial notice and application of the rules on proof of foreign law. These can also be utilized to enhance the role of community law in member states.

In many African countries, some form of executive or parliamentary act is required for international law to have the force of law within the national legal system. However, it is legally possible for courts to give domestic effect to a treaty, and hence community law, even though it has not been incorporated into national law. The extent to which a court can do this depends on the character of the relevant law, what the government has already done in relation to that law, the state of the existing law and the court's approach to the doctrine of separation of powers. In Africa, courts' reliance on unincorporated treaties has been very visible in cases involving human rights issues. In a number of cases, courts have relied on unincorporated human rights treaties. Courts have had recourse to unincorporated treaties in interpreting ambiguous statutes.

In *Dow* v. *AG*,[98] the applicant challenged the constitutionality of provisions of Botswana's Citizenship Act 1984 as being discriminatory and an infringement on her constitutional rights and freedoms. The relevant provisions of the Act, in essence, denied citizenship to children born to female citizens of Botswana who were married to foreign men. The High Court's interpretation of a statute was 'strengthened' by the fact that Botswana was a signatory to the OAU Convention on Non-Discrimination, even though Botswana had not ratified it, a fact which the judge expressly acknowledged. On appeal, the Attorney General specifically took issue with the court's reliance on unincorporated

96 Kufour (2008), pp. 110–13.
97 *Von Abo* v. *The Government of the Republic of South Africa* 2009 (2) SA 526.
98 1991 BLR 233.

treaties, but the Court of Appeal affirmed the trial court's use of unincorporated treaties.[99] It held that, even if treaties and conventions do not confer enforceable rights on individuals within the state until parliament gave them the force of law, they could still be used as aids to interpretation. In Ghana, Justice Archer in *New Patriotic Party* v. *Inspector General of Police*[100] held that the fact that Ghana had not passed specific legislation to give effect to the African Charter on Human and Peoples' Rights did not mean that it could not be relied upon in adjudication.[101] In Kenya, the Court of Appeal has held that, even though Kenya subscribes to the common law view that international law is only part of domestic law where it has been specifically incorporated, current thinking on the common law theory is that both international customary law and treaty law can be 'applied by state courts where there is no conflict with existing state law, even in the absence of an implementing legislation'.[102] The judicial philosophy that gives effect to unincorporated treaties has also been felt in other areas. In Ghana, Justice Ocran was influenced in *Delmas America Africa Line Inc.* v. *Kisko Products Ghana Ltd*[103] by the UN Convention on the Carriage of Goods by Sea. He found Article 5 on the liability of carriers 'highly relevant', even at a time when the convention had not been incorporated into Ghanaian law. In South Africa, the Supreme Court of Appeal in *De Gree* v. *Webb* was influenced by the principles of the Hague Convention on the Protection of Children and Cooperation in respect of Inter-Country Adoption, which, although ratified by South Africa, had not been implemented domestically at the time.[104] Similarly, in *Roger Parry* v. *Astral Operations Ltd*,[105] the South African Labour Court was prepared to be 'guided by' article 6 of the EU's Rome Convention on the Law Applicable to Contractual Obligations.

[99] *AG* v. *Dow* 1992 BLR 119.

[100] [1993–94] 2 GLR 459 at 466. Compare *Chihana* v. *Republic*, MSCA Criminal Appeal No. 9 of 1992, where the Supreme Court of Malawi held that the UN Universal Declaration of Human Rights is part of the law of Malawi, but the African Charter on Human and People's Rights is not and added: 'Malawi may well be a signatory to the Charter and as such is expected to respect the provisions of the Charter but until Malawi takes legislative measures to adopt it, the Charter is not part of the municipal law of Malawi and we doubt whether in the absence of any local statute incorporating its provision the Charter would be enforceable in our Courts.'

[101] Botha and Olivier (2004).

[102] *Rono* v. *Rono* [2005] KLR 538 at 550. [103] [2005] SCGLR 75.

[104] *De Gree* v. *Webb* 2007 (5) SA 184. See also *K* v. *K* 1999 (4) SA 691.

[105] 2005 (10) BLLR 989.

All of these cases suggest that it is possible for courts to give effect to community law even when it has not been expressly incorporated into national law. This should be encouraged. The extent to which this can be done will vary from case to case. It will also depend on the ability of counsel, at times, to draw the court's attention to the relevant community law. As discussed below, there are cases emerging in which this has been done.

Apart from using community law as an aid to interpretations with a view to enhancing its effectiveness in member states, judicial philosophy may also be used to allow community law to confer rights on individuals under the doctrine of legitimate expectation. This doctrine is well accepted in the public law of many common law jurisdictions, including those in Africa.[106] It began its life as a doctrine aimed at safeguarding procedural fairness and legal certainty, but it is now well accepted that it can, albeit rarely, create substantive rights for individuals. In some countries, the doctrine has been extended to treaties that have been ratified but not incorporated into national law.[107] In Africa, decided cases on this issue are scant.

Dicta in *Abacha* v. *Fawehinmi*;[108] suggest that the Nigerian Supreme Court accepts that an unincorporated treaty might give rise to a legitimate expectation that the government would observe the terms of the treaty.[109] However, in the Zimbabwean case of *Movement for Democratic Change* v. *The President of the Republic of Zimbabwe*,[110] the court rejected this possibility. The applicant argued that, although the Southern African Development Community Principles and Guidelines Governing Democratic Elections (hereafter, the SADC Guidelines) had not been

106 *Administrator, Transvaal* v. *Traub* 1989 (4) SA 731 at 761; *Lisse* v. *The Minister of Health and Social Services* 2004 NR 107; and *Republic* v. *Kenya Revenue Authority, ex parte Aberdare Freight Services Ltd* [2004] 2 KLR 530 at 545–6. Forsyth (2006b).

107 *Minister of Immigration and Ethnic Affairs* v. *Teoh* (1995) 183 CLR 273. Although doubt has been cast on *Teoh* in subsequent Australian decisions, it has not been overruled. Kirby (2010), p. 42.

108 [2000] 6 NWLR 228.

109 Ibid. at [12]–[13], Ogundare JSC delivering the lead judgment, and subsequently Achike JSC cited with approval the Privy Council opinion in *Higgs* v. *Minister of National Security* [2000] 2 WLR 1368 at 1375 to the effect that an unincorporated treaty 'may have an indirect effect upon the construction of statutes . . . Or may give rise to a legitimate expectation on the part of the citizens that the government, in its acts affecting them, would observe the terms of the treaty', and added that this 'represents the correct position of the law, not only in England but in Nigeria as well'.

110 HC 1291/05 (High Court, Zimbabwe, 2007).

incorporated into domestic law, the court could use the doctrine of legitimate expectation to hold that the provisions of the SADC Guidelines are relevant and applicable in the court. The court rejected this argument. It held that although the SADC Guidelines had been approved by the Zimbabwean Government, they were not a direct source of rights and obligations under Zimbabwean law. In the court's view, by assenting to the SADC Guidelines, the government indicated to both the national and international communities that it subscribed to the minimum standards set out in the guidelines. Indeed, the court noted that after approving the SADC Guidelines, the government 'initiated and piloted through Parliament, two specific pieces of legislation aimed at regulating the conduct of elections in accordance with the SADC Principles and Guidelines'. However, it did not give the applicant, or any other citizen of Zimbabwe, a cause of action that was enforceable in a domestic law court.

Admittedly, this is the correct position in law. However, the court's failure to investigate whether at least some procedural rights could have been indirectly founded on the SADC Guidelines can be criticized. This is especially so since the court noted that after approving the SADC Guidelines, the government initiated and piloted through Parliament two specific pieces of legislation that were aimed at regulating the conduct of elections, in accordance with the SADC Guidelines. In seeking a foundation for a decision based on legitimate expectation arising out of an unincorporated community law, a national court will have to pay attention to the conduct of its executive – at both the international and national levels. The fact that the relevant community law has been signed or ratified, pronouncements of the government during the negotiations on the law and the government's action on the law since signing may all be relevant considerations.

It remains to be seen whether and how African courts will help to implement community law, especially in the light of the fact that, generally, governments have been reluctant to implement community laws through incorporation. Interestingly, in such a setting, relying on the doctrine of legitimate expectation and the principle of consistent interpretation to give effect to those laws nationally will be an important step forward. It could send a positive – and strong – signal to governments that the community laws are worth more than the papers they are written on; they can have consequences at the national level. Such a judicial stance may well deter governments from negotiating and ratifying treaties and other community laws. However, this is purely conjectural. And, in any case, it may be better not to have a treaty at all than to have one which has no meaningful effect.

There have been a few cases in which reliance has been placed on the communities' objectives or goals. Although they are not laws as such, the objectives and goals of the communities can shape courts' jurisprudence, and the remedies they provide, in a manner that enhances economic integration. In *R.* v. *Obert Sithembiso Chikane*,[111] the Swaziland court held that 'in cases where cross-border criminals are convicted, the Courts must [through the sentence] express the displeasure of the Southern African Development Community that serious cross-border crime shall not be tolerated'. Furthermore, in *Shah* v. *Manurama Ltd*,[112] the Ugandan court held that, in East Africa, there could no longer be an automatic and inflexible presumption for the courts to order security for costs against a plaintiff resident in the EAC. One factor that influenced the court in its decision was the fact that, among the objectives of the community, as outlined in article 5 of the EAC Treaty, was the need to develop policies and programmes aimed at widening and deepening cooperation among the member states in legal and judicial affairs for their mutual benefit. Judicial reliance on community objectives when deciding cases is important at the present stage of the communities' development, in which the body of community law is not enormous and states have been slow to incorporate community law. By paying attention to the objectives of the communities, courts can fashion remedies or produce judgments that ultimately strengthen integration. Areas where this could be useful include the enforcement of judgments from other African countries, national restrictions on cross-border commerce, migrant workers' rights and treatment of foreigners' assets.

In addition to relying on the communities' objectives, there have been instances where courts drew on substantive community laws to bolster their decisions. In *Friday Anderson Jumbe* v. *Humphrey Chimpando*,[113] the Malawian court relied on the Southern African Development Protocol against Corruption for guidance on principles relating to corruption. In *S* v. *Shaik*, the South African Constitutional Court cited an article in the AU Convention on Preventing and Combating Corruption as evidence of the seriousness of corruption as a crime and its potential to undermine important constitutional values.[114] In *Chloride Batteries Ltd* v.

[111] Crim. Case No. 41/2000 (High Court, Swaziland, 2003).

[112] [2003] 1 East Afr. LR 294.

[113] Constitutional Case Nos. 1 and 2 of 2005 (High Court, Malawi, 2005).

[114] 2008 (5) SA 354 at 384.

Viscocity,[115] the Malawian court took judicial notice of article 55 of the COMESA Treaty, which deals with competition, in granting an injunction restraining the defendant from marketing in Malawi alleged counterfeit batteries imported from Kenya.[116] In *Hoffman* v. *South African Airways*,[117] which dealt with the constitutionality of South African Airways' practice of refusing to employ as cabin attendants people who are living with HIV, the South African Constitutional Court referred to the Code of Conduct on HIV/AIDS and Employment in the Southern African Development Community 1997. The court took cognizance of the fact that under the Code: HIV status should not be a factor in job status, promotion or transfer; pre-employment testing for HIV is discouraged; and no compulsory workplace testing for HIV is required. Finally, in the Lesotho case of *Molifi* v. *Independent Electoral Commission*,[118] the male applicant challenged the constitutionality of legislation that designated particular electoral divisions as reserved for women candidates only, including the one in which he wanted to stand for election into the local assembly. One of the international instruments found to be useful by the court in rejecting the applicant's challenge was the SADC Declaration on Gender and Development 1997.

In many of the above cases, the courts did not engage in depth with the community laws or objectives they used. Had this been done, one would have had a better sense of the courts' attitude towards community law and the goals of economic integration. One would also have been able to predict better the extent to which future legal submissions based on community law, even if unincorporated, would be received. Notwithstanding this limitation, the cases are important first steps. They demonstrate a level of awareness on the part of lawyers and judges of the existence and relevance of community law. It is hoped that, with time, this awareness will translate into more rigorous judicial and legal engagement with community law and its place in member states. In furtherance of this, academics and institutions have a crucial role to play. They must sow the seeds of community law in the minds of future generations of lawyers and judges. This can be done through specific courses on

[115] Civil Cause No. 1896 of 2006 (High Court, Malawi 2006).

[116] Article 55(1) provides that: 'The Member States agree that any practice which negates the objective of free and liberalised trade shall be prohibited. To this end, the Member States agree to prohibit any agreement between undertakings or concerted practice which has as its objective or effect the prevention, restriction or distortion of competition within the Common Market.'

[117] 2001 (1) SA 1.

[118] Civil No. 11/05, CC: 135/05 (Court of Appeal, Lesotho, 2005).

economic integration in Africa or integrating relevant aspects of community law into already existing courses, such as international law and commercial law. Economic integration studies should not be confined to postgraduate students. The presence of a strong juristic community with interest in community law is one of the surest ways to guarantee the effective implementation of community law in member states.

From the above, it is evident that, apart from instances where community law has been directly incorporated into national law or expressly made a source of national law, the doctrine of legitimate expectation, the principle that legislation should be interpreted consistently with international law, and a judicial philosophy that generally allows courts to be guided by foreign norms, may be used to give effect to community law in member states. In other words, they can provide an avenue through which unincorporated community laws can be implemented in member states. This will be advantageous to the communities and individuals. Admittedly, in the absence of specific national legislation implementing community law, the role courts can play is limited. Courts are constrained by constitutional arrangements on the separation of powers. Equally important is the degree to which judges and lawyers are aware of community laws and are willing to deploy them in adjudication and litigation. Also, the role of courts is contingent on litigation in which community law is engaged and legal arguments in which community issues are raised. Where, perhaps due to a lack of awareness and financial constraints, there is a culture of settling disputes out of court or of not invoking community law in litigation, there is not much courts can do through their jurisprudence to facilitate the implementation of community law.

7.3.3 *National legal culture and community law*

An examination of the implementation of law is incomplete without an assessment of the effect of factors outside the 'formal' structures of institutions, judicial decisions, statutes and constitutions that make up the legal system. These factors, which include legal culture, affect the implementation of law. Friedman has emphasized that law is best understood and described as a system that is a product of social forces. Social forces shape the evolution, content, enforcement and efficacy of law.[119]

[119] Friedman (1975). Earlier, Friedman described legal culture as 'the network of values and attitudes relating to law'. See Friedman (1969), p. 34. For a critique of Friedman's approach to the concept of legal culture, see Cotterrell (1997).

Unlike legal principles, legal culture – which is an aspect of culture, the way of life of a people – is largely country-specific, diverse and evolutionary.[120] Indeed, legal culture may vary across different branches of law and even within parts of the same country. Thus, it may not be entirely accurate or appropriate to talk about an African legal culture as if there were a homogenous 'African' way of life as regards the law.

Notwithstanding these caveats, there are a number of factors about legal systems in Africa that could potentially affect the implementation of community law. These factors include the underdeveloped nature of the legal systems, legal pluralism and the minimal use of litigation as a channel for addressing disputes. Griffiths defines legal pluralism as 'the state of affairs, for any social field, in which behaviour pursuant to more than one legal order occurs'.[121] So defined, it can be said that most, if not all, states are pluralistic. What is distinct in Africa is that the existence of multiple legal orders is statutorily recognized, and laws and conduct founded on those legal orders are legitimized by the state.[122]

Legal pluralism in Africa provides for multiple legal regimes and avenues for legal redress. In some countries, native courts administering customary (and Sharia) law coexist with the national courts.[123] In others, the national courts administer both customary and general law. The existence of multiple legal orders implies multiple demands on people's commitment to law; some may feel more attached to customary law, some to the general state law and others possibly to community law. The making and implementation of community law will have to take these into account. A pluralistic tradition can be adaptable to specific situations and problems. However, it also suggests the need for a robust private international law regime that can offer certainty for foreign investors and economic transactions. Unfortunately, the current regime in most African legal systems is underdeveloped and cannot adequately cope with the challenges of integration.[124]

Legal pluralism's potential adverse impact on the implementation of community law and, generally, on economic integration in Africa should not be exaggerated. In many African countries, legal pluralism is mostly manifest in family-, succession- and property-law-related issues. Areas of commercial law, such as contracts, torts, banking and insurance, are

[120] Nelken (2004). [121] Griffiths (1986), p. 2.
[122] Ghana Constitution, art. 11; the Gambia Constitution, art. 7(e)(f); and Constitution of the Republic of Malawi, art. 200.
[123] Zimbabwe: Customary Law and Local Courts Act, Chapter 7:05.
[124] Oppong (2006d).

regulated mainly by generally applicable and uniform state laws. Family law and succession may not be directly relevant for economic transactions at the present stage of economic integration in Africa, but they will become so as the communities start the process of integrating the 'social and cultural'[125] dimensions of life in member states. Although there are similarities in the rules, customary law is, of course, not uniform in Africa.[126]

When people move freely within the communities and form personal relationships with people subject to different customs, questions on the content and application of customary law will emerge. What happens when community law provides for rights not recognized under a group's customary law? What happens when community law conflicts with customary law? Will community law prevail in such instances? Will customary law be deemed of such importance to the lives of its adherents that it will remain unaffected by community law? Will traditional private international law rules be appropriate in this context? Surely, social issues addressed by customary law also have economic dimensions and the communities cannot remain neutral or ambivalent towards them. Thus, it is not surprising that the EU has legislated in the area of family law[127] and is currently working on wills and succession.[128] In Africa, these issues will also have to be addressed, with customary law being a complicating factor. This complication is exacerbated by the fact that customary laws are diverse across the continent and are largely unwritten. Accordingly, there is no written

[125] AEC Treaty, art. 6(2)(f)(ii), which envisages the integration of the 'social and cultural sectors' at the final stage in the establishment of the AEC. The EAC aims to deepening cooperation among the member states in 'social and cultural fields'. See EAC Treaty, art. 5(1). The ECOWAS aims at adopting common policies in the 'social and cultural sectors'. See ECOWAS Treaty, art. 3(2)(e).

[126] Abiodun has argued that a '"United African Customary Law" will be instrumental to the proposed project for a "United African States" by the African Union' (Abiodun (2007), p. 80). Historically, an attempt in this direction, namely the Restatement of African Law Project which began under the direction of Professor Allot of the School of Oriental and African Studies, was eventually abandoned.

[127] See Council Regulation (EC) No. 2201/2003 of 23 November 2003, concerning Jurisdiction and the Recognition and Enforcement of Judgments in Matrimonial Matters and the Matters of Parental Responsibility, repealing Regulation (EC) 1347/2000.

[128] Proposal for a Regulation of the European Parliament and of the Council on Jurisdiction, Applicable Law, Recognition and Enforcement of Decisions and Authentic Instruments in Matters of Succession and the creation of a European Certificate of Succession, Brussels, 14 November 2009, COM(2009)154 Final.

law to 'look up', but there are many laws that one may have to investigate on site, rather than in the comfort of a library.

The impact on economic integration of legal pluralism in property law is, however, more immediate and can be adverse. Multiple regimes for the transfer and ownership of property, as well as customary law restrictions on alienation of property, can be a disincentive to establishing business and undertaking commercial activities.[129] The land tenure system in Ghana, which mixes customary law with state law, has been noted as a major obstacle to foreign investment.[130] In general, legal pluralism in Africa has economic significance, since it will ultimately increase transaction costs for businesses to investigate multiple sources of law. One writer has also noted legal pluralism as being a potential source of conflict, a state of affairs that undermines commerce.[131]

Another feature of African legal culture that is likely to impact on the implementation of community law is the minimal use of law and litigation as channels for redressing wrongs. Friedman has observed that legal culture 'determines when and why and where people turn to law or government, or turn away'.[132] African legal culture emphasizes reconciliatory and non-adversarial modes of settling disputes. Adjudication is 'guided negotiation' for a settlement.[133] Customary arbitration is a key aspect of dispute settlement in most African countries. Dispute settlement in traditional African societies also made minimal use, if at all, of specialist legal professionals. The rise of lawyers, the emergence of adjudicators who are neutral, ignorant of the facts and disinterested, and their roles in settling disputes appear to be products of colonization.[134] These features of African legal culture can be problematic for community law.

This book has consistently emphasized the role of law, lawyers, litigation and the courts as mechanisms for promoting the development of community law in member states. In a setting where these mechanisms are not frequently resorted to, this can be problematic. For example, the ECOWAS protocols on free movement of persons have been implemented in member states for more than thirty years. However, there is not a single decided case in the principal law reports of the English-speaking member states dealing with this issue or invoking the protocols. National borders have been arbitrarily closed, illegal fees have been

129 Akuffo (2009); and Yagba (1996).
130 Amponsah (2007), p. 122.
131 Schmid (2001).
132 Friedman (1969), p. 34.
133 Allott (1968a), p. 144.
134 Menski (2006), pp. 435–44.

levied at border posts and nationals have been deported from member states, but, to my knowledge, apart from one case, none of these issues has been challenged judicially.[135] It has already been noted that, notwithstanding many years of economic integration processes in Africa, reliance on community law before national courts has been minimal. Indeed, law reporting is itself something that is not approached seriously in most African countries; such reports often do not keep pace with current judgments or may even be non-existent.

To an extent, the above state of affairs reflects the realities in Africa and cannot be wholly attributed to a deep-seated and immutable cultural bias. Historical accounts of African legal culture reveal deep attachment to the law. This was due to the fact that there was popular participation in lawmaking and the administration of justice was highly localized rather than remote.[136] Furthermore, contrary to perceptions today, in the past, Africans were labelled as 'naturally and typically litigious, ready to resort to law at the slightest opportunity'.[137] Allott has argued that this claim was borne out by judicial statistics at the time, but it could be explained on the ground of the traditional availability of courts of law. In his words, 'the judicial arena was not something strange and forbidden; it was rather like a football pitch, to which everyone might resort for entertainment and excitement and to challenge'.[138] Surely, this is not the case today. The judicial system of many countries, as a channel for addressing legal wrongs, remains inaccessible to a significant proportion of the population. Among the factors contributing to this are litigation costs, poverty, physical inaccessibility of legal and judicial institutions, mistrust in the ability and independence of judges to deliver justice, political instability and politicization of the judicial process, ignorance of individual rights and illiteracy. These could be overcome through the provision of legal aid, education, greater protection of the integrity and independence of the judicial process, and improving people's physical access to legal and judicial institutions.

An important lesson from African legal culture that is relevant in the implementation of community law is the fact that customary law is inextricably linked with the societies in which it operates. In other words, there is an intimate linkage between customary law and the socio-cultural environment; customary law evolves from within and is

[135] *Afolabi Olajide* v. *Federal Republic of Nigeria* [2004] 52 WRN 1.

[136] Allott (1968a), p. 135.

[137] Allott (1968a), p. 147; and Blankenburg (1997).

[138] Allott (1968a), p. 147.

not imposed from above.[139] This intimate linkage is the basis for the continued endurance of customary law, even on matters on which attempts have been made by states (and formerly by colonial powers) to impose uniform law. This suggests that a top-down approach regarding community lawmaking and implementation may not always be appropriate. In some instances, the communities should leave decision-making and implementation to the member states, so policies will be localized and not seen as imposed from above and, accordingly, ignored. It is significant in this respect that one of the EAC's operational principles is the principle of subsidiarity, which emphasizes multi-level participation of a wide range of participants in the process of economic integration.[140]

7.4 Conclusion

This chapter has examined the implementation of community law in African states. The approach of the community treaties to the issue has left uncertainties in its wake. Member states have not fully implemented obligations assumed at the community level. National laws have not systematically dealt with the issue of implementing community law. This is reflected in the constitutions and the courts' jurisprudence. In some instances, existing constitutional provisions may be inimical to implementing community law effectively. Currently, community law does not enjoy any preferential legal status in member states. It is treated like any other international law. Community law's genesis in international law cannot be denied. However, the effective implementation of community law will demand a very different approach from that dealing with the reception of international law into national legal system.

After many years of economic integration, the above state of affairs on the implementation of community law in member states is difficult to fathom. The lack of attention to the issue of implementation creates a disjunction between community and national legal systems, and works against the effectiveness of economic integration. Given that the communities envisage progression through the various stages of integration – from free trade areas into customs unions, common markets and economic communities – they should become more attentive to this issue. It will become increasingly important as economic

139 Menski (2006), p. 407. 140 EAC Treaty, art. 7(1)(d).

integration progresses; the further economic integration moves through the stages, the more intensive the interactions between community and national law will become. The communities and member states will have to provide a more robust and defined legal framework to manage these interactions. Member states should analyze the challenges posed by their laws and jurisprudence for implementing community law and, where necessary, effect amendments or legislate to overcome the challenges. This task for member states should be founded on their undertakings in the communities' treaties to create conditions favourable for the development and achievement of the communities' goals, abstaining, at the same time, from measures likely to jeopardize the achievement of their aims.[141] The traditional explanation of the lack of political will as the main obstacle to progress of economic integration in Africa is inadequate. This chapter reveals that, even if governments are willing politically to implement community law, serious legal limitations exist that must be addressed first.

[141] COMESA Treaty, art. 5(1); EAC Treaty, art. 8(1)(a)(c); and ECOWAS Treaty, art. 5(1).

8

Inter-institutional relations: public–private international law dimensions

8.1 Introduction

For centuries, private international law has been used to address legal problems generated by interactions among legal systems. It deals with problems that arise when transactions or legal claims involve a foreign element. Private international law issues are most frequent in settings that allow for the growth of international relationships or activities with transnational implications. Economic integration provides this setting: it compels interaction among multiple legal systems; allows for the free movement of persons, goods, services and capital across national boundaries; and fosters the intensification of transnational economic activity. These circumstances generate problems that private international law can help to resolve. Accordingly, a developed private international law regime is an indispensable part of economic integration. Private international law impacts on the free movement of persons, goods, services and capital. It affects economic transactions within a community and, therefore, merits attention in any economic integration process. An economic community does not, and cannot, function solely on the basis of substantive rules. The procedural rules for resolving issues arising in cross-border transactions are equally important. These rules may be useful in dispute settlement at both the community and national levels. In other words, true integration should aim not only at the removal of barriers to the movement of persons, goods, services and capital, but also the strengthening of the legal infrastructure for settling cross-border disputes. A developed private international law regime is a key aspect of this infrastructure.

Private international law provides a means through which the horizontal and vertical relations between the multiple legal systems in a community can be structured and managed. It creates linkages between legal systems without necessarily unifying them. The rules on recognition and enforcement of foreign judgments allow effect to be given to the judicial acts of foreign states. International civil procedure rules enable states to work together for the smooth and effective administration of justice in transnational disputes. Choice of law rules allow parties to choose which legal system will govern their transactions. These rules often operate outside the context of economic integration. But their true foundation is in the interactions of legal systems that result from the transnational activities of their inhabitants. As Foote has noted, 'if society of each legislating State was entirely isolated, so that the individuals composing it were cut off from intercourse with all but their fellow subjects, the law of each State would have full operation within its own domain, and could claim to extend itself no further'.[1] Transactions between people subject to different legal systems, which is made more prevalent by community economic integration, provide the *raison d'être* for private international law.

However, as discussed in Chapter 9, the utility of private international law in economic integration is not limited to its impact on individual economic transactions or interstate relations. Its principles can also be important in how community institutions relate to each other, as well as to national institutions. I characterize this as inter-institutional relational issues. These issues would ordinarily be the domain of public international law, or the internal relationships between the relevant institutions. Private international law may, however, be relevant in addressing some of the issues. Indeed, increasingly scholars are exploring the interactions between public and private international law problems, including interactions between international institutions.[2] Inter-institutional relational issues are the focus of this chapter. It assesses how community institutions in Africa interact with each other, as well as with national institutions, through the lens of public–private international law principles. Some writers have, albeit cursorily, identified a role for private international law in Africa's economic integration.[3] Their focus has been on how private international law affects individual economic transactions. This chapter advances the discourse in a new direction by examining how private international law is equally important for community institutional arrangements.

[1] Foote (1904), p. 23.

[2] Mills (2006); Reed (2003), pp. 199–240; and Shany (2003).

[3] Thompson (1990), pp. 99–100; Thompson and Mukisa (1994), p. 1454; Omorogbe (1993), p. 364; Ndulo (1993a), pp. 111–12; and Ringo (1993).

8.2 Inter-institutional relational issues

Palpably missing from the discourse on economic integration under the AEC Treaty, and the constitutive treaties of the other communities, is any discussion of the role of private international law.[4] Ignoring reciprocal agreements for the recognition and enforcement of judgments in national statutes, there is no international convention on a private international law issue negotiated by African states. This state of affairs is troubling. As discussed in Chapter 9, the underdeveloped nature of private international law in Africa is a key obstacle to economic transactions. It may equally handicap the utility of private international law in addressing inter-institutional relational issues. Africa's economic integration treaties have been inattentive to potential private international law issues arising from their design of community institutions, especially in cases where it is envisaged that community and national institutions will interact. This may hamper the effective operation of community institutions and undermine their relations with national institutions. Consistent with the thesis that effective economic integration results from properly structuring and managing relational issues, this section examines how the effective operation of one community institution, the community courts, can be enhanced or constrained by private international law. It will be argued that, although developed for individual cross-border transactions, attention to private international law rules can enhance institutional effectiveness. However, it will be shown that these rules may not be wholly appropriate in the context of inter-institutional relational issues.

8.2.1 Arbitration in community courts – jurisdiction, choice of law and enforcement

The courts of justice of the COMESA, EAC and ECOWAS have jurisdiction to determine cases that are referred to them by persons (the community, its institutions or individuals) who choose them (not the individual judges in their personal capacity) as forums for the arbitration of disputes.[5] The SADC Tribunal has no arbitral jurisdiction. Judges

[4] Oppong (2006d).

[5] EAC Treaty, art. 32; COMESA Treaty, art. 28; art. 16 of the ECOWAS Treaty establishes an Arbitration Tribunal of the Community. The status, composition, powers, procedure and other issues concerning the Arbitration Tribunal are to be set out in a Protocol relating to it. Until that time, art. 9(5) of the ECOWAS Court Protocol provides that the court of justice should exercise the powers of the Tribunal. See generally Koh (1996).

hearing such arbitrations sit as the court and not as *persona designata*. The arbitral jurisdiction is conferred on the court, not on individual judges. In other words, when the community courts arbitrate a dispute, they sit as a 'court of arbitration'.[6] The judges do not sit in their personal capacity. Individual judges are designated to sit on this court of arbitration[7] just as they are when the court sits to settle a dispute through litigation. As in any arbitration proceedings, the parties retain a measure of control over the process on issues such as the judges who are to sit as arbitrators,[8] the place of arbitration[9] and the applicable law.[10]

As a marked departure from what is assumed, traditionally, to be the preference for the settlement of disputes in Africa,[11] neither the AEC Treaty nor the Protocol on the African Court of Justice[12] contains any provision conferring arbitral jurisdiction on the African Court of Justice and Human Rights (hereafter, African Court of Justice). Comparatively, it appears that the combination of an adversarial and arbitral jurisdiction in the same community court is largely unique to Africa.[13] Indeed,

[6] Rule 6(1) of the Common Market for Eastern and Southern Africa Court of Justice Arbitration Rules 2002, online: www.comesa.int/institutions/court_of_justice/arbitration_rules/ARBITRATION%20RULES/en (hereafter, COMESA Arbitration Rules).

[7] COMESA Arbitration Rules, r. 6(2).

[8] Ibid., r. 6(2). [9] Ibid., r. 7. [10] Ibid., r. 24.

[11] At the continental level, the preference for arbitration was reflected in the establishment of a Commission on Mediation, Conciliation and Arbitration as the 'judicial' organ of the OAU. The OAU did not have a court of justice. Charter of the Organization of African Unity, 25 May 1963, 3 ILM 766; and Protocol on the Commission of Mediation, Conciliation and Arbitration, 21 July 1964, 3 ILM 1116 (hereafter, Protocol on the Commission of Mediation). The commission's jurisdiction was not compulsory and it only had jurisdiction over disputes between states. See arts. XII–XIV of the Protocol on the Commission of Mediation. Article 56 of the ECOWAS Treaty 1975 made an attempt at the amicable settlement of disputes by direct agreement, a prerequisite for submission of the dispute to the tribunal established for the Community. This provision is repeated in art. 76 of the ECOWAS Treaty. It applied to any dispute that may arise among the member states regarding the interpretation or application of the Treaty. See also art. 40 of the Treaty for the Establishment of the Preferential Trade Area for Eastern and South African States, 21 December 1981, 21 ILM 479 (hereafter, PTA Treaty). A principal issue unaddressed by these provisions is whether all member states were (or will be) bound by the outcome of an amicable settlement between disputing states on an issue of interpretation of the treaty. For a commentary on the PTA Treaty, see Sinare (1989).

[12] Annexed to the protocol is the Statute of the African Court of Justice.

[13] The Court of Justice of the Andean Community, the Court of Justice of the European Free Trade Area and the Court of Justice of the Caribbean Community do not have arbitral jurisdiction. However, art. XXIII of the Agreement Establishing the Caribbean Court of Justice enjoins member states to 'encourage and facilitate the use of arbitration and other means of alternative dispute resolution for the settlement of international commercial disputes' by providing appropriate procedures to ensure observance of

it appears to be a recent phenomenon; the first generation of African economic integration treaties did not provide for any such dual jurisdiction in their respective community courts.[14]

It is difficult to identify the specific rationale for the inclusion of the dual jurisdiction provisions; the treaties have no explanatory memoranda to them and academic writings do not address this issue. However, it can be speculated that they reflect the preference for arbitration as a mode of settling disputes in Africa,[15] the general rise of arbitration as a means of dispute settlement and a consolidation of existing practice.[16] It may also be a sign of interest in investing in institutions with multiple responsibilities – the African Court of Justice is a clear example of that trend. Historically, there were also calls for the establishment of permanent arbitration centres in Africa.[17] Indeed, one organization to respond early to such calls was the Preferential Trade Area (PTA) for Eastern and Southern African States, which helped to establish the PTA Center for Commercial Arbitration in Djibouti. It is also possible that these provisions were inspired by the EC Treaty, but, as noted below, their wording and scope are very different. Article 272 of the EU Treaty confers an arbitral jurisdiction on the European Court of Justice (ECJ). However, as Craig and de Búrca have accurately noted, article 238 (now 272) of the EC Treaty does not make the ECJ 'simply an arbitrator in the normal sense of that term'.[18] Accordingly, it can be argued that the arbitral jurisdiction of community courts is novel and, apparently, African.

Both arbitration in interstate disputes and commercial arbitration are covered by the arbitral jurisdiction of the COMESA, EAC and

agreements to arbitrate and for the recognition and enforcement of arbitral awards in such disputes. The Court of Justice and Arbitration of the Organization for the Harmonization of Business Law in Africa does not settle cases through arbitration. However, the treaty gives it what can be described as supervisory jurisdiction of 'private' arbitration. See OHADA Treaty, arts. 21–26.

14 ECOWAS Treaty 1975; Treaty for East African Cooperation, 6 June 1967, 6 ILM 932; and PTA Treaty.

15 One writer has observed that arbitration is 'the norm' in most sub-Saharan African countries, but this is mainly the case for inter-tribal and personal disputes. As a system for resolving international commercial disputes, arbitration is a relatively recent phenomenon. Sempasa (1992), p. 407. See generally Chukwuemerie (2006).

16 The Preferential Trade Area for Eastern and Southern African States had a tribunal established under the PTA Treaty and an independent Centre for Commercial Arbitration, which was responsible for facilitating international arbitration of private commercial disputes. It appears that the dual jurisdiction of the current COMESA Court of Justice merges the jurisdiction of both bodies.

17 Tiewul and Tsegah (1975), p. 418; and Sempasa (1992), p. 412.

18 Craig and de Búrca (2003), p. 577.

ECOWAS courts. Indeed, the EAC Treaty provision, which is cited below, specifically refers to an arbitration clause in 'a commercial contract or agreement'.

Article 28 of the COMESA Treaty provides that:

> The Court shall have jurisdiction to hear and determine any matter: (a) arising from an arbitration clause contained in a contract which confers such jurisdiction to which the Common Market or any of its institutions is a party; and (b) arising from a dispute between the Member States regarding this Treaty if the dispute is submitted to it under a special agreement between the Member States concerned.

Article 32 of the EAC Treaty is wider in scope. It provides:

> The Court shall have jurisdiction to hear and determine any matter: (a) arising from an arbitration clause contained in a contract or agreement which confers such jurisdiction to which the Community or any of its institutions is a party; or (b) arising from a dispute between the Partner States regarding this Treaty if the dispute is submitted to it under a special agreement between the Partner States concerned; or (c) arising from an arbitration clause contained in a commercial contract or agreement in which the parties have conferred jurisdiction on the Court.

Article 16 of the ECOWAS Treaty is less definite. It provides that:

> 1. There is hereby established an Arbitration Tribunal of the Community.
> 2. The status, composition, powers, procedure and other issues concerning the Arbitration Tribunal shall be as set out in a Protocol relating thereto.

At present, the arbitral jurisdiction of the court is seldom invoked. The Registrar of the EAC court has bemoaned this state of affairs, observing that 'although the East African Court of Justice as arbitrator has many advantages against other arbitrators, no one has appointed it and if any has there has not been any dispute to lead the parties to the Court for arbitration. Even the three Governments [Kenya, Tanzania and Uganda] have not been able to utilise the free services of the Court as far as arbitration is concerned but find it easier to go to France and London for exorbitant arbitration and leave out an institution of their own creation'.[19] In the case of *Building Design Enterprise* v. *Common Market for Eastern and Southern Africa*,[20] the COMESA court sat as a court of arbitration. However, the parties settled and the arbitral proceedings

[19] Ruhangisa (2006).
[20] Application No. 1 of 2002 (COMESA Court of Justice, 2002).

were discontinued. Notwithstanding its current minimal invocation, the arbitral jurisdiction is important. It creates an avenue for individuals to become active participants in the economic integration processes by providing forums for the settlement of disputes that may be generated by their transactions within communities. For people who seek a neutral, expedited and party-controlled forum for dispute settlement while conducting commercial transactions in Africa, the arbitral jurisdiction may be equally useful.

Indeed, the community courts can be developed into forums for the resolution of inter-African commercial and political disputes through arbitration. The arbitral jurisdiction may serve to ensure harmonious interstate relations within the communities by providing a non-adversarial means of settling interstate disputes. This is important for the development of the communities; harmonious interstate relations will allow the communities to focus on economic integration. African governments are reluctant to choose international litigation as a means of settling disputes *inter se*. Indeed, as already noted, of all the cases so far brought before the COMESA, EAC, ECOWAS courts and the SADC Tribunal, only one involved interstate parties.[21] It appears that African governments give preference to non-adversarial means of settling disputes.[22] The arbitral jurisdiction injects a measure of rule orientation into the processes of amicably settling interstate disputes.

Despite the importance of the arbitral jurisdiction and its apparent novelty, the relevant provisions in the treaties are scant. Left on their own, they could not provide meaningful guidance for the community courts when exercising that jurisdiction.[23] To address this problem, both the COMESA and EAC courts have adopted detailed rules on arbitration.[24] However, the rules still leave complex issues unaddressed. If the issues are not addressed, they could undermine the utility of the jurisdiction. Among the issues are: the role that the goals or objectives of economic integration should play in the arbitral

[21] *Eritrea* v. *Ethiopia* [1999] LawAfr. LR 6.

[22] The first continental instrument for the settlement of disputes between independent African states emphasized 'mediation, conciliation and arbitration' as the modes of settling disputes. See Protocol on the Commission of Mediation, art. XIX.

[23] EAC Treaty, art. 32; COMESA Treaty, art. 28; and ECOWAS Treaty, art. 16.

[24] East African Court of Justice Arbitration Rules 2002, online: www.eac.int/EACJ_Arbitration_Rules.pdf (hereafter, EAC Arbitration Rules); and COMESA Arbitration Rules. It appears that the ECOWAS court has not yet published any such rules.

process; the administrative costs of the community courts' dual jurisdiction; the competence of the judges to perform the dual role; whether the community courts lose their 'community' character and become private, international, commercial arbitration centres when they are exercising their arbitral jurisdiction; and the extent to which principles developed in the context of international commercial arbitration could be extended to arbitration in the context of economic integration.

From a public–private international law perspective, other issues emerge. Firstly, what substantive law governs arbitral proceedings before the community courts? Secondly, will arbitral proceedings before the community courts be subject to the supervisory jurisdiction of national courts of the place of arbitration? Presumably parties to arbitration could specify the governing law.[25] In cases where they do not, the issue becomes more difficult. On the issue in dispute, should the court apply community law, if there is any, international law, the laws of the member states or the law of a non-member state? The arbitration rules of the COMESA and EAC courts address these issues. Under Rule 6 of the EAC Arbitration Rules:

> (1) The Tribunal shall decide the dispute in accordance with the law chosen by the parties. But if the parties expressly authorise it to do so, the Tribunal shall decide on the substance of the dispute according to considerations of justice and fairness without being bound by the rules of law.
> (2) The choice of the law or legal system of a designated state shall be construed, unless otherwise agreed by the parties, as directly referring to the substantive law of that state and not its rules of conflict of laws.
> (3) Failing a choice of the law by the parties, the Tribunal shall apply the rules of law it considers to be appropriate given all the circumstances of the dispute.
> (4) In all cases, the Tribunal shall decide, in accordance with the terms of the particular contract, and shall take into account the usages of the trade applicable to the particular transaction.[26]

[25] Under art. XXIX:2 of the Protocol of the Commission of Mediation, the parties could specify which law was to be applied by the Arbitral Tribunal. In the absence of an agreement of the applicable law, the tribunal was to decide the dispute according to treaties concluded between the parties, international law, the Charter of the Organization of African Unity, the Charter of the United Nations and, if the parties agree, *ex aequo et bono*.

[26] This rule appears to have been borrowed from art. 29 of Kenya's Arbitration Act 1995, Ch. 4 of which has a similarly worded provision.

Under Rule 24 of the COMESA Arbitration Rules:

> 1. (a) The Court shall apply the law designated by the parties as applicable to the substance of the dispute.
>   (b) Failing such designation by the parties, the Court shall apply the law determined by the conflict of law rules, which it considers applicable.
> 2. The Court shall decide as amiable *compositeur* or *ex aequo et bono* only if the parties have expressly authorized the Court to do so, and if the law applicable to the arbitral procedure permits such arbitration.
> 3. In all cases, the Court shall decide in accordance with the terms of the contract and shall take into account the usage of the trade applicable to the transaction.[27]

An issue unaddressed by either the treaty provisions or the Arbitration Rules of the courts is the extent to which community goals should, or would, inform the choice of law processes when the courts are exercising their arbitral jurisdiction. Party autonomy is upheld under the rules. However, they are silent on what limitations could or should be placed on parties' choice of the applicable law. It is now generally recognized that the choice of law process is not a neutral or disinterested exercise. Substantive and policy considerations underlie, or may even compel, the choice of the applicable law.[28] Communities definitely have an interest in ensuring that laws are not circumvented, through ingenious choice of law agreements, by parties who conduct business within them.[29] An illustration of how parties' choice of the applicable law can be used to circumvent community law, and how this may be judicially overcome, is provided by the ECJ's case of *Ingmar GB Ltd* v. *Eaton Leonard Technologies Inc.*[30]

Ingmar GB Ltd (hereafter, Ingmar) was a company established in the United Kingdom, and Eaton Leonard Technologies Inc. (hereafter, Eaton) was a company established in California. They concluded a contract, under which Ingmar was appointed as Eaton's commercial agent in the

27 This section appears to have been borrowed from s. 28 of the UNCITRAL Model Law on International Commercial Arbitration, which has a similarly worded provision. The Model Law's provision that 'any designation of the law or legal system of a given State shall be construed, unless otherwise expressed, as directly referring to the substantive law of that State and not to its conflict of laws rules' was omitted.

28 Martinek (2007); Roodt (2003); and Brilmayer (1995).

29 Wai (2002).

30 *Ingmar GB Ltd* v. *Eaton Leonard Technologies Inc.* (C-381/98) [2000] ECR I-9305.

United Kingdom. The contract was governed by the law of the state of California. The contract was terminated in 1996. Ingmar instituted proceedings in England seeking, pursuant to Regulation 17 of Commercial Agents (Council Directive) Regulations 1993, compensation for damages suffered as a result of the termination of the contract. The regulation implemented Council Directive 86/653/EEC of 18 December 1986 on the Coordination of the Laws of the Member States relating to Self-employed Commercial Agents.[31] The directive was intended to harmonize the laws of member states.

The English Court of Appeal made a preliminary reference to the ECJ, and asked whether articles 17 and 18 of the directive must be applied where the commercial agent carried on his activity in a member state although the principal was established in a non-member state and a clause of the parties' contract stipulated that it was to be governed by the law of the non-member state. The court reasoned that articles 17 and 18 were mandatory. They were to protect, for all commercial agents, the freedom of establishment and the operation of undistorted competition in the internal market, and must be observed throughout the EC to achieve the objectives of the EC Treaty. The court held that it was essential for the community legal order that a principal established in a non-member state, whose commercial agent carried on his activity within the community, could not evade those provisions by the simple expedient of a choice of law clause. To the court, the purpose served by the articles requires that they be applied where the situation is closely connected with the community, in particular where the commercial agent carries on his activity in the territory of a member state, irrespective of the law by which the parties intended the contract to be governed.

Rule 6(3) of the EAC court's arbitration rules provides a basis on which the interests of the EAC can be made to influence the choice of law process. In the absence of the parties' choice, the court can apply 'the rules of law it considers to be appropriate given all the circumstances of the dispute'. I argue that the interest of the EAC will be one such circumstance. Even in the absence of this provision, it can still be argued that the court should, and indeed has the inherent power to, protect community interest. It should refuse recognition to a choice of law agreement that would undermine essential community objectives or laws.

[31] [1986] OJ L382/17.

In addition to being forums for the settlement of disputes, the community courts should also see themselves as being entrusted with a mandate for serving as an engine for economic integration through their decisions.

An equally difficult issue is whether the community courts, when exercising their arbitral jurisdiction, would be subject to the supervisory jurisdiction of the courts of the place of arbitration. Naturally, these courts are located and sit in a specific country. However, unlike other arbitral tribunals, they are not governed by the procedural laws of the country in which they sit or, at least, this issue is unsettled. Nor is it settled whether, as in international commercial arbitration, arbitral proceedings before the community courts may be regulated by the national courts of the states in which they sit. Can national courts exercise supervisory jurisdiction over the community courts? Can national courts restrain arbitral proceedings before the community courts? Can national courts grant remedies in aid of the arbitration proceedings? The possibility of subjecting the arbitral proceedings of the community courts to national laws and the supervisory jurisdiction of national courts will upset the balance of relations between community and national legal systems. Writing from the perspective of article 238 of the EC Treaty, Hartley has rightly observed that 'in many countries the activities of arbitrators are subject to the supervision of the court. There cannot, of course, be any question of this with regard to the European Court [of Justice]'.[32] In the case of the community courts, the issue remains open and needs to be clarified.

Another issue arising from the arbitral jurisdiction of the community courts is the enforceability of their awards. As discussed below, it is envisaged that national courts will be used to enforce judgments of the community courts.[33] The same procedure is anticipated for the awards of the community courts.[34] Accordingly, it is to national laws on the enforcement of foreign arbitral awards that we must turn to examine whether community awards can be effectively enforced, and how the national laws might impact on the relations between community and national legal systems.

[32] Hartley (2003), p. 443.

[33] EAC Treaty, art. 44; COMESA Treaty, art. 40; ECOWAS Court Protocol, art. 24; and SADC Tribunal Protocol, art. 32(1)(2)(3).

[34] Rule 27(3) of the EAC Arbitration Rules provides that 'enforcement of arbitral awards shall be in accordance with the enforcement procedures of the country in which enforcement is sought'. Rule 22(1) of the COMESA Arbitration Rules also provides that the arbitration award 'shall be in the form of a judgment and shall be enforceable in terms of article 40 of the [COMESA] Treaty'.

In African states, the enforcement of foreign arbitral awards is regulated mainly by statute.[35] If an award does not qualify for enforcement under statute, many of which operate on the basis of reciprocity,[36] it is possible that it may be enforced at common law.[37] As of September 2010, thirty-one African countries were parties to the UN Convention on the Recognition and Enforcement of Foreign Arbitral Awards.[38] Therefore, the convention may also be important in the enforcement of awards in these countries. Subject to specified limitations, even under the convention, the enforcement of an arbitral award should be 'in accordance with the rules of procedure of the territory where the award is relied upon'.[39] Equally important for the enforcement of community awards may be the UNCITRAL Model Law on International Commercial Arbitration.[40] Its award enforcement provisions are very similar to those of the convention. As of September 2010, ten African countries – Egypt, Kenya, Madagascar, Mauritius, Nigeria, Rwanda, Tunisia, Uganda, Zambia and Zimbabwe – had enacted legislation based on the model law.

A perennial issue concerning the enforcement of foreign arbitral awards is the extent to which the enforcing court can, or may, review, set aside or modify an award. This power exists under the statutes of various African states that deal with the enforcement of foreign awards. For example, under sections 35 and 36 of Kenya's Arbitration Act 1995, the court may, on application of a party or *suo motu*, set aside or refuse to enforce an arbitral award. No exceptions have been made for awards from the community courts. In other words, an award from the EAC or COMESA court enjoys no privileged position regarding enforcement in

35 Kenya – Arbitration Act 1995, ss. 36–7; Zimbabwe – Arbitration Act 1996, First Schedule, arts. 35–6; Uganda – Arbitration and Conciliation Act 2000, ss. 39–47; Zambia – Arbitration Act 2000, ss. 30–1; and Nigeria – Arbitration and Conciliation Act 1990, ss. 51–2.

36 With the exception of Djibouti and Rwanda, all African countries that are parties to the UN Convention on the Recognition and Enforcement of Foreign Arbitration Awards have entered a reservation that they will apply the convention only to recognition and enforcement of awards made in the territory of another contracting state.

37 Fawcett and Carruthers (2008), pp. 652–4.

38 10 June 1958, 330 UNTS 3 (hereafter, New York Arbitration Convention). The following countries are parties to it: Algeria, Benin, Botswana, Burkina Faso, Cameroon, Central African Republic, Côte d'Ivoire, Djibouti, Egypt, Gabon, Ghana, Guinea, Kenya, Lesotho, Liberia, Madagascar, Mali, Mauritania, Mauritius, Morocco, Mozambique, Niger, Nigeria, Rwanda, Senegal, South Africa, Tunisia, Uganda, United Republic of Tanzania, Zambia and Zimbabwe.

39 Ibid., art. III.

40 21 June 1985, 24 ILM 1302 (hereafter, UNCITRAL Model Law).

Kenya and, indeed, in other African countries where similar provisions exist.[41] In the context of economic integration, and with a view to ensuring vertical community–state relations, this is an important issue. If national courts can review, set aside or modify a community court's award, this upsets vertical relations that should exist between community and national courts. Generally, it will undermine the utility of the community arbitration process.

The national statutes on the enforcement of foreign awards usually codify the grounds of non-enforcement contained in international conventions. The conventions provide grounds for non-enforcement, which must be decided under 'the law of the country where the award was made' or 'in accordance with the law of the country where the arbitration took place'.[42] From a relational perspective, and in the context of economic integration, this raises two difficulties. The first, as noted above, is the possibility that the award may be denied recognition with the consequence that a judicial act of a community – an arbitration award – is rendered ineffective within a member state. The second is that a community judicial act will be validated in a member state using a national law instead of community law. The non-enforcement of a community award, on grounds of non-compliance with the laws of the state in which the community court sat, will upset vertical community–state relations. Let us assume, for example, that the High Court of Kenya refuses to enforce an award from the EAC court because the court did not comply with Tanzanian law – the law of the place where the court is currently located. Such a position will mean that the Kenyan court privileges the law of another member state rather than a judicial act of the EAC.

Perhaps, with a view to maintaining vertical community–state relations, a solution to these enforcement issues would be for communities to adopt a rule comparable to Articles 53 and 54 of the International Centre for the Settlement of Investments Disputes Convention on the Settlement of Investment Disputes between States and Nationals of other States (hereafter, ICSID Convention).[43] Under Article 54(1), each contracting state is obliged to recognize an award, rendered pursuant to the convention, as binding and enforce the pecuniary obligations imposed

41 Uganda: Arbitration and Conciliation Act, s. 34.

42 See UNCITRAL Model Law, s. 36(a)(i)(iv)(v); and New York Arbitration Convention, s. V(a)(d)(e).

43 Convention on the Settlement of Investment Disputes between States and Nationals of other States, 18 March 1965, 575 UNTS 159.

by that award within its territories as if it were a final judgment of a court in that state. Article 53 provides that:

> The award shall be binding on the parties and shall not be subject to any appeal or to any other remedy except those provided for in this Convention. Each party shall abide by and comply with the terms of the award except to the extent that enforcement shall have been stayed pursuant to the relevant provisions of this Convention.

This provision prevents national courts from modifying or setting aside an award from the centre. In other words, there can be no external review of an ICSID award. The ICSID Convention has its own self-contained procedures for reviewing awards. A party to an ICSID proceeding cannot initiate action before a national court to set aside or review the award; the court of a state that is party to the convention is under an obligation to dismiss any such action. This distinct feature of the convention is important for the finality of ICSID awards. It provides a clear advantage over other international arbitration forums.[44]

As of January 2010, forty-five African countries were parties to the ICSID Convention.[45] Indeed, some have enacted legislation implementing the convention. Examples are Zimbabwe's Arbitration (International Investment) Act, Zambia's Investment Dispute Convention Act and Kenya's Investment Dispute Convention Act.[46] Significantly, and compared with other statutes for the enforcement of foreign awards, none of the ICSID Convention-implementing statutes contains a provision that allows the court enforcing an award from the centre to refuse to enforce it on any ground. Consistent with the provisions of the convention, what is provided is that the enforcing court should stay the enforcement proceedings for the parties to return to the centre to settle their differences as regards the award.

If African states are willing to privilege awards from an institution that is not of their creation, and which sits in distant Washington DC in the United States, they should be more willing, or at least less reluctant, to

[44] Schreuer (2001), pp. 1082–4.

[45] Recently, the South African High Court criticized the fact that South Africa was not party to the Convention. See *Von Abo* v. *The Government of the Republic of South Africa* 2009 (2) SA 526.

[46] See also Botswana – Settlement of Investment Disputes (Convention) Act No. 65 of 1970; Lesotho – Arbitration International Investment (Disputes) Act 23 of 1974; Malawi – Investment Disputes (Enforcement of Awards) Act 46 of 1966; and Nigeria – International Centre for Settlement of Investment Disputes (Enforcement of Awards) Decree No. 49 of 1967. For a survey of statutes implementing the ICSID Convention, see Asouzu (2001), pp. 370–8.

extend similar privileges to awards emanating from a community court of their own creation which sits on their doorstep – the judges of which are chosen by them. A national or community enactment comparable to Article 53 of the ICSID Convention has the advantage of ensuring that an award from a community court will not be subject to national law in a manner that will undermine its effectiveness or enforceability, or upset vertical community–state relations. A privileged status for community awards might improve the chances of individuals choosing the community courts as the place to settle their disputes.

Another issue worth noting relates to the position of states and community institutions in arbitral proceedings before the community courts. Because arbitration is consensual, a claim of immunity by a state or community institution from the jurisdiction of the community courts is unlikely to be made, let alone accepted. That may not be so when it comes to enforcing the award. This issue is left unaddressed in the treaties, as well as the existing rules of the community courts on arbitration. It is submitted that the public policy considerations which underlie the doctrine of sovereign immunity from execution[47] can be consistently maintained, even for awards emanating from community courts in the context of economic integration. Unlike the non-recognition of a community arbitral award on the basis of non-compliance with a national law, restrictions on the scope of assets available to satisfy a community arbitral award do not adversely affect the balance of the relations between community and national legal systems. It is also likely that community institutions will enjoy immunity from execution in respect of assets in member states. Comparatively, it is worth noting, in this regard, that despite the attempts to insulate ICSID awards from the vagaries of national legal systems, the immunity of states from execution is recognized under section 55 of the convention.

On the whole, the above exposition reveals that for the effective implementation of the arbitral jurisdiction of the community courts a number of issues must be addressed. This will ensure that the arbitral jurisdiction aids economic integration and also avoids unnecessary tensions between community and national legal systems. Perhaps the fact that, at present, the arbitral jurisdiction is seldom invoked has made these issues less immediate and concrete. Even so, these issues are important, and will become increasingly so as individuals become aware of the jurisdiction and utilize it to settle their disputes.

[47] *Republic of Angola* v. *Springbok Investment Ltd* 2005 (2) BLR 159.

8.2.2 *Enforcing judgments of community courts by national courts*

There has been a proliferation of community and international courts in recent decades. Currently, Africa is host to at least four active community courts. The proliferation of international courts has been matched by an improvement in the legal status of individuals appearing before them. Historically, individuals have been granted no or restricted standing rights before international courts.[48] In this context, individuals include all non-state entities, such as natural persons, companies, associations and NGOs. The traditional view prevailed: only states are subjects of public international law. Recently, individuals have been granted *locus standi* to litigate before some international courts. What was essentially the preserve of states has undergone a fundamental shift: individuals can now bring action against states, international organizations and their institutions under various treaties.[49]

The granting to individuals of the rights of action has not been matched by a clear articulation, in the realm of private and public international law, of how successful individuals may enforce judgments secured from international courts. This is especially so when an individual wants to enforce the judgment before a national court. How does an individual, in whose favour a pecuniary award has been made against a community institution or a state, go about enforcing the judgment? Should he rely on the goodwill of the community to pay? Can he rely on his country to assist him diplomatically to secure the judgment? Can he proceed to a national court and enforce the judgment as a foreign judgment? What about a judgment that orders a state or community institution to do something, for example, an order to release goods unlawfully seized in breach of community law? These are not academic questions. In Africa, developments surrounding recent attempts – which are discussed below – to enforce judgments of the SADC Tribunal in various national courts, and the difficulties encountered in the process, render addressing these questions of more than theoretical importance.

48 Statute of the International Court of Justice, 26 June 1945, 59 Stat. 1055, art. 34(1). However, as far back as 1907, individuals had standing before the Central American Court of Justice.

49 COMESA Treaty, art. 26; SADC Tribunal Protocol, art. 15(1)(2); EAC Treaty, art. 30; ECOWAS Court Protocol, art. 10; Agreement Establishing the Caribbean Court of Justice, 14 February 2001, art. XXIV; and Statute of the Central American Court of Justice, art. 22(g).

Historically, various mechanisms have been used to enforce judgments of international courts. They include the use of international non-judicial institutions, self-help and diplomatic negotiations. Generally, these mechanisms were devised at a time when the individual had no *locus standi* before international courts.[50] It was reasoned that 'the function of enforcing a decision of an international tribunal is an executive function, and as such should be confined, in the ordinary case at any rate, to a body which is invested with executive powers. It becomes, in any event, *a political as distinguished from a judicial matter*'.[51] To Rosenne, 'in international law the separation of the adjudicative from the post-adjudicative phase is a fundamental postulate of the whole theory of judicial settlement . . . this leads to the consequence that enforcement partakes of the quality of an entirely new dispute to be regulated *by political means*'.[52] These observations suggest that international law did not contemplate direct enforcement of international courts' decisions by national courts. Rather, it contemplates enforcement through diplomatic means. As between states, such an enforcement mechanism, which is power-oriented, is unproblematic. As between an individual and a state or international institution judgment debtor, the absence of a rule-oriented enforcement mechanism can be disadvantageous.

In the few cases that exist on the subject, national courts have been reluctant to recognize or enforce international courts' judgments at the instance of individuals who are directly or indirectly affected by the judgments. In *Socobel* v. *Greek State*,[53] a company sought to enforce a judgment of the Permanent Court of International Justice before a Belgian national court. The action failed because the company was not, and indeed could not have been, a party to the action before the Permanent Court. To the Belgian court, it was inconceivable that 'a party which, by definition, was not admitted to the bar of an international court should be able to rely on a decision in a case to which it was not a party'.[54] More recently, the Supreme Court of the United States held that a judgment of the International Court of Justice (ICJ) was not directly enforceable as domestic law, and could therefore not

[50] It is not being suggested here that these mechanisms have been ineffective in securing compliance with decisions of international courts. Paulson (2004); and Schulte (2004).

[51] Hudson (1944), p. 128. [52] Rosenne (1957), p. 102.

[53] *Socobel* v. *Greek State* (1951) 18 Int'l L. Rep. 3.

[54] Ibid., at 5. See also *Committee of United States Citizens Living in Nicaragua* v. *Ronald Wilson Reagan* 859 F.2d 929, 934, 938.

prevail over state procedural rules.[55] Like *Socobel*, this action was instituted by an individual who was not, and could not have been, a party to the ICJ proceedings. It is open to question whether both judgments would have been different had the international judgments been issues as a result of actions instituted directly by the affected individuals.

Notwithstanding national courts' reluctance to enforce decisions of international courts at the instance of individuals, it has long been recognized that diplomatic protection is ineffective for, or often inaccessible to, individuals who seek to rely on or enforce judgments of international courts. Accordingly, some commentators have advocated using national courts to enforce international courts' judgments.[56] Reisman argued for an enhanced role for national courts in enforcing the ICJ's judgments.[57] He proposed a Draft Protocol for the Enforcement of ICJ Judgments. Signatories to this protocol were to undertake 'to enact such internal legislation as is necessary to require domestic courts and tribunals to enforce international judgments, and rights arising thereon, solely and exclusively upon certification of the authenticity of said judgment'.[58] Schachter had earlier suggested that there seemed to be 'good reasons' for national courts to recognize international awards.[59] Nantwi left open the possibility of using national courts to enforce judgments of international courts, and noted that 'the special circumstances of any particular case' may merit this.[60] Jenks also discussed the possibility that specific judgments of international courts may be treated as equivalent to a foreign judgment and enforceable by municipal procedures available for the enforcement of such foreign judgments.[61]

These suggestions have now found their way into treaties.[62] Some of Africa's economic integration treaties contain provisions that seek to use national courts to enforce judgments of their respective community courts. Article 44 of the EAC Treaty provides that 'the execution of a

[55] *Jose Ernesto Medellin* v. *Texas* 128 S. Ct 1346 (2008). But see *Hombre Sobrido* v. *The French State*, Judgment No. 266/2000 (Court of Appeal of Saint Denis, 2000); and *Merce Pesca Co.* v. *The French State*, Judgment No. 267/2000 (Court of Appeal of Saint Denis, 2000). Both judgments are reported in (2000) 4 *Yearbook of the International Tribunal of the Law of the Sea* 151 and 155.

[56] O'Connell (1990); Reilly and Ordonez (1995–6); and Alford (2003), pp. 715–31.

[57] Reisman (1969), p. 25. See generally Charnovitz (2009).

[58] Reisman (1969), p. 27. [59] Schachter (1960), p. 13. [60] Nantwi (1966), p. 145.

[61] Jenks (1964), pp. 681–2 and 706–15.

[62] It must be noted that, even before these suggestions, the use of national courts to enforce international judgments – in this case decisions of the Council of Ministers and the European Commission of the European Economic Community – had been provided for in what is now art. 299 of the Treaty on the Functioning of the European Union.

judgment of the [EAC court] which imposes a pecuniary obligation on a person shall be governed by the rules of civil procedure in force in the Partner State in which the execution is to take place'. Similar provisions are found in the ECOWAS and COMESA treaties and the SADC Tribunal Protocol.[63] There are two notable differences in the provisions. Firstly, while the EAC and COMESA provisions refer to judgments that impose 'a pecuniary obligation', the ECOWAS Court Protocol and SADC Tribunal Protocol refer to 'any judgments' and 'judgment' respectively.[64] For individuals litigating before community courts, this is significant, as some of the courts' judgments are likely to be for non-pecuniary relief. Secondly, it appears that national courts in COMESA and the EAC have the discretion to enforce such judgments. Under the ECOWAS Court Protocol, enforcement, which is to be made by a designated competent national authority, is mandatory.

The Statute on the African Court of Justice and Human Rights adopts a different approach to enforcing judgments of the court. It does not envisage using national courts to enforce its judgments. Under article 46(3), parties 'guarantee' execution of judgments. Non-compliance may be referred by the court to the Assembly of Heads of State and Government, which will decide on measures to be taken to give effect to the judgment. There is also a general undertaking by the contracting parties to refrain from measures that will hinder the attainment of the AEC's objectives.[65] This expectation has been described as 'naive' given past experience with the enforcement of judgments from international courts in Africa.[66]

The provisions which seek to adopt national rules for enforcing foreign judgments to enforce the judgments of community courts provide a means of linking community and national legal systems. They aim to integrate community and national judicial structures and offer an opportunity for cooperation and dialogue between them. This opportunity to enhance integration in their respective sub-regions should be explored. For individuals, these provisions represent a positive change in the direction of international law. The post-adjudicative phase of litigation before international courts is often politicized. There is inherent in the traditional international law enforcement mechanisms elements of

[63] SADC Tribunal Protocol, art. 32(1)(2)(3); OHADA Treaty, art. 25; Agreement Establishing the Caribbean Court of Justice, art. 26; Statute of the Central American Court of Justice, art. 39; and EU Treaty, art. 299.

[64] COMESA Treaty, art. 40; ECOWAS Court Protocol, art. 24(2); EAC Treaty, art. 44; and SADC Tribunal Protocol, art. 32(1).

[65] AEC Treaty, art. 5.

[66] Naldi and Magliveras (1999), p. 614.

power relations that weigh heavily against individual judgment creditors. Although it has its own challenges, enforcement through national courts is rule-oriented, and can therefore be beneficial to individuals.

Until recently, the provisions that seek to use national courts to enforce community judgments remained untested. This was so even though there have been a few instances in which the community courts have made pecuniary awards in favour of individuals. For example, in *Muleya* v. *Common Market for Eastern and Southern Africa (No. 3)*,[67] the COMESA court awarded damages of $2,000 against the respondent for publishing defamatory matter about the applicant. The ECOWAS court also awarded damages of $100,000 in favour of an applicant, a journalist who was unlawfully detained by the Gambian Government,[68] and compensation of CFA Francs 100,000 in favour of an applicant who was adjudged to have been enslaved in Niger.[69]

In 2010, the High Courts of Zimbabwe and South Africa decided two separate applications that were made to register and enforce judgments of the SADC Tribunal.[70] In *Mike Campbell (Pvt) Ltd* v. *The Republic of Zimbabwe*,[71] the applicants challenged aspects of Zimbabwe's land-reform policy as inconsistent with the SADC Treaty. The tribunal found the respondent in breach of its obligations under the SADC Treaty. It ordered the respondent to take all necessary measures to protect the possession, occupation and ownership of applicants' lands and to take all appropriate measures to ensure that no action be taken which interfered with their peaceful residence on the farms. It further ordered the respondent to pay fair compensation to the applicants. It was those orders that the applicants sought to enforce in Zimbabwe and South Africa. The High Court of Zimbabwe declined to register the tribunal's judgment. The court held that it is generally not contrary to Zimbabwe's public policy to enforce the tribunal's judgements because Zimbabwe is

67 [2004] 1 East Afr. LR 173.

68 *Manneh* v. *The Gambia*, ECW/CCJ/JUD/03/08 (ECOWAS Court of Justice, 2008).

69 *Mme Hadijatou Mani Koraou* v. *The Republic of Niger*, ECW/CCJ/JUD/06/08 (ECOWAS Court of Justice, 2008).

70 *Gramara (Pvt) Ltd* v. *Government of the Republic of Zimbabwe*, HC 33/09 (Zimbabwe, High Court, 2010); and *Fick* v. *Government of the Republic of Zimbabwe*, Case No. 77881/2009 (North Gauteng High Court, South Africa, 2010). On the relationship between the SADC Tribunal and Zimbabwean courts, the Supreme Court has observed that the SADC Tribunal 'enjoys no legal status in Zimbabwe' (*Commercial Farmers Union* v. *Minister of Lands and Rural Resettlement*, Judgment No. SC 31/10 (Supreme Court, Zimbabwe, 2010)).

71 Case No. SADC (T) 2/2007 (SADC Tribunal, 2008). For a comprehensive account on the background to this case and judgments, see Naldi (2009).

under an international obligation to do so. However, in the instant case, the legal and practical consequences of recognizing and enforcing the tribunal's judgment were such that the court should refuse to register it. The court reasoned, legally, that the land-reform programme was mandated by the Zimbabwean Constitution and that its constitutionality was upheld by the Supreme Court of Zimbabwe. Practically, registering the tribunal's judgment will compel Zimbabwe's government to act contrary to the law enacted by parliament. Furthermore, it will necessitate the government having to reverse all of the land acquisitions that have taken place since 2000 under the programme, with all of the ramifications. In contrast, the High Court of South Africa, in a short judgment that contained no reasons, registered the tribunal's judgment. The opposing judgments from the Zimbabwean and South African courts expose some of the challenges that persons who obtain judgments from the community courts are likely to face when they seek to enforce the judgments.

8.2.3 Using national courts to enforce community judgments – challenges

There are a number of challenges in trying to use national courts to enforce community judgments. Among them are the following: firstly, can the existing national common law and statute law regimes for the enforcement of foreign judgments be suitably adapted for the purpose of enforcing community judgments? Secondly, if they can be suitably adapted, can national courts review community judgments? Thirdly, will the use of civil procedure rules, which differ from country to country, afford equal or adequate protection to individual judgment creditors? If these challenges are not addressed, then they may deny individuals the benefits of the judgments and could also undermine the relations between national and community courts. In general, given the demands of economic integration, the extant national regimes for the enforcement of foreign state court judgments cannot, unthinkingly, be extended to community judgments.

The effective enforcement of community judgments will demand review of national laws. For example, it is envisaged under Rule 41(4) of the Rules of the Court of Justice of the Common Market for Eastern and Southern Africa (hereafter, COMESA Court Rules)[72] that penalties imposed on non-attending witnesses will be enforced by national courts under the provision of article 40 of the COMESA Treaty. However, this

[72] COMESA Legal Notice No. 6 of 2003, 8 April 2003, online: www.comesa.int/institutions/court_of_justice/rules/view (accessed 1 September 2010).

may not be possible in some COMESA countries. Under both the common law and statute law, the court will not enforce a judgment that is a penalty.[73] Thus, the effective implementation of this rule, which is essential for the administration of justice within the COMESA, will demand changes in some member states' laws.

The use of national courts to enforce community judgments also raises constitutional questions as to the relations between community and national courts: what limitations exist on the constitutionally conferred jurisdictional powers of national courts when it comes to enforcing community judgments? Can national courts review those judgments, set them aside or modify them? So far, there appear to be no answers to these questions. Although it did not involve a review of the SADC Tribunal's judgment, the decision of the Zimbabwe High Court not to enforce the tribunal's judgment on the ground that enforcement will, inter alia, be inconsistent with a decision of the Supreme Court of Zimbabwe provides a concrete illustration of a national court refusing to enforce a community decision on the basis of national law.[74] National courts are slow to review foreign state judgments, but the power to review remains, especially where there is an allegation of fraud. If national courts review community judgments, it will undermine the administration of justice within the community, and render the community's legal system subject to the varying demands of member states' laws. On the other hand, it can be argued that review by national courts introduces a measure of accountability in international adjudication. However, in the context of economic integration, it is likely that the destabilizing effect of such national judicial reviews will far outweigh the benefits of accountability. Accordingly, it is proposed that, firstly, in the context of economic integration, national courts in Africa should not have the power to review or invalidate community judgments; that power should reside with the community courts.[75] Secondly, national courts should not have jurisdiction to decline to enforce community judgments. This is

[73] See, e.g. Kenya – Foreign Judgment (Reciprocal Enforcement) Act, Cap 43, s. 3(b); and Zimbabwe – Civil Matters (Mutual Assistance) Act 14 of 1995, s. 6(h)(ii).

[74] *Gramara (Pvt) Ltd* v. *Government of the Republic of Zimbabwe*, HC 33/09 (Zimbabwe, High Court, 2010).

[75] COMESA Treaty, art. 31(3); EAC Treaty, art. 35(3); SADC Tribunal Protocol, art. 26; ECOWAS Court Protocol, art. 25; and *Tokunbo Lijadu Oyemade* v. *Council of Ministers*, Suit No. ECW/CCJ/APP/02/08 (ECOWAS Court of Justice, 2009). See generally Brown (2007), pp. 152–84.

especially so when the applicable law for such a decision will, as in *Gramara (Pvt) Ltd*,[76] be national law.

The former proposition finds support in international law. In the *Chorzow Factory* case,[77] the Permanent Court of International Justice held that a national court did not have the power to invalidate an international judgment. Both propositions are also consistent with the view that the community legal system should not be subjected to national legal systems. Admittedly, both propositions offend the long-established discretion in national courts to enforce foreign judgments. They also challenge national constitutions that make the judiciary the ultimate source of judicial power. To grant community judgments this privileged status will require amendment of national laws. At the community level, the acceptance of these propositions will demand greater responsibility from community courts to ensure the integrity of the processes that result in their judgments. This will make up for the proposed absence of discretion in national courts to decline to enforce them.

Another drawback in using the existing national regimes to enforce community judgments is that some do not provide for the enforcement of non-monetary judgments. However, in the context of economic integration, non-monetary judgments are more likely to be a major component of community judgments.[78] There is a movement in some countries towards enforcing foreign non-monetary judgments.[79] With the exception of South Africa, which is currently considering proposals to enforce non-monetary judgments, Africa remains largely insulated from this movement.[80] In *Gramara (Pvt) Ltd*,[81] one of the arguments against the enforcement of the SADC Tribunal's judgment was that aspects of it entailed administrative consequences and it was not for the payment of a fixed sum of money. The High Court held that it would be 'contrary to principle to restrict the scope of recognition proceedings by reference to the specific remedies enjoined by a given foreign judgment'. In other

[76] *Gramara (Pvt) Ltd* v. *Government of the Republic of Zimbabwe*, HC 33/09 (Zimbabwe, High Court, 2010).
[77] PCIJ Ser. A., No. 17, 1928, p. 33.
[78] For a discussion of the various kinds of judgments given by international courts and their implications for enforcement, see Jenks (1964), pp. 667–88.
[79] Examples are Australia, New Zealand, Singapore, Canada and the European Community. See Oppong (2006a), pp. 276–82; Oppong (2007a); and Pitel (2007).
[80] See South African Law Reform Commission (2006).
[81] *Gramara (Pvt) Ltd* v. *Government of the Republic of Zimbabwe*, HC 33/09 (Zimbabwe, High Court, 2010).

words, the mere fact that a judgment of a community court did not entail the payment of money should not automatically lead a national court to dismiss an application to enforce it. This is an important pronouncement, given that some community court judgments are likely to be of non-pecuniary character.

Most community judgments are likely to be against sovereign states. Thus, it is troubling that the treaties are silent on the issue of state immunity from enforcement actions at the national level. States often enjoy exemption from execution against their assets in their own territory or elsewhere.[82] Therefore, national law on this issue will be highly relevant regarding enforcement actions brought by individual judgment creditors. A successful claim of immunity from execution will rob individuals of the benefits of a community judgment. Although there has been a perceptible trend towards restrictive state immunity, it still remains a formidable challenge.[83]

The above has assumed that the provisions in the community treaties that seek to use national courts to enforce community judgments are binding on national courts. However, the absence of domestic legislation, especially in dualist countries, implementing the community treaties[84] raises questions as to the binding effect of the provisions. A treaty is not effective within a state unless implemented by domestic legislation. Without domestic legislation, courts may be incompetent to give effect to the provisions and use them as the basis to enforce community judgments. From a comparative perspective, this problem appears to have been explicitly acknowledged by the drafters of article 26 of the Agreement establishing the Caribbean Court of Justice. Accordingly, they provided: 'The Contracting Parties agree to take all the necessary steps, *including the enactment of legislation* to ensure that . . . any judgment, decree, order or sentence of the Court given in the exercise of its jurisdiction shall be enforced by all courts and authorities in any territory of the Contracting Parties as if it were a judgment, decree, order or sentence of a superior court of that Contracting Party.' Reisman's Draft Protocol for the Enforcement of ICJ Judgments also suggested the need to enact

[82] See *Republic of Angola* v. *Springbok Investment Ltd* 2005 (2) BLR 159; and *Emmanuel Bitwire* v. *The Republic of Zaire* [1998] I Kampala LR 21.

[83] See generally Ostrander (2004); and Crawford (1981).

[84] The exception is the EAC Treaty, which has been given the force of law in Kenya, Uganda and Tanzania. See Tanzania – Treaty for the Establishment of East African Community Act 2001 (Act No. 4); Kenya – Treaty for the Establishment of East African Community Act 2000 (Act No. 2); and Uganda – East African Community Act 2002.

'internal legislation'. It is unfortunate that the community treaties do not recognize, or at least are silent on, the need for domestic legislation, especially on this issue. To my knowledge, no African country has as yet enacted legislation on the enforcement of community judgments.

In *Gramara (Pvt) Ltd*, the court rightly noted that Zimbabwe has not taken any specific internal measures to domesticate the SADC Treaty or the Protocol of the Tribunal. More specifically, no legislative or administrative steps have been taken to implement Zimbabwe's obligations under article 32 – the provision calling for the use of national civil procedures to enforce the tribunal's judgment – or to transform those obligations into effectual provisions of the municipal law. Rather than address this prior and important question, the court appeared to have wrongly assumed that the mere fact that Zimbabwe is subject to the jurisdiction of the tribunal (by virtue of the fact that it ratified the treaty, which then binds it in international law) gives it jurisdiction to hear the application to enforce the tribunal's judgment. Although comity provides the basis for enforcing decisions of foreign state courts,[85] it is suggested that it cannot provide the basis for enforcing judgments of community courts in national courts. This proposition may appear unconvincing on a first reading, as it can be argued that whatever arrangement governs the output of another state's judiciary, it should apply to a judiciary operating on behalf of a number of states, i.e. an international court. However, it is worth noting that a community court judgment is, in a sense, international law. By assuming jurisdiction to enforce it and consequently enforcing it on the basis of comity rather than an express national legislation, a national court will be circumventing national constitutional provisions on the reception of international law.

Legislation that gives national courts jurisdiction to enforce community judgments and deals with other issues attendant with the exercise of that jurisdiction is particularly important.[86] Enforcement of a community judgment raises issues that are not present with a foreign state judgment for which the existing national regimes have been designed. For example, unlike a foreign state judgment, which has its sole source in a

[85] Collins (2002).

[86] See, e.g. UK – European Communities (Enforcement of Community Judgments) Order, SI 1972/1590; Ireland – European Communities (Enforcement of Community Judgments, Orders and Decisions) Order, SI 2007/121; and Malta – European Communities (Enforcement of Community Judgments) Order 2007, LN 387 of 2007. See generally Fawcett (1963), pp. 63–5.

foreign state, a judgment from a community court may actually be a 'review' of an earlier decision of a court of the country in which the enforcement is sought. Ordinarily, this would be a conflicting judgment and, therefore, unenforceable.[87] Let us assume that, after exhausting local remedies, an individual proceeds to a community court.[88] He obtains a judgment contrary to that of national courts 'exhausted' by the individual. His attempt to enforce the community judgments may meet significant challenges. Firstly, a national court will be reluctant to enforce a judgment that contradicts its own judgment and, even more so, if the first judgment was from a superior court in that country. It is worth pointing out that, at present, there are no constitutionally mandated hierarchical relations between national and community courts. The community courts exist outside national judicial structures. Accordingly, without legislation, a national court is not bound by decisions of any community court, no matter how exalted the community court is.

Secondly, from the above illustration the community judgment will, in principle, be a review of earlier decisions of national courts. In some countries, this will raise a constitutional question as to the *locus* of final judicial power.[89] For example, under article 125(3) of the Constitution of the Republic of Ghana, the judicial power of Ghana shall be vested in the judiciary and neither 'the President nor Parliament nor any organ or agency of the President or Parliament shall have or be given final judicial power'.[90] Ordinarily, this is a classic separation of powers provision. However, when read in the context of international adjudication and its effect on states, it is debatable whether it would be constitutional to give the ECOWAS court final judicial power in Ghana, even if that power was restricted to defined matters. In the absence of a specific constitutional provision, which makes community law supreme over domestic law, transfers some state powers to the community or provides legislation to regulate enforcement in such cases, enforcing a community judgment could amount to an unconstitutional subjection of Ghana's legal systems to the community legal system.[91]

87 Various solutions to the enforcement of conflicting foreign judgments have been suggested. See Wolff (1962), p. 263; *Showlag* v. *Mansour* [1995] 1 AC 431; Brussels I Regulation, s. 34(4); and American Law Institute (1971), s. 114.

88 See, e.g. COMESA Treaty, art. 26.

89 Ku (2006).

90 Constitution of the Republic of Sierra Leone 1991, art. 120; and Constitution of the Republic of South Africa, art. 165.

91 Similar concern has been raised in the United States about the possibility of NAFTA's Chapter 11 Tribunals reviewing decisions of US courts. *Loewen Group Inc.* v. *United States*, 42 ILM 811; *Mondev International Ltd* v. *United States*, 42 ILM 85; and Bekker (2004–5).

The above exposition reveals that, as in the case of community arbitral awards, the proposed use of national courts to enforce community judgments is riddled with problems. So far, these problems have not been carefully thought through, let alone resolved. Member states of the communities should examine these problems and legislate to resolve them. There is the need for community input here to ensure that community judgments are not subjected to varying national laws, which might result in dissimilar effects of community judgments. For example, regarding pecuniary judgments, national law may vary on issues such as prescription, the currency in which the obligation may be discharged and the mode of calculating interest on the judgment. Indeed, what is needed is detailed and well-considered community law setting out the legal framework for the enforcement of community judgments in member states. It is not enough simply to provide that the execution of community judgments shall be governed by the rules of civil procedure in force in the member state in which enforcement is sought. Various reasons have been given for non-compliance with community judgments, including arguments about national sovereignty, absence of strong economic interdependence among African countries and a preference for negotiation in place of adjudication.[92] It remains to be seen whether the use of national courts to enforce community judgments will assist individuals to overcome or bypass these arguments.

What is certain is that the existing national laws are inadequate to meet the community treaties' demands that national civil procedure rules on enforcement of foreign judgments be used to enforce judgments of the community courts. Section 8.3.1 of this chapter provides model legislation on the enforcement of judgments of community courts that could overcome some of the challenges identified above.

8.2.4 *Conflict of jurisdiction between community courts*

Recent decades have witnessed a proliferation of international and community courts. This has raised the issue of conflict of jurisdictions among the courts and how it impacts the effective administration of justice. Conflict of jurisdiction exists when the same issue between the same parties is pending before two or more courts.[93] A feature of Africa's

[92] Kufour (1996), pp. 6–11. [93] Shany (2003), pp. 24–8.

economic integration is the multiplicity of communities and their respective courts with potentially overlapping jurisdictions.[94] Overlapping jurisdictions result from the fact that states are often members of more than one community and the subject matter jurisdiction of community courts is primarily identical, namely, to interpret and apply the often similarly worded treaties of the communities. States and individuals may have standing before two or more community courts on the same subject matter. This is especially so since it does not appear that the jurisdiction of the community courts is exclusive to the jurisdiction of other courts and, thus, parties may forum shop in a manner that is currently unregulated. This state of affairs may lead to conflict of jurisdictions and other related problems, such as parallel proceedings and conflicting judgments. This problem of conflicting judgments should be distinguished from issues of conflict of jurisdictions. Conflicting judgments deal with conflicts between the jurisprudence, both in terms of the principles developed and the remedies provided, by the relevant courts. However, the two problems are related. Inconsistent principles developed by community courts may encourage forum shopping and give rise to the prospect of conflict of jurisdictions.

The issue of conflicting jurisdictions between international courts, and how to approach or resolve them, is not an 'African problem'.[95] Nor will such conflicts be limited to inter-African community courts. They can take the form of a conflict between the jurisdiction of an African community court and another international court. For example, article 28(d) of the Statute on the African Court of Justice and Human Rights gives the court jurisdiction over 'any question of international law'. This sets up a potential direct conflict with the ICJ's jurisdiction[96] and the WTO dispute-settlement institutions. In principle, there is nothing that prevents two African states from submitting a trade dispute arising under a WTO agreement – which is 'international law' – to the African Court of Justice. Similarly, conflict may exist between the jurisdiction of the community courts and that of the WTO dispute-settlement institutions on issues relating to international trade.[97] Proceedings before the judicial

[94] Oduor (2005); Pauwelyn (2004); Kiplagat (1995–6); and Leal-Arcas (2007).

[95] Shany (2003).

[96] See Charter of the United Nations, 26 June 1945, 1 UNTS XVI, arts. 33 and 95; and Statute of the International Court of Justice, art. 36(2).

[97] So far, Africa's participation in the WTO dispute settlement process has been minimal. This lowers, but does not eliminate, the prospect for such conflicts. Mosoti (2006); Alavi (2007); and Jobodwana (2009).

institutions of the EU and NAFTA have been fertile sources of conflict with WTO dispute-settlement proceedings.[98] Another source of conflict could be Africa's economic communities and the jurisprudence of their respective courts.

In contrast with developments elsewhere,[99] there are at present no treaty provisions for resolving potential conflicts between the community courts, and between the community courts and other international courts. Articles 17, 18 and 19 of the SADC Tribunal Protocol grant the tribunal exclusive jurisdiction over all disputes between the member states and the community, natural or legal persons and the community, and between the community and its staff. However, it can be argued that this is not enough since the provisions do not appear to bar parties from litigating elsewhere, even if the latter court may subsequently decline jurisdiction. The Protocol on Relations between the African Union and the Regional Economic Communities (hereafter, Protocol on Relations)[100] is equally silent on this issue. The absence of conflict-of-jurisdictions-resolution provisions is troubling. In international law, jurisdictional coordination between international courts is largely not mandatory. It is often subject to the goodwill of individual judges.[101] There is, therefore, no defined set of rules to which African judges confronted with this problem can readily resort. In general, one would have expected that, with a view to ensuring jurisdictional harmony among the community courts, conflict-of-jurisdictions-resolution provisions would have been included in the Protocol on Relations. Conflict of jurisdictions between community courts can undermine the effectiveness of the overarching AEC legal system.

Historically, the EAC was attentive to the problem of conflict of jurisdictions. Article 41(1) of the Treaty for East African Cooperation[102] provided that 'the Partner States undertake not to submit a dispute concerning the interpretation or application of this Treaty, so far as it

[98] Shany (2003), pp. 54–9.

[99] EU Treaty, art. 292; Treaty Creating the Court of Justice of the Cartagena Agreement, 28 May 1979, 18 ILM 1203 (as amended by the Treaty Creating the Court of Justice of the Andean Community, 28 May 1996), art. 42(1); NAFTA, art. 2005; and Olivos Protocol for the Settlement of Disputes in Mercosur, 18 February 2002, 2251 UNTS A-37341, 42 ILM 2, art. 1(2). The issue of whether the WTO will uphold these forum selection clauses in matters over which it too has jurisdiction remains undecided. See *Mexico-Tax Measures on Soft Drinks and other Beverages* (2006), WT/DS308/AB/R at [54] (Appellate Body).

[100] Online: www.afrimap.org/english/images/treaty/AU-RECs-Protocol.pdf.

[101] Shany (2003), p. 109.

[102] Treaty for East African Cooperation, 6 June 1967, 6 ILM 932.

relates to or affects the Common Market, to any method of settlement other than those provided for in this Treaty'. It is quite intriguing that this provision is neither present in the EAC Treaty nor the two protocols establishing the EAC Customs Union and Common Market. Indeed, given the proliferation of community and international courts, this is the time when such a provision would be very much needed.

In the absence of conflict-of-jurisdiction-resolution provisions, community judges may have to resort to jurisdiction regulating norms that have been applied by national judges to address similar issues in the area of international litigation. In private international law, the common law doctrines of comity[103] and *forum non conveniens, lis alibi pendens* and respect for party autonomy as regards choice of forum agreements serve as jurisdiction-regulating norms between national courts.[104] They may provide a solution to the problem of conflicting jurisdictions between the community courts. Indeed, it can be argued that basic rules, such as respect for choice of forum agreements, *lis pendens, res judicata*, abuse of right and comity are part of customary international law, or general principles of law, and community courts may resort to them in resolving problems of jurisdictional conflicts. The ECOWAS court has already invoked one of the doctrines. In *Chukwudolue* v. *Republic of Senegal*,[105] it declared itself incompetent to hear the case on the grounds of a choice of forum clause in a document submitted by the plaintiff. The clause provided that claims were to be referred to 'the World Court at the Hague or the International Court of Arbitration'. *Chukwudolue* affirms the relevance of private international law doctrines in resolving conflict of jurisdictions between community courts. However, it is suggested that in their application of private international law doctrines, community courts should prioritize the community's interests. Given the nature and demands of economic integration, disputes affecting a community's interests should be submitted exclusively to its community court or, at least, there should be a presumption in favour of litigating such disputes before its community court.[106] Accordingly, community courts should be slow to decline jurisdiction or stay proceedings in favour of another court in such disputes.

The use of private international law doctrines, or general principles of law such as comity, *forum non conveniens* and *lis alibi pendens*, to resolve

[103] Henckels (2008), pp. 594–6. [104] Bell (2003).
[105] Judgment No. ECW/CCJ/APP/07/07 (ECOWAS Court of Justice, 2007).
[106] Shany (2003), pp. 211–12.

conflict of jurisdictions represents a second-best solution. A better alternative is through the inclusion of explicit conflict and overlap clauses in the relevant community treaties.[107] Applying such clauses, to which the parties have expressly agreed in a treaty, provides a more robust and legitimate foundation for a community court's decision when faced with conflict of jurisdiction problems than applying analogues from national law. Indeed, given the differences in legal traditions, such analogues may not be similarly present in the legal systems of the disputing parties, and they can hardly be elevated to the status of general principles of law in international law. In light of the above, it is recommended that COMESA, EAC, ECOWAS and SADC amend the constitutive treaties to include the following provision:

1. Member states undertake not to submit a dispute concerning the interpretation or application of this treaty or a law made pursuant to it to any court, arbitral tribunal or proceeding whatsoever except for those provided for in this treaty.
2. A violation of paragraph 1 is a breach of community law and entitles the member state that was sued in the foreign forum to receive compensation. Such compensation shall not be limited to the cost of taking part in the foreign proceedings.
3. Without prejudice to the above, the fact that a member state has, in breach of paragraph 1, instituted proceedings in a foreign forum does not prevent other member states from invoking the dispute settlement provisions of this treaty.

8.2.5 *Judicial cooperation between community and national courts*

The jurisprudence of African national courts reveals instances where they have grappled with issues on judicial cooperation with foreign courts. In these instances, issues including the service of documents abroad and admissibility of foreign evidence were discussed.[108] International judicial cooperation is now indispensable for the effective administration of justice in cases involving a foreign element. Some African countries have responded to this by becoming parties to

[107] Pauwelyn and Salles (2009).

[108] *Fonville* v. *Kelly* [2002] 1 East Afr. LR 71; *Willow Investment* v. *Mbomba Ntumba* [1997] TLR 47; *Microsoft Corp.* v. *Mitsumi Computer Garage Ltd* [2001] KLR 470; *Pastificio Lucio Garofalo SPA* v. *Security & Fire Equipment Co.* [2001] KLR 483; *Mashchinen Frommer GmbH* v. *Trisave Engineering & Machinery Supplies (Pty) Ltd* 2003 (6) SA 69; and *Blanchard, Krasner & French* v. *Evans* 2004 (4) SA 427.

international treaties dealing with judicial cooperation. Four African countries – Egypt, Botswana, Malawi and Seychelles – are parties to the Hague Convention on the Service Abroad of Judicial and Extra-Judicial Documents in Civil or Commercial Matters,[109] and two – South Africa and Seychelles – are parties to the Hague Convention on the Taking of Evidence Abroad in Civil or Commercial Matters.[110] There are also national statutes dealing with international judicial cooperation in civil and criminal matters.

Presently, no regional or continental convention on judicial cooperation exists in Africa. The legal framework for judicial cooperation with foreign state courts in civil matters is regulated by national statutes.[111] However, the same cannot be said of cooperation with international courts, especially when they are exercising 'civil' jurisdiction.[112] Admittedly, when most of these statutes were enacted, international courts were rare, especially in Africa. With the emergence of community courts, the importance of providing a legal framework to regulate judicial cooperation between community courts and national courts, and perhaps among community courts themselves, is evident. As Rosenne has observed, 'the principle of the independence of the judiciary makes it difficult if not impossible for a decision of an international court or tribunal to impose an obligation directly on an internal tribunal unless the national legislation makes provision for that'.[113]

There are a number of questions that could arise as regards cooperation between community and national courts for which no clear answers exist at present. Do national courts have jurisdiction to assist community courts to gather evidence from member states? Do national courts have jurisdiction to assist community courts to serve documents on natural and legal persons within the former's jurisdiction? What will be the legal basis and procedures for such cooperation? Do the legal basis and procedures provide an adequate regime to ensure efficient administration of justice at the community level? Will a community court stay its proceedings if a similar issue is pending before a national court?[114]

[109] 15 November 1965, 20 UST 361. [110] 18 March 1970, 23 UST 2555.

[111] Kenya – Civil Procedure Act, Chapter 21, s. 55; Uganda – Foreign Tribunals Evidence Act, Chapter 10 and Civil Procedure Act, Chapter 71, s. 56.

[112] See generally Shany (2007). [113] Rosenne (2004), p. 66.

[114] *Richard Thomas Etheredge* v. *Minister of State for National Security Responsible for Lands, Land Reform and Resettlement*, Suit No. 3295/08 (High Court, Zimbabwe, 2008); and Ebobrah and Nkhata (2010).

Will procedures adopted by national courts in cooperating with community courts be conducive to the effectiveness of community law?

These are important questions that have not been examined in the discourse on community courts in Africa. Apart from legislation in Zimbabwe, there does not appear to be any statute that explicitly envisages judicial cooperation with an international court. Section 3(2) of Zimbabwe's Civil Matters (Mutual Assistance) Act 1995 allows the Minister of Justice to extend provisions of the Act to 'any international tribunal'. An international tribunal is defined as any court or tribunal which, in pursuance of any international agreement or any resolution of the General Assembly of the United Nations: (a) exercises any jurisdiction or performs any function of a judicial nature or by way of arbitration, conciliation or inquiry; or (b) is appointed, whether permanently or temporarily, for the purpose of exercising any jurisdiction or performing any such function. This definition is broad enough to cover community courts in Africa. The provision appears to be the first of its kind in the field of judicial cooperation in civil matters in Africa.[115] But it does not appear that the ministerial power has been exercised in respect of any international tribunal. With the proliferation of community courts in Africa, the importance of cooperation between community and national courts for the effective administration of justice cannot be overemphasized. Unfortunately, treaties and laws on the community courts have also not provided a clear legal framework for cooperation between them and national courts on issues such as taking evidence, summoning witnesses and serving documents.[116] It appears that the only area where cooperation is explicitly anticipated, and a framework provided for, is that of enforcing community judgments. Surely, judicial cooperation goes beyond this. The need for cooperation with national courts is important, especially as the community courts allow individuals to litigate directly before them and also have jurisdiction to arbitrate disputes between individuals.

The lack of a legal framework on the issue of judicial cooperation between national and community courts in the community treaties is somewhat remedied by the community courts' rules of procedure. Under

[115] This section appears to have been borrowed from some countries. United Kingdom – Evidence (Proceedings in Other Jurisdictions) Act 1975, s. 6(1); and US Code, chapter 28, s. 1782(a).

[116] Compare Agreement Establishing the Caribbean Court of Justice, art. XXVI(a), which obliges national governments to enact legislation to ensure that all national authorities 'act in aid of the Court'.

Rule 74(1)(a) of the COMESA Court Rules, the court may, *suo motu* or on application, stay its proceedings where the court and a national court are seized of a case in which the same relief is sought, the same issue of interpretation is raised or the validity of the same act is called into question. Such a stay of proceedings will be an act of deference by the community court to the national court. It is likely to improve relations between the two courts. From the perspective of national courts, the existence of *lis pendens* is a factor that weighs heavily in their decisions to stay proceedings, but they still retain the discretion not to do so under both common and statute law.[117]

Under Rule 27 of the East African Court of Justice Rules of Procedure 2008 (hereafter, EAC Court Rules),[118] a national court may be requested to serve notice on a person. A national court to which a request for service of notification is sent *may*, upon receipt, proceed as if the notification had been issued by it, and then return the notification to the EAC court together with the record, if any, of its related proceedings. In other words, national courts have discretion to serve the notification. What happens when discretion is exercised against the service of a notification is left unanswered? Article 74(1) of the Rules of the Court of Justice of the Economic Community of West African States (hereafter, ECOWAS Court Rules) seems not to envisage the need to use national courts for serving documents.[119] It provides that where the rules require that a document be served on a person, the Chief Registrar of the court should ensure that service is effected at that person's address either by the dispatch of a copy of the document by registered post with a form for acknowledgement of receipt, or by personal delivery of the copy against a receipt. It is very likely that such a process of serving documents will be considered an infringement of state sovereignty.[120] Bypassing a state's institutions, including its courts, to assume jurisdiction over its subjects

[117] *Jammal* v. *Abdalla Hashem* 1975 (2) ALR Comm. 141; *Owens* v. *Owens* [1959] EA 909; *Baldwin* v. *Baldwin* [1967] RLR 289; *Fattal* v. *Fattal* [1999–2000] 1 GLR 331; *Berrange NO* v. *Hassan* 2009 (2) SA 339; and Uganda – Civil Procedure Act, Chapter 71, s. 6, which provides that the pendency of a suit in a foreign court shall not preclude a court from trying a suit in which the same matters or any of them are in issue in that suit in the foreign court.

[118] Available at www.eac.int/rules-applicable.html.

[119] Online: www.ecowascourt.org/site2.html. Rule 43(5) provides that an order summoning witnesses shall be served on the parties and the witnesses, but there is no statement on how this service is to be made.

[120] It is envisaged under art. 99(a) of the ECOWAS Court Rules that the court will adopt supplementary rules on letters rogatory.

is likely to be a cause for concern by the state. Also, without the use of national legal processes, it is unlikely that any sanction can be imposed on an individual who does not acknowledge service from a community court.

Under article 41(6) and (7) of the COMESA Court Rules, the court may order that a witness or expert be heard by the judicial authority of his place of permanent residence. The order shall be sent for implementation to the competent judicial authority under conditions laid down in its rules of procedure.[121] Under article 41(8), a member state shall treat any violation of an oath or affirmation by a witness or expert in the same manner as if the offence had been committed before one of its courts with jurisdiction in civil proceedings. At the request of the court, the member state concerned *shall* prosecute the offender before its competent court. This provision is unlikely to sit well with constitutional provisions in member states that confer the discretion to prosecute criminal offences solely with the Attorney General. In the absence of legislation, it is unlikely that contempt of or perjury before a community court can be similarly treated and punished by a national court.[122]

The above suggests that the community courts acknowledge the limitations on their jurisdiction. They seek to overcome their limitations through cooperation with national courts. However, it does not appear that careful thought has been given to the issue of whether the existing national laws are tailored to facilitate this cooperation. To ensure effective cooperation, it is important for member states to enact statutes regulating cooperation between community and national courts. A particular issue that demands attention should be whether national courts should still maintain the discretion they currently enjoy in deciding whether or not to meet the demands of a foreign court. Section 8.3.2 provides model legislation on judicial cooperation between national and community courts in Africa. Pending such legislation, it is suggested that national courts should treat the community courts as foreign courts for the purposes of their civil procedure rules. However, it must be admitted

121 COMESA Court Rules, r. 41(7)(a).

122 South Africa – Rome Statute of the International Criminal Court Act 2002, s. 37; United Kingdom – International Criminal Court Act 2001, s. 54; Scotland – International Criminal Court (Scotland) Act 2001, s. 4; and Ireland – International Criminal Court Act 2006, s. 11. In *George Lipimile* v. *Mpulungu Harbour Management*, Judgment No. 22 of 2008 (Zambian Supreme Court, 2008), the court held that it had jurisdiction to try a person (in this case a Zambian) for contempt committed in France. However, the act of contempt related to an order of a Zambian court and not a French court.

that, in their current form, the definition of a foreign court in national statutes often tends to mean a foreign state's courts.[123]

8.3 Model legislation on community judgments enforcement and judicial cooperation

The preceding discussion reveals that the issues of enforcing community court judgments by national courts and judicial cooperation between both courts to ensure the effective administration of justice by the former has not been carefully thought through. This section provides two model statutes intended to overcome some of the challenges identified in the discussion.

8.3.1 Enforcement of Community Judgments Act

1. Citation

This Act may be cited as the [*insert name of community*] (Enforcement of Community Judgments) Act.

2. Interpretation

In this Act –

'Community' means [*insert name of community*].

'Community court' means [*insert name of community court or tribunal*].

'Community judgment' means any decision, judgment, order or arbitration award that is enforceable under or in accordance with [*article 40 of the Treaty establishing the Common Market of Eastern and Southern Africa*] [*article 24 of the Protocol on the Court of Justice of the Economic Community of West African States*] [*article 44 of the Treaty establishing the East African Community*] [*article 32 of the Protocol on Tribunal and Rules of Procedure thereof of the Treaty establishing the Southern African Development Community*].

123 Kenya's Civil Procedure Act, Ch. 21 defines a foreign court as a court situated outside Kenya which has no authority in Kenya. Uganda's Civil Procedure Act, Ch. 71 and s. 1 of Tanzania's Civil Procedure Code 1966 contain a similar definition. It remains an open question as to whether it can be argued that the COMESA and EAC courts, neither of which is geographically situated in either Kenya or Uganda, has authority in either country. The EAC Court and COMESA Court are geographically situated in Tanzania and Zambia respectively.

'Registration order' means an order made by the High Court under section 3(1) of this Act.

'Treaty' means [*insert title of community constitutive treaty*].

3. Registration orders for Community judgments

(1) The High Court shall, upon application duly made at any time for the purpose by the person entitled to enforce it, forthwith, make an order permitting the registration of a Community judgment.
(2) An application to the High Court for a registration order may be made without notice.
(3) An application for a registration order must be supported by an authenticated copy of the Community judgment for which the registration order is sought.
(4) Where the Community judgment is not in [*insert official language of the High Court*], a translation of it into [*insert official language of the High Court*] shall be provided by the person seeking the registration order. The translated copy must be certified by a notary public or other qualified person; or accompanied by written evidence confirming that the translation is accurate.
(5) Where the application for a registration order is for a Community judgment that is a money judgment, the application must state –
    (a) the name of the judgment creditor and his address for service within the jurisdiction;
    (b) the name of the judgment debtor and his address or place of business, if known; and
    (c) the amount in respect of which the judgment is unsatisfied.
(6) Where it appears that a Community judgment, under which a sum of money is payable, has been partly satisfied at the date of the application for a registration order, the order shall be made only in respect of the balance remaining payable at that date.

4. Challenging registration orders

(1) A copy of the registration order must be served on every person against whom the Community judgment was given.
(2) The registration order must state the name and address for service of the person who applied for registration, and must exhibit a copy of the Community judgment for which the registration order was made.
(3) The registration order must also state the right of the person against whom the order was made to apply within twenty-eight days for the variation, suspension or cancellation of the order.

(4) An application for a variation, suspension or cancellation of a registration order shall be made within twenty-eight days of the date on which the registration order was served on the person against whom it was made, and it shall state the grounds for the application.
(5) A registration order may be varied, suspended or cancelled, as the case may be on the ground that:
    (a) the Community judgment has been wholly or partly satisfied;
    (b) the applicant intended to challenge the Community judgment using the procedures set out in the Treaty, and has in fact taken material steps in that direction; or
    (c) the Community court has varied, cancelled or suspended the Community judgment.
(6) The person against whom a registration order is made must satisfy the court on the balance of probabilities that one or more or the grounds stated in section 4(5) exist. There shall be no other basis for varying, cancelling or suspending a Community judgment.
(7) The High Court may in the case of a Community judgment, which is not a money judgment, dispense with the requirement for notice under section 4(1) or stipulate a duration shorter than that provided under section 4(3) within which the person against whom a registration order has been made can apply for its variation, cancellation or suspension.

5. No review on the merits

In proceedings under this Act the High Court shall not enter into the merits of the Community judgment.

6. Registration of Community judgment

(1) Where a person against whom a registration order is made fails to satisfy the court under section 4(6) or fails to apply for a variation, cancellation or suspension of the registration order under section 4(4), the High Court shall forthwith register the judgment and issue an order for its enforcement.
(2) A Community judgment that is a money judgment shall be registered and enforced in the currency in which it is expressed.

7. Effect of registration of Community judgment

(1) A Community judgment registered in accordance with Article 6(1) shall, for all purposes of execution, be of the same force and effect, and proceedings may be taken on the judgment as if the judgment

had been a judgment or order given or made by the High Court on the date of registration.

(2) Unless otherwise provided in the Community judgment, any sum payable under the Community judgment shall carry interest from the date on which the Community judgment was made, and at such rate, as if the Community judgment, order or decision had been a judgment or order given or made by the High Court.

(3) The High Court shall have jurisdiction over complaints that enforcement of a Community judgment is being carried out in an irregular manner.

8. Immunity

Nothing in this Act shall be construed as derogating from the law of [*insert name of country*] relating to immunity of that State or of any foreign State from execution.

8.3.2 *Judicial Cooperation with Community Courts Act*

1. Citation

This Act may be cited as the Judicial Cooperation with the [*insert name of community court*] Act.

2. Interpretation

In this Act –

'Community' means [*insert name of community*].

'Community court' means [*insert name of community court or tribunal*].

3. Application for assistance in obtaining evidence for Community court proceedings

Where an application is made to the High Court for an order for evidence to be obtained from a person within [*insert name of state*] and the court is satisfied –

(a) that the application is made in pursuance of a request issued by or on behalf of the Community court exercising jurisdiction under the [*insert title of constitutive treaty of community*]; and

(b) that the evidence to which the application relates is to be obtained for the purposes of proceedings, which either have been instituted before the Community court or whose institution before that court is contemplated, the High Court shall have the powers conferred on it by the provisions of this Act.

4. Power of High Court to give effect to application for assistance

(1) Subject to the provisions of this section, the High Court shall have power, on an application made under section 3, to make an order for obtaining evidence. The order may require a person specified therein to take such steps as the court may consider appropriate for that purpose.

(2) Without prejudice to the generality of subsection (1), but subject to the provisions of this section, an order under this section may, in particular, make provision –
- (a) for the examination of witnesses, either orally or in writing;
- (b) for the production of documents;
- (c) for the inspection, photographing, preservation, custody or detention of any property.

(3) An order under this section shall not require a person –
- (a) to state what documents relevant to the proceedings to which the application for the order relates are or have been in his possession, custody or power; or
- (b) to produce any documents other than particular documents specified in the order as being documents appearing to the court making the order to be, or to be likely to be, in his possession, custody or power.
- (c) to produce an official document, if in the opinion of the court its production or the disclosure of its contents will be prejudicial to the security of the State or will be injurious to the public interest.

(4) Every person whose attendance is required by virtue of an order made under subsection 1 of this section shall be entitled to the same allowances as a witness appearing at a trial in the High Court.

(5) Any order of the High Court made under this section may be enforced in the same manner as an order made in a cause pending in the High Court.

5. Privilege of witnesses

(1) A person shall not be compelled by virtue of an order under section 4 above to give any evidence that he could not be compelled to give in proceedings before the High Court.

6. Service of Community documents

(1) The High Court shall, on an application made before it for that purpose, have jurisdiction to make an order for the service of any document issued by the Community court on any person in [*insert name of country*].
(2) An application for an order under subsection 1 shall be made by the Registrar of the Community court or his appointed representative.
(3) In order for service of the process to be effected in accordance with this Act, a letter of request shall be submitted and two copies of the document are to be served. Provided that where the documents are in a language other than [*insert official language of the court*], translations of them shall also be submitted.
(4) Without prejudice to any enactment that mandates specific procedures for service on particular persons, service of documents on an order made under subsection 1 shall be effected by leaving the original document or a copy of it, as indicated in the letter of request, and a copy of the translation with the person to be served.
(5) After service of the process has been effected, or attempts to effect service of it have failed, the serving officer shall file with the Registrar of the High Court an affidavit made by the officer, stating when, where and how he or she did or attempted to do so.
(6) The Registrar of the High Court shall send to the Registrar of the Community court a certificate certifying that the document or a copy thereof was served on the person, at the time, and in the manner specified in the certificate or that service of the process could not be effected for the reason specified.
(7) The certificate issued by the Registrar of the High Court under subsection 6 shall be sealed with the seal of the Court.

7. Offences against administration of Justice in the Community court

(1) A person who commits any act certified by the [*insert name of community court*] as an offence against the administration of justice in the Community court may be dealt with as for the corresponding domestic offence under the law of [*insert name of country*] committed in relation to the High Court.
(2) Without prejudice to the generality of the above, the High Court shall have jurisdiction to try and punish a person for an act of

contempt committed before the Community court, even though the act or omission constituting the contempt is not defined in a written law in [*insert name of state*] and the penalty is not so prescribed.

(3) A person convicted for an offence under this section shall be subject to a fine not exceeding [*insert amount*] or a term of imprisonment not exceeding [*insert term*].

(4) Proceedings for an offence under this section shall not be instituted, except by or with the consent of the Attorney General.

8.4 Conclusion

This chapter has examined how inter-institutional relations can be enhanced using the rules of public and private international law. The effectiveness of community institutions can be affected by how they relate to each other and also to national institutions. The chapter has argued that inattention to important public and private international law issues is likely to affect the relations between national and community courts and, concomitantly, the effectiveness of the latter. Community laws in Africa acknowledge the role that national courts can play in enhancing community courts' effective operations. However, community and national laws have been largely inattentive to whether the existing national laws provide an adequate legal framework for performing that role. In general, national courts relate to each other using private international law principles. With the community courts, there are added dimensions for principles of public international law. It is unlikely that the existing principles can be wholly or without modification adopted as the legal framework for the relations between community and national courts. They have to be complemented by specifically tailored national and community laws. So far, it appears that community and national laws have been drafted on the unwritten assumption that private international law principles provide an adequate legal framework for the relations between community and national courts. This chapter has exposed difficulties relating to this assumption and has provided two draft laws specifically designed to address some of the challenges identified.

9

Interstate relations, economic transactions and private international law

9.1 Introduction

Interstate relational issues are a feature of economic integration. Regional economic communities operate within the context of multiple state legal systems. The legal relations between the member states of a community are just as important for effective community development as community–state relations. Such relations directly impact on economic transactions within a community. There are socio-political and economic dimensions of interstate relations, but from a legal perspective a number of issues arise in this context. Are normative acts in one state recognized and enforced in other member states?[1] Are there any constraints attached to the recognition and enforcement of foreign normative acts? Do member states share the same legal traditions – common law, civil law, Roman–Dutch law and so on – and how does that impact upon their relations with one another? What is the degree of harmonization of laws between the member states? Should harmonization of laws be pursued as part of the integration processes? In the absence of harmonization, are there any approaches or techniques that could be adopted? To what extent do judges take account of each other's jurisprudence? These are weighty issues likely to be faced by communities in Africa, especially as they progress through the stages of economic integration.

This chapter investigates the extent to which African states relate to each other using private international law as the barometer. Economic integration fosters interaction among states. These interactions provide evidence of the strength of the integration process. The deeper the level of integration, the stronger one would expect the level of interaction to be.

[1] Normative acts are acts within a member state that create legal consequences. These include enacted laws, court judgments, arbitration awards and administrative acts, such as the registration of companies.

Put differently, there should be a positive correlation between the intensity of interstate legal relations and the strength of an economic integration process. The choice of private international law as the barometer is appropriate. Apart from public international law and, to a lesser extent, comparative law, no other law subject deals with interstate legal relations more than private international law. This chapter assesses how private international law can affect economic transactions generated by strengthened economic integration in Africa. It also makes proposals for reforming private international law in Africa so that it can better serve the needs of cross-border economic transactions. This chapter complements parts of Chapter 4 dealing with the harmonization of laws in Africa.

9.2 Function of private international law in communities

Private international law is concerned with claims or matters within a state that involve a foreign element. In addition to its principal function of ensuring justice for individuals whose relations touch more than one state,[2] private international law performs a regulatory function between states. It can be used to regulate the conduct of persons who transact across states, with a view to achieving the objectives of an economic community.[3] Choice of law rules could be used to ensure adherence to standards set by a community, and protect community interests by preventing any resort to laws that may defeat community goals. The rules on the enforcement of foreign judgments can be used to ensure greater effectiveness of judgments and, thus, aid cross-border settlement of disputes within a community.[4] Put differently, private international law can be used to manage interstate relations and the intense economic relationships fostered by economic integration.[5] Without an effective

[2] Wai (2001), p. 187.

[3] Wai (2001); Wai (2005); Watt (2006); Tzouganatous (1986); and Seck (1999).

[4] Significantly, four of the current international conventions on the enforcement of foreign judgments have been spearheaded by economic integration organizations. Inter-American Convention on the Extraterritorial Validity of Foreign Judgments and Arbitral Awards, 8 May 1979, 1439 UNTS I-24392, 18 ILM 1224; Inter-American Convention on Jurisdiction in the International Sphere for the Extraterritorial Validity of Foreign Judgments, 24 May 1984, 24 ILM 468; Brussels I Regulation; and the Lugano Convention on Jurisdiction and Enforcement of Judgments in Civil and Commercial Matters, [2007] OJ L339/3 (hereafter, Lugano Convention). So far, attempts by the Hague Conference on Private International Law to have a global convention on the subject have failed.

[5] Boggiano (2000), pp. 79–94; Siehr (2004); and Hay, Lando and Rotunda (1986).

private international law regime, important community goals might not be achieved. There can be no meaningful implementation of factor mobility, which is the free movement of persons, goods, capital and services, without attention to the facilitative role of private international law. Factor mobility is envisaged by Africa's economic communities.[6] Private international law affects the functioning of any economic community that promotes factor mobility. Indeed, it was social and commercial relations between individuals of independent European states that set the stage for the emergence and development of private international law as a subject.[7]

In economic communities, and the world at large, private international law can be a tool for multi-level governance. Through cooperation between national courts, a state can maintain adherence to its norms even though litigation is pursued outside its borders. Indeed, private international law is a force for ensuring order and stability in legal relationships that transcend national legal systems.[8] This role is most visible in federal states – a more advanced form of economic integration – where, in some jurisdictions, rules are deployed to ensure legal harmony or unity within the federation.[9] Private international law also provides an avenue for harmony in decision-making in the face of legal pluralism. In other words, regardless of the multiplicity and diversity of legal traditions, the application of private international law rules can provide some comfort for individuals transacting across states. Indeed, this is the very essence of the role of private international law in economic integration. Economic integration assumes and fosters the dismantling of state boundaries. Private international law is founded on the existence of boundaries, but it provides principles for managing cross-border coexistence.

Politically, private international law's approach to managing the coexistence of states is suitable for states that may want to maintain

6 AEC Treaty, art. 6(2)(f)(i); COMESA Treaty, art. 84; EAC Treaty, art. 104; and ECOWAS Treaty, art. 55(1)(ii).

7 Foote (1904), p. 23.

8 Watt (2005); Hay, Lando and Rotunda (1986), p. 168; and Drobnig (1966–7).

9 Canada and Australia have witnessed the constitutionalization of private international law. The Supreme Court of Canada has held that private international law has a role to play in fulfilling the intention of the framers of the Canadian constitution to create a single country. *Morguard Investments Ltd* v. *De Savoye* [1990] 3 SCR 1077, 76 DLR (4th) 256; *Hunt* v. *T & N plc* [1993] 4 SCR 289, 109 DLR (4th) 16; *Tolofson* v. *Jensen* [1994] 3 SCR 1022, 120 DLR (4th) 289; *John Pfeiffer Ltd* v. *Rogerson* (2000) 203 CLR 503; Edinger (1995); Walker (2003); and Stellios (2005).

their distinct legal traditions and laws while integrating.[10] Private international law maintains the integrity of the national legal systems; it defines the applicable law for the resolution of a particular problem, but leaves the content of that applicable law untouched. This characteristic can be useful in the harmonization of laws, since it reassures executives and legislatures of their control over their substantive laws. African states are in the early stages of economic integration. They have concerns about sovereignty and some might equally be concerned about the erosion of the ideals of their legal traditions. In such a setting, a developed private international law regime can provide legal certainty for cross-border transactions and, at the same time, ensure that substantive national laws are not fundamentally changed.

However, the virtues of private international law as a tool for addressing interstate relational issues and promoting economic transactions should not blind us to its limitations. The need to ascertain foreign law and the possibility that courts may be *pro lex fori* can be costly for businesses. It is also arguable that within an integrated economy, *pro lex fori* tendencies, if carried to the extreme, may be deemed a non-tariff barrier to trade. The guarantees offered by private international law for maintaining the integrity of the substantive laws of national legal systems may also be thwarted by other community laws, which may displace national laws.

Given the importance of private international law in economic integration, it comes as no surprise that it is an essential component of economic integration in parts of the world.[11] Considerable institutional and academic attention is given to it within the EU. From its inception, a sound private international law regime was identified as having a key role to play in the creation and sustenance of the internal market.[12] The Organization of American States (OAS) is another body with economic integration among its objectives.[13] Through its Inter-American

[10] The demands of economic integration may, however, compel a different result. An example of this is the Europeanization of English private international law. *Allianz SpA* v. *West Tankers Inc.* (C-185/07) [2009] ECR I-663; *Turner* v. *Grovit* (C-159/02) [2004] ECR I-3565; *Owusu* v. *Jackson* (C-281/02) [2005] ECR I-1383; Hartley (2005); and Harris (2008).

[11] Casad (1981); and Caffrey (1985).

[12] See art. 220 of the Treaty of Rome. The Convention (now Regulation) on Jurisdiction and the Recognition and Enforcement of Judgment in Civil and Commercial Matters was the direct product of art. 220.

[13] Charter of the Organization of American States, 30 April 1948, 119 UNTS 3, art. 42.

Conference on Private International Law, the OAS has supervised the negotiation and adoption of over twenty conventions by its members.[14] These conventions cover various issues, including the recognition and enforcement of judgments and choice of law in contracts.[15] The topics for recent conferences have focused on the region's free trade agenda.[16] The Common Market of the Southern Cone (MERCOSUR) sees the 'harmonization of legislation in relevant areas' as a key to strengthening its integration process.[17] Private international law has attracted MERCOSUR's attention, and progress there has been described as 'impressive'.[18] Indeed, the history of cooperation on private international law issues in the Americas dates back to the nineteenth century. As early as 1928, the Pan-America Code on Private International Law, better known as the 'Bustamante Code', was adopted.

Against this background, it is baffling that, despite decades of economic integration in Africa, none of the communities has, or has had, private international law on its agenda. This is so despite the fact that the treaties contain provisions that may be interpreted as enjoining the communities to adopt private international law initiatives. In article 57(1) of the ECOWAS Treaty, member states undertook 'to co-operate in judicial and legal matters with a view to harmonizing their judicial and legal systems'. The modalities for the implementation of this article were to be the subject matter of a protocol. So far, none has been concluded. Article 126 of the EAC Treaty also obliges member states to 'encourage the standardization of judgments of courts within the community' and 'harmonize all their national laws appertaining to the community'. At present, no initiative of private international law of significance has been undertaken under it.

9.3 Measuring strength of interstate legal relations in Africa

9.3.1 Through a private international law lens

As noted above, private international law provides a barometer for measuring the extent to which states interact with each other, especially

[14] Juenger (1994); Garro (1992); Amado (1990–1); Castro (1992); and O'Hop (1995), pp. 163–6.
[15] Inter-American Convention on the Law Applicable to International Contracts, 17 March 1994, 33 ILM 732; and Inter-American Convention on Jurisdiction in the International Sphere for the Extraterritorial Validity of Foreign Judgments, 24 May 1984, 24 ILM 468.
[16] Arroyo and Kleinheisterkamp (2002), p. 254.
[17] Asuncion Treaty, art. 1. See also Arroyo (2000), pp. 157–63.
[18] Arroyo (2000), p. 172.

through the medium of litigation. It creates linkages between legal systems without unifying them. As states become more interconnected – a concomitant of economic integration – and their residents interact, the number of private international law issues should, in theory, increase and the need to address those issues should become more immediate. In other words, the theory is that strong economic integration enhances cross-border activities, which results in disputes the resolution of which will engage private international law principles. Admittedly, private international law is only one of the means through which legal systems interact. And even if it was the only means, it is unlikely to give a wholly accurate picture. Many cross-border economic disputes do not make it to the courts, and where they do the court may miss the private international law issue at stake.

The extent to which African states are interacting with one another on private international law issues provides an insight into how they are related and the strength of the economic integration process. It can be argued that an appreciable volume of inter-African private international law cases (cases in which the foreign element is from an African country) is evidence of interactions between African countries. These interactions could be the result of cross-border trade, or investment and movement of people, all of which are being promoted by the various communities. Evidence of interaction could be located in the extent to which African courts assume jurisdiction over persons domiciled or resident in each other's states, apply each other's laws, assist in judicial proceedings in each other's countries and enforce each other's judgments. The findings on these points can inform us about the state of the strength of economic integration in Africa.

Africans have been promoting African unity for over forty years.[19] Indeed, African economic integration initiatives date back to 1910, when the Southern African Customs Union (SACU), which now consists of Botswana, Lesotho, Namibia, South Africa and Swaziland, was created. So what does the level of inter-African private international law problems teach us about the interconnectedness of African legal systems? To answer that question, a case study of over 350 private international law judgments given by courts at all levels in thirteen Commonwealth African

[19] The Organization of African Unity (now African Union) was established in 1963. Under art. 2(1)(a) of the Charter of the Organization of Africa Unity, 25 May 1963, 479 UNTS 39, 2 ILM 766, a principal purpose of the organization was to 'promote the unity and solidarity of the African States'.

countries over a decade (1997–2007) was conducted.[20] The decade coincided with the emergence of the communities examined in this book. From the examination, fewer than 10 per cent of the cases involved inter-African private international law issues.[21]

From a private international law perspective, enforcing foreign judgments is, perhaps, the best evidence of interstate relations. An effective foreign judgment enforcement regime is a key component of any integration initiative likely to achieve significant success. Indeed, in federal states, it is often given constitutional foundation.[22] So far, it appears that careful thought has not been given to this issue in Africa. From the case study, there were cases in which judgments from other African countries were denied recognition or enforcement by national courts. This was due to the fact that the foreign judgment emanated from a country that had not been designated as a beneficiary under the statutory regime for registration of foreign judgments. In the Commonwealth countries, the statutory regime for the registration of foreign judgments coexists with a common law regime. A judgment that is not eligible for registration under statute may be enforced at common law. In *Heyns* v. *Demetriou*,[23] it was held that a South African judgment could not be registered under Malawi's British and Commonwealth Judgments Act 1922 and the Judgment Extension Act 1922. In *Barclays Bank of Swaziland* v. *Koch*,[24] it was held that a Swaziland judgment could not be registered under Botswana's

[20] The countries studied were: Botswana, Ghana, Kenya, Lesotho, Malawi, Namibia, Nigeria, South Africa, Swaziland, Tanzania, Uganda, Zambia and Zimbabwe. Oppong (2007b); and Oppong (2008a). The case study has been updated to reflect cases decided after 2007.

[21] See, e.g. *Ssebaggala & Sons Electric Centre Ltd* v. *Kenya National Shipping Line Ltd* [2000] LawAfr. LR 931 (enforcement of judgment from Uganda); *Willow Investment* v. *Mbomba Ntumba* [1997] TLR 47 (enforcement of judgment from Zaire); *Mtui* v. *Mtui* 2000 (1) BLR 406 (recognition of divorce decree from Tanzania); *Molly Kiwanuka* v. *Samuel Muwanga* [1999] Swaziland High Court 13 (maintenance of a child in Uganda); and *Sello* v. *Sello (No. 2)* 1999 (2) BLR 104 (order to return child in Lesotho to Botswana).

[22] Constitution of the Commonwealth of Australia, art. 118; and Constitution of the United States of America, art. 4(1).

[23] [2001] Malawi High Court 52. See also *Willow Investment* v. *Mbomba Ntumba* [1997] TLR 47 (the Tanzanian court refused to enforce a judgment from Zaire); *SDV Transmi (Tanzania) Ltd* v. *MS STE Datco*, Civil Application No. 97 of 2004 (Court of Appeal, Tanzania, 2004), in which the absence of a regime for the reciprocal enforcement of judgments between Tanzania and Democratic Republic of Congo was the determinative consideration that made the court grant a stay of execution in favour of the applicant against the Democratic Republic of Congo resident respondent judgment creditor who had no assets in Tanzania.

[24] 1997 BLR 1294.

Judgments (International Enforcement) Act (Cap 11: 04).[25] It is worth remembering that Botswana, Malawi, South Africa and Swaziland are all members of the Southern African Development Community (SADC).

The cases in which judgments from African courts were denied registration in other national courts reflect a wider problem, namely that under the statutes on the registration of foreign judgments, not many African countries have been designated as beneficiaries.[26] Even for the designated countries, only judgments from specified courts, usually the designated state's superior courts, can be registered. This state of affairs evinces inattention to a pertinent relational issue in economic integration. It can undermine economic transactions in the communities as they progress. Perhaps the paucity of inter-African judgment enforcement cases has made this less than an immediate issue. But it is a damning indictment on Africa's economic integration that a judgment from the United Kingdom – a former colonial power – is more likely to be registered in member states of the various communities than judgments from their respective member states.

After years of promoting economic integration, this is troubling. National statutes deny judgments from other African countries the expedited and simplified procedure for enforcing foreign judgments through registration. Registration is a simplified and expedited procedure for enforcing foreign judgments. One would have expected that African governments, in their 'determination to promote unity, solidarity, cohesion and cooperation among the peoples of Africa and African States',[27] would make the procedure available to African judgments. Under the existing statutes for the registration of foreign judgments, *the executive* designates countries whose judgments may benefit from that regime. Of all the communities, it is only between the founding

[25] For similar cases outside the scope of the case study, see, e.g. *Italframe Ltd* v. *Mediterranean Shipping Co.* [1986] KLR 54 (judgment from Tanganyika (now Tanzania) denied registration in Kenya); and *Re Lowenthal and Air France* 1966 (2) ALR Comm. 301 (judgment from Zambia denied registration in Kenya).

[26] South Africa's regime designates only Namibia. Namibia's regime designates only South Africa. Swaziland's regime has been extended to Lesotho, Botswana, Zimbabwe, Zambia, Zanzibar, Malawi, Kenya and Tanzania. Ghana's regime designates only Senegal (see First Schedule of Foreign Judgments and Maintenance Orders (Reciprocal Enforcement) Instrument, 1993, LI 1575). Tanzania's regime designates Lesotho, Botswana, Mauritius, Zambia, Seychelles, Somalia, Zimbabwe and the Kingdom of Swaziland (see Reciprocal Enforcement of Foreign Judgments Order, GN Nos. 8 and 9 of 1936); and Kenya's regime designates Malawi, Seychelles, Tanzania, Uganda, Zambia and Rwanda (Foreign Judgments (Reciprocal Enforcement) (Extension of Act) Order, s. 2).

[27] Constitutive Act, preamble.

members of the East African Community (EAC)[28] – Kenya, Tanzania and Uganda – that judgments can be registered in each other's countries.[29] To be certain, it is not being argued here that a judgment from an African country should be automatically enforced in another African country. Indeed, there are factors that can justify the non-registration of an African judgment.[30] What is being argued is that an effective economic community should have judgments easily enforceable among member states. Currently, in Africa, as far as enforcement through registration is concerned, this is not the case.

It is recommended that, to remedy this problem, each African state should designate many more African states as beneficiaries of its statutory regime for the registration of foreign judgments. A more ambitious and long-term project would be to conclude an African foreign judgment enforcement convention.[31] However, given the paucity of inter-African judgment enforcement cases, the similarities in the provisions of existing national statutes on foreign judgment enforcement, the challenges of negotiating an international convention and the general ambivalence towards private international law issues, the statutory designation of more African states may be the only feasible option, at least for the immediate future. Statutory designation is an easier course to take and can be done immediately. Negotiating an African convention could take years. However, with the benefit of the experiences of others such as the EU and OAS, this need not be the case.

The application of each other's laws is also another manifestation of relations between states. Comity sometimes demands that individuals are not allowed to evade foreign state laws merely by litigating in another state or choosing a different applicable law. Thus, in *Herbst* v. *Surti*,[32] the Zimbabwean court refused to enforce a contract that was illegal under the proper law of the contract, in this instance South African law. From

[28] Burundi and Rwanda recently became members of the EAC. Under Kenya's Foreign Judgments (Reciprocal Enforcement) (Extension of Act) Order, judgments from Rwanda can be registered. Thanawalla (1970).

[29] See, e.g. *Ssebaggala & Sons Electric Centre Ltd* v. *Kenya National Shipping Line Ltd* [2000] LawAfr. LR 931; *Pioneer General Assurance Society Ltd* v. *Zulfikarali Nimji Javer* [2006] eKLR (Kenyan court registered judgments from Uganda); *Société de Transports International Rwanda* v. *H. Abdi*, Civil Application No. NAI 298 of 1997 (Court of Appeal, Kenya, 1997) (appeal against a decision setting aside the registration in Kenya of a Rwanda judgment); and *Pioneer General Assurance Society Ltd* v. *Zulfikarali Nimji Javer* [2006] eKLR (payment of interest on a Ugandan judgment registered in Kenya).

[30] *Cairo Bank* v. *Mohamed Ali Bahaydar* 1966 (1) ALR Comm. 33.

[31] Oppong (2007e), p. 704.

[32] 1990 (2) ZLR 269.

the case study, choice of forum agreements that designate an African state and choice of law agreements that adopt an African state's law were at issue in some cases. Courts have been prepared to uphold these agreements. In *Friendship Container Manufacturing Ltd* v. *Mitchell Cotts Ltd*,[33] the Kenyan court upheld an exclusive choice of forum agreement contained in a bill of lading that vested jurisdiction in South African courts. In *Barlows Central Finance Corp. Ltd* v. *Joncon Ltd*,[34] a sales agreement contained a South African choice of law and forum clause. The Swaziland court upheld the choice of law clause, but declined to enforce the choice of forum agreement. One factor that influenced the court's latter determination was that Swaziland and South African law were similar in many respects. As economic integration in Africa strengthens and spurs on cross-border transactions, issues of applying other African countries' laws are likely to increase. In this regard, the present judicial attitude of generally upholding party autonomy, which sometimes translates into an application of foreign law, is important.

In the absence of such agreements, the courts applied various tests, including the place of performance and the real and substantial connection test. In *Georgina Ngina* v. *Inter Freight East Africa Ltd*,[35] a contract was entered into in Kigali, Rwanda. The place of performance was in Kenya. It was held that the Kenyan courts had jurisdiction. The central issue in *Roger Parry* v. *Astral Operations Ltd*[36] was the applicable law for a contract of employment that was performed in Malawi. The South African court rejected the respondent's argument that the contract was governed by Malawi law as that was the place of performance. The court found that there were strong-enough factors connecting the contract with South Africa to make its law the applicable law.

Admittedly, neither *Friendship Container Manufacturing* nor *Barlows Central Finance Corp.* involved the direct application of the law of another African country. But the fact that courts uphold parties' choice of law or forum will ultimately prove important for economic transactions within the communities in Africa. As discussed in Chapter 4, apart from the initiatives of the Organization for the Harmonization of Business Laws in Africa and the East African Community, there appears to be no present or immediate future initiative on the agenda of the other

[33] [2001] East Afr. LR 338.

[34] Case No. 2491/99 (High Court, Swaziland, 1999). *Afinta Financial Services (Pty) Ltd* v. *Luke Malinga T/A Long Distance Transport*, Civ. Case No. 123/2001 (High Court, Swaziland, 2001).

[35] [2006] eKLR. [36] 2005 (10) BLLR 989.

communities to harmonize member states' laws. In the absence of harmonized substantive laws among member states, judicial enforcement of parties' choice of law and forum agreements is an alternative that individuals may use to regulate the law that governs their transactions. There are definitely limitations on this alternative. The courts may not give effect to a choice of law agreement which violates mandatory rules of the forum[37] or public policy. A badly drafted choice of law clause may place the courts in a difficult position regarding the parties' intentions, which will then affect the willingness of the courts to enforce the clause.[38] Notwithstanding these limitations, this alternative is one with which individuals may have to be content for some time.

While courts are prepared to uphold African choice of law and choice of forum agreements, few such choices are made compared with agreements that choose non-African states and laws.[39] The minimal use of African state choice of law and forum agreements tells us much about individuals' perceptions of the adequacy of courts and laws in Africa to deal with the complex issues involved in cross-border transactions. These adverse perceptions about African legal systems' lack of ability in this regard will have to be addressed through institutional reform and the enhancement of resources, including training of personnel, available to the judiciary.

9.3.2 *Through a comparative law lens*

To the extent that it deals with an analysis of the operation of rules in different legal systems, comparative law bears some affinity with private international law. Both subjects deal with foreign legal systems, albeit from different perspectives. Reimann describes the relationship between the two disciplines as 'intimate'.[40] However, the importance of comparative law as a means for creating and strengthening relations between states goes beyond its affinity with private international law. To Tunc, comparative law could be a source of peace among nations.[41] Harmonious coexistence among states is an essential condition for effective

[37] Ibid.

[38] *Afinta Financial Services (Pty) Ltd* v. *Luke Malinga T/A Long Distance Transport*, Civ. Case No. 123/2001 (High Court, Swaziland, 2001); and *Ekkehard Creutzburg* v. *Commercial Bank of Namibia* [2006] All SA 327.

[39] *Raytheon Aircraft Credit Corp.* v. *Air Al-Faraj Ltd* [2005] 2 KLR 47; *Fonville* v. *Kelly* [2002] 1 East Afr. LR 71; *Valentine Investment Co. Ltd* v. *Federal Republic of Germany* [2006] eKLR; and *Nika Fishing Co. Ltd* v. *Lavinia Corp.* [2001] 16 NWLR 556.

[40] Reimann (2006), p. 1364. [41] Tunc (1961).

economic integration. In Chapter 2, it was argued that inter-system jurisprudential communication, which often takes the form of a comparative law exercise, is useful in all branches of law. It can be used to strengthen relations between member states within a community and aid the harmonization of law. This section examines the state of jurisprudential communication among African states using private international law. However, the discussion here may equally apply to other branches of law relevant to strengthening economic integration in Africa, such as contract, investment and labour laws.

Comparative law and the use of comparative foreign materials enrich judicial decisions. For private international lawyers, this has been argued as a path to harmonization in the absence of international conventions.[42] Southern Africa provides a good example of how comparative law aids international (in this case regional) harmonization of law.[43] Judgments of Southern African courts, but mainly those of South Africa, have been relied on frequently in other Southern African countries. As Justice Tebbutt once observed, 'the common law of Botswana is the Roman–Dutch law . . . The courts of Botswana have never been reluctant, in their own adaptation of the common law to the requirements of modern times, to have regard to the approach of the South African courts and to the writings of authoritative South African academics'.[44] In part, this may be attributed to the fact that they all share the same legal tradition – the Roman–Dutch law. Also, law reporting (and access to legal materials) is fairly up to date in the major states of the region, namely, South Africa, Namibia, Botswana and Zimbabwe.

As noted above, there has been no systematic examination of the significance of private international law in Africa's economic integration. Nor has there been any attempt to harmonize private international law in the communities. Given this state of affairs, jurisprudential communication can be used to achieve a degree of harmonization in laws across the communities. Indeed, it is refreshing to note that there is a high level of harmony between the jurisprudence of the various Roman–Dutch law countries that are members of the SACU, SADC and COMESA. Through judicial decisions, and recent proposed legislative reforms, the Roman-Dutch law jurisprudence is also converging with the common law.[45]

[42] Forsyth (2005).

[43] *American Flag plc* v. *Great African T-shirt Corp.* 2000 (1) SA 356; and *Bizy Holdings Ltd* v. *Eso Management Ltd* 2002 (2) BLR 125.

[44] *Silverston Ltd* v. *Lobatse Clay Works* 1996 BLR 190 at 195.

[45] Oppong (2008b); and South African Law Reform Commission (2006).

The jurisprudence of the common law countries within the EAC and ECOWAS is also largely similar.[46] However, unlike the Roman–Dutch law countries, there is infrequent jurisprudential communication between them. In other words, the common law countries, especially those in West Africa, do not demonstrate an appreciable level of reliance on each other's case law.[47] Rather, the source of the harmony in their jurisprudence is England, from where they borrow principles of law. From the perspective of economic integration, and with a view to strengthening interstate relations, this state of affairs among the common law countries is problematic. With the increasing Europeanization of English private international law, a development currently reflected in the minimal amount of textbook space devoted to 'the traditional rules', there is a need for the common law African countries to diversify their sources of persuasive authority. Southern Africa may be a good place to examine in this respect. There are a number of issues on which the common law converges with Roman–Dutch law.[48] Indeed, two recent judgments from the South African Supreme Court of Appeal have brightened up the prospect of closer convergence on the issue of jurisdiction in international matters.[49] This is the area where the Roman–Dutch law diverges most from the common law. Communication between judges of the common law and Roman–Dutch law traditions can be an important step in creating a judicially engineered harmonized private international law regime in Africa. A study that distils the common core of principles between both legal traditions will be an important aid to this pursuit.

In general, there is a need to enhance jurisprudential communication within the communities by making jurisprudence – case law,

[46] Ghana, Gambia, Kenya, Nigeria, Tanzania, Sierra Leone and Uganda.

[47] But see *Eastern and Southern African Trade* v. *Hassan Basajjabalaba* [2007] Uganda Commercial Court 30. The Ugandan court referred to two decisions on the effect of choice of law agreements on the court's jurisdiction: *Fonville* v. *Kelly* [2002] 1 East Afr. LR 71 and *Tononoka Steels Ltd* v. *East & Southern African Trade & Development Bank* [2002] 2 East Afr. LR 536. It was noted in respect of one of the cases, 'it is a case from a Sister Republic, with comparable jurisprudence. The decision, though not binding upon the High Court of Uganda, is pleasantly persuasive'. The court followed that decision. The demise of the West African Court of Appeal Reports and the East African Law Reports (recently revived), which reported cases from the common law countries of West and East Africa respectively, accounts in part for the infrequent jurisprudential communication between the courts in these regions.

[48] Kutner (1990).

[49] *Richman* v. *Ben-Tovim* 2007 (2) SA 283; and *Bid Industrial Holding* v. *Strang* 2008 (3) SA 355.

statute and academic commentary – more accessible. The case study revealed that occasionally courts in two neighbouring states faced a similar issue, and yet came to different conclusions, often in ignorance of an earlier decision on the same point in the other country.[50] This can be illustrated with two pairs of cases addressing two different issues. The first related to whether or not a plaintiff, who was resident in an EAC country, should be ordered to pay security for costs when litigating in another. In the Kenyan case of *Healthwise Pharmaceuticals Ltd* v. *Smithkline Beecham Consumer Healthcare Ltd*,[51] the court rejected the applicant's argument that it was a resident of the EAC and therefore the defendant would have no difficulties in recovering any costs that may be awarded. However, in the Ugandan case of *Shah* v. *Manurama Ltd*,[52] the court held that, given the establishment of the EAC, there could no longer be an automatic and inflexible presumption for the courts to order security for costs with regard to plaintiffs who are resident in the EAC.

The second issue related to whether a court might assume jurisdiction to grant an *in personam* interdict against an *incola* in respect of conduct in another country. In *Bozimo Trade and Development Ltd* v. *First Merchant Bank of Zimbabwe Ltd*,[53] the Zimbabwean court drew a distinction between mandatory and prohibitory interdicts. It held that it had no jurisdiction to grant a mandatory injunction for acts committed abroad, as that would infringe the sovereignty of the foreign country. A different conclusion was reached in the South African case of *Metlika Trading Ltd* v. *Commissioner, South African Revenue Service*:[54] the court held that it had jurisdiction to issue such an interdict and it did not matter that it was mandatory or prohibitory. Fortunately, in both examples, the later decision (given without reference to the earlier case) appeared to be better than the earlier one. The prospect that a better decision could be taken in one state by taking into account persuasive jurisprudence from a sister jurisdiction should be encouraged.

Although the above has focused on jurisprudential communication between courts in Africa, it is important that jurisprudential

[50] But see *Coutts* v. *Ford* 1997 (1) ZLR 440; *Society of Lloyd's* v. *Price* 2006 (5) SA 393; *Detmold* v. *Minister of Health and Social Services* 2004 NR 175; and *Minister for Welfare and Population Development* v. *Fitzpatrick* 2000 (3) SA 422.

[51] [2001] LawAfr. LR 1279. [52] [2003] 1 East Afr. LR 294.

[53] 2000 (1) ZLR 1. [54] 2005 (3) SA 1.

communication should not be limited to that between African states. National legal systems and, indeed, the communities' legal systems should also communicate with the international legal system. They must demonstrate awareness of and partake in relevant developments on the international plane. Judges and lawyers must show awareness of the growing volume of private international law jurisprudence by international and regional institutions. This is especially so if the private international law regimes in the communities are not to be isolationist. It is reassuring that in a number of cases in the case study, judges and counsel showed an awareness of relevant international conventions and their potential influence on judicial decisions.[55]

9.4 Private international law and economic transactions

9.4.1 History and relevance

Historically, the first major private international law legislation in common law Africa was aimed at facilitating commerce in the colonies. It was legislation for the enforcement of foreign judgments. Patchett[56] traces the genesis of the first Gold Coast (now Ghana) legislation in this area, the Foreign Judgment Extension Ordinance 1907, to a complaint to a District Commissioner from a trading company in the Gold Coast regarding debtors who absconded to the Ivory Coast (now Côte d'Ivoire), which was then under French rule, ostensibly to avoid payment. The company suggested that extradition arrangements should be instituted, but the Colonial Secretary did not respond positively to this idea. He was of the view that the fault lay with the traders who allowed credit indiscriminately. This response incensed the company. They wrote directly to the Secretary of State. They reiterated their earlier plea, and further suggested that the problem of fleeing debtors existed even among the British colonies in West Africa. The colonial office, after some hesitation, took a second look at the matter. It suggested that the system of registration of judgments then in force in the United Kingdom would be a better solution. This led to the enactment in the Gold Coast of the Foreign Judgment Extension Ordinance. Similar statutes were enacted

[55] *Sello* v. *Sello (No. 2)* 1999 (2) BLR 104 at 109; *De Gree* v. *Webb* 2007 (5) SA 184 at [11], [17], [47]–[55], [85]–[94]; *Roger Parry* v. *Astral Operations Ltd* 2005 (10) BLLR 989; and *Delmas America Africa Line Inc.* v. *Kisko Products Ghana Ltd* [2005–6] SCGLR 75.

[56] Patchett (1984), p. 20.

for the other colonies.[57] In our present climate of easier communication and movement of assets, the dangers of 'absconding debtors' and 'absconding assets' is an even greater reality.

At present, private international law, like any domestic private law regime, can in effect be a non-tariff barrier to international trade and a disincentive to economic transactions.[58] Unbridled application of the *lex fori*, disrespect for choice of law and forum agreements, and the non-recognition or enforcement of foreign judgments by states may all evince protectionism. These can act as a hindrance regarding the free flow of 'wealth, skills and people' across national boundaries.[59] Diversity in private international rules can impose undue transaction costs on businesspeople and encourage forum shopping and other strategic behaviour inimical to international trade. Rules that clearly allocate international jurisdiction, respect parties' choice of law and forum agreements, and provide certain and expedited means of enforcing foreign judgments are an essential part of a private international law regime meant to facilitate economic transactions.

The need to make private international law responsive to the needs of international economic transactions has been recognized in academic writing and judicial decisions.[60] African courts have also recognized this need. South African courts have emphasized the need for the country's trade and commercial relations to be an important consideration in applying its laws on jurisdiction.[61] Namibia's High Court has held that commercial considerations influence parties in agreeing to choice of law and forum clauses, and that this should be considered when assessing the international competence of foreign courts in an action to enforce a foreign judgment.[62] In *MAK (Pty) Ltd* v. *St Paul Insurance Co. SA Ltd*,[63] the Botswana High Court took into account the fact that this was an 'age of intense international trade involving cross-border transactions' in rejecting the Roman–Dutch law principle that *peregrini* parties cannot

[57] Gambia – Foreign Judgment Extension Ordinance 1908; Northern Nigeria – Foreign Judgment Extension Ordinance 1908; Southern Nigeria – Foreign Judgment Extension Ordinance 1908; and Sierra Leone – Foreign Judgment Extension Ordinance 1908.

[58] Mengozzi (2001).

[59] *Morguard Investments Ltd* v. *De Savoye* [1990] 3 SCR 1077 at 1096; 76 DLR (4th) 256 at 269.

[60] Brand (1997); and Sykes (2008).

[61] *American Flag plc* v. *Great African T-shirt Corp.* 2000 (1) SA 356 at 375; and *Hay Management Consultants (Pty) Ltd* v. *P3 Management Consultants (Pty) Ltd* 2005 (2) SA 522.

[62] *Argos Fishing Co. Ltd* v. *Friopesca SA* 1991 NR 106.

[63] 2007 (1) BLR 210.

by agreement (prorogation) confer jurisdiction on a court without at least one other recognized *rationes jurisdictionis*, such as residence, domicile or cause of action.

Private international law can be a direct source of investment in Africa's economic communities if, working with some member states, they create a climate that encourages what I characterize as 'jurisdictional tourism'. Note the British pride in Lord Denning's famous statement that England is a good place to forum shop.[64] Private international lawyers have generally shied away from statistical or empirical measures of the subject's effect on issues like international business decision-making, international corporate behaviour or even economic development. However, these issues are often the unarticulated background to the development and application of private international law rules and judicial decisions.[65] Undeniably, the status of London as an international commercial litigation centre provides money and employment to the Queen's Counsel and to many others who practise there. This provides foreign currency for the country. Contracting parties with no association to England are attracted to litigate there because of its accommodating jurisdiction rules and respect for choice of law and forum agreements. This is not to suggest that the English rules have been deliberately developed to encourage jurisdictional tourism, but, in practice, they facilitate it. Of course, these rules must be combined with a judicial system that is neutral, modern, efficient and independent.

Reflecting on the Roman–Dutch rules on jurisdiction in South Africa, Forsyth has noted the impossibility of a *peregrine* (foreigner) suing another *peregrine* in South Africa unless they have some other association with the jurisdiction other than their choice-of-forum agreement.[66] At common law, this will not ordinarily be a problem; the presence of an exclusive jurisdiction agreement, without more, will be enough to confer jurisdiction.[67] As economic integration in Africa progresses and trade and investment grows, African countries with

64 *The Atlantic Star* [1973] QB 364 at 382.

65 An explicit admission of this is art. 65 of the EU Treaty, which provides that private international law issues may be necessary for the 'proper functioning of the internal market'.

66 Forsyth (2006a). For judicial support for this position, see *Chong Sun Wood Products Ltd* v. *K & T Trading Ltd* 2001 (2) SA 651; and *Hulse-Reutter* v. *Godde* 2001 (4) SA 1336.

67 The importance of choice-of-forum agreements has been given a further boost under the Hague Convention on Choice of Court Agreements 2005. The convention is not yet in force and there are no African countries currently party to it. As of August 2010, it had been signed by the EU and the United States, and ratified by Mexico. Beaumont (2009).

advanced and independent legal systems should, with the support of their respective communities, explore the possibility of developing into jurisdictional tourist sites for the resolution of commercial disputes, including those involving non-African parties.[68] A contract between a Ghanaian and a Kenyan businessperson or a Ghanaian and a Dutch exporter could have a South African choice of law and forum clause rather than an English one. Jurisdictional tourist sites will provide a neutral, easily accessible and potentially less costly forum for resolving commercial disputes in Africa. They will also be a source of investment, employment and foreign exchange for the countries involved.

Aside from national courts, it has been discussed in Chapter 8 that some community courts also have jurisdiction to determine cases referred to them by private parties who choose them as forums for arbitration of their commercial disputes.[69] For people transacting in Africa and seeking a neutral forum to settle disputes, the community courts can provide a viable dispute settlement forum. The community courts' arbitral jurisdiction can be used to develop them into forums for the resolution of commercial disputes in Africa. To develop national and community courts into jurisdictional tourist sites, corruption within the judiciary must be eliminated. This can be achieved through institutional reforms, independent oversight of the operations of courts – which should not compromise their independence – and the adoption of strict and enforceable codes of judicial conduct.

9.4.2 *Enforcement of foreign judgments*

Enforcing a judgment from another state is, perhaps, the best testament to the recognition that an enforcing state gives to validity of normative acts performed in the foreign state. As noted above, in economic integration, a regime for the enforcement of foreign judgments is needed to

[68] Forsyth (2003), p. 216, where he advocates South African courts to develop an international role akin to that of the Commercial Court in London for Southern and Central Africa.

[69] EAC Treaty, art. 32; and COMESA Treaty, art. 28. Article 16 of the ECOWAS Treaty also establishes an Arbitration Tribunal for the community. The status, composition, powers, procedure and other issues concerning the Arbitration Tribunal are to be set out in a Protocol relating thereto. Until that time, art. 9(5) of the Protocol A/P.1/7/91 on the Community Court of Justice of the High Contracting Parties as Amended by Supplementary Protocol A/SP/.1/01/05 Amending the Protocol Relating to the Community Court of Justice (herafter, ECOWAS Court Protocol) provides that the ECOWAS Court of Justice exercises the powers of the Arbitration Tribunal.

facilitate commercial transactions. A judgment given against a person resident in one state should easily be enforced in a state in which that person has assets. Individuals who transact across national boundaries are concerned about the extent to which foreign judgment enforcement regimes are cheap, rapid and uncomplicated. In summary, an effective regime for foreign judgment enforcement offers practical benefits for individuals. At present, there are limitations on existing regimes for the enforcement of foreign judgments in member states of the communities under review. These adversely affect the extent to which they can give effect to each other's judgments.

We have already noted the reciprocity requirement in the statutory regimes for the enforcement of foreign judgment in common law countries, and the limited number of African countries that have been designated. However, it is worth adding here that under South Africa's Enforcement of Civil Judgment Act 32 of 1988, reciprocal treatment from a designated country is not mandatory, but the country must be designated nonetheless. Reciprocity also exists for some of the civil law regimes, but it appears that, unlike in the common law countries, it is a judicial rather than an executive decision.[70] The fact that very few African countries have been designated under these statutory regimes means that not many countries benefit from statutory regimes.

Another problem relates to the diversity in bases of international competence. This implies that not all judgments from other countries will be enforced despite having been validly decreed in the foreign country. The principle that the foreign court should have been competent, in accordance with the enforcing court's rules of private international law, is a requirement in all of the countries.[71] What differs is what each country treats as international competence. In South Africa, and indeed the other Roman–Dutch law jurisdictions of Southern Africa, namely Botswana, Lesotho, Namibia, Swaziland and Zimbabwe, residence and submission are recognized bases of international competence. More recently, mere presence was also accepted as a basis of international competence in South Africa.[72] It remains to be seen whether the other

[70] Examples are Ethiopia, Egypt and Tunisia. They entrust the reciprocity assessment to the judiciary. Ethiopian Civil Procedure Code 1965, art. 457; Egyptian Civil and Commercial Procedure 1968, art. 296; and Tunisian Code of Civil and Commercial Procedure 1959, art. 319. Teshale (2000).

[71] *John Holt* v. *Christoph Nutsugah* (1929–31) Gold Coast Divisional Court 75; *Pakou* v. *Rudnap Zambia Ltd* (1998) ZR 233; *Steinberg* v. *Cosmopolitan National Bank of Chicago* 1973 (4) SA 564; and *Argos Fishing Co. Ltd* v. *Friopesca SA* 1991 NR 106.

[72] Oppong (2007a).

Roman–Dutch law countries will also adopt this basis of international competence. There is continuing debate as to whether other grounds such as nationality, domicile and attachment of property should suffice for international competence in Roman–Dutch law.[73] At common law, and for the common law countries in Africa, presence, residence and submission appear to be the only recognized bases of international competence.

When these differences in the bases of international competence are read with the differences in the bases of domestic competence in international matters, it becomes evident that the scope of judgments, from some African countries that can be enforced in other African countries, is reduced. This is so despite the fact that such judgments might have been legitimately decreed in the foreign jurisdiction. For example, attachment of property and, aside South Africa, arrest of a *peregrine* defendant are bases of jurisdiction in international matters in Roman–Dutch law jurisdictions of Southern Africa.[74] However, it is unlikely that a judgment given on either ground will be enforced in the common law jurisdiction where, as noted above, presence, residence and submission are the only recognized bases of international competence.

Indeed, even where countries have the same basis of international competence, they may interpret it differently or require different standards of proof. Submission is a case in point. In *Blanchard, Krasner & French* v. *Evans*,[75] the Full Bench of the Witwatersrand Local Division rejected the trial court's ruling that submission must be proved as a matter of legal certainty. It held that submission must be proved on the balance of probabilities.[76] In *Richman* v. *Ben-Tovim*,[77] the trial court laid down the test as being conduct, which clearly indicated, and was consistent only with, an unqualified acceptance of or acquiescence to jurisdiction. These cases appear to suggest, although the South African courts have accepted that submission to jurisdiction may be express or implied, they have set a high threshold test for it, especially where it is to be inferred from conduct. It is arguable whether other jurisdictions adhere to this high threshold test. What is certain from the case study I have

[73] Leon (1983), pp. 338–9.

[74] South Africa has abolished arrest as a basis of jurisdiction in international matters. Sibanda (2008); and Oppong (2008a). However, arrest remains a basis of competence in international matters in other countries. Zimbabwe – High Court Act, Ch. 7.06, s. 15; Namibia – Rules of the High Court of Namibia, s. 9(1); Lesotho – High Court Rules 1980, r. 6(8); and *Lesotho Express Delivery Services Ltd* v. *Ravin Panambalana*, Civ/T/634A/02, Civ/T/APN/469/02 (High Court, Lesotho, 2006).

[75] 2002 (4) SA 144. [76] Ibid., at 148. [77] 2006 (2) SA 591 at 602.

carried out is that, in the Ugandan and Nigerian cases where submission was also argued, enforcement was refused.[78]

To facilitate the free flow of judgments among members of the African communities, there is a need for reform of the bases of international competence. Adopting a broad and flexible basis of international competence will be a step in the right direction. It will enable courts to enforce foreign judgments given on bases hitherto not recognized under their law, but which support a conclusion that the foreign court legitimately exercised jurisdiction over the judgment debtor. The real and substantial connection test, which is a basis of international competence developed by the Canadian Supreme Court and applied to the enforcement of both inter-provincial and international judgments,[79] is an example of a broad and flexible basis of jurisdiction.

There is a South African case in which real and substantial connection was invoked, albeit unsuccessfully. In *Supercat Inc.* v. *Two Oceans Marine*,[80] the plaintiff sought enforcement of a Florida (United States) judgment against the defendant South African company. The Florida court assumed jurisdiction on the basis that the tort involved, fraud, was committed within its jurisdiction. At the time of the action, the defendant was neither resident nor domiciled in Florida. However, it entered appearance, denied the jurisdiction of the court and thereafter failed to proceed with its defence. The court held that the Florida court was not internationally competent under South African law. Counsel referred to Canada's real and substantial connection bases of international competence. He argued that the traditional approach to the recognition of foreign judgments was obsolete and that the exigencies of international trade called for a new approach. The judge found the Canadian cases 'informative', but felt 'not inclined or, sitting as a single judge, entitled to ignore the considerable weight of judicial authority in this country'. It is recommended that member states of the African communities should adopt this basis of international competence to expand the scope of foreign judgments that could potentially be enforced in their respective countries.

Equally constraining to the enforcement of foreign judgments within the communities is the fact that the present enforcement regimes,

[78] *Transroad Ltd* v. *Bank of Uganda* [1998] UGA J. No. 12; and *Ghassan Halaoui* v. *Grosvernor Casinos Ltd* [2002] 17 NWLR 28.

[79] *Morguard Investments Ltd* v. *De Savoye* [1990] 3 SCR 1077; *Beals* v. *Saldanha* [2003] 3 SCR 416, 234 DLR (4th) 1; and Blom and Edinger (2005).

[80] 2001 (4) SA 27.

especially those of the common law countries, are restricted to the enforcement of foreign money judgments. At common law, only judgments for a fixed sum of money can be enforced.[81] This means that injunctions, orders of specific performance and other non-monetary remedies cannot be enforced in many states. These remedies are important in international litigation. Occasionally, there may be the need to seek their recognition and enforcement in other countries. If, in these instances, they cannot be enforced, this can be problematic for the relevant party.

The demands of modern-day, international commercial transactions and litigation suggest a need for the re-assessment of the rule restricting the enforcement of *in personam* foreign judgments to those for a sum of money. The emergence of new forms of relief, hitherto unknown to the common law, and their frequent deployment to serve the cause of justice have become a common feature of modern international commercial litigation. Provisional and protective remedies like the Mareva injunction, the Anton Piller order, the anti-suit injunction and negative declarations are examples of such relief. These remedies have benefits for the individual litigant and, indeed, society as a whole. They preserve the status quo, ensuring that a party does not dissipate his assets to defeat a prospective judgment and generally prevent him from taking actions to defeat the cause of justice. They may also be tactically deployed to the beneficial end of achieving a settlement. Such a settlement, from a public policy perspective, is good for society as it reduces judicial workload. Additionally, and especially in this electronic age, time is of the essence in these remedies. International cooperation in their enforcement is sometimes necessary. A party's ability to bring an action for the enforcement of non-money judgments will be a great boost to securing these benefits. A similar case can be made for other substantive reliefs that are not money judgments, such as orders to transfer shares, permanent injunctions, orders for the restitution of chattel and specific performance generally.

In various countries outside Africa, there have been both judicial and legislative moves to abrogate the rule against the enforcement of non-money judgments.[82] In the context of economic integration, the regimes for the enforcement of judgments between member states of the EU, and

[81] *Re Lowenthal and Air France* 1966 (2) ALR Comm. 301; *Re the Maintenance Orders Enforcement Ordinance* (1954) 27 KLR 94; and *Coluflandres Ltd* v. *Scandia Industrial Product Ltd* 1969 (2) RLR 431.

[82] Examples are Australia, New Zealand, Singapore and Canada. See Oppong (2006a); Oppong (2007a); Pitel (2007); and Pham (2008).

between member states of the EU and the European Free Trade Area, allow the recognition and enforcement of non-money judgments.[83] To support economic transactions within the African communities, it is suggested that national courts and legislators should consider abrogating the common rule against the enforcement of foreign non-money judgments. This will facilitate the free flow of judgments among member states of the communities.

Another limitation worth examining relates to the bases on which a foreign judgment can be denied recognition. There are both common law and statutory defences to actions to enforce foreign judgments. The common law bases include the judgment being contrary to public policy, infringing the rules of natural justice or having been procured by fraud. These grounds often give rise to interpretive difficulties and leave much room for judicial discretion. Public policy is an example of an ill-defined basis for non-recognition. Its unbridled invocation and application, especially in the context of economic integration, where states are expected to respect each other's laws and legal acts, can affect the horizontal relations between states and impact negatively on economic transactions. Comparatively, it is significant that within the EU the jurisprudence of the ECJ favours restricting the scope of public policy in actions to enforce foreign judgments.[84]

From the case study, it does not appear that public policy is often invoked as a defence in actions to enforce foreign judgments. Indeed, the study revealed only two cases, both involving judgments from non-African countries, in which the courts grappled with the defence and its scope. In *Eden* v. *Pienaar*,[85] the respondent challenged the recognition and enforcement of an Israeli judgment as contrary to South African public policy. The judgment contained a linkage provision, the effect of which was to ensure that depreciation of the Israeli currency did not redound to the benefit of the judgment debtor. The trial court refused enforcement on the grounds that the linkage provision escalated the face value of the debt to an unconscionable amount, and that the Israeli statute, on which the action was based (the statute created liability for failure to negotiate in good faith), was contrary to South African law. In allowing the appeal, the court held that the linkage provision was an aspect of revalorization, which increased the face value of the debt, but

[83] Brussels I Regulation, art. 32; and Lugano Convention, art. 32.

[84] *Krombach* v. *Bamberski* (C-7/98) [2000] ECR I-1935; and *Regie Nationale des Usines Renault SA* v. *Maxicar SpA* (C-38/98) [2000] ECR I-2973.

[85] 2001 (1) SA 158. See also *Patel* v. *Bank of Baroda* [2001] 1 East Afr. LR 189.

did not affect its real value. The purchasing power of the debt remained the same, and there was nothing unconscionable or *contra bonos mores* about revalorization. It was further held that the mere fact that a foreign statute embodied concepts not recognized by South African law did not of itself constitute a ground for refusing to enforce the judgment. There was nothing contrary to South African public policy in requiring a party to pay damages for not negotiating in good faith.

Statutes may also afford specific defences to actions to enforce foreign judgments. At present there are some statutes with inappropriate nationalistic or protectionist undertones that need to be re-examined to ensure the free flow of judgments within communities in Africa. The much-criticized South African Protection of Business Act 99 of 1978 is an example. The Act provides that, except with the permission of the Minister of Economic Affairs, no judgment, order, direction, arbitration award or letter of request, or any other request delivered, given or issued or emanating from outside the Republic, shall be enforced in the Republic if it arises from an act or transaction that took place at any time and is connected with the following defined matters: mining, production, importation, exportation, refinement, possession, use, or sale of, or ownership of any matter or material, of whatever nature, whether within, outside, into or from the Republic.[86] Regardless of the Minister's consent, the recognition and enforcement of a foreign judgment for punitive or multiple damages arising out of the defined matters is prohibited.[87] A defendant who has already paid part of such an award can recover it from the judgment creditor.[88] The Act was to protect South Africans from the adverse effects of foreign laws, such as those allowing for penal or multiple damages. Indeed, other countries outside Africa have statutes with a similar purpose.[89]

However, the South African Act is unique in its breadth and has rightly been described as the clearest example of 'legislative overkill',[90] and conveying a 'discouraging message to foreigners seeking the assistance of [South African] courts'.[91] If applied to the letter, its effect on business confidence might be devastating. Schulze has observed that it is nothing but a stumbling block to much-needed foreign investment in

[86] Protection of Business Act 99 of 1978, s. 1(1)(a).

[87] Ibid., s. 1A(1). [88] Ibid., s. 1B.

[89] UK – Protection of Trading Interest Act 1980; Australia – Foreign Anti-Trust Judgments (Restrictions on Enforcement) Act 1979 (Cth); and Canada – Foreign Extra-territorial Measures Act 1984, ss. 8 and 9.

[90] Forsyth (2003), p. 435. [91] South African Law Reform Commission (2006) at [5.2.2].

South Africa.[92] Happily, it has seldom been invoked and, even where it has, the courts have been careful to construe its scope narrowly.[93] Indeed, the South African Law Reform Commission has recommended repeal of the Act.[94]

Thomashausen's study of the judgment-enforcement regimes in Angola and Mozambique,[95] both civil law countries in Southern Africa, also reveals a protectionist tenor. One of the conditions that must be met by a foreign judgment before it will be recognized and enforced is that where the enforcing court's rules of private international law provide that its substantive law should have been applied, a foreign court's decision, which affects an Angolan or Mozambican, must not disadvantage that citizen in relation to the decision that would have been reached had the law of the enforcing court been applied. In other words, a national of the forum should not be treated by the foreign court less favourably than he would have been in his national court. Furthermore, the foreign judgment must originate from a court that had jurisdiction in accordance with Angolan or Mozambican law. However, unlike in the Roman–Dutch law and common law countries, the foreign court's international jurisdiction will be acknowledged only when the Angolan or Mozambican courts do not claim international jurisdiction of their own as regards the dispute at issue. Thomashausen rightly describes the enforcement regimes in the two countries as a '"home-bound" system'.[96]

The constraining effect that the defences to the recognition and enforcement will have in the member states is difficult to judge. Much will depend on how national courts interpret and apply them. It is suggested that, without prejudice to the need to ensure that justice is served in individual cases, in approaching the defences national courts should have the broader objective of facilitating the free circulation of judgments within the communities in mind.

Another area of interest to business relates to currency issues in foreign judgment enforcement. Should foreign judgments be converted into the local currency? When should the conversion be effected[97] and at whose rate? Given the currency inconvertibility and fluctuating exchange rate problems in Africa, these issues are particularly important. Some of

92 Schulze (2005), p. 32. 93 Ibid., p. 31.
94 South African Law Reform Commission (2006) at [5.3.1]–[5.3.4].
95 Thomashausen (2002). 96 Ibid., p. 33.
97 Some countries use the date of the original judgment as the conversion date. Ghana – Courts Act 459 of 1996, s. 82(7); and South Africa – Enforcement of Foreign Civil Judgment Act 32 of 1988, s. 3(4).

these issues were raised in *Ssebaggala & Sons Electric Centre Ltd* v. *Kenya National Shipping Line Ltd.*[98] The applicant sought to register and enforce, in Kenya, a Ugandan judgment that, interestingly, was denominated in British pounds. The application was brought under the Foreign Judgment (Reciprocal Enforcement) Act. Two issues that arose for determination were the currency in which the judgment was to be registered and the time for conversion of currency. The court held that under section 7 of the Act, a foreign currency judgment *may* be registered as a judgment for a sum payable in such sums in Kenya's currency as are equivalent thereto on the basis of the exchange rate prevailing at the time of registration. Also, the time of conversion was when the judgment was registered and not the date of enforcement.

Ssebaggala can be contrasted with the Ghanaian case of *Broderick* v. *Northern Engineering Product.*[99] Although this case dealt with a judgment from England, the principles are equally applicable to judgments from any African state. The plaintiff obtained judgment in England against the defendants, who were resident in Ghana. After registering the judgment under the Courts Act 1971 (Act 372), the plaintiff went into execution and realized part of the amount. When the plaintiff sought to levy further execution, the defendants called for accounts. The issue that had to be determined was whether the rate of conversion of the Cedi to pound Sterling to be used in calculating the defendants' indebtedness to the plaintiff should be the rate prevailing at the time the judgment was given in England or the rate prevailing at the time of execution. The plaintiff pleaded for the application of the rate prevailing at the date of execution because at that time, the Cedi had depreciated considerably against Sterling such that if the plaintiff were to convert the Cedis he would realize from sales on execution into Sterling, he would receive much less than the value of the English judgment. It was held that it was common knowledge in Ghana that the exchange rate was very volatile and changed almost daily. Accordingly, an application of the exchange rate prevailing at the time of execution of the judgment would ensure that the plaintiff obtained what was properly due to him and thus would be the best way to do justice in the case. However, under section 77(5) of the Courts Act 1971 (now section 82(7) of the Courts Act 1993, Act 459), the rate of exchange to be used in determining the value of the judgment registered in Ghana was the exchange rate prevailing at the time the judgment was given in England. The court was attentive to the fact that, under the circumstances,

[98] [2000] LawAfr. LR 931. [99] [1991] 2 GLR 88.

conversion at the date of judgment placed the plaintiff at a disadvantage: if the plaintiff converted the Cedis he would realize from execution into pounds Sterling, he would receive much less than the value of the judgment he obtained in England. This problem is exacerbated if the Cedi depreciates and there is a delay in executing the judgment. The potential injustice inherent in the date of judgment conversion rule is obvious.

Some African countries have departed from the common law rule that the courts cannot give judgments in foreign currency.[100] In the absence of other exchange control restrictions, the courts' jurisdiction to grant judgments in foreign currency inures to the benefit of judgment creditors who bring common law actions to enforce foreign judgments or secure payment of other debts denominated in foreign currency.[101] However, where a party seeks to register a foreign judgment, as noted in the two cases above, a number of the registration statutes compel the conversion of the judgment into the currency of the enforcing forum.[102] The provision in the Ghanaian legislation, which can be said to be representative of those in other jurisdictions, reads:

> Where the sum payable under a judgment, which is to be registered, is expressed in a currency other than the currency of Ghana, the judgment shall be registered as if it were a judgment for a sum in the currency of Ghana based on the rate of bank exchange prevailing at the date of the judgment of the original court.[103]

Some jurisdictions, such as Kenya, however, make the date of registration rather than the date of the original judgment the conversion date.

[100] *Barclays Bank of Swaziland Ltd* v. *Mnyeketi* 1992 (2) SA 425; *Makwindi Oil Procurement Ltd* v. *National Oil Co. of Zimbabwe* 1988 (2) SA 690; *Makwindi Oil Procurement Ltd* v. *National Oil Co. of Zimbabwe* 1989 (3) SA 191; *Royal Dutch Airlines (KLM)* v. *Farmex Ltd* [1989–90] 1 GLR 46; Bannermah (1993–5); Niewoudt (1992–3); and Black (2010), pp. 90–4.

[101] See generally *Echodelta Ltd* v. *Kerr and Downey Safaris* 2004 (1) SA 509; *Chiraga* v. *Msimuko* 2004 (1) SA 98; *Eden* v. *Pienaar* 2001 (1) SA 158; and *Charles Thys* v. *Herman Steyn* [2006] eKLR, in which the court held that it will be contrary to public policy for judicial procedure to be exploited to rake in supernormal profits associated with the rapid fluctuations of the Kenyan shilling on the international money markets.

[102] Botswana – Judgments (International Enforcement) Act 1981, Ch. 11:04, s. 5(5); Namibia – Enforcement of Foreign Civil Judgments Act 1994, Act 28 of 1994, s. 3(4); Tanzania – Foreign Judgments (Reciprocal Enforcement) Ordinance 1935, s. 4(3); Ghana – Courts Act 1996, Act 459, s. 82(7); Zambia – Foreign Judgments (Reciprocal Enforcement) Act, Ch. 76, s. 4(3); Uganda – Foreign Judgments (Reciprocal Enforcement) Act, Ch. 9, s. 3(3); and Nigeria – Foreign Judgments (Reciprocal Enforcement) Act 1990, Ch. 152 LFN, s. 4(3). But see Kenya – Foreign Judgment (Reciprocal Enforcement) Act, s. 7(1), which uses the discretionary language 'may be registered'.

[103] Ghana – Courts Act 1996, Act 459, s. 82(7).

These currency conversion provisions may be of great financial significance to individuals, especially in an era of fluctuating exchange rates that may work to the prejudice of one party. Recognizing the potential hardship and injustice that can result, especially to the foreign judgment creditor, legislation in Australia and New Zealand gives a judgment creditor the option to state in his application for registration whether he wishes the judgment to be registered in the currency of the original judgment.[104] This choice mitigates the potential hardship that can be caused by the provisions, at least from the perspective of the judgment creditor. It appears from the discretionary language of Kenya's legislation that such an option is available to foreign judgment creditors.[105] It is recommended that subsequent reform of legislation for the enforcement of foreign judgments in Africa should incorporate a provision similar to New Zealand and Australia's statutes. This will facilitate the free circulation of judgments within the communities.

With a view to strengthening interstate relations and facilitating economic integration in Africa, the above limitations must be reviewed either nationally or, more appropriately, through an African convention on the enforcement of foreign judgments. A well-thought-out foreign judgment enforcement regime is indispensable to the success of any economic community. Judgments must freely circulate in member states of a community. Where the enforcement of private legal claims, including claims founded on foreign judgments, is impossible, unduly complicated, time-consuming or expensive, it hinders closer economic relations and hampers the development of a stable economic community.[106] The development of a harmonized regime for the enforcement of foreign judgments in Africa will benefit individuals who utilize the regime. It will also strengthen the relational bond existing between legal systems in Africa.

9.5 Developing a private international law regime to aid integration

9.5.1 State of existing regime

The above discussion demonstrates the importance of private international law in economic integration, but, as suggested above, there is

[104] Australia – Foreign Judgments Act 1991, s. 6(11)(a); and New Zealand – Reciprocal Enforcement of Judgments Act 1934, s. 4(3).

[105] Kenya: Foreign Judgments (Reciprocal Enforcement) Act, s. 7(1).

[106] Hay (1968); Koh (1996); and Casad (1980–1).

palpable inattention to it in Africa's economic communities. To strengthen interstate relations and aid economic transactions, there is a need for African countries to embark on a comprehensive examination and reform of their private international law regimes. This is especially important as the communities progress through the stages of integration. The goal of ensuring 'the free movement of persons, goods, services and capital and right of establishment and persons' outlined in the AEC Treaty,[107] and also pursued in other communities, will be seriously hampered or fail to materialize without these reforms.[108] With deeper integration, one can foresee not only increased development of cross-border personal relationships, such as through marriages, but also an increase in cross-border economic transactions. This will mean greater resort to private international law principles to resolve disputes arising from such transactions. Parties to such transactions may also want to be certain of the principles in order to take them into account when structuring or negotiating transactions with a view to avoiding conflict of laws situations.[109] Against this background, there may be a need to harmonize private international law rules to govern the operation of divergent national substantive rules.[110] At the continental level, although the vision of an African common market under the AEC Treaty looks distant, it can be inferred from the treaty that it must happen within the next fifteen years. It is recommended that the time to begin preparation for this is now. For the RECs communities, this call is even more immediate and strong. Luckily, Africa has the benefit of learning from other regions' efforts.

Among the areas that should receive immediate attention are choice of law in contract and tort, *in personam* jurisdiction in international matters, and the recognition and enforcement of foreign judgments and international civil procedure. These areas are of direct and immediate impact on economic transactions, and there is either inappropriate diversity of rules across Africa or an absence of any authoritative legal positions. Choice of law in torts is illustrative of this. Industrial and technological developments, as well as advancements in international transportation, have made international torts a fertile area of private international law problems. However, so far, the position in many African countries is unclear due to the absence of strong judicial authority, legislation or treaties on the subject.

[107] AEC Treaty, art. 4(2)(1). [108] Ovrawah (1994).
[109] Schmitthoff (1956). [110] Tebbens (1990), p. 62.

In the common law African countries, a recent opportunity to discuss the subject came in the Kenyan case of *Rage Mohammed Ali* v. *Abdullahim Maasai.*[111] The case arose out of an accident in Uganda. Both parties were citizens and residents of Kenya. The plaintiff brought a claim in contract (instead of tort) for general and special damages arising from injuries sustained in an accident. The court disallowed the claim. The plaintiff was unable to prove that he was an employee of the defendant. To the court, 'this is a simple and straightforward case of a motor vehicle accident that took place in a foreign country outside the limits of the jurisdiction of the courts in Kenya'. Neither counsel nor the court raised the possibility of a claim in tort and the concomitant choice of law issues that would have called for resolution.

Until recently, in South Africa and the other Roman–Dutch law countries,[112] the consensus among scholars was that the issue of the applicable law in tort was *res nova*, and thus it was for the courts to decide which of the various approaches to choice of law in torts they wanted to adopt.[113] *Burchell* v. *Anglin*[114] put this state of affairs to rest. The plaintiff brought a claim for damages and loss of profit in the South Africa High Court for damages arising from alleged defamatory statements made by the defendant in the state of Nebraska (the United States). At issue was whether the applicable law was South African or some foreign law. The court held that even though the *lex loci delicti* was Nebraska, this was not the end of the inquiry to find the *lex causae.* The court noted that doubt existed as to whether the application of a single formula, such as the *lex loci delicti*, led to adequate results or was a sufficient test to achieve justice between the parties. In light of this doubt, the court advocated a balancing test in which it determines the jurisdiction with the most significant relationship to the parties and the delict. The law of that jurisdiction is to be applied. In the instant case, the court followed this route: having decided that the *lex loci delicti* was Nebraska, it moved on to decide whether Nebraska was indeed the jurisdiction with the most significant relationship to the parties and the delict. It found that Nebraska's relationship to the parties and the

[111] [2005] eKLR. In *Riddlesbarger* v. *Robson* [1958] East Afr. LR 375, the Kenya Court of Appeal held that an action will lie in Kenya for a libel published abroad if the libel was wrongful and actionable both in Kenya and the country of publication.

[112] The exception is Lesotho. In *Lepota* v. *Hyland*, CIV/APN/280/87 (High Court, Lesotho, 1991), the court held that the law governing a tort alleged to have been committed abroad is the *lex loci delicti.*

[113] Forsyth (2003), pp. 326–7 and the writers cited therein.

[114] 2010 (3) SA 48.

delict was more significant than the relationship of South Africa thereto. Before deciding that Nebraska's law was applicable, the court noted that moral values or public policy should be taken into consideration in the choice of law process, and the prospective applicable law should be placed under and pass the scrutiny of South African constitutional law. In this instance, Nebraska's law passed the scrutiny and it was held that the *lex causae* was the law of Nebraska. The court expressly left open the question of whether this holding meant that the law of Nebraska was applicable in the quantification of damages.

Internationally, there is currently a trend towards upholding the *lex loci delicti commissi* as the choice of law rule in torts.[115] Australian[116] and Canadian[117] courts have abandoned the English double actionability rule. The United Kingdom has also reformed its law on this issue by statute.[118] Within the EU, it also has a central role to play in choosing the applicable law in non-contractual obligations.[119] Whether African countries will follow this trend remains to be seen. In Nigeria, case law relating to intra-state torts supports both the double actionability rule and the *lex loci delicti* principle.[120] However, the position on international torts is unclear. A Ghanaian court has expressed a preference for parties to sue in the state in which 'the cause of action arose and according to whose law the liability is to be determined',[121] but it is yet to be decided what law will apply if the court decides to assume jurisdiction.[122] The uncertainties on the issue of the applicable law in torts do not serve the interest of facilitating economic transactions within the communities.

In the area of international civil procedure, the existing laws are often very dated, and most African countries have not taken advantage of international developments in the area. Indeed, the case study suggests

115 Kiggundu (2006).
116 *Regie National des Usines Renault SA* v. *Zhang* (2002) 210 CLR 491.
117 *Tolofson* v. *Jensen* [1994] 3 SCR 1022, 120 DLR (4th) 289.
118 Private International Law (Miscellaneous Provisions) Act 1995.
119 Regulation (EC) No. 864/2007 of the European Parliament and of the Council of 11 July 2007 on the Law Applicable to Non-contractual Obligations (Rome II), [2007] OJ L199/40.
120 See Agbede (2004), pp. 39–40; Agbede (1989), pp. 159–79; and *A.O. Agunanne* v. *Nigeria Tobacco Co. Ltd* [1979] 2 FNLR 13.
121 *Signal Oil & Gas Co.* v. *Bristow Helicopters Ltd* [1976] 1 GLR 371 at 379.
122 The earlier case of *Wachter* v. *Harlley* [1968] GLR 1069, which involved slander allegedly committed in Switzerland, supports the double actionability rule.

that it is a difficult area.[123] This can be problematic when courts are invited to settle disputes arising from cross-border economic transactions and there is a need for cooperation with another African state's court in terms of serving documents, or securing witnesses or evidence.

9.5.2 *Role of various constituencies*

The development of private international law to enhance interstate relations and aid economic transactions within the communities demands constituencies with interest in the subject and a consciousness that allows them to look beyond the confines of their own legal systems. These constituencies have a role to play in reforming private international law to meet the challenges of economic integration in Africa. The reform agenda should be approached at both national and community levels. The ultimate aim should be to ensure a well-thought-out private international law regime that will engender stability, security and predictability in international commercial transactions within an economically integrated Africa. African academics and academic institutions have a crucial role to play. Through their research and writings, they can expose areas in need of reform and suggest ways of addressing them.

It is noteworthy that there are efforts to enhance the institutional development of the subject. In 2000, the Institute for Private International Law in Southern Africa was established as a part of the University of Johannesburg. Its current goal is to draft a code of private international law of contract for the Southern African Development Community and/or the African Union. The Institute of Foreign and Comparative Law of the University of South Africa strives to be the

[123] From the case study, among the areas of difficulty identifiable from the judgments were the following: procedures for serving documents abroad (*Fonville* v. *Kelly* [2002] 1 East Afr. LR 71; and *Willow Investment* v. *Mbomba Ntumba* [1997] TLR 47); the procedures for taking evidence abroad (*Kells* v. *Ako Adjei*, Case No. CA 8/2000 (Supreme Court, Ghana)); rules on the formalities and admissibility in court of affidavits taken abroad (*Microsoft Corp.* v. *Mitsumi Computer Garage Ltd* [2001] KLR 470; and *Pastificio Lucio Garofalo SPA* v. *Security & Fire Equipment Co.* [2001] KLR 483); the law regarding the relevance and effect of rules on the authentication of foreign documents (*Blanchard, Krasner & French* v. *Evans* 2004 (4) SA 427; *Lamus Agricultural Services Co. Ltd* v. *Gwembe Valley Dev. Ltd* [1999] Zambia LR 1; and *Slyvanus Juxon-Smith* v. *KLM Royal Dutch Airline*, Civil Appeal No. J4/19/2005 (Supreme Court, Ghana)); and deposit of security for costs by foreign plaintiffs (*Fasco Trading Co. Ltd* v. *Goodearth Ltd* [2000] LawAfr. LR 1236; *Noble Builders (U) Ltd* v. *Sandhu* [2004] 2 East Afr. LR 228; and *B & W Industrial Technology Ltd* v. *Baroutsos* 2006 (2) SA 135).

premier research institution in the development and application of private international law, public international law and comparative law in Africa. It aims to maintain and develop a database of private international law, particularly in the area of family law. The Institute of International and Comparative Law in Africa is being established in the University of Pretoria in recognition of the lack of institutional and resource capacity in the areas of international and comparative law in Africa. This institute aims to develop an internationally recognized institution on African soil with expertise in public and private international law, as well as comparative law. It will inter alia constitute a repository: where knowledge and material on the legal systems of African countries and the conflicts between these legal systems are available; where the international treaties and other instruments influencing domestic regulation can be assessed; and which will act as a point of convergence where networks of legal scholars in Africa can be centered and come together with people from the rest of the world. The Hague Conference on Private International Law has also established a document centre for Southern Africa at the University of Johannesburg. These efforts have so far been concentrated in Southern Africa and are likely to benefit the economic integration processes there. There is a need to expand these initiatives into other African regions and the various law faculties have a crucial role to play.

The lack of written rules is very much a feature of the common law and Roman–Dutch law countries; very few areas of private international law have legislation on them in Africa. There is an urgent need to legislate or reform existing legislation on some private international law issues.[124] Law Reform Commissions and parliaments are important here. Legislation takes time. Until then, courts will be the principal institution for reform. Indeed, historically, courts have been at the forefront of the development of private international law and they will continue to perform that role in Africa.[125]

National constitutions and the courts' visions of their roles in the development of law will influence the extent to which they can be helpful on this score. In a number of cases in the case study, African judges have encountered difficult private international law issues and chosen to defer to the appropriate legislative institution for a solution. For example, in

[124] Some countries have recently adopted private international law legislation and their experiences could be useful. Deskoski (2008); Tekinalp (2007); Jessel-Holst (2007); Zhu (2007); Fiorini (2005); and von Schwind (1968).

[125] Blom (2002).

Raytheon Aircraft,[126] the Kenyan court found as problematic the absence of rules of court on how a defendant, who had been sued in Kenya for being in breach of a choice of forum agreement, could challenge the court's jurisdiction. It did not create a rule to fill that vacuum. Instead, it called on the Rules Committee to look at the issue. There were other cases in which courts reformed the law without reference to parliament. In *Bid Industrial Holding* v. *Strang*,[127] the South African court abolished the rule that a foreign *peregrinus* can be arrested to found or confirm jurisdiction in a claim relating to money.[128] It also sanctioned mere presence as a basis of jurisdiction in international matters, a basis of jurisdiction previously unknown to South African law. Earlier, in *Richman* v. *Ben-Tovim*,[129] the court held that mere physical presence suffices as a basis of international competence in actions to enforce foreign judgments.

The challenges of economic integration coupled with the underdeveloped state of private international law in Africa is likely to raise issues that courts may have to address without a national precedent. On such issues, attention to international developments and a judicial philosophy informed by the needs of economic integration will be useful. 'Internationalist policy consciousness'[130] in private international law refers to an approach to resolving problems on the basis of internationalist visions or goals. The internationalist objectives of promoting international trade and commerce, aiding international uniformity or harmonization of rules and fostering harmonious interstate relations are examples of these goals. All of these objectives are relevant in economic integration. Internationalist consciousness is a source of reform in private international law through the adoption of international conventions and judicial decisions informed by its goals. African states are parties to a small number of private international law conventions. Therefore, international conventions are unlikely to be a significant and immediate source of reform and development of private international law to aid Africa's economic integration. Rather, it is to the courts that we must look.

[126] [2005] 2 KLR 47; *Drive Control Services Ltd* v. *Troycom Systems Ltd* 2000 (2) SA 722; and *Nku* v. *Nku* 1998 BLR 187.

[127] 2008 (3) SA 355.

[128] Under South African law, the courts will not assume jurisdiction over a foreign defendant in claims relating to money, unless his assets within the jurisdiction have been attached to found or confirm jurisdiction.

[129] 2007 (2) SA 283. [130] Wai (2004).

The case study revealed judgments that already reflect the existence of this internationalist consciousness in African judges. However, it must be admitted that the way in which the courts approached internationalist objectives was often superficial. In *Barclays Bank of Swaziland* v. *Koch*,[131] the Botswana court held that 'the comity of nations and international commerce required that foreign judgments be recognised and enforced in each other's countries as far as possible'. In *Sunrise Travel and Tours Ltd* v. *Wanjigi*,[132] the Kenyan court suggested that, in an 'era of increased globalization', it would be a good thing for defendants to be sued where they are domiciled.

The radical changes in South African law introduced by *Richman* and *Bid Industrial Holding* were also in part justified by internationalist objectives. In *Richman* v. *Ben-Tovim*,[133] the court found 'compelling reasons why . . . in this modern age, traditional grounds of international competence should be extended, within reason, to cater for itinerant international businessmen'. In *Bid Industrial Holding*,[134] the fact that neither counsel nor the court was able to identify any other countries that required arrest as a prerequisite for jurisdiction over foreign defendants in claims relating to money influenced the court's decision to abolish arrest as a basis of jurisdiction.

However, perhaps the most significant reform informed by internationalist objectives was in the Ugandan case of *Shah* v. *Manurama Ltd*.[135] In *Shah*, the court held that, given the re-establishment of the East African Community, there could no longer be an automatic and inflexible presumption for the courts to order security for costs with regard to plaintiffs resident in the EAC when they bring claims against Ugandan residents. Among the factors that informed this decision were that the EAC Treaty made express provision for the unification and harmonization of the laws of the member states and there existed a regime for the reciprocal enforcement of judgments among the member states.

It must be admitted that advancing internationalist objective can sometimes unfairly subject the parties' interests to systemic and states' interests. As Wai has observed:[136]

> Private international law in the Commonwealth traditions . . . has traditionally focused on the conflicts between the interests and preferences of individual parties. A significant danger in promoting international system objectives is that the interests and values of individual parties are dealt with unfairly.

131 1997 BLR 1294 at 1297. 132 [2002] LawAfr. LR 5933 at [12].
133 2007 (2) SA 283. 134 *Bid Industrial Holding* v. *Strang* 2008 (3) SA 355.
135 [2003] 1 East Afr. LR 294. 136 Wai (2001), p. 187.

I have also argued that the *Richman* decision, which was informed by various internationalist objectives, potentially undermines defendants' rights to a fair hearing and defeats their legitimate expectations as to the venue of trial. Notwithstanding these objections, it is worth emphasizing that, for the purpose of using private international law to aid Africa's economic integration, courts cannot be inattentive to internationalist objectives, especially when they will enhance integration by facilitating economic transactions.

9.5.3 *Need for continental and international engagement*

National efforts to reform private international law should be complemented by continental efforts, spearheaded by the African Union (of which the AEC is an integral part) and aimed at harmonizing private international law rules. Despite their diverse legal traditions, it is definitely possible for African nations to achieve this. The Institute for Private International Law in Southern Africa is already doing some work in this direction in Southern Africa. The work of the institute should be encouraged, possibly adopted, by the AU and made a continent-wide initiative. In Chapter 4, I outlined a path to harmonization of laws in Africa that builds on its diverse legal traditions. Indeed, as argued there, the extent to which African laws are diverse should not be exaggerated, at least as between countries belonging to the same legal tradition.

From the AEC's perspective, this work advocates the establishment of a body with a specific mandate to look into Africa's private international law rules and how they relate to economic integration. Article 25(2) of the AEC Treaty, which allows the Assembly of Heads of State or Governments to establish additional specialized technical committees, can provide the basis for establishing such an institution. A similar case can be made for the various RECs. In this regard, it is significant that the Assembly of Heads of State and Government of the African Union adopted, in February 2009, the Statute of the African Union Commission on International Law.[137] The eleven-member commission, the members of which have now been elected, is to undertake activities relating to the codification and progressive development of international law in Africa.[138] It is also mandated to conduct studies on legal matters

[137] 1 February 2009, online: www.africa-union.org/root/au/Documents/Treaties/treaties.htm.

[138] Ibid., art. 4(a).

of interest to the African Union and its member states.[139] It is suggested that, in addition to the many public international law problems identified in this book, private international law should also find a place on the commission's agenda. The commission could be used as a forum for developing private international law conventions in Africa.

Parallel to these, there is a need for states and the communities to increase their cooperation with the international institutions working on private international law.[140] The principal institution in this regard is the Hague Conference on Private International Law. Cooperation could start with the ratification of Hague conventions by African countries. The Hague conventions and methods of the Conference could also serve as a model for the development of African conventions on private international law. The Conference can make an input in the development of African regional conventions.[141] Significantly, the idea of an African convention on private-international-law issues has already been advocated by scholars[142] and, as noted above, is being pursued by the Institute of Private International Law.

Cooperation with the Conference could also take the form of sending official delegations to participate in the Conference's proceedings as a prelude to membership. Currently, only three African countries – Egypt, Morocco and South Africa – are members of the Conference.[143] In an era of globalization, Africa and its economic communities cannot be oblivious to international developments.[144] It is significant that although all members of the EU are members of the Conference, the EU itself has recently become a member.[145] MERCOSUR also cooperates with the Conference and an agreement has been concluded between the Conference and the Inter-American Children's Institute, a specialized body of the Organization of American States. A strong relationship with the Conference should be a key aspect of any strategy within the African communities to develop their private international law regimes.

139 Ibid., art. 4(d). 140 Oppong (2006a); and Castellani (2008).

141 Currently, UNIDROIT is helping the Organization for the Harmonisation of Business Law in Africa (OHADA) to develop a uniform law of contract. This can provide a model of cooperation between the Conference and Africa in the area of private international law.

142 Forsyth (2002).

143 In September 2010, excluding the three member states, nineteen African countries (Botswana, Burkina Faso, Burundi, Cape Verde, Guinea, Kenya, Lesotho, Liberia, Madagascar, Malawi, Mali, Mauritius, Namibia, Niger, Sao Tome and Principe, Seychelles, Swaziland, Togo and Zimbabwe) have ratified various Hague Conventions.

144 Kruger (2005); Kotuby (2001–2); and Fawcett (1997).

145 The EU became a member on 3 April 2007. See Schulze (2007).

9.5.4 *Values to inform Africa's private international law regime*

The above discussion suggests that to meet the challenges and demands of economic integration, the communities will need to develop a private international law regime that suits the ends of economic integration. As noted above, similar regimes, founded principally on treaties and community legislation, have already been developed by some economic communities outside Africa. So far, such a regime is absent in Africa. At best, what the case study reveals is an emerging, judicially led, academically unexplored and institutionally inactive body of law that provides adequate, appropriate and fair solutions to private international law problems. It is also receptive to the influence of external values, such as human rights, internationalism and the use of comparative foreign materials. These can be useful for the ends of economic integration.

This body of law is currently riddled with difficult, unsettled and underdeveloped areas. Its evolution into a regime comparable to those of the economic communities outside Africa is inextricably linked with the progress of economic integration in Africa.[146] Any movement to develop a regime that suits Africa's economic integration should combine community laws with national case law. This book proposes ten values that should influence the regime:

- It should not be isolationist. It should be sensitive to and participate in international processes in the field.
- It should emphasize the importance of harmonizing and/or unifying private international law rules across Africa. This can be achieved through the adoption of international conventions and the active use of comparative law in resolving private international law problems.
- It should recognize the multiple interests at stake in the resolution of private international law problems and, as far as possible, prioritize the interests of the disputing parties.
- It should not be overtly discriminatory, but be sensitive to the interests of African residents and domiciliaries when deciding private international law cases or adopting rules.
- It should ensure a proper balance between the role of courts in the development of private international law and legislative interventions in areas where the law is undeveloped, underdeveloped or uncertain.

[146] Oppong (2006d).

- It should have rules that are sensitive to the demands of international human rights laws.
- It should aim at making Africa an attractive place for the resolution of international commercial disputes by adopting and providing rules conducive to that goal.
- It should be responsive and receptive to alternative modes of settling disputes, such as international arbitration and litigation before regional courts, by providing rules to facilitate their processes, including supportive judicial remedies.
- It should respect party autonomy in international transactions and uphold parties' rights to regulate their transactions through choice of law and forum agreements.
- It should pay attention to the institutional development of the subject by acknowledging, supporting and facilitating the work of academics and academic institutions working in the field.

9.6 Conclusion

Private international law can perform a dual role in Africa's economic integration. Its principles may be used to strengthen interstate relations and facilitate cross-border economic transactions within the communities. However, given the existing state of the subject, its principles are unlikely to perform both roles effectively. To achieve this, there is a need for radical reform of Africa's private international law. The reform should be approached at both national and community levels. The rules adopted should be tailored to meet the needs of economic integration in Africa. To this end, a set of values has been suggested. Reform at national and community levels should be combined with increased participation in international institutions working on private international law. It is only through participation that Africa can learn, be heard and make the emerging international conventions take account of its needs and interests.

10

Conclusion

10.1 The current state of affairs

This book set out to examine how relational issues of law in economic integration are being approached in Africa. At their core, relational issues deal with the legal interactions among community, national, regional and international legal systems within the context of economic integration. The theory was that effective economic integration is the product of properly structuring and managing, within well-defined legal frameworks, vertical, horizontal and vertico-horizontal relations among states, legal systems, laws and institutions. Put differently, an economic community must have well-structured and well-managed relations between itself and other legal systems as a necessary condition for its effectiveness.

After expounding the theory and applying it to four of the African Union's recognized regional economic communities and the African Economic Community, the findings of the book can be captured in a few words: Africa's economic integration processes have not paid systematic or rigorous attention to relational issues. The interactions between community and member states' legal systems, among the various communities, as well as among member states' legal systems, have neither been carefully thought through nor placed on a solid legal framework. Where attempts have been made to provide a legal framework, they have been incomplete, unsatisfactory and, sometimes, grounded on questionable assumptions. This book has argued consistently that unless these shortfalls are remedied, the growth and effectiveness of Africa's economic integration will be seriously undermined. Put differently, even if all the socio-economic and political challenges that bedevil Africa's economic integration were to disappear, there remains much in the realm of law which, if unaddressed, will hinder its success and effectiveness. To remedy some of these shortfalls, this book, in various parts, proposes amendments to community and national laws. It also provides model legislation for that purpose.

The discussions and arguments in the book have been founded on a vision of the AEC and the other communities as supranational organizations. However, not all commentators support the idea of supranational institutions to push forward Africa's economic integration processes. Kufuor argues that there is probably very little real demand for supranational institutions and organizations within ECOWAS.[1] He provides a number of reasons to support this stance. However, a careful assessment of these reasons suggests that, while he might have been successful in demonstrating that the conditions conducive for supranationalism are not yet present in West Africa, a reader would still be left unconvinced as to whether such institutions are not demanded. Indeed, it is arguable that conditions conducive to supranationalism, such as the rule of law and democratic governance, are gradually emerging in some African countries. The UN Economic Commission for Africa has identified the absence of supranational authority to enforce the commonly agreed policies of the communities as a principal weakness of African economic communities.[2] And, as far back as 1977, Chime described the appalling lack of supranational institutions as 'a serious handicap'.[3] A number of provisions and principles in the communities' treaties also support a claim that they are founded on a supranational vision. In theory and practice, it is difficult to conceive how the communities can proceed to become or operate as common markets and economic unions without supranational institutions.

So far, the impact of relational issues has not been seriously felt due to the slow pace at which Africa's economic integration is progressing. That will not remain so forever. The communities are progressing through the various stages of integration – from free trade areas to customs unions, common markets, economic unions and complete economic integration. The Common Market for Eastern and Southern Africa (COMESA) became a customs union in 2009; the Southern African Development Community (SADC) became a free trade area in 2008, planned

[1] Kufuor (2006); and Mazzeo (1984), pp. 164–5.

[2] UN Economic Commission for Africa (2004), p. 7. In addition to this, one must note the absence of strong state 'powerhouses' within the communities to push forward politically and be the paymasters for the integration processes. Within the EAC and ECOWAS, this role is weakly performed by Kenya and Nigeria respectively. The success and endurance of the SACU can, in part, be attributed to the leadership and financial commitment of South Africa.

[3] Chime (1977), p. 403.

(albeit unsuccessfully) to become a customs union in 2010 and plans to become a common market by 2015; the Economic Community of West African States (ECOWAS) is edging closer to creating a customs union; and the East African Community (EAC) became a common market in July 2010. Relational issues become more evident as integration progresses: the deeper the level of integration, the greater the demands made by the community on member states become. Accordingly, sooner rather than later, the inadequacies in the existing legal framework will be exposed and will have to be addressed if the communities are to operate effectively.

In terms of their architecture, as reflected in their constitutive treaties and other laws, some communities have utilized a number of the relational principles and mechanisms discussed in Chapter 2. The COMESA, ECOWAS, EAC and SADC treaties provide for a preliminary reference procedure,[4] envisage a role for national courts in the implementation and enforcement of community laws and judgments,[5] and allow individuals to access their community courts.[6] Also, within the EAC, a fairly adequate regime for enforcing member states' judgments and jurisprudential communication among the three founding members – Kenya, Tanzania and Uganda – exists. These are important first steps. The first generation of Africa's economic integration treaties were very much inattentive to relational issues, and did not utilize the relational principles examined in Chapter 2 as a means for integrating community and national legal systems.[7]

Although the community treaties adopt some relational principles, they have also shied away from others. Only the Treaty Establishing the East African Community provides for the supremacy of community law. All of the treaties provide that the implementation of community law will be done through national legislation.[8] Although the treaties

[4] COMESA Treaty, art. 30; ECOWAS Court Protocol, art. 10(f); and EAC Treaty, art. 34. See also SADC Tribunal Protocol, art. 16.

[5] EAC Treaty, art. 44; COMESA Treaty, art. 40; ECOWAS Court Protocol, art. 24; and SADC Tribunal Protocol, art. 32(1)(2)(3).

[6] COMESA Treaty, art. 26; SADC Tribunal Protocol, art. 18; EAC Treaty, art. 30; and Protocol of the ECOWAS Court, art. 10.

[7] Treaty Establishing a Central African Economic and Customs Union, 8 December 1964, 4 ILM 699; Charter of the Union of Central African States, 2 April 1968, 7 ILM 725; and Treaty Establishing the Economic Community of West African States, 28 May 1975, 1010 UNTS I-14843. The only exception appears to be the Treaty for East African Cooperation, 6 June 1967, 6 ILM 932.

[8] AEC Treaty, art. 5(2); SADC Treaty, art. 6(5); ECOWAS Treaty, art. 5(2); COMESA Treaty, art. 5(2); and EAC Treaty, art. 8(2).

provide for various categories of community laws with varying legal effects, these categories appear to be largely ignored in the making of community laws. For example, we noted that the law of the African Union, of which the AEC is an integral part, provides for various categories of decisions – including regulations. Regulations are directly applicable and member states are obliged to align their laws with the demands of regulations. However, since the AU's inception, the categorization of decisions has been ignored, and no use has so far been made of regulations. It was argued in Chapter 7 that reliance on national legislation to implement all community laws is likely to create a disjunction between community and national legal systems, and adversely affect the status of community law in member states. National governments may not prioritize implementation of community laws.[9] This stalls the development of the communities and poses significant problems for individuals who seek to rely on community law in member states. Indeed, Chapter 7 examined cases in which individuals in dualist countries unsuccessfully relied on community laws because of the absence of domestic implementing legislation. A more selective approach in which some defined categories of community laws would be directly applicable and effective was advocated as a means for implementing community laws.

The full practical impacts of the adopted relational principles on Africa's integration processes remain to be seen. The principles have not been invoked by individuals or national and/or community institutions. In view of Africa's long-standing commitment to economic integration, and in light of the demonstrated significance of relational issues in economic integration, it is ironic that not much practical use has been made of relational principles. National courts appear to be largely unaware of their roles in economic integration and the nature of their relations with the communities' legal systems. In a few instances, community law was invoked in national courts, and a preliminary reference or recognition of community decisions would have been appropriate.

[9] Article 8(2) laid down a twelve-month period within which member states were to enact legislation to give the force of law to the EAC Treaty in their national legal systems. This provision has been complied with. See Tanzania – Treaty for the Establishment of East African Community Act 2001; Kenya – Treaty for the Establishment of East African Community Act 2000; and Uganda – East African Community Act 2002. However, these Acts are not detailed enough. They do not take into account all of the consequences of giving force of law to community law in member states. Compare, for example, the UK's European Communities Act 1972, which gave force of law to the treaties of the European communities.

However, in those instances, national courts seemed oblivious to their duties under community law. For example, the supremacy of the community law principle is enshrined in the EAC Treaty[10] and Kenya has implemented the treaty, which also provides for preliminary reference to the East African Court of Justice. However, a Kenyan court, without resort to the East African Court of Justice, has held that if the treaty were in conflict with the Kenyan constitution, the municipal court's first duty would be to uphold the supremacy of the constitution.[11] To be fair, it has been noted that some national courts have relied on the interpretative and adjudicative relational principles. They have utilized community law and the goals of the communities in their decisions.[12] This is a commendable development that is likely to help in integrating community law into national legal systems in Africa.

The rare invocation of the adopted relational principles raises an important question: Is Africa suitably conditioned to make effective use of them? Socio-cultural, economic, political and constitutional factors condition the effectiveness of relational principles. Africa is plagued by issues that may work against their effective operation, including: the lack of activist and independent national and regional judiciaries; the presence of potentially inimical constitutional provisions; the dominance of politics in the integration processes; the perceived absence of a litigation culture;[13] the lack of public awareness about the activities and laws of the communities; and the lack of interest of African lawyers[14] and private institutions[15] in economic integration processes. Empirical studies on how these issues truly affect Africa's integration processes are generally lacking, and should form an important research agenda.[16]

[10] EAC Treaty, art. 8(4).

[11] *Peter Anyang' Nyong'o* v. *AG* [2007] eKLR (High Court, Kenya, 2007).

[12] *R.* v. *Obert Sithembiso Chikane*, Crim. Case No. 41/2000 (High Court, Swaziland, 2003); *Friday Anderson Jumbe* v. *Humphrey Chimpando*, Constitutional Case Nos. 1 and 2 of 2005 (High Court, Malawi, 2005); *Chloride Batteries Ltd* v. *Viscocity*, Civil Cause No. 1896 of 2006 (High Court, Malawi, 2006); and *Hoffman* v. *South African Airways* 2001 (1) SA 1.

[13] Shaw (1983); and Maluwa (1989).

[14] Kulusika (2000), p. 47.

[15] The absence of private sector involvement and the domination of intergovermentalism have been identified as a key obstacle to the success of Africa's regional economic integration processes. Fine and Yeo (1999), pp. 434–5; and Asante (1997), p. 147. One notable exception is the Trade Law Center for Southern Africa, www.tralac.org.

[16] Friedrich Ebert Foundation (Botswana) (2007). The report found that there is great and widespread support from the business community and civil society organizations for deepening integration within the SADC.

Individuals are an important medium for linking the communities with member states. They have invoked community law before national courts with varying degrees of success, but have achieved greater success before the community courts. In a number of actions brought directly to the community courts by individuals, member states' measures have been found to be in breach of community law. Indeed, in Chapter 5, it was noted that, but for actions brought by individuals, the community courts would have fallen into desuetude. In general, there do not appear to have emerged in Africa constituencies which have an interest in the integration processes, and which are prepared to champion it at both domestic and community levels. This is in part because economic integration and community law are not taught in most African universities, either as a freestanding undergraduate course or as sections of courses such as commercial, constitutional or public international law. As a result, awareness of Africa's economic integration processes remains limited. Most lawyers do not view them as being relevant to their practice. Scholars have not taken much interest, and there are yet to emerge journals, private institutions or NGOs dedicated to economic integration.

Despite the fact that some community courts have found national measures that are in breach of community law, their jurisprudence does not demonstrate a conscious attempt to articulate the place of relational principles in Africa's economic integration. Indeed, in *Anyang' Nyong'o* v. *AG*,[17] the East African Court of Justice was presented with an opportunity to affirm the principle of supremacy of community law enshrined in article 8(4) of the EAC Treaty. However, the court did not even make reference to the article, let alone expand on its significance for community law. In *Frank Ukor* v. *Alinnor*,[18] the ECOWAS court held that the ECOWAS treaty was 'the supreme law of the ECOWAS, and it may be called its Constitution'. This dictum may be favourably interpreted as supporting the supremacy of ECOWAS law, but, admittedly, it is too cursory for one to launch a forceful argument on it. In *Jerry Ugokwe* v. *The Federal Republic of Nigeria*,[19] the ECOWAS Court observed that the kind of relationship existing between the ECOWAS court and national courts of member states is not of a vertical nature, but demands an 'integrated

[17] [2008] 3 KLR 397.
[18] Suit No. ECW/CCJ/APP/01/04 (ECOWAS Court of Justice, 2005) at [21].
[19] Case No. ECW/CCJ/APP/02/05 (ECOWAS Court of Justice, 2005) at [32].

Community legal order'.[20] One can infer from the court's vision of an 'integrated community legal order' that it recognizes the importance of the bond that should exist between the community and national legal systems. The jurisprudence of national and community courts on matters directly related to economic integration is comparatively scant and cursory. However, the jurisprudence suggests that there is prospect for integrating community law into national legal systems in Africa. This should be exploited for the purposes of strengthening Africa's economic integration.

In economic integration, it is not only community–state relations that matter. Interstate relations are equally important. Indeed, integration is principally concerned with the latter. In this regard, the discussion in this book has revealed a number of worrying issues that can affect interstate relations and hinder integration. Cross-border economic activity thrives in a setting where the relations between states are harmonious. Inadequate foreign judgment enforcement regimes, diversity in laws and the absence of any systematic attempt to harmonize aspects of national law were identified as potential obstacles to integration. Innovative solutions to overcoming them have been proffered, including model laws.

On interstate relations, private international law has an important role to play. However, its role in integrating legal systems has been largely ignored by the communities, despite calls by many writers.[21]This book has suggested values that should inform the development of a private international law regime that can serve the needs of an economically integrated Africa. In addition to private international law, jurisprudential communication between courts is useful for strengthening interstate relations. It was offered in Chapter 4 as a path to harmonization of national laws. Jurisprudential communication currently exists among African courts, but it is largely sporadic and concentrated within geographical regions and legal traditions. This book has suggested improved access to legal materials and a study that distils the common core of African laws as undertakings that could improve communication between courts.[22]

[20] This observation was made in the context of the issue of whether one can appeal, to the Community court, a decision of a national court.

[21] Oppong (2006d); Thompson (1990), pp. 99–100; Thompson and Mukisa (1994), p. 1454; Omorogbe (1993), p. 364; and Ndulo (1993a), pp. 111–12.

[22] As regards private international law, the author is working on a book, *Private International Law in Commonwealth Africa*, to be published by Cambridge University Press. It aims to distil the common core private international law principles in the Commonwealth countries.

Another important issue is how the communities relate to each other and the international legal system. Africa's integration treaties have paid some attention to community–state relations. However, the same cannot be said of the communities' relations with each other and the international legal systems, especially that of the World Trade Organization (WTO). There are treaty references to international law as a source of community law[23] and the need for the communities to coordinate with other communities, especially the AEC.[24] However, these references are not enough. They do not provide a concrete or structured legal framework for the many complex issues that could arise in this area. Chapter 3 addressed some of the complex issues that arise from the relations between the communities and the AEC. Many more issues remain unexamined, let alone addressed. Does AEC law enjoy supremacy over a conflicting law of a community? Are there any subjects on which only the AEC can legislate? How are breaches of AEC decisions and directives by the communities to be remedied? How is AEC law enforceable in the communities? Are the regional communities competent before the African Court of Justice? Can the AEC intervene in an action before a community in which the interest of the AEC is affected? These issues deserve further exploration and discussion by institutions responsible for and scholars interested in Africa's economic integration.

Equally important, but not discussed in this book, are the relations between Africa's communities and the WTO. The status of WTO law within the legal systems of the communities, how to reconcile the multiple commitments of African states under community law and WTO law, and the rules for resolving conflicts between WTO law and the communities' laws are all important issues that have not been addressed, comprehensively, either by the communities' treaties or in academic writing.[25] These are important issues for the stability of both the world trade system and Africa's economic integration. Recent developments and the jurisprudence of the WTO Appellate Body suggest that the interaction between regional economic communities and the WTO is an issue of more than theoretical importance. For Africa, these issues will become even weightier as economic integration progresses. Differences between community laws, or national laws founded on community law, and WTO law are susceptible to challenge under the WTO's dispute-settlement system.

[23] ECOWAS Court Protocol, art. 20(1); and SADC Tribunal Protocol, art. 21(1).

[24] COMESA Treaty, preamble, arts. 178–9; ECOWAS Treaty, preamble, arts. 78–9; EAC Treaty, preamble, art. 130(2); and SADC Treaty, preamble, art. 24.

[25] Ng'ong'Ola (1999); Oduor (2005); and Pauwelyn (2004).

So far, the WTO trade policy reviews of some of the communities have not found them to be directly or significantly in breach of WTO laws.[26] It remains to be seen whether this will be the case as they progress and strengthen their integration processes. Indeed, already, concerns have been expressed about overlapping African states' membership of regional communities, and the tendency of the communities to detract from the multilateral trade regime.

10.2 Moving forward

Relational issues of law are endemic in economic integration. Broadly, these issues focus on the interactions among community, national, regional and international legal systems. The extent to which relational issues manifest themselves and the degree of attention devoted to them often varies with the level or stage of integration reached. Economic communities around the world have acknowledged the challenge posed by relational issues for their development and effectiveness. They have used various relational principles and mechanisms as part of the legal framework to address relational issues.

Africa's economic communities have deployed some relational principles and mechanisms, but they have also shied away from others. As regards the relational principles adopted, their true impact on economic integration in Africa remains to be seen. Indeed, it remains an open question whether Africa is socio-culturally, economically, politically and constitutionally conditioned for the effective use of them. However, in the few instances in which they have been invoked before the courts, their potential to aid economic integration has been evident. To an extent, the future success of Africa's economic integration will depend on how relational principles are utilized to bridge the gap between the communities and member states.

Moving forward, it is worth recalling that this book has exposed a number of unaddressed relational issues that currently bedevil Africa's economic integration processes. All of the issues cannot be addressed at the same time. There should be prioritization in any attempt to address them. In my opinion, the most important and immediate first steps are the rationalization of the relations between the various communities,

[26] See World Trade Organization, *Trade Policy Review – Southern African Customs Union*, 2003, WT/TPR/S/114; and World Trade Organization, *Trade Policy Review – East African Community*, 2006, WT/TPR/S/171.

overcoming the canker of multiple memberships of the communities, and putting the path to the formation of the AEC on solid legal foundations, with a clear legal framework to regulate the relations between the communities and the AEC. Another important step would be for member states to enact legislation implementing the respective community treaties. This should be preceded by detailed national studies on any potential conflicts between existing community and national laws. Member states should iron out any differences to ensure smooth national implementation of the treaties and other community laws. At the continental level, there should also be a clear separation of the political integration agenda from the economic integration agenda. While maintaining its status as an 'integral part' of the African Union, the AEC should be allowed to maintain an independent existence, especially from an institutional perspective.

These steps should be followed by concrete community and national measures aimed at creating constituencies with interest in community law. In this regard, important constituencies are judges, lawyers, law enforcement and training institutions, companies and businesspersons. The integration of community law into national education curricula, educational campaigns aimed at creating awareness about the communities and litigation aimed at testing unsettled aspects of community law should be encouraged and pursued. As the communities move up the stages of integration – and they are – relational issues will become more important. The earlier the communities, states, policy-makers, businesses and scholars devote some time to them, the better it will be for Africa.

BIBLIOGRAPHY

Abiodun, B. O., 2007. 'Towards an African Concept of Law' **1** *African Journal of Legal Theory* 71

Adede, A. O., 1999. 'Constitutionalism, Culture and Tradition: African Experiences on the Incorporation of Treaties into Domestic Law' **7** *African Yearbook of International Law* 239

Adepoju, A., Boulton, A. and Levin, M., 2007. *Promoting Integration through Mobility: Free Movement and the ECOWAS Protocol* (UN Refugee Agency, New Issues in Refugee Research, Research Paper No. 150)

Adewoye, O., 1997. 'Constitutionalism and Economic Integration' in R. Lavergne (ed.), *Regional Integration and Cooperation in West Africa – A Multidimensional Perspective* (Dakar, Senegal: IDRC/Africa World Press)

Agbede, I. O., 1989. *Themes on Conflict of Laws* (Ibadan, Nigeria: Shaneson C. I. Ltd)

2004. 'Nigeria' in B. Verschraegen (ed.), *Encyclopedia of Laws – Private International Law* (The Hague: Kluwer Law International)

Agu, C., 2009. 'Obstacles to Regional Integration: The Human Factor Challenge to Trade Facilitation and Port Reforms in Nigeria' **2** *International Journal of Private Law* 445

Ajomo, M. A., 1976. 'Regional Economic Organisations: The African Experience' **25** *International and Comparative Law Quarterly* 59

1993. 'International Legal Status of the African Economic Community' in M. A. Ajomo and O. Adewale (eds.), *African Economic Community Treaty, Issues Problems and Prospects* (Lagos: Nigerian Institute of Advanced Legal Studies)

Ajomo, M. A. and Adewale, O. (eds.), 1993. *African Economic Community Treaty, Issues Problems and Prospects* (Lagos: Nigerian Institute of Advanced Legal Studies)

Ajulo, S. B., 1989. 'The Economic Community of West African States and International Law' **27** *Journal of Modern African Studies* 233

2001. 'Sources of the Law of the Economic Community of West African States (ECOWAS)' **45** *Journal of African Law* 45

Akinrinsola, I., 2004. 'Legal and Institutional Requirements for West African Economic Integration' **10** *Law and Business Review of Americas* 493

Akintan, S. A., 1977. *The Law of International Economic Institutions in Africa* (Leiden: A. W. Sijthoff)

Akiwumi, A. M., 1972. 'Judicial Aspects of Economic Integration Treaties in Africa' in Hague Academy of International Law (ed.), *Legal aspects of Economic Integration Colloquium 1971* (Leiden: A. W. Sijthoff)

Akuffo, K., 2009. 'The Conception of Land Ownership in African Customary Law and its Implications for Development' **17** *African Journal of International and Comparative Law* 57

Alavi, A., 2007. 'African Countries and the WTO Dispute Settlement Mechanism' **25** (1) *Development Policy Review* 25

Albarrancin, G., 1998. 'The Relationship between the Laws Derived from the Organs of MERCOSUR and the Legal Systems of the Countries that Comprise MERCOSUR' **4** *ILSA Journal of International and Comparative Law* 897

Alford, R. P., 2003. 'Federal Courts, International Tribunals and the Continuum of Deference' **43** *Virginia Journal of International Law* 676

Allott, A. N., 1965. 'Towards the Unification of Laws in Africa' **14** *International and Comparative Law Quarterly* 366

1968a. 'The Unification of Laws in Africa' **16** *American Journal of Comparative Law* 51

1968b. 'African Law' in J. D. M. Derrett (ed.), *An Introduction to Legal Systems* (New York: Frederick A. Praeger)

Alter, K. J., 2001. *Establishing the Supremacy of European Law: The Making of an International Rule of Law in Europe* (Oxford: Oxford University Press)

2008a. 'Agents or Trustees? International Courts in their Political Context' **14** *European Journal of International Relations* 33

2008b. 'Delegating to International Courts: Self-Binding vs. Other Binding Delegation' **71** *Law and Contemporary Problems* 37

2009. *The European Court's Political Power – Selected Essays* (Oxford: Oxford University Press)

Alter, K. J. and Helfer, L. R., 2010. 'Nature or Nurture? Judicial Lawmaking in the European Court of Justice and the Andean Tribunal of Justice' **64** *International Organization* 563

Alter, K. J. and Meunier, S., 2009. 'The Politics of International Regime Complexity' **7** (1) *Perspectives on Politics* 13

Amado, J. D., 1990–1. 'Recognition and Enforcement of Judgment in Latin American Countries: An Overview and Update' **31** *Virginia Journal of International Law* 99

Amerasinghe, C. F., 2004. *Local Remedies in International Law* (Cambridge: Cambridge University Press, 2nd edn)

2005. *Principles of the Institutional Law of International Organizations* (Cambridge: Cambridge University Press, 2nd edn)

American Law Institute, 1971. *Restatement of the Law, Second: Conflict of Laws* (St Paul, Minnesota: American Law Institute)

Amponsah, N., 2007. 'Institutional and Economic Performance: Ghana's Experience under the Fourth Republic, 1992–2002' in K. Boafo-Arthur (ed.), *Ghana: One Decade of the Liberal State* (London: Zed Books)

Amuwo, K., 1999. 'France and the Economic Integration Project in Francophone Africa' **4** *African Journal of Political Science* 1

Arroyo, D. P. F., 2000. 'International Contracts Rules in Mercosur: End of an Era or Trojan Horse?' in P. J. Borchers and J. Zekoll (eds.), *International Conflict of Laws for the Third Millennium, Essays in Honour of Friedrich K. Juenger* (New York: Transnational Publishers)

Arroyo, D. P. F. and Kleinheisterkamp, J., 2002. 'The VIth Inter-American Specialized Conference on Private International Law (CIDIP VI): A New Step towards Inter-American Legal Integration' **4** *Yearbook of Private International Law* 237

Asante, S. K. B., 1997. *Regionalism and Africa's Development* (London: Macmillan Press)

Asante, S. K. B., Nwonwa, F. O. C. and Muzvidziwa, V. N. (eds.), 2001. *Towards an African Economic Community* (Pretoria: African Institute of South Africa)

Asare, S. K., 2006. 'Plain Meaning v. Purposive Interpretation: Ghana's Constitutional Jurisprudence at a Crossroad' **3** *University of Botswana Law Journal* 93

Asouzu, A. A., 2001. *International Commercial Arbitration and African States: Practice, Participation and Institutional Development* (Cambridge: Cambridge University Press)

Aust, A., 2007. *Modern Treaty Law and Practice* (Cambridge: Cambridge University Press, 2nd edn)

Austin, J., 1995. *The Province of Jurisprudence Determined* (trans. Rumble, W. R.; Cambridge: Cambridge University Press)

Balassa, B., 1962. *The Theory of Economic Integration* (London: Allen and Unwin)

Bamodu, G., 1994. 'Transnational Law, Unification and Harmonization of International Commercial Law in Africa' **38** *Journal of African Law* 125

Bannermah, R. E., 1993–5. 'Award of Damages in Foreign Currency: A Critical Look at the Judgments' **19** *Review of Ghana Law* 231

Barents, R., 2003. *The Autonomy of Community Law* (The Hague: Kluwer Law International)

Beaumont, P., 2009. 'Hague Choice of Court Agreements Convention 2005: Background, Negotiations, Analysis and Current Status' **5** *Journal of Private International Law* 125

Bebr, G., 1971. 'Law of the European Communities and Municipal Law' **34** *Modern Law Review* 481

1977. 'Article 177 of the EEC Treaty in the Practice of National Courts' **26** *International and Comparative Law Quarterly* 241

Bekker, P. H. F., 2004–5. 'The Use of Non-domestic Courts for Obtaining Domestic Relief: Jurisdictional Conflicts between NAFTA Tribunals and U.S. Courts?' **11** *ILSA Journal of International and Comparative Law* 331

Bell, A., 2003. *Forum Shopping and Venue in Transnational Litigation* (Oxford: Oxford University Press)

Bentil, K. J., 1969. 'The Legal Framework and the Economic Aspects of the East African Common Market' **4** *Journal of Law and Economic Development* 27

Bethlehem, D., 1998. 'International Law, European Community Law, National Law: Three Systems in Search of a Framework' in M. Koskenniemi (ed.), *International Law Aspects of the European Union* (The Hague: Martinus Nijhoff Publishers)

2005. 'International Economic Relations' in J. Dugard (ed.), *International Law: A South African Perspective* (Lansdowne, South Africa: Juta & Co. Ltd)

Betlem, G. and Nollkaemper, A., 2003. 'Giving Effect to Public International Law and European Community Law before Domestic Courts: A Comparative Analysis of the Principle of Consistent Interpretation' **14** *European Journal of International Law* 569

Bhattacharyya, S., 2009. 'Root Causes of African Underdevelopment' **18** *Journal of African Economies* 745

Bhuiyan, S., 2007. *National Law in WTO Law, Effectiveness and Good Governance in the World Trading System* (Cambridge: Cambridge University Press)

Biukovic, L., 2006. 'Compliance with International Treaties: Selective Adaptation Analysis' **44** *Canadian Yearbook of International Law* 451

2008. 'Selective Adaptation of WTO Transparency Norms and Local Practices in China and Japan' **11** *Journal of International Economic Law* 803

Black, V., 2010. *Foreign Currency Claim in the Conflict of Laws* (Oxford: Hart Publishing)

Blankenburg, E., 1997. 'Civil Litigation as Indicator of Legal Cultures' in D. Nelken (ed.), *Comparing Legal Cultures* (Aldershot: Dartmouth Publishing Company)

Blom, J., 2002. 'Reform of Private International Law by Judges: Canada as a Case Study' in J. J. Fawcett (ed.), *Reform and Development of Private International Law: Essays in Honour of Sir Peter North* (Oxford: Oxford University Press)

Blom, J. and Edinger, E., 2005. 'The Chimera of the Real and Substantial Connection Test' **38** *University of British Columbia Law Review* 373

Boas, M., 2001. 'Regions and Regionalisation: A Heretic's View' in M. Bods Page (ed.), *Regionalism and Regional Integration in Africa: A Debate of Current Aspects and Issues* (Uppsala: Nordiska Afrikainstitutet)

Boggiano, A., 2000. 'The Law of Relations between Legal Systems: A Methodological Analysis' in J. Basedow (ed.), *Private Law in the International Arena: From National Conflict Rules towards Harmonization and Unification – Liber Amicorum Kurt Siehr* (The Hague: TMC Asser Press)

Botha, N. and Olivier, M., 2004. 'Ten Years of International Law in South African Courts: Reviewing the Past and Assessing the Future' **29** *South African Yearbook of International Law* 42

Brand, R. A., 1997. 'Recognition and Enforcement of Judgments as a Trade Law Issue: The Economics of Private International Law' in J. Bhandari and A. O. Sykes (eds.), *Economic Dimensions of International Law: Comparative and Empirical Perspectives* (Cambridge: Cambridge University Press)

Breytenbach, W., 2008. 'Peacekeeping and Regional Integration in Africa' **8** *Monitoring Regional Integration in Southern Africa Yearbook* 249

Brilmayer, L., 1995. 'The Role of Substantive and Choice of Law Policies in the Formation and Application of Choice of Law Rules' **252** *Recueil des Cours* 9

Broberg, M. and Fenger, N., 2010. *Preliminary References to the European Court of Justice* (Oxford: Oxford University Press)

Brown, C., 2007. *The Common Law of International Adjudication* (Oxford: Oxford University Press)

Brown, M. L., 1989. 'Nigeria and the ECOWAS Protocol on Free Movement and Residence' **27** *Journal of Modern African Studies* 251

Brownlie, I., 2003. *Principles of Public International Law* (Oxford: Oxford University Press, 6th edn)

Caffrey, B. A., 1985. *International Jurisdiction and the Recognition and Enforcement of Foreign Judgment in the LAW ASIA Region: A Comparative Study of the Laws of Eleven Asian Countries Inter-se and with the E.E.C. Countries* (North Ryde: CCH Australia Ltd)

Cameron, J. and Gray, K., 2001. 'Principles of International Law in the WTO Dispute Settlement Body' **50** *International and Comparative Law Quarterly* 248

Cappelliti, M. and Golay, D., 1986. 'The Institutional Economics of European Integration' in M. Cappelliti, M. Seccombe and J. Weiler (eds.), *Integration through Law, Europe and the American Experience* (New York: Walter de Gruyter), Vol. 1, Bk 1

Carrubba, C. J. and Murrah, L., 2005. 'Legal Integration and the use of the Preliminary Ruling Process in the European Union' **59** *International Organization* 399

Casad, R. C., 1980–1. 'Civil Judgment Recognition and the Integration of Multi-State Associations: A Comparative Study' **4** *Hastings Journal of International and Comparative Law Review* 1

1981. *Civil Judgment Recognition and the Integration of Multi-State Associations: Central America, the United States of America, and the European Economic Community* (Lawrence: Regent Press of Kansas)

Cassese, A., 1985. 'Modern Constitutions and International Law' **192** (3) *Recueil des Cours* 341

Castellani, L. G., 2008. 'International Trade Law Reform in Africa' **10** *Yearbook of Private International Law* 547

Castro, L. P., 1992. 'Some Aspects Concerning the Movement for Development of Private International Law in the Americas through Multilateral Conventions' **39** *Netherlands International Law Review* 243

Charnovitz, S., 2009. 'The Enforcement of WTO Judgments' **34** *Yale Journal of International Law* 558

Chayes, A. and Chayes, A. H., 1995. *The New Sovereignty: Compliance with International Regulatory Agreements* (Cambridge: Harvard University Press)

Chime, C., 1977. *Integration and Politics among African States* (Uppsala: Scandinavian Institute of African Studies)

Chukwuemerie, A., 2006. 'The Internationalisation of African Customary Law Arbitration' **14** *African Journal of International and Comparative Law* 143

Cichowski, R. A., 2007. *The European Court and Civil Society: Litigation, Mobilization and Governance* (Cambridge: Cambridge University Press)

Collins, L., 2002. 'Comity in Modern Private International Law' in J. J. Fawcett (ed.), *Reform and Development of Private International Law – Essays in Honour of Sir Peter North* (Oxford: Oxford University Press)

Cotterrell, R., 1997. 'The Concept of Legal Culture' in D. Nelken (ed.), *Comparing Legal Cultures* (Aldershot: Dartmouth Publishing Company)

Craig, P. P., 1992. 'Once Upon a Time in the West: Direct Effect and the Federalization of EEC Law' **12** *Oxford Journal of Legal Studies* 453

Craig, P. P. and de Búrca, G., 2003. *EU Law: Text, Cases and Materials* (Oxford: Oxford University Press, 3rd edn)

Crawford, J., 1981. 'Execution of Judgments and Foreign Sovereign Immunity' **75** *American Journal of International Law* 820

Cronje, J. B., 2010. 'Implementation of SADC Protocols', online: www.tralac.org/cgi-bin/giga.cgi?cmd=cause_dir_news_item&cause_id=1694&news_id=91436&cat_id=1059

Dashwood, A., 1977. 'The Principle of Direct Effect in European Community Law' **16** *Journal of Common Market Studies* 229

Davidson, P. J., 2008. 'The Role of International Law in the Governance of International Economic Relations in ASEAN' **12** *Singapore Yearbook of International Law* 213

de Búrca, G., 2010. 'The European Court of Justice and the International Legal Order after *Kadi*' **51** *Harvard International Law Journal* 1

de la Torre, F. C., 2005. 'TEC, Article 240 on National Courts Jurisdiction' in H. Smit, P. Herzog, C. Campbell and G. Zegel (eds.), *Smit and Herzog on the Law of the European Union* (New York: Matthew Bender, LexisNexis)

de Mestral, A. and Winter, J., 2004. 'Giving Direct Effect to NAFTA: Analysis of Issues' in D. Savoie and D. Schwanen (eds.), *Thinking North America, the Art of the State* (Montreal: Institute for Research on Public Policy) de Richemont, J., 1978. *Integration of Community Law within the Legal Systems of the Member States: Article 177 of the Treaty of Rome* (Paris: Journal des Notaires et des Avocats)

Deen-Swarray, M. and Schade, K., 2006. 'Perception of Business People and Non-State Actors on Regional Integration – A SADC-wide Survey' **6** *Monitoring Regional Integration in Southern Africa Yearbook* 51

Deskoski, T., 2008. 'The New Macedonian Private International Law Act of 2007' **10** *Yearbook of Private International Law* 441

Devuyst, Y. and Serdarevic, A., 2007–8. 'The World Trade Organization and Regional Trade Agreements: Bridging the Constitutional Gap' **18** *Duke International and Comparative Law Journal* 1

di Delupis, I. D., 1970. *The East African Community and Common Market* (London: Longmans)

Dickerson, C. M., 2005. 'Harmonizing Business Laws in Africa: OHADA Case Calls the Tune' **44** *Columbia Journal of Transnational Law* 17

Dowrick, F. E., 1983. 'A Model of the European Communities' Legal System' **3** *Yearbook of European Law* 169

Drake, S., 2005. 'Twenty Years after Van Colson: The Impact of "Indirect Effect" on the Protection of Individual's Community Rights' **30** *European Law Review* 329

Draper, P., Halleson, D. and Alves, P., 2007. 'SACU, Regional Integration and the Overlap Issue in Southern Africa: From Spaghetti to Cannelloni?' (South African Institute of International Affairs, Trade Policy Report No. 15)

Drezner, D. W., 2009. 'The Power and Peril of International Regime Complexity' **7** (1) *Perspectives on Politics* 65

Drobnig, U., 1966–7. 'Conflict of Laws and the European Economic Community' **15** *American Journal of Comparative Law* 204

Duffy, H., 2009. '*Hadijatou Mani Korouar* v. *Niger*: Slavery Unveiled by the ECOWAS Court' **9** *Human Rights Law Review* 151

Dunoff, J. L., 2008. '"Less than Zero": The Effects of giving Effect to WTO Law' **6** *Loyola University Chicago International Law Review* 279

Dworkin, R. M., 1967–8. 'The Model of Rules' **35** *University of Chicago Law Review* 14

Ebobrah, S. T., 2007. 'A Rights Protection Goldmine or a Waiting Volcanic Eruption? Competence of, and Access to the Human Rights Jurisdiction of the ECOWAS Community Court of Justice' **7** *African Human Rights Law Journal* 307

2009. 'Litigating Human Rights before Sub-Regional Courts in Africa: Prospects and Challenges' **17** *African Journal of International and Comparative Law* 79

Ebobrah, S. T. and Nkhata, M. J., 2010. 'Is the SADC Tribunal under Judicial Siege in Zimbabwe?' **43** *Comparative and International Law Journal of Southern Africa* 81

Edinger, E., 1995. 'The Constitutionalization of the Conflict of Laws' **25** *Canadian Business Law Journal* 38

Eeckhout, P., 2004. *External Relations of the European Union – Legal and Constitutional Foundations* (Oxford: Oxford University Press)

Eisenberg, G. S., 1993–4. 'The GATT and the WTO Agreements: Comments on their Legal Applicability to the Republic of South Africa' **19** *South African Yearbook of International Law* 127

Enonchong, N., 2007. 'Harmonization of Business Law in Africa: Is Article 42 of the OHADA Treaty a Problem?' **51** *Journal of African Law* 95

Erasmus, G., 2003. 'The Incorporation of Trade Agreements and Rules of Origin: The Extent of Constitutional Guidance' **28** *South African Yearbook of International Law* 157

European Court of Auditors, 2010. *Effectiveness of EDF Support for Regional Integration in East Africa and West Africa* (Luxembourg: Publications Office of the European Union)

Ewing-Chow, M., 2008. 'Culture Club or Chameleon: Should ASEAN Adopt Legalization for Economic Integration?' **12** *Singapore Yearbook of International Law* 225

Fagbayibo, B., 2009. 'Towards the Harmonization of Laws in Africa: Is OHADA the Way to Go?' **42** *Comparative and International Law Journal of Southern Africa* 309

Fallon, M. and Meeusen, J., 2002. 'Private International Law in the European Union and the Exception of Mutual Recognition' **4** *Yearbook of Private International Law* 37

Fawcett, J. E. S., 1963. *The British Commonwealth in International Law* (London: Stevens & Sons)

Fawcett, J. J., 1997. 'The Europeanization of Private International Law: The Significance for Singapore' **1** *Singapore Journal of International and Comparative Law* 69

Fawcett, J. J. and Carruthers, J. M., 2008. *Cheshire, North & Fawcett Private International Law* (Oxford: Oxford University Press, 14th edn)

Fine, J. and Yeo, S., 1999. 'Regional Integration in Sub-Saharan Africa: Dead End or a Fresh Start?' in A. Oyejide (ed.), *Regional Integration and Trade Liberalisation in Sub-Saharan Africa* (London: Macmillan Press Ltd)

Fiorini, A., 2005. 'The Codification of Private International Law: The Belgian Experience' **54** *International and Comparative Law Quarterly* 499

Fitzke, S., 1999. 'The Treaty for East African Co-operation: Can East Africa Successfully Revive One of Africa's Most Infamous Economic Groupings?' **8** *Minnesota Journal of Global Trade* 127

Foote, J. A., 1904. *Foreign and Domestic Law: A Concise Treatise on Private International Jurisprudence, Based on the Decisions in the English Courts* (London: Stevens and Haynes)

Foroutan, F. and Pritchett, L., 1993. 'Intra-Sub-Saharan African Trade: Is it little?' **2** *Journal of African Economies* 74

Forsyth, C. F., 2002. 'The Provenance and Future of Private International Law in Southern Africa' *Journal of South African Law* 60

2003. *Private International Law: The Modern Roman-Dutch Law Including the Jurisdiction of the High Court* (Cape Town: Juta & Co)

2005. 'The Eclipse of Private International Law Principle? The Judicial Process, Interpretation and the Dominance of Legislation in the Modern Era' **1** *Journal of Private International Law* 93

2006a. 'The Impact of the Domestic on the International: Some Crucial Deficiencies in the South African Law of Jurisdiction with their Regional and International Consequences' **18** *South African Mercantile Law Journal* 1

2006b. 'The Protection of Legitimate Expectations: Some Pitfalls for Botswana to Avoid' **3** *University of Botswana Law Journal* 5

Franck, T. M., 1964. *East African Unity through Law* (New Haven: Yale University Press)

Friedman, L. M., 1969. 'Legal Culture and Social Development' **4** *Law and Society Review* 29

1975. *The Legal System: A Social Science Perspective* (New York: Russel Sage Foundation)

Friedrich Ebert Foundation (Botswana), 2007. *Deepening Integration in the SADC: A Comparative Analysis of 10 Country Studies and Surveys of Business and Non-State Actors* (Gabarone: Friedrich Ebert Foundation (Botswana))

Fumagalli, L., 2004. 'EC Private International Law and the Public Policy Exception – Modern Features of a Traditional Concept' **6** *Yearbook of Private International Law* 171

Garro, A., 1992. 'Unification and Harmonization of Private Law in Latin America' **40** *American Journal of Comparative Law* 587

Gathii, J. T., 2009–10. 'African Regional Trade Agreements as Flexible Legal Regimes' **35** *North Carolina Journal of International Law and Commercial Regulation* 571

Geda, A. and Kebret, H., 2007. 'Regional Economic Integration in Africa: A Review of Problems and Prospects with a Case Study of COMESA' **17** *Journal of African Economies* 357

Ghai, Y. P., 1969. 'East African Community' **III** *Annual Survey of African Law* 76

1976. *Reflections on Law and Economic Integration in East Africa* (Uppsala: Scandinavian Institute of African Studies)

Ginsburg, T., Chernykh, S. and Zachary, E., 2008. 'Commitment and Diffusion: How and Why National Constitutions Incorporate International Law' **1** *University of Illinois Law Review* 201

Gondwe, M., 1998. 'From PTA to COMESA: The Quest for Sub-Regional Economic Integration in Eastern and Southern Africa' **6** *African Yearbook of International Law* 3

Gonidec, P. F., 1998. 'The Relationship of International Law and National Law in Africa' **10** *African Journal of International and Comparative Law* 244

Goode, R., 2005. 'Rule, Practice, and Pragmatism in Transnational Commercial Law' **54** *International and Comparative Law Quarterly* 539

Graewert, T., 2008. 'Conflicting Laws and Jurisdictions in the Dispute Settlement Process of Regional Trade Agreements and the WTO' **1** *Contemporary Asia Arbitration Journal* 287

Griffiths, J., 1986. 'What is Legal Pluralism?' **24** *Legal Pluralism and Unofficial Law* 1

Guzman, A. T., 2002. 'The Cost of Credibility: Explaining Resistance to Interstate Dispute Resolution Mechanisms' **31** *Journal of Legal Studies* 303

Harris, J., 2008. 'Understanding the English Response to the Europeanisation of Private International Law' **4** *Journal of Private International Law* 347

Harris, J. W., 1979. *Law and Legal Science: An Inquiry into the Concepts of Legal Rule and Legal System* (Oxford: Clarendon Press)

Hart, H. L. A., 1994. *The Concept of Law* (Oxford: Clarendon Press)

Hartley, T. C., 2001. 'International Law and the Law of the European Union – A Restatement' **72** *British Yearbook of International Law* 1

2003. *The Foundations of European Community Law* (Oxford: Oxford University Press)

2005. 'The European Union and the Systematic Dismantling of the Common Law Conflict of Laws' **54** *International and Comparative Law Quarterly* 813

Hass, E. B., 1958. *The Uniting of Europe: Political, Social and Economic Forces 1950–1957* (Stanford: Stanford University Press)

Hay, P., 1965. 'International and Supranational Organizations: Some Problems of Conceptualization' *University of Illinois Law Forum* 733

1966. *Federalism and Supranational Organizations: Patterns for New Legal Structures* (Urbana: University of Illinois Press)

1968. 'The Common Market Preliminary Draft Convention on the Recognition and Enforcement of Judgments – Some Considerations of Policy and Interpretation' **16** *American Journal of Comparative Law* 149

Hay, P., Lando, O. and Rotunda, R., 1986. 'Conflict of Laws as a Technique for Legal Integration' in M. Cappelliti, M. Seccombe and J. Weiler (eds.), *Integration through Law Europe and the American Experience* (New York: Walter de Gruyter), Vol. 1, Bk 2

Hazlewood, A., 1967. 'Problems of Integration among African States' in A. Hazlewood (ed.), *African Integration and Disintegration – Case Studies in Economic and Political Union* (Oxford: Oxford University Press)

Helfer, L. R., Alter, K. and Guerzovich, M. F., 2009. 'Islands of Effective International Adjudication: Constructing an Intellectual Property Rule of Law in the Andean Community' **103** *American Journal of International Law* 1

Helfer, L. R. and Alter, K. J., 2009. 'The Andean Tribunal of Justice and Its Interlocutors: Understanding Preliminary Reference Patterns in the Andean Community' **41** *New York Journal of International Law and Politics* 871

Helfer, L. R. and Slaughter, A.-M., 1997. 'Towards a Theory of Effective Supranational Adjudication' **107** *Yale Law Journal* 273

Henckels, C., 2008. 'Overcoming Jurisdictional Isolationism at the WTO – FTA Nexus: A Potential Approach for the WTO' **19** *European Journal of International Law* 571

Hilf, M., 1997. 'The Role of National Courts in International Trade Relations' in E.-U. Petersmann (ed.), *International Trade Law and GATT/WTO Dispute Settlement System* (The Hague: Kluwer Law International)

Hilf, M. and Petersmann, E.-U. (eds.), 1993. *National Constitutions and International Economic Law* (Deventer: Kluwer Law International)

Houben, P.-H. J. M., 1965–6. 'The Merger of the Executives of the European Communities' **3** *Common Market Law Review* 37

Hu, J., 2004. 'The Role of International Law in the Development of WTO Law' **7** *Journal of International Economic Law* 143

Hudson, M. O., 1944. *International Tribunals, Past and Future* (Washington: Carnegie Endowment International Peace and Brookings Institute)

Hunter, I. A., 1977–8. 'Proving Foreign and International Law in the Courts of England and Wales' **18** *Virginia Journal of International Law* 665

Inglehart, R., 1970. 'Public Opinion and Regional Integration' **24** *International Organization* 764

Ingram, P., 1983. 'Effectiveness' **86** *Archiv fur Rechts und Sozialphilosophie* 484

International Law Commission, 2007. *Most Favoured-Nation Clause – Report of the Working Group* (New York: International Law Commission, ILC Document A/CN.4/L.719)

Jackson, C., 2003a. 'Constitutional Structure and Governance Strategies for Economic Integration in Africa and Europe' **13** *Transnational Law and Contemporary Problems* 139

Jackson, J. H., 2003b. 'Sovereignty-Modern: A New Approach to an Outdated Concept' **97** *American Journal of International Law* 782

2003–4. 'The Varied Policies of International Juridical Bodies – Reflections on Theory and Practice' **25** *Michigan Journal of International Law* 869

Jakobeit, C., Hartzenberg, T. and Charalambides, N. (eds.), 2005. *Overlapping Membership in COMESA, EAC, SACU and SADC: Trade Policy Options for the Region and for EPA Negotiations* (Eschborn: GTZ)

Jenks, C. W., 1964. *The Prospect of International Adjudication* (London: Stevenson & Sons)

Jessel-Holst, C., 2007. 'The Bulgarian Private International Law Code of 2005' **9** *Yearbook of Private International Law* 375

Jessup, P. C., 1948. *A Modern Law of Nations – An Introduction* (New York: Macmillan Company)

Jobodwana, Z. N., 2009. 'Participation of African Member States in the World Trade Organization Dispute Settlement Mechanism' **2** *International Journal of Private Law* 206

Joerges, C., 1996. 'Taking Law Seriously: On Political Science and the Role of Law in the Process of European Integration' **2** *European Law Journal* 105

2002–3. 'Law, Economics and Politics in the Constitutionalisation of Europe' **5** *Cambridge Yearbook of European Legal Studies* 122

Johnson, O. E. G., 1991. 'Economic Integration in Africa: Enhancing Prospects for Success' **29** *Journal of Modern African Studies* 1

Jones, M. L., 1984. 'The Legal Nature of the European Community: A Jurisprudential Analysis using H.L.A. Hart's Model of Law and a Legal System' **17** *Cornell International Law Journal* 1

Juenger, F., 1994. 'The Inter American Convention on the Law Applicable to International Contracts: Some Highlights and Comparisons' **42** *American Journal of Comparative Law* 381

Jyranki, A. (ed.), 1999. *National Constitutions in the Era of Integration* (The Hague: Kluwer Law International)

Kaahwa, W., 1999. 'The Treaty Establishing the New East African Community: An Overview' **7** *African Yearbook of International Law* 61

Karuuombe, B., 2008. 'The Role of Parliament in Regional Integration – the Missing Link' **8** *Monitoring Regional Integration in Southern Africa Yearbook* 222

Keck, A. and Schropp, S., 2008. 'Indisputably Essential: The Economics of Dispute Settlement Institutions in Trade Agreements' **42** *Journal of World Trade* 785

Kelsen, H., 1967. *The Pure Theory of Law* (trans. Knight, M.; Berkeley: University of California Press)

1991. *General Theory of Norms* (trans. Hartney, M.; Oxford: Clarendon Press)

Kessie, E., 1999. 'Trade Liberalisation under ECOWAS: Prospect, Challenges and WTO Compatibility' **7** *African Yearbook of International Law* 31

Kiggundu, J., 2006. 'Choice of Law in Delict: The Rise and Rise of the *Lex Loci Delicti Commissi*' **18** *South African Mercantile Law Journal* 97

Kiplagat, P. K., 1995. 'Dispute Recognition and Dispute Settlement in Integration Processes: The COMESA Experience' **15** *Northwestern Journal of International Law and Business* 437

1995–6. 'Jurisdictional Uncertainties and Integration Process in Africa: The Need for Harmony' **4** *Tulane Journal of International and Comparative Law* 43

Kirby, M., 2010. 'The Common Law and International Law – A Dynamic Contemporary Dialogue' **30** *Legal Studies* 30

Klabbers, J., 2009. *An Introduction to International Institutional Law* (Cambridge: Cambridge University Press, 2nd edn)

Koch, C., 2005. 'The Doctrine of Supremacy of European Community Law as a Condition Precedent for the Doctrine of Direct Effect' **9** *International Trade & Business Law Review* 201

Koh, P. M. C., 1996. 'Foreign Judgments in ASEAN – A Proposal' **45** *International and Comparative Law Quarterly* 844

Kotuby, C. T., 2001–2. 'Internal Developments and External Effects: The Federalization of Private International Law in the European Community and its Consequences for Transnational Litigants' **21** *Journal of Law and Commerce* 157

Kouassi, R. N., 2007. 'The Itinerary of the African Integration Process: An Overview of the Historical Landmarks' **1** *African Integration Review* 1

Kronenberger, V., 2000. 'A New Approach to the Interpretation of the French Constitution in Respect of International Conventions: From Hierarchy of Norms to Conflict of Competence' **47** *Netherlands International Law Review* 323

Kruger, T., 2005. 'The South African Litigant and European Union Rules of Civil Procedure' **38** *Comparative and International Law Journal of Southern Africa* 75

Ku, J. G., 2006. 'International Delegation and the New World Court Order' **81** *Washington Law Review* 1

Kufuor, K. O., 1994. 'Law, Power, Politics and Economics: Critical Issues Arising out of the New ECOWAS Treaty' **6** *African Journal of International and Comparative Law* 429

1996. 'Securing Compliance with the Judgments of the ECOWAS Court of Justice' **8** *African Journal of International and Comparative Law* 1

2005. 'The Collapse of the Organization of African Unity: Lessons from Economics and History' **49** *Journal of African Law* 132

2006. *The Institutional Transformation of the Economic Community of West African States* (Aldershot: Ashgate Publishing Company)

2008. 'Ban on the Importation of Tomato Paste and Concentrate in Ghana' **16** *African Journal of International and Comparative Law* 100

Kulusika, S. E., 2000. 'The Lawyer and the Challenges of Economic Integration' **32** *Zambia Law Journal* 20

Kutner, P. B., 1990. *Common Law in Southern Africa: Conflict of Laws and Torts Precedents* (New York: Greenwood Press)

Kwak, K. and Marceau, G., 2006. 'Overlaps and Conflicts of Jurisdiction between the World Trade Organization and Regional Trade Agreements' in L. Bartels and F. Ortino (eds.), *Regional Trade Agreements and the WTO Legal System* (Oxford: Oxford University Press)

Lauterpacht, H., 1929. 'Decisions of Municipal Courts as a Source of International Law' **10** *British Yearbook of International Law* 65

Leal-Arcas, R., 2007. 'Choice of Jurisdiction in International Trade Disputes: Going Regional or Global?' **16** *Minnesota Journal of International Law* 1

Lenaerts, K., 2003. 'Interlocking Legal Orders in the European Union and Comparative Law' **52** *International and Comparative Law Quarterly* 873

Leon, P. S. G., 1983. 'Roma non Locuta est.: the Recognition and Enforcement of Foreign Judgments in South Africa' **26** *Comparative and International Law Journal of Southern Africa* 325

Lesser, C. and Moise-Leeman, E., 2008. 'Informal Cross-border Trade and Trade Facilitation in Sub-Saharan Africa' (OECD, Trade Policy Working Paper No. 86)

Lester, S. and Mercurio, B. (eds.), 2009. *Bilateral and Regional Trade Agreements – Commentary and Analysis* (Cambridge: Cambridge University Press)

Lindberg, L. N., 1963. *The Political Dynamics of European Economic Integration* (Stanford: Stanford University Press)

Linthorst, H. J., 1965–6. 'The Merger of the European Communities' **3** *Common Market Law Review* 397

Mackenzie, R. and Sands, P., 2004. 'International Courts and Tribunals and the Independence of the International Court of Justice' **44** *Harvard International Law Journal* 271

Magliveras, K. D. and Naldi, G. J., 2002. 'The African Union – A New Dawn for Africa?' **51** *International and Comparative Law Quarterly* 415

Maher, I., 1996. 'Limitations on Community Regulation in the UK: Legal Culture and Multi-level Governance' **3** *Journal of European Public Policy* 577

1998. 'Community Law in the National Legal System: A Systems Analysis' **36** *Journal of Common Market Studies* 237

Maluwa, T., 1989. 'The Peaceful Settlement of Disputes among African States, 1963–1983: Some Conceptual Issues and Practical Trends' **38** *International and Comparative Law Quarterly* 299

1998. 'The Incorporation of International Law and its Interpretational Role in Municipal Legal Systems in Africa' **23** *South African Yearbook of International Law* 45

1999. *International Law in Post-Colonial Africa* (The Hague: Kluwer Law International)

2001. 'Reimagining African Unity: Preliminary Reflections on the Constitutive Act of the African Union' **9** *African Yearbook of International Law* 3

2007. 'From the Organisation of African Unity to the African Union: Rethinking the Framework for Inter-State Cooperation in Africa in the Era of Globalisation' **5** *University of Botswana Law Journal* 5

Mancuso, S., 2007. 'Trends on the Harmonization of Contract Law in Africa' **13** *Annual Survey of International and Comparative Law* 157

Mann, C. J., 1972. *The Function of Judicial Decision in European Economic Integration* (The Hague: Nijhoff)

Martinek, M. G., 2007. 'Look Back before you Leap? Fateful Tendencies of Materialization and of Parallelism in Modern Private International Law Theory' *Journal of South African Law* 277

Martinez, J. S., 2003–4. 'Towards an International Judicial System' **56** *Stanford Law Review* 429

Martor, B., Pilkington, N., Sellers, D. S. and Thouvenot, S., 2007. *Business Law in Africa: OHADA and the Harmonization Process* (London: Kogan Page Ltd, 2nd edn)

Maus, D., 1999. 'The Influence of Contemporary International Law on the Exercise of Constituent Power' in A. Jyranki (ed.), *National Constitutions in the Era of Integration* (The Hague: Kluwer Law International)

Mazzeo, D., 1984. 'The Experience of the East African Community: Implications for the Theory and Practice of Regional Cooperation in Africa' in D. Mazzeo (ed.), *African Regional Organizations* (Cambridge: Cambridge University Press)

McCarthy, C., 2008. 'Is African Economic Integration in Need of a Paradigm Change? Thinking Out of the Box on African Integration' **8** *Monitoring Regional Integration in Southern Africa Yearbook* 4

McDonald, S. A., 2004. 'The Caribbean Court of Justice: Enhancing the Law of International Organizations' **27** *Fordham International Law Journal* 930

McMahon, J. and Young, M. A., 2007. 'The WTO's Use of Relevant Rules of International Law: An Analysis of the Biotech Case' **56** *International and Comparative Law Quarterly* 907

Meagher, K., 2001. 'Throwing Out the Baby to Keep the Bathwater: Informal Cross-Border Trade and Regional Integration in West Africa' in M. Bods Page (ed.), *Regionalism and Regional Integration in Africa: A Debate of Current Aspects and Issues* (Uppsala: Nordiska Afrikainstitutet)

Mengozzi, P., 2001. 'Private International Law and the WTO Law' **292** *Recueil des Cours* 249

Menski, W., 2006. *Comparative Law in Global Context – the Legal Systems of Asia and Africa* (Cambridge: Cambridge University Press, 2nd edn)

Michaels, R. and Pauwelyn, J., 2011. 'Conflict of Norms or Conflict of Laws?: Different Techniques in the Fragmentation of International Law' in T. Broude and Y. Shany (eds.), *Multi-Sourced Equivalent Norms in International Law* (Oxford: Hart Publishing, 2011)

Miller, N., 2002. 'An International Jurisprudence? The Operation of "Precedent" Across International Tribunals' **15** *Leiden Journal of International Law* 483

Mills, A., 2006. 'The Private History of International Law' **55** *International and Comparative Law Quarterly* 1

2008. 'The Dimensions of Public Policy in Private International Law' **4** *Journal of Private International Law* 201

Mistry, P. S., 2000. 'Africa's Record of Regional Co-operation and Integration' **99** *African Affairs* 553

Moravcsik, A., 1997. 'Taking Preferences Seriously: A Liberal Theory of International Politics' **51** *International Organization* 513

Mosoti, V., 2006. 'Africa in the First Decade of WTO Dispute Settlement' **9** *Journal of International Economic Law* 427

Mujuzi, J. D., 2010. '*Michelot Yogogombaye* v. *The Republic of Senegal*: The African Court's First Decision' **10** *Human Rights Law Review* 372

Mulat, T., 1998. 'Multilateralism and Africa's Regional Economic Communities' **32** (4) *Journal of World Trade* 115

Murphy, S., 2009. 'Does International Law Obligate States to Open their National Courts to Persons for the Invocation of Treaty Norms that Protect or Benefit Persons' in D. Sloss (ed.), *The Role of Domestic Courts in Treaty Enforcement – A Comparative Study* (Cambridge: Cambridge University Press)

Mutai, H. K., 2007. *Compliance with International Trade Obligations: The Common Market for Eastern and Southern Africa* (Alphen aan den Rijn: Kluwer Law International)

Mvungi, S. E. A., 2002a. 'Legal Analysis of the Draft Treaty for the Establishment of the East African Community' in S. Mvungi (ed.), *The Draft Treaty for the Establishment of the EAC: A Critical Review* (Dar es Salaam: Dar es Salaam University Press)

2002b. *The Draft Treaty for the Establishment of the EAC: A Critical Review* (Dar es Salaam: Dar es Salaam University Press)

Naldi, G. J., 2009. '*Mike Campbell (Pvt) Ltd et al* v. *The Republic of Zimbabwe*: Zimbabwe's Land Reform Programme Held in Breach of the SADC Treaty' **53** *Journal of African Law* 305

Naldi, G. J. and Magliveras, K. D., 1999. 'The African Economic Community: Emancipation for African States or Yet Another Glorious Failure?' **24** *North Carolina Journal of International Law and Commercial Regulation* 601

Nantwi, E. K., 1966. *The Enforcement of International Judicial Decisions and Arbitral Awards in Public International Law* (Leyden: A. W. Sijthoff)

Ndulo, M., 1993a. 'Harmonization of Trade Laws in the African Economic Community' **42** *International and Comparative Law Quarterly* 101

1993b. 'The Promotion of Intra-African Trade and the Harmonisation of Laws in the African Economic Community: Prospects and Problems' in M. A. Ajomo and O. Adewale (eds.), *African Economic Community Treaty, Issues, Problems and Prospects* (Lagos: Nigerian Institute of Advanced Legal Studies)

1996. 'The Need for the Harmonisation of Trade Laws in the Southern African Development Community (SADC)' **4** *African Yearbook of International Law* 195

Ndulu, B. J., 2006. 'Infrastructure, Regional Integration and Growth in Sub-Saharan Africa: Dealing with the Disadvantages of Geography and Sovereign Fragmentation' **15** *Journal of African Economies* 212

Nelken, D., 2004. 'Using the Concept of Legal Culture' **29** *Australian Journal of Legal Philosophy* 1

Ng'ong'Ola, C., 1999. 'Regional Integration and Trade Liberalisation in Africa – The Treaty for the Establishment of an African Economic Community Revisited in the Context of the WTO System' **33** *Journal of World Trade* 145

Ngolele, E. M., 2006. 'The Content of the Doctrine of Self-Execution and Its Limited Effect in South African Law' **31** *South African Yearbook of International Law* 141

Niewoudt, L., 1992–3. 'The Power of the South African Court to Give Judgment in Foreign Currency' **18** *South African Yearbook of International Law* 147

Nijman, J. and Nollkaemper, A. (eds.), 2007. *New Perspectives on the Divide between National and International Law* (Oxford: Oxford University Press)

Njenga, F. X., 1968. 'Contrast between the Effect of Laws of E.E.C. and E.A.C.' **4** *East African Law Journal* 138

Nollkaemper, A., 2002. 'The Direct Effect of Public International Law' in J. M. Prinssen and C. Schrauwen (eds.), *Direct Effect: Rethinking a Classic of EC Legal Doctrines* (Groningen: Europa Law Publishing)

Nyman-Metcalf, K. and Papageorgiou, I., 2005. *Regional Integration and Courts of Justice* (Belgium: Intersentia Publishing)

Obilade, A. O., 1993. 'The African Court of Justice: Jurisdictional, Procedural and Enforcement Problems' in M. A. Ajomo and O. Adewale (eds.), *African Economic Community Treaty: Issues, Problems and Prospects* (Lagos: Nigerian Institute of Advanced Legal Studies)

O'Brien, D., 2009. 'Accessing the Original Jurisdiction of the Caribbean Court of Justice' **36** *Legal Issues of Economic Integration* 339

O'Connell, M. E., 1990. 'The Prospect for Enforcing Monetary Judgments of the International Court of Justice: A Study of Nicaragua's Judgment against the United States' **30** *Virginia Journal of International Law* 891

Oduor, M., 2005. 'Resolving Trade Disputes in Africa: Choosing between Multilateralism and Regionalism: the Case of COMESA and the WTO' **13** *Tulane Journal of International and Comparative Law* 177

O'Hop Jr, P. A., 1995. 'Hemispheric Integration and the Elimination of Legal Obstacles under a NAFTA-Based System' **36** *Harvard International Law Journal* 127

O'Keefe, R., 2008. 'The Doctrine of Incorporation Revisited' **79** *British Yearbook of International Law* 7

Oliver, P., 1997. 'Joint Liability of the Community and the Member States' in T. Heukels and A. McDonnell (eds.), *The Action for Damages in Community Law* (The Hague: TMC Asser Institute)

Olowu, D., 2003. 'Regional Integration, Development and the African Union Agenda: Challenges, Gaps and Opportunities' **13** *Transnational Law and Contemporary Problems* 211

Oluoch, L. O. W., 2009. 'Legitimacy of the East African Community' **53** *Journal of African Law* 194

Omorogbe, Y., 1993. 'The Legal Framework for Economic Integration in the ECOWAS Region: An Analysis of the Trade Liberalisation Scheme' **5** *African Journal of International and Comparative Law* 355

Oppong, R. F., 2006a. 'Enforcing Foreign Non-Money Judgments: Some Recent Developments in Canada and Beyond' **39** *University of British Columbia Law Review* 257

2006b. 'The Hague Conference and the Development of Private International Law in Africa: A Plea for Cooperation' **8** *Yearbook of Private International Law* 189

2006c. 'Observing the Legal System of the Community: The Relationship between Community and National Legal Systems under the African Economic Community Treaty' **15** *Tulane Journal of International and Comparative Law* 41

2006d. 'Private International Law and the African Economic Community: A Plea for Greater Attention' **55** *International and Comparative Law Quarterly* 911

2007a. 'Canadian Courts Enforce Foreign Non-Money Judgments' **70** *Modern Law Review* 670

2007b. 'A Decade of Private International Law in African Courts 1997–2007 Part I' **9** *Yearbook of Private International Law* 223

2007c. 'Mere Presence and International Competence in Private International Law' **3** *Journal of Private International Law* 321

2007d. 'Re-Imagining International Law: An Examination of Recent Trends in the Reception of International Law into National Legal Systems in Africa' **30** *Fordham International Law Journal* 297

2007e. 'Private International Law in Africa: The Past, Present and Future' **55** *American Journal of Comparative Law* 677

2008a. 'A Decade of Private International Law in African Courts 1997–2007 Part II' **10** *Yearbook of Private International Law* 367

2008b. 'Roman-Dutch Law Meets the Common Law on Jurisdiction in International Matters' **4** *Journal of Private International Law* 311

2009. 'The AU, African Economic Community and Africa's Regional Economic Communities: Untangling a Complex Web' **17** *African Journal of International and Comparative Law* 92

Orakhelashvili, A., 2006. *Peremptory Norms in International Law* (Oxford: Oxford University Press)

Orloff, N., 1968. 'Economic Integration in East Africa: The Treaty for East-African Co-Operation' **7** *Columbia Journal of Transnational Law* 302

Ostrander, J., 2004. 'The Last Bastion of Sovereign Immunity: A Comparative look at Immunity from Execution of Judgments' **22** *Berkeley Journal of International Law* 540

Ovrawah, O. A., 1994. 'Harmonization of Laws within the Economic Community of West African States' **6** *African Journal of International and Comparative Law* 76

Palmeter, D., 2000. 'The WTO as a Legal System' **24** *Fordham International Law Journal* 444

Patchett, K. W., 1984. *Recognition of Commercial Judgments and Awards in the Commonwealth* (London: Butterworths)

Paulson, C., 2004. 'Compliance with Final Judgments of the International Court of Justice since 1987' **98** *American Journal of International Law* 434

Paulson, S. L., 1983. 'On the Status of the *Lex Posterior* Derogating Rule' **5** *Liverpool Law Review* 5

Pauwelyn, J., 2003. *Conflict of Norms in Public International Law* (Cambridge: Cambridge University Press)

2004. 'Going Global, Community, or Both – Dispute Settlement in the Southern African Development Community (SADC) and Overlaps with the WTO and Other Jurisdictions' **13** *Minnesota Journal of Global Trade* 231

Pauwelyn, J. and Salles, L. E., 2009. 'Forum Shopping Before International Tribunals: (Real) Concerns, (Im)Possible Solutions' **42** *Cornell International Law Journal* 77

Pelkmans, J., 1986. 'The Institutional Economics of European Integration' in M. Cappelliti, M. Seccombe and J. Weiler (eds.), *Integration through Law: Europe and the American Federal Experience* (New York: Walter de Gruyter), Vol. 3, Bk 1

Pernice, I., 1998. 'Constitutional Law Implications for a State Participating in a Process of Regional Integration. German Constitution and "Multilevel Constitutionalism"' in E. Riedel (ed.), *German Reports on Public Law Presented to the XV International Congress on Comparative Law* (Baden-Baden: Nomos)

Pescatore, P., 1974. *The Law of Integration: Emergence of a New Phenomenon in International Relations Based on the Experience of the European Communities* (Leiden: A. W. Sijthoff)

Peters, A., 2007. 'The Globalization of State Constitutions' in A. Nollkaemper and J. E. Nijman (eds.), *New Perspectives on the Divide between National and International Law* (Oxford: Oxford University Press)

Pham, K., 2008. 'Enforcement of Non-Money Foreign Judgments in Australia' **30** *Sydney Law Review* 663

Pirker, B., 2011. 'Interpreting Multi-Sourced Equivalent Norms: Judicial Borrowing in International Courts' in T. Broude and Y. Shany (eds.), *Multi-Sourced Equivalent Norms in International Law* (Oxford: Hart Publishing, 2011)

Piscitello, D. P. and Schmidt, J. P., 2007. 'In the Footsteps of the ECJ: First Decision of the Permanent MERCOSUR-Tribunal' **34** *Legal Issues of Economic Integration* 283

Pitel, S. G. A., 2007. 'Enforcement of Foreign Non-Monetary Judgments in Canada (and Beyond)' **3** *Journal of Private International Law* 241

Posner, D. N. and Young, D. J., 2007. 'The Institutionalization of Political Power in Africa' **18** *Journal of Democracy* 126

Raustiala, K. and Victor, D. G., 2004. 'The Regime Complex for Plant Genetic Resources' **58** *International Organization* 277

Raz, J., 1970. *The Concept of a Legal System: An Introduction to the Theory of a Legal System* (Oxford: Clarendon Press)

Reed, L., 2003. 'Mixed Private and Public International Law Solutions to International Crisis' **306** *Recueil des Cours* 177

Reilly, D. M. and Ordonez, S., 1995–6. 'Effect of the Jurisprudence of the International Court of Justice on National Courts' **28** *New York Journal of International Law and Politics* 435

Reimann, M., 2006. 'Comparative Law and Private International Law' in M. Reimann and R. Zimmermann (eds.), *Oxford Handbook of Comparative Law* (Oxford: Oxford University Press)

Reinisch, A., 2000. *International Organizations before National Courts* (Cambridge: Cambridge University Press)

Reisman, W. M., 1969. 'The Enforcement of International Judgments' **63** *American Journal of International Law* 25

Riechenberg, K., 1995. 'The Merger of Trading Blocks and the Creation of the European Economic Area: Legal and Judicial Issues' **4** *Tulane Journal of International and Comparative Law* 63

Riesenfeld, S. A., 1996–7. 'Legal Systems of Regional Economic Integration' **20** *Hastings Journal of International and Comparative Law Review* 539

Ringo, F. S., 1993. 'The Recognition and Enforcement of Foreign Arbitral Awards in the COMESA/SADC Region: Analysis of Legal Development' **9** *Lesotho Law Journal* 185

Romano, C. P. R., 2007. 'The Shift from Consensual to the Compulsory Paradigm in International Adjudication: Elements for a Theory of Consent' **39** *New York Journal of International Law and Politics* 791

Roodt, C., 2003. 'The Integration of Substantive Interests and Material Justice in South African Choice of Law' **36** *Comparative and International Law Journal of Southern Africa* 1

Rosenne, S., 1957. *The International Court of Justice: An Essay in Political and Legal Theory* (Leiden: A. W. Sijthoff)

2004. *The Perplexities of Modern International Law* (Leiden: Martinus Nijhoff Publishers)

Ross, S., 1972. 'The Common Market Tribunal: The Solution to the Conflict between Municipal and International Law in East Africa' **21** *International and Comparative Law Quarterly* 361

Ruhangisa, J. E., 2006. 'Litigation in the East African Court of Justice' **65** The African Executive, online: www.africanexecutive.com/modules/magazine/articles.php?article=807

Ruppel, O. C. and Bangamwabo, F.-X., 2008. 'The SADC Tribunal: A Legal Analysis of its Mandate and Role in Regional Integration' **8** *Monitoring Regional Integration in Southern Africa Yearbook* 179

Salami, I., 2008. 'Legal Considerations for Devising a Governance Structure for the African Union' **16** *African Journal of International and Comparative Law* 262

Sarooshi, D., 2005. *International Organizations and the Exercise of Sovereign Powers* (Oxford: Oxford University Press)

Sawyer, K., 2007. 'The Principle of "Interpretation Conforme": How Far Can or Should National Courts Go When Interpreting National Legislation Consistently with European Community Law' **28** *Statute Law Review* 165

Schachter, O., 1960. 'Enforcement of International Judicial and Arbitral Decisions' **54** *American Journal of International Law* 1

Schermers, H. G., 1972. *International Institutional Law* (Leiden: A. W. Sijthoff)

Schilling, T., 1996. 'The Autonomy of the Community Legal Order: An Analysis of Possible Foundations' **37** *Harvard International Law Journal* 389

Schlemmer, E. C., 2004. 'South Africa and the WTO Ten Years into Democracy' **29** *South African Yearbook of International Law* 125

Schmid, U., 2001. 'Legal Pluralism as a Source of Conflict in Multi-Ethnic Societies: The Case of Ghana' **46** *Journal of Legal Pluralism and Unofficial Law* 1

Schmitthoff, C. M., 1956. 'Conflict Avoidance in Practice and Theory' **21** *Law and Contemporary Problems* 429

Schneider, A. K., 1998–9. 'Getting Along: The Evolution of Dispute Resolution Regimes in International Trade Organizations' **20** *Michigan Journal of International Law* 679

Schreuer, C. H., 2001. *The ICSID Convention: A Commentary* (Cambridge: Cambridge University Press)

Schulte, C., 2004. *Compliance with Decisions of the International Court of Justice* (Oxford: Oxford University Press)

Schulze, A., 2007. 'The Accession of the European Community to the Hague Conference on Private International Law' **56** *International and Comparative Law Quarterly* 939

Schulze, C., 2005. *On Jurisdiction and the Recognition and Enforcement of Foreign Judgments* (Pretoria: UNISA Press)

Schwelb, E., 1960. 'Republican Constitution of Ghana' **9** *American Journal of Comparative Law* 634

Sebalu, P., 1972. 'The East African Community' **16** *Journal of African Law* 345

Seck, S., 1999. 'Environmental Harm in Developing Countries Caused by Subsidiaries of Canadian Mining Corporations: The Interface of Public and Private International Law' **37** *Canadian Yearbook of International Law* 139

Sempasa, S. L., 1992. 'Obstacles to International Commercial Arbitration in African Countries' **41** *International and Comparative Law Quarterly* 387

Senghor, J. C., 1990. 'Theoretical Foundations for Regional Integration in Africa: An Overview' in P. A. Nyong'o (ed.), *Regional Integration in Africa: Unfinished Agenda* (Nairobi: African Academy of Sciences)

1993. 'The Treaty Establishing the African Economic Community: An Introductory Essay' **1** *African Yearbook of International Law* 183

2007. 'Institutional Architecture for Managing Integration in the ECOWAS Region: An Empirical Investigation' in J. C. Senghor and N. K. Poku (eds.), *Towards Africa's Renewal* (Aldershot: Ashgate Publishing Ltd)

Shaffer, G. C., 2003. *Defending Interests: Public-Private Partnerships in WTO Litigation* (Washington DC: Brookings Institution Press)

Shams, R., 2005. *The Drive towards Economic Integration in Africa* (Hamburg Institute of International Economics, Discussion Paper No. 316)

Shany, Y., 2003. *The Competing Jurisdictions of International Courts and Tribunals* (Oxford: Oxford University Press)

2007. *Regulating Jurisdictional Relations between National and Internationl Courts* (Oxford: Oxford University Press)

2009. 'No Longer a Weak Department of Power? Reflections on the Emergence of a New International Judiciary' **20** *European Journal of International Law* 73

Shaw, M., 1983. 'Dispute Settlement in Africa' **37** *Yearbook of World Affairs* 149

2003. *International Law* (Cambridge: Cambridge University Press, 5th edn)

Sibanda, O., 2008. 'Jurisdictional Arrest of a Foreign Peregrinus Now Unconstitutional in South Africa: *Bid Industrial Holdings* v. *Strang*' **4** *Journal of Private International Law* 329

Siehr, K., 2004. 'Coordination of Legal Systems in Private International Law' in T. Einhorn and K. Siehr (eds.), *Intercontinental Cooperation through Private International Law: Essays in Memory of Peter Nygh* (The Hague: TMC Asser Press)

Sinare, H., 1989. 'The Treaty for the Establishment of the Preferential Trade Area for Eastern and Southern African States and Its Relevance to Economic Integration' **5** *Lesotho Law Journal* 77

Slaughter, A.-M., 2004. *A New World Order* (Princeton: Princeton University Press)

Smith, J. M., 2000. 'The Politics of Dispute Settlement Design: Explaining Legalism in Regional Trade Pacts' **54** *International Organization* 137

Sohn, L. S., 1972. 'Organs of Economic Co-Operation in Africa' **16** *Journal of African Law* 212

Sorensen, M., 1983. 'Autonomous Legal Orders: Some Considerations Relating to a Systems Analysis of International Organizations in the World Legal Order' **32** *International and Comparative Law Quarterly* 559

South African Law Reform Commission, 2006. *Consolidated Legislation Pertaining to International Judicial Co-operation in Civil Matters – Project 121* (Pretoria: SALRC)

Starr, W. C., 1977. 'Hart's Rule of Recognition and the E.E.C.' **28** *Northern Ireland Legal Quarterly* 258

Stellios, J., 2005. 'Choice of Law and the Australian Constitution: Locating the Debate' **33** *Federal Law Review* 8

Sundström, G. O. Z., 1972. 'The Legal Procedures and Techniques of Economic Co-operation' **16** *Journal of African Law* 229

Sykes, A. O., 2008. 'Transnational Forum Shopping as a Trade and Investment Issue' **37** *Journal of Legal Studies* 339

Taylor, C. O. N., 1996–7. 'Dispute Resolution as a Catalyst for Economic Integration and an Agent for Deepening Integration: NAFTA and MERCOSUR?' **17** *Northwestern Journal of International Law and Business* 850

Tebbens, H. D., 1990. 'Private International Law and the Single European Market: Coexistence or Cohabitation' in *Forty Years on: The Evolution of Postwar Private International Law in Europe*, Symposium, Centre of Foreign Law and Private International Law, University of Amsterdam, October 1989 (Deventer: Kluwer International)

Tekinalp, G., 2007. 'The 2007 Turkish Code Concerning Private International law and International Civil Procedure' **9** *Yearbook of Private International Law* 313

Teshale, S., 2000. 'Reciprocity with Respect to Enforcement of Foreign Judgments in Ethiopia: A Critique of the Supreme Court's Decision in the Paulos Papassinous Case' **12** *African Journal of International and Comparative Law* 569

Thanawalla, S., 1970. 'Foreign *Inter Partes* Judgments: Their Recognition and Enforcement in the Private International Law of East Africa' **19** *International and Comparative Law Quarterly* 430

Thomashausen, A., 2002. 'The Enforcement and Recognition of Foreign Judgments and Other Forms of Legal Cooperation in the SADC' **35** *Comparative and International Law Journal of Southern Africa* 26

Thompson, B., 1990. 'Legal Problems of Economic Integration in the West African Sub-Region' **2** *African Journal of International and Comparative Law* 85

Thompson, B. and Mukisa, R. S., 1994. 'Legal Integration as a Key Component of African Economic Integration: A Study of Potential Legal Obstacles to the Implementation of the Abuja Treaty' **20** *Commonwealth Law Bulletin* 1446

Tiewul, S. A. and Tsegah, F. A., 1975. 'Arbitration and the Settlement of Commercial Disputes: A Survey of African Practice' **24** *International and Comparative Law Quarterly* 393

Trachtman, J. P. and Moreman, P. M., 2003. 'Cost and Benefit of Private Participation in WTO Dispute Settlement: Whose Right is it Anyway' **44** *Harvard International Law Journal* 221

Trindade, A. A. C., 1983. *The Application of the Rule of Exhaustion of Local Remedies in International Law* (New York: Cambridge University Press)

Tshosa, O., 2007. 'The Status and Role of International Law in the National Law of Botswana' in C. M. Fombad (ed.), *Essays on the Law of Botswana* (Cape Town: Juta & Co)

2010. 'The Status of International Law in Namibian National Law: A Critical Appraisal of the Constitutional Strategy' **2** *Namibian Law Journal* 3

Tunc, A., 1961. 'Comparative Law, Peace and Justice' in K. H. Nadelmann, A. T. von Mehren and J. N. Hazard (eds.), *XXth Century Comparative and Conflicts Law* (Leiden: A. W. Sythoff)

Tzouganatous, D., 1986. 'Private International Law as a Means to Control the Multinational Enterprise' **19** *Vanderbilt Journal of Transnational Law* 477

Udombana, N. J., 2002. 'A Harmony or a Cacophony? The Music of Integration in the African Union Treaty and the New Partnership for Africa's Development' **13** *Indiana International and Comparative Law Review* 185

2002–3a. 'An African Human Rights Court and an African Union Court: A Needful Duality or a Needless Duplication' **28** *Brooklyn Journal of International Law* 811

2002–3b. 'The Institutional Structure of the African Union: A Legal Analysis' **33** *California Western International Law Journal* 69

Uganda Law Reform Commission, 2004. *Report on the Background Study on the Legal Implementation of the World Trade Organization Agreements* (Kampala: Uganda Law Reform Commission)

UN Conference on Trade and Development, 2009. *Economic Development in Africa Report 2009: Strengthening Regional Economic Integration for Africa's Development* (Geneva: UNCTAD)

UN Economic Commission for Africa, 2002. *Economic Report on Africa 2002: Tracking Performance and Progress* (Addis Ababa: UNECA)

2004. *Assessing Regional Economic Integration in Africa* (Addis Ababa: UNECA)

2006. *Assessing Regional Integration in Africa II: Rationalizing Regional Economic Communities* (Addis Ababa: UNECA)

2008. *Assessing Regional Integration in Africa III: Towards Monetary and Financial Integration in Africa* (Addis Ababa: UNECA)

2010. *Assessing Regional Integration in Africa IV: Enhancing Intra-African Trade* (Addis Ababa: UNECA)

Van den Bossche, P., 1996. 'In Search of Remedies for Non-Compliance: The Experience of the European Community' **3** *Maastricht Journal of European and Comparative Law* 371

Van der Mei, A. P., 2009. 'The East African Community: The Bumpy Road to Supranationalism – Some Reflections on the Judgments of the Court of Justice of the East African Community in *Anyang' Nyong'o and others* and

East African Law Society and others' (Maastricht Faculty of Law Working Paper No. 2009–7, available at http://ssrn.com/abstract=1392709)

Vaubel, R., 2003. 'International Organization' in C. K. Rowley and F. Schneider (eds.), *The Encyclopedia of Public Choice* (New York: Springer)

Vereshchetin, V. S., 1996. 'New Constitutions and the Old Problem of the Relationship between International Law and National Law' **7** *European Journal of International Law* 29

Viljeon, F. and Louw, L., 2007. 'State Compliance with the Recommendations of the African Commission on Human and Peoples' Rights, 1994–2004' **101** *American Journal of International Law* 1

Voeten, E., 2007. 'The Politics of International Judicial Appointments: Evidence from the European Court of Human Rights' **61** *International Organization* 669

von Schwind, F., 1968. 'Problems of Codification of Private International Law' **17** *International and Comparative Law Quarterly* 428

Wai, R., 2001. 'In the Name of the International: The Supreme Court of Canada and the Internationalist Transformation of Canadian Private International Law' **39** *Canadian Yearbook of International Law* 117

2002. 'Transnational Liftoff and Transnational Touchdown: The Regulatory Function of Private International Law in an Era of Globalization' **40** *Columbia Journal of Transnational Law* 209

2004. 'International Trade Agreements, Internationalist Policy Consciousness, and the Reform of Canadian Private International Law' in Canadian Council on International Law (ed.), *The Measure of International Law: Effectiveness, Fairness and Validity (Proceedings of the 31st Annual Conference of the Canadian Council on International Law)* (The Hague: Kluwer Law International)

2005. 'Transnational Private Law and Private Ordering in a Contested Global Society' **46** *Harvard International Law Journal* 471

Walker, J., 2003. 'Must There be Uniform Standards for Jurisdiction within a Federation?' **119** *Law Quarterly Review* 567

Wallace, C. J., 1999. 'European Integration and Legal Culture: Indirect Sex Discrimination in the French Legal System' **19** *Legal Studies* 397

Watt, H. M., 2005. 'European Integration, Legal Diversity and the Conflict of Laws' **9** *Edinburgh Law Review* 6

2006. 'Integration and Diversity: The Conflict of Laws as a Regulatory Tool' in C. Fabrizio (ed.), *The Institutional Framework of European Private Law* (Oxford: Oxford University Press)

Weatherill, S., 1995. *Law and Integration in the European Union* (Oxford: Clarendon Press)

Weiler, J. H. H., 1981. 'The Community System: The Dual Character of Supranationalism' **1** *Yearbook of European Law* 267

1991. 'The Transformation of Europe' **100** *Yale Law Journal* 2403

Weyland, I., 2002. 'The Application of Kelsen's Theory of the Legal System to European Community Law – The Supremacy Puzzle Resolved' **21** *Law and Philosophy* 1

Winter, J. A., 1972. 'Direct Applicability and Direct Effect: Two Distinct and Different Concepts in Community Law' **9** *Common Market Law Review* 425

Winters, L. A., 1997. 'What Can European Experience Teach Developing Countries about Integration?' **20** *World Economy* 889

Wolff, M., 1962. *Private International Law* (Oxford: Clarendon Press)

Wouters, J., 2000. 'National Constitutions and the European Union' **27** *Legal Issues of Economic Integration* 25

Yagba, T. A. T., 1996. 'Legal Pluralism and Economic Integration in Africa: Policy and Research Imperatives' *Nigerian Current Law Review* 100

Yakubu, J. A., 1999. *Harmonization of Laws in Africa* (Lagos: Malthouse Press Ltd)

Zamora, S., 1989. 'Is There Customary International Economic Law?' **32** *German Yearbook of International Law* 9

Zhu, W., 2007. 'China's Codification of the Conflict of Laws: Publication of a Draft Text' **3** *Journal of Private International Law* 283.

INDEX